THE HERITAGE OF
AMERICAN SOCIAL WORK

THE HERITAGE OF
AMERICAN
SOCIAL WORK

READINGS IN ITS
PHILOSOPHICAL AND INSTITUTIONAL
DEVELOPMENT

Edited by Ralph E. Pumphrey
and Muriel W. Pumphrey

COLUMBIA UNIVERSITY PRESS
NEW YORK AND LONDON

COPYRIGHT © 1961 COLUMBIA UNIVERSITY PRESS

ISBN 0-231-08619-9

LIBRARY OF CONGRESS CATALOG CARD NUMBER: 61-8989
PRINTED IN THE UNITED STATES OF AMERICA

10 9 8 7 6 5 4

PREFACE

Social workers, like many other persons in the helping professions, tend to be absorbed with the burdens of people with whom they are presently working. Sometimes they see these difficulties as common to large groups in the nation or the world, and they look forward to the long, slow processes of social, economic, or political change that are requisite if conditions are to be modified. Seldom do they look backward to learn how we arrived where we are, and to get perspective on the magnitude and character of today's problems.

In fact, social work as it is now practiced is the product of a long, evolutionary growth of effort to remedy undesirable conditions that have resulted from persistent, if not inherent, traits of human nature and social organization. Identification of some of these persistent behaviors which have created personal and social complications in the past, and some of the ways which have been used in trying to deal with them, can help the worker in the present to judge not only what methods may be most useful but also what may be the prospects of their success.

It is the experience of the editors in teaching both undergraduate and graduate students that such information as they receive about early social welfare activities and the beginnings of the profession of social work comes to them as secondary descriptions, colored by the prejudices and criticisms of a later generation. The literature of social welfare is voluminous, but most of it has been ephemeral, found in the reports of thousands of small local associations or departments, in journals and other publications of limited circulation and long out of print. Most collections of readings have concentrated on single specialties with little opportunity to get a comprehensive sense of how the many services of modern social work were provided and to see how the predecessors of the profession expressed themselves.

It is our hope that this book will be of general interest to social workers. We also hope that it will provide enrichment material for both graduate and undergraduate courses in social work and social history.

Our choice of materials has been based on three primary purposes: (1) To assist in social work's task of professional identification. There have been certain classic positions with respect to personal and social need which long antedated social work as a profession and which have tended either to unify or to divide the profession. By becoming acquainted with some of these, the profession will, we believe, be helped out of adolescence into a maturity which builds upon, rather than rejects, its history. (2) To assist in the understanding of present professional and social issues through the recognition that many of these are current manifestations of choices which are seemingly ageless. Sometimes these can be recognized more clearly when seen against a less emotionally charged background than the present. (3) To acquaint prospective members of the profession, members of other professions, and historians with something of the origins and social function of social work.

We have included some description of what was done and some philosophical discussion of why something should or should not be done. The mass of material and our hope of achieving a sense of breadth precluded exhaustive treatment of any one aspect. Our basic criterion was that each item should contain something with which *every* member of the social work profession should be familiar. This does not mean that the selections are always well-known, but that they are brief, articulate statements which are either typical of a period or descriptions of great innovations that caused later repercussions. Except in the case of indubitable classics, such as the Pierce veto, preference has been given to items which may not be accessible to many readers, such as unpublished documents, early agency reports, and journals which are not on usual social work reading lists. Such criteria involve much personal judgment; many readers will find that their favorite "gems" from the past have been omitted.

The readings are organized into four periods in relation to five turning points in social welfare history rather than by an arbitrary application of political or social landmarks. The first is the codification of English experience in the Elizabethan Poor Law of 1601, just before the beginning of colonization in America. This provided the legal framework for the meeting of need in the colonies down to the end of the revolution, our second landmark, when the new states, freed of English political control, began to develop their own digressions and expansions. The third turning point was the Pierce veto in 1854, which arrested a movement in the direction of Federal acceptance of responsibility in the field of social welfare. It is not so easy to point to a single event to mark the next period, but it is clear that by the close of the 1893 depression social welfare activities were taking on new forms and the nebulous profession of social work was beginning to take shape. The final document in the book, one of the Supreme Court decisions affirming the constitutionality of the Social Security Act, clearly marks a change of eras. With a comprehensive governmental system of economic provision assured, social work as a profession could turn its attention to the perfection of methods and the formulation of a more integrated philosophy.

To give as much of the flavor of the past as possible, we have retained original spelling and most punctuation. Where words are used with meanings so different from current usage as to endanger understanding, footnote interpretations have been added. In order to afford as wide a sampling as possible, only brief excerpts of most items are included. Omissions are indicated by ellipses (. . .) and editorial interpolations by brackets ([ ]). Wherever possible, the descriptive titles are those of the author himself, or are derived from the text. The rest have been provided by the editors.

Documents are grouped within each period, with an introduction for each group to indicate the problem being dealt with, varying positions or solutions, and its significance in the evolution of the profession. The source of each reading is given in the heading, while additional information is included in foot-notes, numbered consecutively for each period. In this way it is hoped that specialists will be enabled to go to the originals if they so desire, while beginning students will be made acquainted with some of the places where they can find for themselves additional information on the subjects covered.

For anyone who may be interested in the interaction of contemporaneous movements, the approximate time covered is given for each period in the Contents. For those who wish to examine a single idea, a particular problem, or a client group, a topical list is in the Appendix.

We owe much to our many friends who have encouraged us to carry out this project, and to the students whose reactions have helped to determine the suitability of various readings. Among those to whom we owe special gratitude are Professor Eveline Burns, Mrs. Margaret Otto, librarian, and Mrs. Grace Bermingham, reference librarian, New York School of Social Work, Columbia University; Frank J. Hertel, general director, and Mrs. Marie Godley, administrative assistant, Community Service Society, New York City; and Mrs. Helen Gleave, librarian, George Warren Brown School of Social Work, Washington University.

The unlimited access to their rich collections of historical materials which was provided to us by the libraries of the New York School of Social Work and of Yale University enabled us to assemble the core of the readings. However, it would not have been possible to complete the book without the whole-hearted cooperation of many other libraries and historical societies, especially the Boston Public Library, the New Haven Colony Historical Society, the Fairfield Historical Society and the Pequot Library, Fairfield, Connecticut, the New York Public Library, the Columbia University Library, the New York University Library, the Johns Hopkins University Library, the Library of Congress, the Legislative Reference Library of the New York State Library, the Washington University Library and the library of the George Warren Brown School of Social

Work, the St. Louis Public Library and the St. Louis Municipal Reference Library, and the Denver Public Library.

We were also greatly helped by the staffs of various national and local social work agencies and organizations, especially the National Association of Social Workers, the National Conference on Social Welfare, the United Community Funds and Councils of America, Inc., the Cleveland Welfare Federation, the Community Service Society of New York, and the Mile High United Fund of Denver.

For permission to quote copyrighted material we are indebted to Barnes and Noble, Inc. (R3, 6); George Allen & Unwin, Ltd. (R58); The Family Service Association of America, Inc. (R79, 102); The National Conference on Social Welfare (R80, 97); the National Association of Social Workers (R81, 82, 83, 84, 94); Miss Helen Hall on behalf of the *Survey* (R88, 103); the Russell Sage Foundation (R91, 92); the Commonwealth Foundation (R93); the University of North Carolina Press (R95); Longmans, Green & Co. (R96); Association Press (R98); Harcourt, Brace and Co. (R105); *Social Forces* (R107, 108); W. W. Norton & Co. (R110); the *Southwestern Social Science Quarterly* (R111).

For permission to use previously unpublished material not in the public domain we are also indebted to the New York School of Social Work, Columbia University (R71, 85, 89, 90), and to the Community Service Society of New York (R32). We also acknowledge our gratitude to Charles DeF. Besoré, Chief Counsel and Executive Director of the State of New Jersey Law Revision and Legislative Services, who loaned us a copy of Miss Dix's Memorial to the Legislature of that state (R37).

Finally, we must say "thank you" to our many typists, not the least of whom, and certainly the most long-suffering, were Jennie Lou and Brooks.

RALPH E. PUMPHREY
MURIEL W. PUMPHREY

Brentwood, Missouri
February, 1961

CONTENTS

GENERAL INTRODUCTION

The tasks which social workers undertake and the auspices under which they carry them out are so varied that outsiders become confused, and even members of the profession have been
unable, as yet, to reach unanimity about its boundaries and
special functions. At least three ways of thinking have been
utilized by those who attempt to reach definitions.

First is what might be termed the "anthropological" approach.
In this, the function of social work is seen as intervention on
behalf of individuals or groups who are in some sort of social
difficulty, or "trouble" or "need." According to this view, social
work helps those who find themselves unable to keep step with
the social system, and eases strains on the system itself, especially
in periods of crisis.

There is also the philosophical approach, which regards social
work as an institutional means for helping men to meet their obligations to their fellows and for helping society to move forward
to higher goals, thereby fulfilling both religious and democratic
ideals.

Pragmatically, social work is what the public or those who are
engaged in it say it is at any given time. New interests and activities are constantly added, while others become obsolete. In
desperation, a theorist once said, "Group work is what the group
worker does."

As one hunts for the antecedents of what is now referred to as
"social work," it is necessary to keep all three types of definition
in mind to see in what ways the present functions of social work
were formerly organized; what goals previous generations set for
themselves; and how the job was done. Through it all, there seems
to be a connecting thread—that of service in helping people to
meet their needs. What has changed more than anything else is
what people have seen as "needs." Many are universal; food,
clothing, and protection from the elements have been recognized

as necessary from earliest times. The attention presently devoted to other requirements, such as love and affection, is the result of quite recent scientific discoveries. While potentialities for physical growth have been known since prehistoric times, universal potentialities for intellectual and personality growth have only been recognized with the advent of modern psychology.

The following readings will be most helpful in illuminating present theory and practice if, in each one, certain components basic to any system of helping are identified: the kind of recipient; the kind of trouble; the kind of help; and the kind of giver.

From the earliest period, there have had to be stipulations concerning eligibility to receive the services offered. Sometimes these have been objective factors, such as residence or age. Sometimes they have been obscure or internal characteristics subjectively determined, such as moral or emotional stamina. They have found expression in such terms as "worthy" or "unworthy," "stable" or "disturbed." Sometimes the recipient has had to be like the usual member of the population; sometimes, different. All children could benefit from education, only the mentally retarded were to be admitted to certain institutions; the whole population would be better off with good sanitary laws, only the sick were to be admitted to hospitals.

Troubles will be found to include external factors, such as economic need and social hardship; and personal factors, such as physical, moral, and personality deviations.

The kind of help extended has varied from donations after a shipwreck to insurance benefits for the aged; from apprenticeship for the potentially dependent or delinquent child to psychiatric treatment. Help has been tailored to the needs of each individual, or generalized to meet the typical needs of all, or nearly all, people.

Finally, the giver may be a neighbor or a fellow citizen; someone like the recipient in some particular, such as religion or national origin; or someone very different, perhaps one who is separated from the recipient by wealth or social status.

In addition to these basic elements in each instance of helping, there are a number of general considerations which may serve to characterize the various efforts to meet personal or social problems. Among those illustrated in the selections in this book are:

1. *The goals* toward which the effort is focused: physical survival, cure, prevention, improvement

2. *The motivations* which stimulated the effort: compassionate response to obvious symptoms; self-protection to avoid physical, moral, or other harm to the giver; economic, to lower costs or to produce gain for the contributor, taxpayer, or recipient

3. *The means, or strategy, for accomplishing the goal:* procedures which may be directed either toward the environment or toward the individual, including stimulation of self-help and compulsion by threat, police power, or suppression

4. *The manpower to do the job:* neighbors, volunteers, elected officials, agents of the giver, or trained specialists

5. *The types of organizational instrumentation* used to accomplish the goals: institutions, methods, techniques, patterns of administration and financing

There are a number of persistent themes which cut across the previously mentioned aspects and considerations. These include the relation of social welfare to religious and democratic ideologies; the personal and social necessity for work; the search for causation; the effort to secure valid information; provision for the needs of children and future generations; the search for assurance that common hazards may be met.

These suggestions for analysis should not be allowed to interfere with an appreciation of what each writer is trying to convey of his own and his associates' hopes, aspirations, and endeavors. Each selection represented creative thinking and substantial accomplishment in its own time. In a number of instances both sides of controversial issues are presented, and there is opportunity to follow the evolution of points of view.

Throughout the readings there is found the conviction that human betterment is possible both for the individual and for society. This is more than a recognition of the mutability of man;

it is an assertion that certain changes are desirable, others undesirable; that it is possible to further desirable and to inhibit undesirable change through conscious, purposive effort. There is also found the conviction that knowledge about man, his needs and potentialities, should be expanded and utilized constantly to enhance the achievements of individuals and of society. Acquaintance with such convictions from the past may help social workers of today to clarify their own convictions.

ABBREVIATIONS

AASW	American Association of Social Workers
AICP	Association for the Improvement of (*or*, Improving) the Condition of the Poor
COS	Charity Organization Society
NASW	National Association of Social Workers
NCCC	National Conference of Charities and Correction
NCCC	*Proceedings*, annual meetings, National Conference of Charities and Corrections
NCSW	National Conference of Social Work (*or*, after 1956, National Conference on Social Welfare)
NCSW	*Proceedings*, annual meetings, National Conference of Social Work and National Conference on Social Welfare, published under varying titles
R	Reading
RSF	Russell Sage Foundation

THE COLONIAL PERIOD
1601–1789

INTRODUCTION

The colonial period was marked by the transfer to America of familiar institutions and concepts, often without thoughtful consideration of the adaptations which might be needed in the primitive conditions of the New World. So extreme were the early deprivations that sheer survival was dependent on mutual aid—compulsory at Jamestown, voluntary at Plymouth and Massachusetts Bay. But once the colonists were past the initial period of settlement, they unquestioningly put into operation the established laws and customs of the homeland for meeting the needs about them.

These were, in most instances, religious people for whom the injunctions of Christianity about the sacredness of human life were of paramount importance. This led to a basic compassionate concern for "impotent" people—young, aged, infirm, and handicapped. At the same time, the austere conditions and the colonists' religious beliefs about the necessity for hard work led to stern measures to protect communities from strangers and able-bodied but idle poor. As life in the colonies became more sophisticated, care for the poor became more highly organized. It began to take on an element of rehabilitation, both for the sake of the recipient and for the sake of the community, which thereby would be relieved of the expense of care. There also began to be sporadic efforts to provide security against some of the economic hazards which might befall the individual. In rural areas the pattern remained much more primitive, while on the great estates there was a strong sense of *noblesse oblige*, a feeling of responsibility toward persons of inferior economic and social status.

I

SURVIVAL THROUGH MUTUAL AID

Disaster is a timeless and poignant human experience, disrupting established precedents and threatening life itself. In such a situation some people become abjectly fearful and dependent, while others recognize potentialities of self-preservation for themselves and the group. Such circumstances prevailed repeatedly on the frontier as it moved across the continent, but never with the same intense awareness of isolation which existed in the first settlements along the seacoast. Excerpts from familiar accounts of the early tribulations at Jamestown, Plymouth, and Boston illustrate basic individual and institutional adjustments to danger, and the values and concepts underlying them.

At Jamestown (R1), John Smith had to rely upon an order, backed by police power, to secure general cooperation with measures deemed essential to group and individual preservation. On the other hand, we learn of the dedicated help given to one another by the settlers at Plymouth (R2), while at Boston (R3) voluntary mutual aid [1] was extended beyond the tight little band of settlers to include the neighboring Indians.

Smith's followers and the fearful Indians who did not take care of their brethren apparently were thinking primarily of their own safety and convenience. John Smith and settlers who gave nursing care in Plymouth and Boston sought to protect and preserve the lives of their entire communities. In the New England accounts we see that these people were moved by concern for the well-being of their fellows, tinged with a missionary zeal to extend the settlers' religious faith and with a desire to win protection from unpredictable neighboring tribes.

Concepts can be discerned here which will recur frequently

---

[1] Mutual aid can be thought of as help given under the generalized assumption that there would be a return in kind under like circumstances.

through the decades and which are fundamental to modern social welfare:

1. Each person has a primary obligation to do all that he can to provide for and care for himself and his family.

2. Each person has a further obligation to govern his own behavior by consideration of the present and future needs of the entire social group. This embraces provision and care for incapacitated persons, including dependent children, because of their membership in the group, their past contributions, and potential future contributions.

3. Beyond personal obligation, governmental authority supports a group obligation to preserve the lives of all its members. Hence, those who obstruct the group or who fail to carry out their personal obligations should be punished, or compelled to change their behavior.

4. The sense of obligation may extend beyond the "in-group" to include all accessible people in trouble, whether they be kin, neighbors, or strangers.

1. He Who Would Not Work Must Not Eat [2]

The Generall Historie of Virginia, New England, and the Summer Isles . . . By Captaine John Smith sometymes Governour in those countryes & Admirall of New England (London: Printed by I. D. and I. H. for Michael Sparkes, 1624), pp. 86–87

Till this present,[3] by the hazard and indeuours of some thirtie or fortie, this whole Colony had ever beene fed. . . . But such was the strange condition of some 150, that had they not beene forced *nolens, volens,* perforce to gather and prepare their victuall they would all haue starued and haue eaten one another. . . . For those Saluage[4] fruites, they would haue had imparted all to the Saluages, especially for one basket of Corne they heard of to be at Powhatas, fifty myles from our Fort. Though he[5] bought

[2] This summary statement of Smith's policy is found in the continuation of the account reproduced here. Captain John Smith, *Works,* ed. Edward Arber (Westminster: Constable, 1895), II, 474.
[3] The year 1609. Anticipated supplies from England had failed to arrive.
[4] I.e., "savage."   [5] John Smith.

neere halfe of it to satisfie their humors, yet to haue had the other halfe, they would haue sould their soules, though not sufficient to haue kept them a weeke. . . . He argued the case in this maner.

Fellow souldiers, I did little thinke any so false to report, or so many to be so simple to be perswaded, that I either intend to starue you, or that *Powhatan* at this present hath corne for himselfe, much lesse for you. . . . But dreame no longer of this vaine hope from *Powhatan*, not that I will longer forbeare to force you, from your Idlenesse, and punish you if you rayle. . . . I protest by that God that made me, since necessitie hath not power to force you to gather for yourselues those fruites the earth doth yeeld, you shall not onely gather for your selues, but those that are sicke. As yet I neuer had more from the store then the worst of you: and all my English extraordinary prouision that I haue,[6] you shall see me diuide it amongst the sick. And this Saluage trash you so scornfully repine at; being put in your mouthes your stomackes can disgest . . . and therefore I will take a course you shall prouide what is to be had. The sick shall not starue, but equally share of all our labours; and he that gathereth not every day as much as I doe, the next day shall be set beyond the riuer, and be banished from the Fort as a drone, till he amend his conditions or starue. . . .

This order many murmured was very cruell, but it caused the most part so well bestirre themselues, that of 200 (except they were drowned) there died not past seuenas.[7]

2. *True Love unto Their Friends and Brethren*

[*Governor William*] *Bradford's History "Of Plimoth Plantation"* (Boston: Wright & Potter, 1898), p. 111

The 2. Booke 1620

In ye time of most distress,[8] there wus but 6. or 7. sound persons, who to their great comendations be it spoken, spared no pains night nor day, but with abundance of toyle and hazard of their owne health, fetched them woode, made them fires, drest them meat, made their beads, washed their lothsome cloaths,

---

[6] I.e., his private stock of goods.
[7] Reads "not past seuen" in *Works*, II, 473.
[8] During a smallpox epidemic.

cloathed and uncloathed them; in a word, did all ye homly & necessarie offices for them . . . all this willingly and cherfully, without any grudging in ye least, shewing herein true love unto their friends & bretheren.

3. *The English Came Daily and Ministered to Them*

[*Governor John*] *Winthrop's Journal "History of New England" 1630–1649*, ed. James Kendall Hosmer (New York: Scribner's, 1908), I, 115

Dec. 5, 1633. John Sagamore [9] died of the smal pox, and almost all his people. . . . The towns in the bay took away many of the children; but most of them died soon after. . . . John Sagamore desired to be brought among the English, (so he was;) and promised (if he recovered) to live with the English and serve their God. He left one son, which he disposed to Mr. Wilson, the pastor of Boston to be brought up by him. . . . When their own people forsook them, yet the English came daily and ministered to them. . . . Among others, Mr. Maverick of Winesemett is worthy of a perpetual remembrance. Himself, his wife, and servants, went daily to them, ministered to their necessities, and buried their dead, and took home many of their children. So did other of the neighbors.

[9] An Indian.

II

THE LEGAL FRAMEWORK

The concepts of individual and group responsibility which Englishmen brought with them to America were embodied in the administrative provisions of the Poor Law which had been hammered out in successive parliamentary enactments during the second half of the sixteenth century and which had assumed classic form in 1601. Fundamental assumptions implicit in this legislation were:

1. The individual's primary responsibility is to provide for himself, his family, and his near relatives.

2. The government's responsibility is to supplement insufficient individual efforts to relieve want and suffering, and to insure the maintenance of life.

3. The government should adapt its activities to the needs of the person in want.

While there were modifications and additions to the administrative arrangements during the succeeding three and a half centuries, the underlying principles and general administrative approach of the Elizabethan Poor Law remained essentially unchanged into the twentieth century.[10] In America, this law provided the pattern for poor laws in the colonies, in the original states, and in many new states as they were added to the nation.

Notable administrative features of the law include:

1. Local governmental responsibility exercised through a small group of "substantial householders" in each parish

[10] For a succinct account of the Poor Law, see Karl de Schweinitz, *England's Road to Social Security, 1349 to 1947* (Philadelphia: University of Pennsylvania Press, 1947). Substantial extracts from Part III of the *Report of the Royal Commission on the Poor Laws and Relief of Distress* (1909) are included in Sophonisba P. Breckinridge, *Public Welfare Administration in the United States: Select Documents* (Chicago: University of Chicago Press, 1938), pp. 18-29. The last vestiges of the Poor Law were repealed in 1948.

2. The classification of those in need, and provision of appropriate kinds of relief for each: apprenticeship for children, so that they might ultimately learn to be self-supporting; work for the able-bodied; almshouses for the incapacitated

3. Financing through taxation, with provision that should the burden on the parish prove excessive, the justices might spread the burden to other parishes

4. Legally enforced family responsibility

One notable addition, in 1662, was the rigid law of settlement. In a period otherwise conducive to mobility of population, this law made it much more difficult for persons of small means to move about freely. If they were unable to support themselves they would not starve, but only if they remained in, or returned to, the parish where they already had settlement. Although unsuited to frontier conditions in the colonies, where economic progress depended on newcomers venturing into strange territory, this law, too, was imported into America and became part of the pattern of measures for the relief of the poor. It thus bound many laudable features of the poor law to the restrictive concepts of a static agricultural society.

4. *The Elizabethan Poor Law*

Anno xliij. Reginae Elizabethae At the Parliament begun and holden at Westminster the xxvij day of October, in the xliij yeere of the Reigne of our most gracious Soueraigne Lady ELIZABETH . . . *1601.* . . . Imprinted at London by Robert Barker, Printer to the Queenes most excellent Maiejtie

An act for the relief of the poore

THE ij CHAPTER

Be it enacted . . . That the Churchwardens of euery Parish, and foure, three, or two substantial Householders there . . . to bee nominated yeerely . . . under the hande and seale of two or more Justices of the Peace in the same Countie . . . shal be called Ouerseers of the poore of the same Parish, And they . . . shall take Order from time to time . . . for setting to worke of the children of all such whose parents shall not . . . bee thought able to keepe and maintaine their children; and also for setting to worke all such persons maried, or unmaried, having no meanes to maintaine them, use no ordinary and dayly trade of life to get their liuing by, and also to rayse weekely or otherwise (by taxation of euery Inhabitant . . . in the said Parish . . .) a conuenient stocke of Flaxe, Hempe, Wool, Threed, Iron, and other necessary ware and stuffe, to set the poore on worke, and also competent summes of money, for, and towards the necessary reliefe of the lame, impotent, old, blinde, and such other among them being poore, and not able to worke, and also for the putting out of such children to bee apprentices. . . .

If the said Justices of peace doe perceiue that the inhabitants of any Parish are not able to leuie among themselues sufficient summes of money for the purposes aforesaid, that then the said two Justices shall and may taxe, rate and assesse, as aforesaide, any other of other Parishes, or out of any Parish, within the Hundred [11] where the sayde Parish is. . . . And if the said Hundred shall not bee thought to the said Justices, able, and fitte to re-lieue the said seuerall Parishes not able to prouide for themselues as aforesayd, Then the Justices of peace at their generall quarter-sessions . . . shall rate and assesse as aforesaid, any other of other Parishes, or out of any Parish within the said Countie for the purposes aforesaid, as in their discretion shall seeme fitte. . . .

It shall bee lawfull for the sayde Churchwardens and Ouerseers . . . to binde any such children, as aforesayd, to be apprentices . . . . And to the intent that necessary places of habitation may more conueniently bee prouided for such poore impotent peo-ple . . . it shall and may be lawfull for the said Churchwardens and Ouerseers . . . to erect, build and set up in fitte and con-uenient places of habitation, in such Waste or Common, at the generall charges of the Parish, or otherwise of the Hundred or Countie, as aforesayd . . . conuenient houses of dwelling for the said impotent poore, and also to place Inmates or more families than one in one cottage, or house . . . Which cottages

---

[11] A subdivision of a county.

and places for Inmates shall not at any time after be used or imployed to or for any other habitation, but onely for impotent and poore of the same Parish. . . .

The Father and Grandfather, and the Mother and Grandmother, and the children of euery poore, old, blinde, lame, and impotent person, or other poore person, not able to worke, being of a sufficient ability, shall at their owne charges relieue and maintaine euery such poore person . . . upon paine that euery one of them shall forfeit twentie shillings for euery moneth which they shall faile therein. . . .

And be it further enacted, that all the surplusage of money which shal be remaining in the sayd stocke of any Countie, shall by discretion of the more part of the Justices of peace in their quarter-Sessions, be ordered, distributed and bestowed for the reliefe of the poore Hospitals of that Countie, and of those that shal sustaine losses by fire, water, the Sea, or other casualties, and to such other charitable purposes, for the reliefe of the poore, as to the more part of the sayd Justices of peace shall seeme conuenient.

5. The Settlement Law

Great Britain, *Statutes of the Realm*, 13 and 14 Charles II
[1662], c. 12

An act for the better Releife of the Poore of this Kingdom.
WHEREAS . . . . by reason of some defects in the law poore people are not restrained from going from one parish to another and therefore doe endeavor to settle themselves in those parishes where there is the best stocke the largest commons or wastes to build cottages and the most woods for them to burn and destroy and when they have consumed it then to another parish and att last become rogues and vagabonds to the great discouragemt. of parishes to provide stocks where it is lyable to be devoured by strangers Be it therefore enacted by the authority aforesaid that it shall and may be lawfull upon complaint made by the churchwardens or overseers of the poore of any parish to any justice of peace within forty dayes after any such person or persons com-

ing so to settle as aforesaid in any tenement under the yearely value of ten pounds for any two justices of the peace . . . by theire warrant to remove and convey such person or persons to such parish where he or they were last legally setled . . . for the space of forty dayes at the least unlesse he or they give sufficient security for the discharge of the said parish to bee allowed by the said justices.

III

THE POOR LAW APPLIED
IN COLONIAL AMERICA

Everywhere the administration of the Poor Law was left to the smallest local units of government. Consequently, local records of towns and parishes provide the basic picture of the law as it actually functioned.[12] Here, previously published accounts from Boston and New York are supplemented by excerpts from the unpublished records of two small Connecticut towns to give some idea of the variety of situations arising and dealt with. These records seem sketchy and incomplete, but among neighbors who were deciding what to do for a person or family whose circumstances were well known, it was not considered necessary to write down details which would be of great interest to us.

We get an idea of the matter-of-fact way in which the Poor Law was applied. While town meetings were preoccupied with establishing boundary lines and property rights, founding schools, and laying out roads, it was taken for granted that when, occasionally, a poor or "impotent" person was to be provided for, the English law and practice were in effect. A "distracted" woman was returned to her parish of settlement in England long before the rigid formal enactment of 1662. Only gradually did colonial legislatures get around to enacting their own poor laws.

In these excerpts orphans and children whose parents were incapacitated were provided for, and children were ordered

[12] Other examples of Poor Law administration in the colonies are found in Grace Abbott, *The Child and the State* (Chicago: University of Chicago Press, 1938); Breckinridge, *Public Welfare Administration;* Carl Breidenbaugh, *Cities in Revolt: Urban Life in America, 1743–1776* (New York: Knopf, 1955), and *Cities in the Wilderness* (New York: Knopf, 1955); Margaret D. Creech, *Three Centuries of Poor Law Administration* (Chicago: University of Chicago Press, 1936); and David M. Schneider, *History of Public Welfare in New York, 1609–1866* (Chicago: University of Chicago Press, 1938). An interesting commentary on the foster care of children in the colonial period is found in Arthur W. James, "Foster Care in Virginia," *Public Welfare,* VIII (1950), 60.

brought up to a "calling." Poor persons had their taxes abated; were given cash or necessary supplies, particularly in times of illness; were provided with medical care; were housed and cared for when incapacitated. Special arrangements were often worked out according to the nature of the case: public and private assistance supplemented each other; children and elderly persons were cared for out of their estates as long as possible; a relative received help from the town for the care of a blind person; articles of clothing were loaned, not given.

In Puritan enclaves the liberty of the town was intended for persons and families who met moral and religious, as well as economic, standards. Hence, some of the "warnings out" may have been based on these grounds rather than on actual or threatened indigency. The records do not say.

6. Distraction and Disaster

Winthrop's Journal, I, 144, 156

Dec. 11, 1634. One Abigail Gifford, widow, being kept at the charge of the parish of Wilsden in Middlesex, near London, was sent by Mr. Ball's ship into this country, and being found to be somewhat distracted, and a very burdensome woman, the governor and assistants returned her back by warrant, 18, to the same parish, in the ship Rebecca. . . .

Aug. 16, 1635. In the same tempest a bark . . . was cast away. . . . None were saved but one Mr. Thatcher and his wife. . . . The General Court gave Mr. Thatcher £26.13.4, towards his losses, and divers good people gave him besides.

7. Boston Records

Second Report of the Record Commissioners of the City of Boston; containing the Boston Records, 1634–1660 . . . (2d ed.; Boston: Rockwell and Churchill, 1881), pp. 132, 160; and A Report . . . Containing the Boston Record from 1660 to 1701 (Boston . . . 1881), p. 51

29:10:56 . . . Goodman Wales hath 6s abated of his rate [13] for his yeare in regard of his poverty.

[13] I.e., taxes.

25:11:56. Itt is agreed upon the complaint against the son of Goodwife Samon living withoutt a calling, that if shee dispose nott of him in some way of employ before the next meeting, that then the townesmen will dispose of him to some service according to law.

1658, 26 of 5th. Margaret Noriss, an Irishwoman, is Admitted into the Town, and David Faulkoner is bound to secure the Town (from any charge as respecting her), In a bond of seven pound. Witness his hand.

David   D. F.   Faulkoner
marke of *s*

29:9:69. Agreed with Henry Taylor Chirurgeon that in consideration of a cure upon good wife Frankline some time since & his promise of attendance for the yeare ensueinge upon any poore, sicke or hurt in the towne, his rate is remited for this yeare.

8. Fairfield, Connecticut, Town Records [14]

Jan. 15, 1665 . . . Jno Banks shall make diligent enquiry who entertains sojourners without ye towns consent contrary to ye Law yrin provided and such as are delinquent he is to psent yt to an authority . . . . Tho Skidmore is accepted as an Inhabitant of ye Town if he pleases to come here to live.

Jan. 23, 1666 . . . Mr. Gold and Sergt Squire should take care yt [the inventoried estate of Mr. Risden] may be forth coming at ye next Court, Casualties excepted . . . they are also Impowered to dispose of ye children of ye deceased untill ye next Court, and whereas ye children do want some clothing for yr absolute necessity, ye Townsmen orders . . . some clothing for ye Childrens use [taken] out of ye estate to supply ye said children wt is absolutely necessary to keep ye warm and clean.

[14] Minutes of town meetings. Original at Connecticut State Library, Hartford.

April 14, 1668 . . . Samll Davis hath Liberty granted him to Inhabit in ye Town untill ye 29th Sepr next . . . . Samll Davis binds himself and heirs in a bond of ten pounds to Inhabit in ye Town no Longer than Michalmas next . . . . (Samll—X his mark —Davis)

Nov. 13, 1669. Whereas Thomas Basset is fallen sicke & is in a suffering condition the Towne Impower the 2 constables of fairfield to take care of him for his necessary supply: upon the Town charge its left to their discretion: the putting out of the children yf they see it nessery, and to remove Bassett yf they see cause to sum other family for his better preservation.

April 16, 1673. The Towne desires and orders Seriant Squire and Sam moorhouse to Take care of Roger knaps family in this time of their great weaknes: and to procure for them such nezssesary comforts . . . as they stand in need of and it shall be satisfied out of the Town treasurie:

Feb. 16, 1673 [*1673/74*]. Goodman Patchin is to continue his worke about the meeting house: The Towne hath given unto Roger knap & goodman loome [Lyon?] what they owe the Towne Treasurie.

April 27, 1681. Joseph Patchin Senr hath this day made: his application to the Townsmen concerning his weakes and age: desiring his owne estate may mayntayne him as far as it will reach and whereas he hath house and Lands in fairfield he Intends to expend it in the first place and . . . yf he sell it he doth Impower mr Jehu Burr and John Wheeler to be Councell to him to sell the said lands without whose councel he will not sell it: This sale to be made for his mayntenance as fare as it will reach.

Nov. 30, 1682. The Towne are willing to give Thomas Bennet Thirteen pounds provided he mayntayn old patchin with meat drink clothing washing and Lodging for the Term of a Twelve month: & render him in clothing at the years end as he is at this present.

Jan. 10, 1683. Whereas Cohoe: in his weaknes and age is in a sufring estate . . . Jehu Bur an agent [is] to provide sum nessary supplyes for him upon the Townes Aco: and . . . such clothing as he lets him have is to be only lent to him:

Aug. 10, 1685 . . . sargant georg squir forthwith to warn william tomson ye shoomaker to remove himself and family out of ye towne . . . sayd squir retorns to ye sam meeting hee hath so warned him out.

Sept. 29, 1685. The town this day by voat giveth ten pounds to John Bennet To be payd out of ye town treasury and to bee husbanded by Leeftenant Nathanill seely and sargent Mathew sherwood about building a haus and what els may be for thar relief in thar aflicted condesion.

Feb. 11, 1685. whereas thomas olivar is in a condission not to manag his afyrs and is much in debt and being willing to put him self in a way to pay his depts and to live in ye best maner hee may and to free ye town of Charg and them and himself of troboll as far as hee may by Resigning himself and estate to sargent John wheeler to ordar ye best way hee may for ye above sayd ends and to prevent Inconveniances . . . the townsmen do apoint [appraisers] . . . to take an Inventory of ye sam.

Feb. 17, 1685 . . . seeing the nessesety of securing thomas olivars goods left in his hous for this two years if anny bee left hee resolving to tak no cayr of them tell he is bettar ye townsmen do ordar . . . an Inventory . . . speedily as may bee and Remove them into security.

April 10, 1685. Aran Fountain being Com to ye town with his family . . . ye townsmen grants him libarty for present to live in ye town till next town meeting on condession he doth remove his mayd he formerly broght to ye town and free ye Town of anny Charge about her provided she bee not with held from him which hee doth hear by Ingag to doe and also to remove himself and family before winter unles he obtain liberty from the town for his stay.

March 4, 1699/1700. The Towne this day grants to Robert Turney ten Pounds to be paid out of the Towne Treasurie in

Consideration of maintaineing his Brother Benjemen who is blinde A year he to leave his Brother as well Cloathed as he now is.

Dec. 18, 1753. voted yt Ann Green when ever she shall be unable to maintain herself shall be maintained by ye Town.

March 14, 1774. Voted yt ye report of ye Com'tee appointed . . . to consider of tje best method to provide for the poor of the Town be accepted.

Also Voted yt the Selectmen deal with such persons who are idle & mispend their time and neglect their families agreable to said Report in reference to the Statute Relating to Rogues Vagabond & Idle persons & c.

Voted yt ye Selectmen Warn all vagrant & Idle persons to depart the Town and if such vagrants & c do not leave the Town forth with according to such warning given by ye Selectmen: Then the Selectmen are directed to prosecute such vagrants & c: and also such persons as Entertain them according to Law.

Dec. 28, 1785. Voted that there be Two of the Selectmen appointed . . . to vendue the Poor and that those who bid them off shall support them at the price bid at.

Aug. 24, 1789. Voted that the Selectmen act their best judgement in vindicating the Town of Fairfield from the claim of Weston respecting the support of Hannah Hodsden.[15]

9. *Joseph Woodden, Blind, Lame, and Impotent*

New Haven, Connecticut, Town Records [16]

1685—April 28. . . . Joseph Woodden. Allsoe Capt. Mansfeild acquainted the towne with a request made by Joseph Woodden (who is blind lame and impotent) that the Towne would

---

[15] A dispute over settlement between adjacent towns.

[16] Entries for April 28 and June 19, 1685, Jan. 18, 1686, Sept. 16 and Dec. 22, 1701, in the town meeting records, 1685–1787, are from the manuscript being edited by Mrs. Zara Powers for publication by the New Haven Colony Historical Society as Vol. III of their *Ancient Town Records.* Other entries are from "Records of the New Haven Townsmen, or Selectmen, 1665–1714," hand copied by Franklin B. Dexter, February, 1917 (in library of New Haven Colony Historical Society).

graunt him a parcell of land containing about 20 acres lieing near to the hous or land that was his fathers. The towne at present did desyer and order that the Townsmen would take the motion into Considderation view the land see what convenienc or inconvenienc they apprehend it may be to the Towne if it be granted and likewise about highwaies, and to make their returne at another Meeting. . . .

1685—June 19. . . . The Townsmen informed that they had according as was appointed in a former meeting veiwed the land mooved for by Joseph Woodden, and they thought ther was about twelve acres might be graunted him on the north or the north East side of the highway. And the towne at present did recommend it to the Townsmen, to Consider the Case on what termes to grant the land and speak with the man and his relations about it and prepare the matter for another meeting. . . .

1686—January 18. . . . *Joseph Woodden his graunt.* It having been at a former towne meeting left with the Townsmen to considder the motion of Joseph Woodden for a graunt of a peec of land neare Wooddens farme and that they would speak with his relations &c, the townsmen now made returne that they had spoken with his brethren and they did Engage that the land should be secured and Emprooved for the use and benefit of theyer Brother Joseph Woodden.

Therupon the Towne did by vote graunt unto the said Joseph Woodden the land according to the returne the Townsmen brought at a meeting the 19th of June 1685, where the place and quantitye is recorded. . . .

3:May [16] 86. A meeting of som of the townsmen they did desier and appoint Sr John Winston and John Alling to lay out the land granted to Joseph Wooden according to town order.

1701—September 16. . . . *Wooden.* The townes men Informed the towne that Joseph wooden was Like to [be] a charg to the towne. After Debate the towne by their voat Left that to the towns men Consideration. . . .

1701—December 22. . . . *Joss. wooden.* Votted that the

Townes men dispose of the 12 acres of Land formerly granted for the use and benefit of Joseph wooden to that end for which it was granted and give Legall conveyances according to Law.

Mr. Joseph Moss Treasurer Cr.

sundry payments for the townes acco'ts . . .

[1704]	to	Benja Wooden for his Bro. Joseph	6. 0.0
[1704/5]	to	Jo. Dormon for Joseph Woodden	6. 0.0
[1704/5]	to	Wm. Willmot for Jo Woodden	0.17.6
[1704/5]	to	Jo Dorman for Jo Woodden	6. 0.0
[1705]	to	Joseph Dormand for Joseph Woodden	13.10.0
[1706]	to	Jo Dormond for Woodden	1.10.0
[1708]	to	Jo Dormond for Woodden	5.10.0

10. A Charge for Transportation

Minutes of the Common Council of the City of New York, V, 365

May 13, 1752. Ordered the Deputy Clerk pay to Amos Paine or his Order Seventeen Shillings and three pence in full of his Account for Transporting a poore person from this City to Staten Island [17] Being his Late Residen[ce].

[17] Staten Island is now the Borough of Richmond in New York City.

IV

PRIVATE PHILANTHROPY
SUPPORTS GOVERNMENTAL ACTIVITY

A generation after its founding, Boston had become an important trading center with wide extremes of wealth and poverty. Casual provisions for the care of the poor were becoming overtaxed and people were seeking new ways of meeting need. The Poor Law itself pointed the way to one innovation—an institution in which to care for the indigent. Between 1656 and 1660 at least three probated wills included bequests to the town for the relief of the poor. These were combined, and an almshouse was built.

English thinking at the time regarded almshouses as a more humane, up-to-date method of care for the poor than haphazard boarding with individual householders. As the population grew during the next century, more and more communities in the colonies turned to this new arrangement.

The pattern of making individual gifts or bequests to the town, rather than setting up isolated foundations, was regarded as natural. Private benevolence thus provided the capital, but the public was expected to maintain the donated facility. This pattern persists to the present day for many libraries, museums, parks, hospitals, mental health clinics, university buildings, and so forth. Henry Webb probably differed from many other donors only in the outspokenness with which he used his gift on behalf of the needy as leverage to promote his personal interests through stipulation of conditions which the town was required to meet.

11. *Three Boston Wills*

"Extracts from the Probate Records of the County of Suffolk, Massachusetts," *New England Historical and Genealogical Register*, VI (1852), 91; VIII (1854), 356; X (1856), 177

ROBERT KEAYNE *or Keane, Will No. 171 (1657)*

Robert Keayne, Citizin and M'chant Taylor of London by freedome and now dwelling in Boston. . . .

[One half of the former grant of £100] with the increase thereof I give to the use of the free Schoole of Boston to Help on the Trayning of some poor mens Children of Boston (that are most hopeful) in the Knowledge of God and learning.

The other fivety pound with the proffit of it, I give for the use and Reliefe of the poore members of our owne Church or to any other good use that shal be accounted as necessary or more necessary than this.

WILLIAM PADDY, *Will No. 189, 1658*

I give £10 to be disposed of by ye select men of ye towne of Boston for ye poore.

HENRY WEBB, *Will No. 246, 1660*

I give unto ye Towne of Boston ye full Vallue of £100, for A Stocke, for ye benefit of ye poore of ye Towne, either to provide Corne, provissions of wood or Coale for ye winters season, out of ye Increase, or otherwise to some meet house for ye annuall Reliefe of such as ye select men of Boston, from time to time, shall see meete, ye whol Towne Engageing to maytayne ye principle, by reedifying in Case of fier, If before my decease I shall not otherwise bestow ye like somme on ye said some, And Provided ye Town of Boston give mee, or my Executrixes, firm Assurance of my land I purchased, with my money, 18 yeeres since and upewords, on fort hill, which if they refuse to doe, one three monethes after it is desired, my will is that legacy of £100, shall Cease, and be, with ye £20 I lent to Mr. Stoddard for ye Towne house, be Repayed and Returne to my Executrixes Vse forever.

12. *Disposition of the Wills*

Boston Records, 1634–1660, p. 158; 1660–1701, pp. 7, 24

5:9:60 . . . Itt is ordered that the select men shall ratify and confirme Mr. Henry Webbs land upon Fort hill to his Executors to their proper use for ever.

Whereas Mr. Henry Webb bequeathed £100 to the Towne to bee improoved for the use of the poore. . . .

Itt is ordered that the said £100 be improoved . . . in some building fitt for that end, and that in case of fire hapning which may consume itt, the Towne shall reedify the like fabrick to the end afore said.

The select men shall have power to make use of a piece of ground in the comon for the erecting an almes house upon, with suitable accommodation.

31:1:62 [*61/62*] . . . Itt is ordered that Mr. Petter Olliver is to Joine with the deacons of the Church of Boston in the receiveing of Capt. Keane legacye of £120 given to the poore, and further heareby ordered to receive Mr. Webbs Legacie of £100. with severall other gifts that are given for the erecting of an Alleme-house, being heareby authorized and impowred by the selectmen of the Town to agree and compound with severall workemen for stones, Timber, &c. for the erecting and finishing of the sd Allemehouse.

26:12:64 . . . Mrs. Jane Woodcock Widdow hath liberty of admittance into the Alleme house duringe the Towne pleasure, Mr. Petter Oliver hath power to order ye same.

V
PRIVATE HELP FOR
SPECIAL RECIPIENTS

Another example of the increasing complexity of Boston phi-lanthropy after the mid-seventeenth century is the Scots' Char-itable Society. This society, based on ties of common nationality in a strange land, took care of its members and their fellow countrymen in what has come to be regarded as the oldest social agency still functioning in the United States. It was the prototype for thousands of nationality, religious, and fraternal organizations which have waxed and waned during the three centuries since its founding.

The obligation to offer succor personally to those in need was assumed to continue over and beyond the "prudentiall care" given by the town, but there was also a strong emphasis on self-help and moral virtues, and on a limited definition of "neighbor." Solicitation of funds in anticipation of need was conducted among those who might become eligible to be recipients. Private donors were assumed to have the right to select their beneficiaries and to set up descriptions of "unworthy" persons who were to be denied aid. Problems of collection, safekeeping, and administra-tion immediately arose, and there was continuing need for re-definition of purpose as mutual aid and neighborly interest became structured and formalized.

13. The Scots' Charitable Society

The Constitution and By-Laws of the Scots' Charitable Society of Boston . . . [2d ed.; Robert B. Adam, ed.] (Boston, 1896), pp. 9–10, 13–14, 22, 25, 29

Laws Rules and Orders of the Poor Boxes Society

At a meating of the 6 of January 1657 we . . . did agree and conclude for the releefe of our selves and any other for the which wee may see cause (to make a box) and every one of us to give as god shall moue our harts . . . . This our benevolence is for the releefe of our selves being Scottishmen or for any of the Scottish nation whom we may see cause to helpe (not excluding the prudentiall care of the respective prudentiall townsmen whose god shall cast any of us or them [)?] (but rather as an addition thereunto) and it is aggred that there shall nothing be taken out of the box for the first sevin yeers for the releefe of any (the box being as yet in its minority). . . .

At Boston in New England This twenty fifth day of Octobr sixteen hundred and eighty four yeirs. 1684.

The Eternall Lord and great Lawgiver to his people heath commanded by his word a Collectione for the necessities one of ane other, for the relieving of them who are under wants and poverty . . . . As it hath been begun in this place formerly in a most laudable manner, But throw some discouradgment hath been left over for a tyme to our griefe & the prejudice of the poor.

Therefore . . . Wee . . . being of one accord most willing to renew the former good example . . . that the poor strangers and families and children of our natione,[18] when under this dispensatione may be more ordourly and better relieved. Wee do recommend this not only on to an other heire present, But unto all our Countriemen in this Colony not present . . . and theirby open the bowells of our compassion, according to our willingness and ability for the reliefe of such of our nation or their children . . . being flesh of our flesh, & bone of our bone may be helped in their distress, And this wee doe not by constraint but by a willing & free heart as in the presence of God . . . .

And Therefore for the better regulating heirof wee have with one Consent maide these rules and lawes Following

VIZ:

1. . . . . their be a sufficient box presently provided, wt two locks & keyes thereon, the box & this book to be delivered by

---

[18] Scotland remained a separate country till 1707.

the Society to him who shall be chosen boxmaster & collector . . . & the two keys to be delivered severally to two Honest men chosen for that effect . . . .

2. That what moneyes shall be given for this charitable use shall be presentlie put in to the said box, with ane accompt thairof insert in this book . . . & that nothing be taken out of the sd box without consent of the foirsd three persons & other two more at leist—being in all five in number.

3. That no money be taken out of the sd box to be given to any but to such as are truly necessitous, & . . . .

8. Ther is no man to be a member of the Society or to have any benefit of the sd charity out of the box but such as contribut theirto, excepting Strangers of our natione that is cast in by shipwrack or otherwayes.

9. It is also heirby provided, that no prophane or diselut person, or openly scandelous shall have any pairt or portione herein, or be a member of the Society. . . .

Nov. 1718. On reading a petition from James Maxwell praying for relief in his old age—alledging yt he was a Contributor while he was in a capacity—The Society voted that he, sd James Maxwell, be allowed out of the box Twenty Shillings, and time to come during life Ten shillings each quarter after this & the Treasurer is ordered to pay the same. . . .

Novr. 5th 1734. Voted Alexander Fyfe and William Ross, as an Act of Charity, not being members of ye box £3 each. . . .

Novr. 7th 1738. Voted that whereas David Snowden is committed to Jaile on an execution for £100 and more pounds due to the box and that the said Snowden designs to swear out of Jaile as the law directs voted that sd Snowden be keeped inn at the Charge of the Box until next quarter. . . .[19]

5th Decr. 1753. Given as Charity to a poor Wdo Stwart a Scots Woman her husband Jno Stewart being Wash'd Overboard in a Storm in their passage from Liverpool to N. York & She much much bruised &c by wch she lost the use of her left arm—

---

[19] Snowden has borrowed from the box and failed to repay. He is being kept in debtors' prison by the Society.

by consent of ye Presidt & Vice Presidt a Crown Sterling . . . £0.68 more given wh consent of ye Presidt a Dollar 0.60.

Memo. *Feby. 11, 1756.* Died Eliza. Wdo Wilson one of the oldest pensioners who was relieved by the Charity of this Society quarterly for these twenty-three years past. She . . . left what Estate she died possessed of to the Society for the use of their poor.

VI

THE PROVISION OF
GUARANTEED SECURITY IN OLD AGE
OR DISABILITY

The kind of assistance, public or private, so far described carried with it a sense of lower class status, if not indeed of disgrace, in colonies which shared the aristocratic backgrounds of the mother country. The clergy, especially in the colonies with established churches, held an elite status, and it is not surprising to find the practice of life tenure of their positions, not unlike the "livings" of the English clergy. As part of their meager compensation they might expect to enjoy an income on an "honorable" basis even after they were too old or infirm to serve their parishes actively.[20] Most such arrangements were probably unwritten and in accord with the custom of the locality.

The following example, in which such an agreement was reduced to writing, illustrates the difficulties which have beset many an attempt to set up social security plans where the unit, in this case a small church, was too small to deal with either the unforeseen personality factors or the financial burden. Note that it is illness "of body and mind" which leads to the dismissal of Mr. Goodsell after more than three decades of service, and to the ensuing controversy over the terms of his agreement.

[20] Church historians have confirmed in correspondence the prevalence of this pattern of tenure in colonial New England. Other instances of written agreements that include a security provision have not been noted, however.

14. Old Age Security for a Local Minister

Church records, Northwest Society of Fairfield, Connecticut, pp. 31–32, 59, 62–63, 65–66, 70–72 [21]

[*Nov. 1, 1725*]. This . . . is to signify . . . that I John Goodsell of Fairfield . . . and we . . . the Northwest Society of sd
Fairfield . . . covenant . . . as follows—

I . . . do promise by God's assistance to . . . efficiate in the
ministry in the sd society according to the present proffession
of this Govermet for a consideration of an hundred pound
per year of bills of credit of this Colony to be paid yearly for
my salory—and we the . . . aforesd society promise that the
abovdsd John Goodsell . . . as long as he shall continue in the
work of ye ministry as abovesd . . . & afterwards when thro—
age or other inability, he is unable, to give him an honourable
support or maintenance shall have one hundred of pounds of
current bills of credit of this colony a year for his yearly sallery
. . . provided the aforesd John Goodsell shall not neglect the
sd servis by his own default. . . .

[*June 22, 1752*]. Voted yt there shall be some fit person agreed
with to supply ye vacancy of ye Revd. Mr. Goodsell "under his
Difficulties."

[*Nov. 20, 1754*]. Put to vote whether ye society of Greenfield
should be willing to be released from Mr. Goodsell's ministry
& was passed in ye affirmative by a majority of 43 men out of
55.—Voted— . . . a committee to treat with Mr. Goodsell for
his maintenance & call a counsell [22] for ye purpose above.

[*Dec. 12, 1754*]. Put to vote whether it appears to this church
that ye Revd. Mr. Goodsell our pastor be capable upon ye
account of his indisposions of body & mind to perform ye work
of ye ministry. passed in ye negative—by a great majority of

[21] The original records are in Connecticut State Library, Hartford. The
Northwest Society was a newly formed parish, within the Town of Fairfield, of the established (Congregational) Church of the colony. An agreement had been reached with the church in Fairfield for a division of the
taxes.
[22] A meeting of representatives of all the churches in the area.

twenty out of twenty one—also Put to vote whether ye consociation [23] of this part of ye county shall be called to consider & Determine what is proper to be Done in our present Deplorable circumstances with respect to ye Dissolution of Mr. Goodsell's pastoral relation to this church. Passed in ye affirmative by ye above majority.

[*May 13, 1756*]. Voted that . . . ye former Committee shall make proposals to Mr. Goodsell concerning sd Goodsell's honorable support or maintenance [24] and make return to ye next society meeting to see if they be Excepttable.

[*Aug. 31, 1756*]. Ye report of ye above committee . . . is: that they have converst and made proposal to Mr. Goodsell Concerning his honorable support or maintenance and said Mr. Goodsell utterly refuseth: to leave ye affair to: judicious men to Decide ye matter: or settel it in: any other method Consistent to reason and Justice.

[*Dec. 23, 1756*]. Ye report of ye Committee: put in ye 17th inst to Decide ye Difficulties Subsisting between Mr. Goodsell and ye Society Respecting his honorabel maintenance & his salary is: That: Mr. Goodsell is so wavering in his mind that they can by no means prevail with him to Settel ye affair in any Just and Resonabel way whatever.

[*May 10, 1757*]. Whereas I, John Goodsell of ye Town and County of Fairfield in ye Colony of Connecticut Did Covenant & agree with ye Northwest Society in sd Fairfield, Called Greenfield Society . . . all which may appear by one Certain writing or Covenant made between me and the said society bearing Date November 1st, 1725.

And whereas I, ye sd John Goodsell, after haveing a Considerabel Time officiated in ye work of ye ministry in sd society, was rendered unabel not by my own default but through ye providence of God to officiate any further in ye work of ye ministry: in sd Society . . . and as There has been a Considerable

---

[23] The association of neighboring churches.

[24] The pastoral relationship has now been dissolved. The church wishes to arrange a settlement of its obligations to Mr. Goodsell so that it will be free to secure a new minister.

Difficulty & Trobel subsisting: between me & ye sd Society, about & Respecting Some arearages of Salary & ye Support or maintenance In sd writing . . . and whereas ye Society: to prevent any further: Difficulty, Touching said arearages of Salary, and sd future maintenance or Support, hath agreed and voted: to give me ye Sum of Two hundred & Eighty pounds Lawfull money: in full for such Arearages, and for Such maintenance or Support, & I, ye sd John Goodsell, for Promoting of peace in sd Society and to prevent any further Difficulty: therein on accompt of Such Arearages or maintenance: and wholly to free sd Society from ye burden Thereof for ye future have agreed to accept ye sd Sum of Two hundred: and eightty pounds . . . in full Satisfaction and Discharge of sd writing or Covenant, or ye Duty therein contained, or that thereby might accrue.[25]

[25] Goodsell accepts a lump-sum settlement of his rights under the agreement.

VII

ORGANIZED PHILANTHROPY FOR
RESTORATIVE PURPOSES

The development of more complex urban patterns was not unique to Boston, and by the middle of the eighteenth century the colonies had assumed the composite character which was to typify the future United States for the first century of its existence. The raw frontier with its hard conditions was and would remain akin to conditions in the early settlements. In the more populous agricultural areas life was stable, though economic levels ranged from marginal to prosperous. Along the coast, there were a number of important commercial cities like Boston, points of interchange between the colonial hinterlands and the commerce, the politics, and the culture of Europe and the rest of the world. None was more sophisticated and wealthy than Philadelphia, and among its citizens none was a more urbane, astute devotee of the "Enlightenment" of the period than Benjamin Franklin. His account of the founding and early days of the Pennsylvania Hospital [26] presents a much more farsighted and modern approach to need than anything previously noted.

Students of community organization will recognize here the classic steps in that process: awareness of need and a compelling impulse to do something about it on the part of informed persons close to the situation (in this instance, a physician); the development of a design for a specialized agency with specialized personnel (a hospital) through which the community as a whole could work together to meet the need; the enlistment of civic leaders in a program of education and social action to put the design into effect; and continuing interpretation and social action to maintain support once the agency was started.

[26] The Pennsylvania Hospital in Philadelphia is the oldest hospital in continuous operation in the United States.

Conceptually, this project moves far beyond the crudities and uncertainties of most colonial social welfare efforts. Instead of merely providing care to keep the ill or injured person alive, the emphasis is on the restoration of the victim to the community as a self-supporting, contributing member; furthermore, the hospital is to be a center of research into, and education in, methods of treatment and prevention. Here, a limited group did not accumulate funds as insurance against their own needs; instead, funds were solicited from those who did not expect to benefit for the sake of unspecified persons whom they did not know. Instead of either incorporating the new agency into the poor relief framework or setting it up entirely separately, the sponsors made the hospital independent but with arrangements whereby it became a facility that could be used by the poor relief authorities. A mutually stimulating utilization of governmental and voluntary concern was achieved through a conditional public appropriation to an incorporated voluntary organization with a highly structured board of directors. The level of governmental participation was raised to the colony as a whole and beyond, through action by the legislative assembly and the proprietary.[27]

Techniques for the provision of care within the hospital were much advanced over the previous haphazard employment of physicians of uncertain abilities to care for the poor; but so, too, were the techniques through which Franklin went about organizing the campaign for raising money, writing informative items for the papers, negotiating with the colonial assembly, and preparing a report of accomplishments.

Above all, Franklin's recollections and public appeals demonstrate skillful utilization of a wide variety of motivations: the professional zeal and humanitarian concern of Dr. Bond and his fellow physicians; the self-protectiveness of those who hoped to avoid illness themselves by reducing the incidence of disease in general; the altruism of those who wished to relieve the suffer-

[27] Thomas Penn, son of William Penn, was proprietor of the colony under the Crown.

ing of others; the thriftiness of those whose charges for poor relief would be lightened if the ill were restored to self-support; the cunning of those who would get something for nothing; and, along with his real concern for the ill and for the good of the community, Franklin's own vanity at being able to accomplish something which others had tried to do and failed.

15. Franklin's Recollections

The Life of Benjamin Franklin, Written by Himself, ed. John Bigelow (Philadelphia: Lippincott, 1874), I, 6–7

In 1751, Dr. Thomas Bond, a particular friend of mine, conceived the idea of establishing a hospital in Philadelphia (a very beneficent design, which has been ascrib'd to me, but was originally his), for the reception and cure of poor sick persons, whether inhabitants of the province or strangers. He was zealous and active in endeavouring to procure subscriptions for it, but the proposal being a novelty in America, and at first not well understood, he met but with small success.

At length he came to me with the compliment that he found there was no such thing as carrying a public-spirited project through without my being concern'd in it. "For," says he, "I am often ask'd by those to whom I propose subscribing, Have you consulted Franklin upon this business? And what does he think of it? And when I tell them that I have not (supposing it rather out of your line), they do not subscribe, but say they will consider of it." I enquired into the nature and probable utility of his scheme, and receiving from him a very satisfactory explanation, I not only subscrib'd to it myself, but engag'd heartily in the design of procuring subscriptions from others. Previously, however, to the solicitation, I endeavored to prepare the minds of the people by writing on the subject in the newspapers, which was my usual custom in such cases, but which he had omitted.

The subscriptions afterwards were more free and generous; but, beginning to flag, I saw they would be insufficient without some assistance from the Assembly, and therefore propos'd to petition for it, which was done. The country members did not at first relish the project; they objected that it could only be serviceable to the city, and therefore the citizens alone should be at the expense of it; and they doubted whether the citizens themselves generally approv'd of it. My allegation on the contrary, that it met with such approbation as to leave no doubt of our being able to raise two thousand pounds by voluntary donations, they considered as a most extravagant supposition, and utterly impossible.

On this I form'd my plan; and, asking leave to bring in a bill for incorporating the contributors according to the prayer of their petition, and granting them a blank sum of money, which leave was obtained chiefly on the consideration that the House could throw the bill out if they did not like it, I drew it so as to make the important clause a conditional one, viz.,

And be it enacted, by the authority aforesaid, that when the said contributors shall have met and chosen their managers and treasurer, *and shall have raised by their contributions a capital stock of* —— *value* (the yearly interest of which is to be applied to the accommodating of the sick poor in the said hospital, free of charge for diet, attendance, advice, and medicines), *and shall make the same appear to the satisfaction of the speaker of the Assembly for the time being,* that *then* it shall and may be lawful for the said speaker, and he is hereby required, to sign an order on the provincial treasurer for the payment of two thousand pounds, in two yearly payments, to the treasurer of the said hospital, to be applied to the founding, building, and finishing of the same.

This condition carried the bill through; for the members, who had oppos'd the grant, and now conceiv'd they might have the credit of being charitable without the expense, agreed to its passage; and then, in soliciting subscriptions among the people, we urg'd the conditional promise of the law as an additional motive to give, since every man's donation would be doubled; thus the clause work'd both ways. The subscriptions accordingly soon exceeded the requisite sum, and we claim'd and receiv'd the public gift, which enabled us to carry the design into execution. A convenient and handsome building was soon erected; the institution has by constant experience been found useful, and flourishes to this day; and I do not remember any of my political manoeuvres, the success of which gave me at the time more pleasure, or wherein, after thinking of it, I more easily excus'd myself for having made some use of cunning.

16. The Pennsylvania Hospital Established

Some Account of the Pennsylvania Hospital: From its First Rise to the Beginning of the Fifth Month, Called May, 1754 (Philadelphia: Printed by B. Franklin and D. Hall, 1754), pp. 6–7, 14–15, 45–47

An Act to encourage the establishing of a Hospital for the relief of the sick poor of this province, and for the reception and cure of lunaticks

WHEREAS the saving and restoring useful and laborious members to a community, is a work of publick service, and the relief of the sick poor is not only an act of humanity, but a religious duty; and whereas there are frequently, in many parts of this province, poor distempered persons, who languish long in pain and misery under various disorders of body and mind, and being scattered abroad in different and very distant habitations, cannot have the benefit of regular advice, attendance, lodging, diet and medicines, but at a great expense, and therefore often suffer for want thereof; which inconveniency might be happily removed, by collecting the patients into one common provincial Hospital, properly disposed and appointed, where they may be comfortably subsisted, and their health taken care of at a small charge, and by the blessing of God on the endeavours of skilful physicians and surgeons, their diseases may be cured and removed: And whereas it is represented to this assembly, that there is a charitable disposition in divers inhabitants of this province to contribute largely towards so good a work, if such contributors might be incorporated with proper powers and privileges for carrying on and completing the same, and some part of the publick money given and appropriated to the providing a suitable building for the purposes aforesaid . . . be it enacted. . . .

[*The Petition to the Proprietors of the Colony*]

The principal difficulty we now labour under, is the want of a commodious lot of ground, in a healthy situation . . . . We are therefore under the necessity of laying the state of our case before our proprietaries, and we hope the same motives which have induced others, will have due weight with them to promote this good work, and that they will generously direct a piece of ground to be allotted for this service. . . .

The interest of the proprietaries and people, are so nearly connected, that it seems to us self-evident that they mutually share in whatever contributes to the prosperity and advantage of the province. . . .

Rules . . . for the admission and discharge of Patients

First, That no patients shall be admitted whose cases are judged incurable, lunaticks excepted. . . .

Secondly, That no person, having the small-pox, itch, or other infectious distempers, shall be admitted, until there are proper apartments prepared. . . .

Thirdly, That women having young children shall not be received, unless their children are taken care of elsewhere, that the Hospital may not be burthened with the maintenance of such children, nor the patients disturbed with their noise. . . .

Eighthly, That at least one bed shall be provided for accidents that require immediate relief.

Ninthly, That if there shall be room in the Hospital to spare, after as many poor patients are accommodated as the interest of the capital stock can support, the managers shall have the liberty of taking in other patients. . . .

17. An Early Appeal for Support

Continuation of the Account of the Pennsylvania Hospital . . . to the Fifth of May, 1761 (Philadelphia: B. Franklin and D. Hall, 1761), pp. 113–14

To give it its proper weight with the publick, let it be considered, that in a city of large trade, many poor people must be employed in carrying on a commerce, which subjects them to frequent terrible accidents. That in a country, where great numbers of indigent foreigners have been but lately imported, and where the common distresses of poverty have been much increased, by a most savage and bloody war, there must be many poor, sick, and maimed. That poor people are maintained by their labour, and, if they cannot labour, they cannot live, without the help of the more fortunate. We all know, many mouths are fed, many bodies clothed, by one poor man's industry and diligence; should any distemper seize and afflict this person; should any sudden hurt happen to him, which should render him incapable to follow the business of his calling, unfit him to work, disable him to labour but for a little time; or should his duty to his aged and diseased parents, or his fatherly tenderness for an afflicted child, engross his attention and care, how great must be the calamity of such a family! How pressing their wants! How moving their distresses! And how much does it behove the community to take them immediately under their guardianship, and have the causes of their misfortunes as speedily remedied as possible! Experience shows, this will be more effectually and frugally done in a publick Hospital, than by any other method whatever.

Can any thing in this checkered world, afford more real and lasting satisfaction to humane minds, than the reflection of having made such a social use of the favours of Providence, as renders them, in some measure, instruments which open the door of ease and comfort to such as are bowed down with poverty and sickness; and which may be a means of increasing the number of people, and preserving many useful members to the publick from ruin and distress.

VIII
NOBLESSE OBLIGE

While the cities were becoming complex and were developing new ways of dealing with human need and suffering, life on the plantations of the South retained a system of social relationships not unlike those of feudal baronies. Here the sense of responsibility for those in need was felt as a personal rather than a corporate one. Hospitality and largesse were parts of that pattern of ethics known as *noblesse oblige* which was widely held by the British aristocracy.

At the very time he was leading the millitary struggle against Britain, George Washington penned a letter to his agent[28] at Mount Vernon which succinctly sets forth his understanding of this aspect of the great landowner's obligations.

18. Washington's Instructions for the Care of the Poor

G. Washington to Lund Washington, Nov. 26, 1775, in *The Writings of George Washington*, ed. Worthington Chauncey Ford (New York: Putnam's, 1889), III, 236-37[29]

It is the greatest, indeed it is the only comfortable reflection I enjoy on this score, that my business is in the hands of a person in whose integrity I have not a doubt, and on whose care I can rely. Was it not for this, I should feel very unhappy, on account of the situation of my affairs; but I am persuaded you will do for me as you would for yourself, and more than this I cannot expect.

Let the hospitality of the house, with respect to the poor, be kept up. Let no one go hungry away. If any of this kind of people should be in want of corn, supply their necessities, provided it does not en-

[28] Lund Washington, a kinsman. The letter was written shortly after Washington assumed command of the Continental Army.

[29] The letter apparently constituted a reaffirmation of his commission to Lund Washington as managing agent for his plantations and business concerns during his absence. The original is on display (A516) in the museum at Mount Vernon.

courage them in idleness; and I have no objection to your giving my money in charity, to the amount of forty or fifty pounds a year, when you think it well bestowed. What I mean by having no objection is, that it is my desire that it should be done. You are to consider, that neither myself nor wife is now in the way to do these good offices. In all other respects, I recommend it to you, and have no doubt of your observing the greatest economy and frugality; as I suppose you know, that I do not get a farthing for my services here, more than my expenses. It becomes necessary, therefore, for me to be saving at home.

The above is copied, not only to remind myself of my promises and requests, but others also, if any mischance happens to

G. Washington

THE FIRST NATIONAL PERIOD
1789–1854

INTRODUCTION

The achievement of national independence brought no immediate, dramatic change with respect to ways of helping the unfortunate. Colonial poor laws were reenacted with the minor changes in terminology required by changes in the monetary system and governmental forms. But the poor laws had not been an issue in the Revolution; the original states retained them and passed them on to the new territories and states as they were erected out of the wilderness to the west. Only gradually came relaxation of the intellectual and emotional, as well as administrative, ties with England. Drawing less and less on the experience of the mother country with respect to poor relief, the states experimented with their own formulations and adaptations of ways of meeting need as they struggled on all fronts for national identity.

The rapid growth of American cities with expanding slums in the first half of the nineteenth century paralleled the experience of English and Continental cities. Human misery and need came to the forefront as a problem of social policy that was debated with vigor. In America, as in England, the shortcomings of purely local administration of poor relief were recognized, and the state began to assume new responsibilities as an investigatory, regulatory, and administrative unit. While some authorities on both sides of the Atlantic believed that public, tax-supported relief was inherently wrong and fostered human weakness, the conclusion reached by most practical-minded men was that the system of public responsibility was too deeply ingrained in the culture to be abolished. Instead, they saw the role of the citizen, both individually and in association with others, as one of exercising vigilance to see to it that the program was carried out efficiently and effectively. To this end voluntary associations were formed to promote more effective approaches to dealing with problems of indigency, while others concentrated on the organization and provision of specialized facilities and services for groups of needy persons with particular handicaps such as blindness, deafness, and insanity.

Of widespread concern was the plight of children caught in a morass of poverty, hopelessness, and neglect. While their other concerns were scattered, almost every thoughtful writer inveighed at the evil, preached at the children or their parents, or offered some scheme for its correction. Among these writers universal public education was frequently seen as an essential first step both for the personal development of the children and for the protection of the social order.

In large measure, the different approaches which were advocated and tried out during this period reflected different philosophical understandings of the origin of individual difficulties, and different insights into what those difficulties meant to the persons in need. Perhaps most universally held was the concept of need as evidence of personal fault, but it was widely alleged that this personal fault might be seriously compounded, or even brought into being, by the faulty operation of the charitable system. Hence the great emphasis on the use of almshouses, on various investigatory techniques, and on cooperation among charitable agencies, both public and private. In the hope of helping individuals to avoid falling into this type of personal fault, educational and advisory programs were recommended which, it was hoped, would enable the individual to compete more effectively in the economic system. The economic system itself was seen in certain quarters as creating conditions beyond the power of the individual to control, negating, in these instances, the doctrine of personal fault and suggesting the need for modifications in the economic system itself. Closely associated with this ideology was a conception of individual psychology which called for the expenditure of the least possible amount of energy: if a person could survive without work, no matter how poorly, he would do so rather than exert himself to earn a living. A contrast to this was the emergent concept of incentive wages embodied in Sarah Josepha Hale's report (R27) to the Boston

Seaman's Aid Society. She pointed out that a do-nothing attitude is related to the impossibility of accomplishing anything positive, no matter how great the effort, and that the possibility of even moderate positive achievement would make a tremendous difference in the attitude and effort of the person in need.

Here and there were a few glimmers anticipatory of the professionalization of persons engaged in philanthropic endeavor. Some well-educated men selected public welfare and private agency administration as full-time vocations. There was discussion of useful technical procedures, with differences of opinion over their effectiveness. Social investigation was the one most talked about, with compilations of instructions on how to approach the needy person as well as lists of pertinent information and hints at where it could be obtained. Mrs. Hale viewed this process of investigation as damaging to the self-respect and future self-sufficiency of the investigated; Joseph Tuckerman (R25) and the AICP (R30–32), while much aware of the responsibility to protect contributors and taxpayers, considered that the essential purpose of the social study was to secure the kind of understanding needed before any attempt was made at reconstruction of the needy person through personal influence.

Tuckerman, John Griscom (R21), his son, John H. Griscom (R29), and Dorothea Dix (R37) attempted to apply survey methods and compile crude statistics concerning costs and numbers served. Thus professional characteristics of full-time effort, specialized skills, and literature were beginning to take form.

With the expansion of the country, improvements in communication, and the spread of education, there was increasing recognition that the problems and catastrophes which overwhelmed people were not isolated incidents, matters of strictly local concern or even of the states alone. Informal exchanges of experience and ideas were supplemented by the beginnings of voluntary associations on a national scale. And since many helpful projects were receiving grants of public lands for their support, it was natural that those concerned with specific categories of needy persons should look to Congress for aid. The passage by

Congress of the Dix bill for Federal assistance to the states for the establishment of hospitals for the insane was the high-water mark of this movement to have the Federal government assume some responsibility in the field of social welfare. The veto of this bill by Franklin Pierce turned back the tide, and for two generations Americans sought ways and means of working out the increasingly difficult welfare problems brought about by urbanization within the framework of state and local organization, both governmental and voluntary.

IX

THE SPREAD OF THE POOR LAW

When the Northwest Territory adopted the Pennsylvania Poor Law, itself an adaptation of the English Poor Law as it had been half a century earlier,[1] Elizabethan philosophical and administrative concepts were indelibly impressed upon nearly all of the country except Louisiana, influenced by the Code Napoleon. While protection against starvation was assured, the limited nature of this protection was indicated in the interim laws adopted in 1790 by the Governor and judges of the Northwest Territory which required that a person be "really suffering" to "render him . . . a wretched and proper object of public charity."[2]

Note the similarity of wording between the 1795 law and the previously quoted English laws of 1601 and 1662 (R4, 5). Changes represented adaptations to a new political framework and attempts at tighter administrative controls, mostly carried over from English experience. The administration remained entirely in the hands of part-time local officials. The undesirability of rigid enforcement of the system of "warning out" in a situation where new settlers were sought and valued led ultimately to its abandonment.[3] Other basic aspects of the Poor Law, including settlement, everywhere remained essentially untouched.[4]

[1] Aileen Elizabeth Kennedy, *The Ohio Poor Law and Its Administration* (Chicago: University of Chicago Press, 1934), p. 14.
[2] *The Statutes of Ohio and of the Northwestern Territory*, ed. Salmon P. Chase (Cincinnati: Corey & Fairbank, 1833), I, 107.
[3] The Ohio Supreme Court in 1827 ruled that a person who had been "warned out" could still establish residence if the warning were not repeated. Warning was dropped from the Ohio law in 1854. Kennedy, *Ohio Poor Law*, pp. 27, 120.
[4] Among detailed studies of the Poor Law are: Alice Shaffer, Mary W. Keefer and Sophonisba P. Breckinridge, *The Indiana Poor Law: Its Development and Administration* (Chicago: University of Chicago Press, 1936); Grace Browning and Sophonisba P. Breckinridge, *The Development of Poor Relief Legislation in Kansas* (Chicago: University of Chicago Press, 1935); Frances Cahn and Valeska Bary, *Welfare Activities of Fed-*

Under the conditions of an expanding frontier community where all men knew each other and were on essentially the same primitive economic level, where people were valued for what they could contribute to the total community, and where mutual aid was a part of daily life, the Poor Law provided a framework for organizing community action to supplement mutual aid in situations of need. How idyllic these conditions would seem to persons accustomed to the grinding poverty of England and the repressive operation of the Poor Law there can be seen from a returned emigrant's account of life in northern Ohio in the early 1830s.

19. Territorial Laws of 1795

The Statutes of Ohio and the Northwestern Territory,
ed. Salmon P. Chase (Cincinnati: Corey & Fairbanks,
1833), I, 175–82

CHAPTER LIV. A LAW FOR THE RELIEF OF THE POOR

1. The justices of the peace of the respective counties of this territory, or any three of them . . . shall nominate and appoint two substantial inhabitants of every township . . . to be overseers of the poor of such townships. . . .

4. It shall and may be lawful to and for the overseers of the poor . . . to make and lay a rate, or assessment . . . on the estimated value of all the real and personal estates within the said townships, respectively . . . to be employed in providing proper houses and places, and a convenient stock of hemp, flax, thread and other ware and stuff, for setting to work such poor persons, as apply for relief, and are capable of working; and also for relieving such poor, old, blind, impotent and lame persons, or other persons not able to work, within the said townships, respectively; who shall therewith be maintained and provided for.

5. . . . The overseers of the poor . . . [may] contract with any person or persons for a house or lodging, for keeping, main-

eral, *State and Local Governments in California, 1850–1935* (Berkeley: University of California Press, 1936); and Emil W. Sunley, *The Kentucky Poor Law, 1792–1936* (Chicago: University of Chicago Press, 1942).

taining and employing any or all such poor . . . as shall be adjudged proper objects of relief; and there to keep, maintain and employ all such poor persons, and take the benefit of their work, labor and service, for and towards their maintenance and support: and if any poor person shall refuse to be lodged, kept, maintained and employed in such house or houses, he or she shall not be entitled to receive relief from the overseers during such refusal. . . .

9. . . . The overseers of the poor . . . [may] put out, as apprentices, all such poor children, whose parents are dead, or shall be by the said justices found unable to maintain them, males till the age of twenty-one, and females till the age of eighteen years. . . .

16. If any person who shall come to inhabit in any township or place within this territory, shall for himself and on his own account, execute any public office, being legally placed therein, in the said township or place, during one whole year; or if any person shall be charged with and pay his or her share towards the public taxes or levies for the poor of such township or place, for two years, successively. . . such person in any of these cases, shall be adjudged and deemed to gain a legal settlement in the same township or place. . . .

19. No person whomsoever coming into any township or place without such certificate, as aforesaid, shall gain a legal settlement therein, unless such person shall give security, if required, at his or her coming into the same, for indemnifying and discharging such township or place, to be allowed by any one justice of the peace respectively.

20. Upon complaint being made by the overseers of the poor . . . any two justices . . . [may] by their warrant or order . . . remove and convey such person, or persons to the county, township, place or state, where he, she or they was or were last legally settled, unless such person or persons shall give sufficient security to discharge and indemnify the said township. . . .

28. The father and grandfather, and the mother and grandmother, and the children of every poor, old, blind, lame and

impotent person, or other poor person not able to work; being of sufficient ability shall at their own charges, relieve and maintain every such poor person, as the justices of the peace . . . shall order and direct, on pain of forfeiting the sum of five dollars for every month they shall fail therein. . . .

[*Adopted from the statutes of Pennsylvania—Published June 19, 1795—To take effect October 1, 1795.*] [5]

20. *Provided with Everything Needful*

D. Griffiths, Jr., *Two Years' Residence in the New Settlements of Ohio, North America: with Direction to Emigrants* (London: Westley and Davis, 1835), pp. 37, 55–56, 75–77, 82

Nor is there, at the entrance of their villages, any signboard nailed up against the walls . . . "Beggars, Gipsies, and Trampers of every description, found in a state of vagrancy in this Parish, will be dealt with according to law." The Traveller's feelings are not harrowed at every turn by the sight of some squalid, ragged, wretched object in human shape. Indeed, during the whole two years of my residence in America, I saw but one beggar. . . .

[The settler] then cuts his logs, etc. for a house; and when everything is ready, he sends round the township to inform the inhabitants of his intended *raising*. On the day appointed, the neighbors assemble, one and all, if necessary, to raise his log-house; and very willingly, too, if they think him a *clever* man, or a man of good character, a well meaning man, as we should say; every such New Settler among them being considered an acquisition. . . .

I have been asked with much anxiety by some . . . "Supposing an emigrant should be unfortunate, and unable to support himself, will they afford him any relief?" . . .

In one township, where I resided, the only person on the town was a disabled Scotchman, who boarded amongst the farmers, sometimes at one house, and sometimes at another. In another township, there was a Dutch family thrown on the town by

---

[5] This editorial note is found in brackets in Chase.

fever, and, being very poor, they were provided with doctor and nurse, and in fact with everything needful for them, until they recovered. In short, I am persuaded that the afflicted and unfortunate meet with as much kindness in the New Settlements of Ohio, as in any part of the world. . . .

There are no *roundsmen*[6] standing at the corners of their streets all day idle. To secure against the inconveniences resulting from a scarcity of labourers, some of the farmers take children of about six or seven years old as apprentices for a certain term of years. The apprentice is clothed, sent to school, and provided for until he is capable of working on the farm, when his master or boss, as they call him, is amply repaid. Poor Emigrants from Europe frequently dispose of their younger children by apprenticing them to farmers or mechanics, since no premium is required.

[6] Able-bodied laborers on relief, obliged to make the rounds of employers in the village, seeking work. See Karl de Schweinitz, *England's Road to Social Security* (Philadelphia: University of Pennsylvania Press, 1947), pp. 74–76.

X
POOR RELIEF IN PUBLIC POLICY

In the coastal cities, where immigration and industrialization were creating concentrations of poverty, and in England, the poor law was not being accepted as uncritically as on the frontier. The famous Poor Law Commission Report of 1834, with the subsequent important reforms of the English law,[7] was the culmination of two generations of concern, investigations, and reports, both official and unofficial. There was activity on both sides of the Atlantic and much exchange of ideas among England, the United States, France, Germany, and other countries.

Variant approaches taken by leading thinkers of the period are here illustrated. John Griscom's "Report on the Subject of Pauperism" (R21), earliest in time and broadest in philosophy of the three, assesses the origin of recipients' attitudes and seeks ways for society to help or to stimulate the poor, whether actually or potentially recipients of relief, so that the need for relief will be obviated. Josiah Quincy, in his "Report on Pauper Laws" (R22), sees the need for guides and bounds for the relief administrator who is otherwise subject to his unregulated emotional response to the appeals of those seeking help and hence may give more than he should. Thomas Chalmers, discussing "The Four Fountains of Charity" (R24), is also concerned with attitudes, both of the recipient, who will become pauperized if he has a right to relief, and of the wealthy person whose attitude will be so much more positive if he acts voluntarily than if he is required to produce the same amount of assistance through taxation.

Each author is concerned with the long-term or recurrent re-

---

[7] See de Schweinitz, *England's Road*, pp. 114–27. The report itself is basic to full understanding of prevailing attitudes: *The Report from His Majesty's Commissioners for Inquiring into the Administration and Practical Operation of the Poor Laws* (London: Published by Authority, 1834).

cipient of relief, who is labeled a "pauper"; each presents an administrative approach to methods of dealing with stereotypes. Only Griscom suggests that part of the basic problem may rest outside the individual in need and puts forward proposals for economic and social action, although he places primary emphasis on better organization of charitable activities. The diverse concepts of governmental function and human motivation held by these writers more than a century before the passage of the Social Security Act are today still expounded in editorial comment and political debate.

One thing all the authors had in common was the prevailing opinion regarding the interrelationship of poverty and antisocial behavior expressed by Quincy (R23).

21. *Report on the Subject of Pauperism*

The First Annual Report of the Managers of the Society for the Prevention of Pauperism in the City of New York [Committee report, John Griscom, Chairman] (New York: Printed by J. Seymour, 1818), pp. 12–22

We were fully prepared to believe, that without a radical change in the principles upon which public alms have been usually distributed, helplessness and poverty would continue to multiply—demands for relief would become more and more importunate, the numerical difference between those who are able to bestow charity and those who sue for it, would gradually diminish, until the present system must fall under its own irresistible pressure, prostrating perhaps, in its ruin, some of the pillars of social order. . . .

The great and leading principles, therefore, of every system of charity, ought to be, *First*, amply to relieve the unavoidable necessities of the poor; and, *secondly*, to lay the powerful hand of moral and legal restriction upon every thing that contributes, directly and necessarily, to introduce an artificial extent of suffering; and to diminish, in any class of the community, a reliance upon its own powers of body and mind for an independent and virtuous support. . . .

To bring the subject committed to our charge more definitely before the Society, we have thought it right, distinctly to enumerate the more prominent of those causes of poverty which prevail within this city; subjoining such remarks as may appear needful.

1st. *Ignorance*, arising either from inherent dullness, or from want of opportunities for improvement. This operates as a restraint upon the physical powers, preventing that exercise and cultivation of the bodily faculties by which skill is obtained, and the means of support increased. The influence of this cause, it is believed, is particularly great among the foreign poor that annually accumulate in this city.

2d. *Idleness.* A tendency to this evil may be more or less inherent. . . .

3d. *Intemperance in drinking.* . . .

4th. *Want of economy.* . . .

5th. *Imprudent and hasty marriages.* . . .

6th. *Lotteries.* . . .

7th. *Pawnbrokers.* . . .

8th. *Houses of ill fame.* . . .

9th. *The numerous charitable institutions of the city.* . . .

In no cases are measures of this kind more prolific in evil, than where they are accompanied by the display of large funds for the purposes of charity; or where the poor are conscious of the existence of such funds, raised by taxation, and of course, as they will allege, drawn chiefly from the coffers of the rich.

How far these evils are remediable, without an entire dereliction of the great Christian duty of charity, is a problem of difficult solution. The principle of taxation is so interwoven with our habits and customs, it would, perhaps, in the present state of things, be impossible to dispense with it. But while our poor continue to be thus supported, to prevent the misapplication and abuse of the public charity, demands the utmost vigilance, the wisest precaution, and the most elaborate system of inspection and oversight.

LASTLY. Your Committee would mention WAR. . . .

Effectually to relieve the poor, is therefore a task far more comprehensive in its nature, than simply to clothe the naked and to feed the hungry. It is, to erect barriers against the encroachments of moral degeneracy; it is to heal the diseases of the mind; it is to furnish that aliment to the intellectual system which will tend to preserve it in healthful operation. . . .

We therefore proceed to point out the means which we consider best calculated to meliorate the condition of the poorer classes, and to strike at the root of those evils which go to the increase of poverty and its attendant miseries. . . .

1st. To divide the city into very small districts, and to appoint, from the members of the Society, two or three Visitors for each district, whose duty it shall be to become acquainted with the inhabitants of the district, to visit frequently the families of those who are in indigent circumstances, to advise them with respect to their business, the education of their children, the economy of their houses, to administer encouragement or admonition, as they may find occasion. . . .[8]

2d. To encourage and assist the labouring classes to make the most of their earnings, by promoting the establishment of a Savings Bank,[9] or of Benefit Societies, Life Insurances, &c. . . .

3d. To prevent, by all legal means, the access of paupers who are not entitled to a residence in the city. . . .[10]

[8] John Griscom, the author, and chairman of the committee which submitted this report, was a Quaker educator known as "the father of all chemistry teachers." He visited Thomas Chalmers (R24) during his European trip, 1818–19, and discussed his plans for the new society. It was less than a year later that Chalmers instituted the parish visitor plan in his newly established parish of St. John's in Glasgow. Both men had probably been influenced by plans for the use of district visitors which had been introduced in Hamburg and Munich in the 1790s.

[9] New York's first savings bank was chartered by the legislature in 1819 "in conformity to a memorial presented to them by the board" of the Society. *2nd Annual Report . . . Society for the Prevention of Pauperism . . .* (New York: E. Conrad, 1820).

[10] "Though ships' masters were required to give bond against the dependency of the passengers they brought, they evaded this provision of the law by landing their poorest ones at Fairfield, Conn., from which point it was only a short walk, in those pedestrian days, to the city." David M. Schneider, "Problems of Poor Relief in 1823," *Quarterly Bulletin of the New York State Conference of Social Work*, IV, No. 1 (1933), 40–41.

4th. To unite with the corporate authorities in the entire inhibition of street begging. . . .

5th. To aid, if it shall be deemed expedient, in furnishing employment to those who cannot procure it, either by the establishment of houses of industry, or by supplying materials for domestic labour.

Although this mode of relieving the necessitous may appear to be entirely exempt from the evils arising from gratuitous aid, it will undoubtedly require a judicious course of management, lest it produce a relaxation of concern on the part of the poor to depend on their own foresight and industry, and the same consequent increase of helplessness and poverty. Yet it must be expected that numerous cases will occur in which employment will furnish by far the most eligible kind of relief. Among the female poor these cases will be the most numerous. Women have fewer resources than men; they are less able to seek for employment; they are more exposed to a sudden reverse of circumstances. Of the wants and the sufferings of this class, their own sex are the best judges. Hence, we are of opinion, that the "Society for the promotion of Industry" deserve the thanks of the community, and . . . an adequate and extended support. . . .

8th. To contrive a plan, if possible, by which all the spontaneous charities of the town may flow into one channel, and be distributed in conformity to a well-regulated system, by which deception may be prevented, and other indirect evils arising from numerous independent associations, be fairly obviated.

22. *Report on Pauper Laws*

Massachusetts, General Court, Committee on Pauper Laws, *Report of Committee to Whom was Referred the Consideration of the Pauper Laws of the Commonwealth* [Josiah Quincy, Chairman] (1821), pp. 3-7, 9-11 [11]

Your Committee . . . have availed themselves of all the light to be derived from . . . the English writers. . . .

[11] The author, Josiah Quincy, was one of several distinguished persons to bear this name. A decade earlier he had been leader of the Federalists in Congress and later was mayor of Boston and president of Harvard College. This report is one of a number on the operation of the Poor

The principle of pauper laws is that of a state, or public, or, as sometimes called, a compulsory provision for the poor. The poor are of two classes. 1. The impotent poor; in which denomination are included all, who are wholly incapable of work, through old age, infancy, sickness or corporeal debility. 2. The able poor; in which denomination are included all, who are capable of work, of some nature, or other; but differing in the degree of their capacity, and in the kind of work, of which they are capable.

With the respect to the first class; that of poor, absolutely impotent, were there none other than this class, there would be little difficulty, either as to the principle, or as to the mode of extending relief.

But another class exists; that of the able poor; in relation to which . . . arise all the objections to the principle of the existing pauper system. The evils, also, which are attributed to this system, of diminishing the industry, destroying the economical habits and eradicating the providence of the labouring class of society may all be referred to the . . . difficulty of discriminating between the able poor and the impotent poor and of apportioning the degree of public provision to the degree of actual impotency.[12]

This difficulty, cannot, apparently, be removed by any legislative provision. There must be, in the nature of things, numerous and minute shades of difference between, the pauper, who, through impotency, can do absolutely nothing, and the pauper, who is able to do something, but that, very little. Nor does the difficulty of discrimination, proportionally, diminish as the ability, in any particular pauper, to do something, increases. There always must exist, so many circumstances of age, sex, previous habits, muscular, or mental, strength, to be taken into the account, that society is absolutely incapable to fix any standard, or

---

Laws which were prepared for state legislatures about this time. The best known of the others was made by J. V. N. Yates, New York Secretary of State, in 1824.

[12] Compare this concept of the basis for granting relief with military disability pensions based on percentage of disability and with old age insurance based on age and premiums paid.

to prescribe any rule, by which the claim of right to the benefit of the public provision shall absolutely be determined. The consequence is that the admission, or rejection, of the claim to such relief is necessarily left to the discretion of Overseers; or to those, who are entrusted by law, with the distribution of the public charity. . . .

From the nature of things, this discretion will always be entrusted to men in good, generally in easy, circumstances; that is, to the prosperous class of society. "The humanity natural to this class, will never see the poor, in any thing like want, when that want is palpably and visibly brought before it, without extending relief." Much less will this be the case, when they have means, placed in their hands by society itself, applicable to this very purpose. In executing the trust, they will, almost unavoidably, be guided by sentiments of pity and compassion, and be very little influenced by the consideration of the effect of the facility, or fullness, of provision, to encourage habits of idleness, dissipation, and extravagance among the class, which labor. "They first give necessaries, then comforts; and often, in the end, pamper, rather than relieve."

If the means, placed under their control, are confined to provision for the poor, in public poor, or alms houses, the effect of these dispositions and feelings appears, in the ease, with which admission is obtained; the kindness with which the poor are treated, during their residence, and in the superiority of the food of the public table, to that, to which they have been accustomed. If those means consist in funds, the same temper and feelings predominate, in their distribution. It is laborious to ascertain the exact merit of each applicant. Supply is sometimes excessive; at others misplaced. The poor begin to consider it as a right; next, they calculate upon it as an income. The stimulus to industry and economy is annihilated, or weakened. . . . The just pride of independence, so honorable to man, in every condition, is thus corrupted by the certainty of public provision. . . .

Your committee in placing, in this strong light the objections to the entire principle of our existing pauper laws, have had no intention to recommend, nor any idea that their investigations would ultimately result in, an abolition of those laws altogether in Massachusetts. . . .

Taking it for granted, therefore, that the present system of making some public, or compulsory provision for the poor is too deeply riveted in the affections, or the moral sentiment of our people to be loosened by theories, however plausible, or supported by, however high names, or authority; [13] your Committee next turn their attention to the various modes, which, it appeared by the returns from the various Overseers of the Poor in this Commonwealth, had been adopted in different towns. . . . Your Committee found these modes to be four.

1. Provision for the poor, by letting them out to the lowest bidder, in families at large, within the town.

2. Provision, by letting them to the lowest bidder, together; that is, all to one person.

3. Provision, by supplies, in money, or articles, at their own houses.

4. Provision, by poor, or alms, houses. . . .

Upon the whole, your Committee apprehend that the experience both of England and of Massachusetts concur in the five following results, which may be well adopted as principles, in relation to the whole subject.

1. That of all modes of providing for the poor, the most wasteful, the most expensive, and most injurious to their morals and destructive to their industrious habits is that of supply in their own families.

2. That the most economical mode is that of Alms Houses; having the character of Work Houses, or Houses of Industry, in which work is provided for every degree of ability in the pauper; and thus the able poor made to provide, partially, at least for their own support; and also to the support, or at least the comfort of the impotent poor.

3. That of all modes of employing the labor of the pauper, agriculture affords the best, the most healthy, and the most cer-

[13] Note the similarity to Griscom's statement that the principle of taxation was too deeply ingrained to be dispensed with (R21).

tainly profitable; the poor being thus enabled, to raise, always, at least their own provisions.

4. That the success of these establishments depends upon their being placed under the superintendence of a Board of Overseers, constituted of the most substantial and intelligent inhabitants of the vicinity.

5. That of all causes of pauperism, intemperance, in the use of spirituous liquors, is the most powerful and universal. . . .

While, therefore, your Committee on the one hand are of opinion, that no subject more imperiously claims the attention and solicitude of the Legislature: that it is the duty of society by general arrangements, to attempt to diminish the increase of pauperism, as well as to make provision for that which is inevitable; that diminution of the evil, is best, and most surely to be effected by making Alms Houses, Houses of Industry, and not abodes of idleness, and denying for the most part all supply from public provision, except on condition of admission into the public institution; and that of all modes of employing the industry of the poor, the best is in agriculture; yet on the other hand, they are also of opinion, that no ultimate system should be founded upon these principles, until they have been laid before their fellow citizens, for their contemplation. Certainty and general satisfaction, being, in cases of this nature, much more important than expedition.

Your Committee, therefore, only recommend that measures should be adopted to [publish] . . . the results of this investigation . . . to insure returns, from the several towns . . . and that a Committee should be appointed, instructed to report at the next session, a system of Town, or District Alms Houses . . . in the form of a bill or bills; having a reference to placing the whole subject of the poor in the Commonwealth, under the regular and annual superintendence of the Legislature.[14]

For the committee,

Josiah Quincy, *Chairman*

[14] A controversial subject is referred to another committee in accordance with the community organization principle that wide public knowl-

23. *Poverty, Vice, and Crime Inseparable*

Josiah Quincy, *Remarks on . . . the Laws of Massachusetts, Affecting Poverty, Vice, and Crime* (Cambridge: Printed at the University Press, 1822), p. 2

Among all the general relations of man, the most interesting to the individual, and the most important to society, are those of poverty, vice, and crime. They are, in truth, often little else than modifications of each other; and, though the class of virtuous poor form an honorable exception to the fact, yet in the more depressed classes, they are so frequently found together, that in every general survey, they may be considered, for the purpose of analysis and remark, in some measure as inseparable.[15]

24. *The Four Fountains of Charity*

Thomas Chalmers,[16] "On the Bearing Which a Right Christian Economy Has upon Pauperism," *The Christian and Civic Economy of Large Towns* (Glasgow: Printed for Chalmers and Collins; Waugh and Ivnes, Edinburgh, 1823), II, 52–61

Poverty is that state in which the occupier is unable of himself to uphold the average subsistence of his family; and . . . pauperism is that state in which the occupier has the ability either entirely, or in part, made up to him out of a public and constitutional fund.

But the truth is, that the invention of pauperism, had it been successful, would have gone to annihilate the state of poverty as well as its sufferings. A man cannot be called poor, who has a

---

edge and participation are essential to the success of community planning. See R39 for the first effective implementation of the concept of annual superintendence.

[15] This opening statement introduced a discussion of the need for houses of correction to avoid imprisonment of children in jails; the desirability of greater judicial discretion, particularly in sentencing children; and the evils of public executions.

[16] Chalmers, a Scottish theologian, put into practice in his parish of St. John's in Glasgow his theories concerning the administration of relief which became a classic demonstration referred to by all authorities on the Poor Law during the rest of the nineteenth century. See de Schweinitz, *England's Road*, pp. 100–13.

legal right, on the moment that he touches the borders of indigence, to demand that there his descending progress shall be
arrested, and he shall be upheld in a sufficiency of aliment for
himself and his family. The law, in fact, has vested him with a
property in the land, which he can turn to account, so soon as
he treads on the confines of poverty: and had this desire been as
effective as was hoped and intended, a state of poverty would
have been impossible. . . . A more real protection would have
been afforded, had the case been abandoned to the unforced
sympathies of our nature—and had it been left to human compassion to soften the wretchedness of a state, against the existence of which no artifice of human policy seems to be at all
available. . . .

On the simple abolition of a compulsory assessment for the relief of new applicants, there would instantly break forth from
innumerable fountains, now frozen or locked up by the hand of
legislation, so many refreshing rills on all the places that had been
left dry and destitute, by the withdrawment from them of public
charity, as would spread a far more equal and smiling abundance
than before over the face of society.

The first, and by far the most productive of these fountains,
is situated among the habits and economies of the people themselves. It is impossible but that an established system of pauperism
must induce a great relaxation on the frugality and providential
habits of our labouring classes. . . . We know not a more urgent
principle of our constitution than self-preservation; and it is a
principle which not only shrinks from present suffering, but
which looks onwards to futurity. . . .

The second fountain which pauperism has a tendency to shut,
and which its abolition would reopen, is the kindness of relatives.
. . . We believe, that were the first fountain restored to its
natural play, there would be discharged, from it alone in the
greatest number of instances, a competency for the closing years
of the labourer; and did this resource fail, that the second fountain would come in aid, and send forth, on the decaying parentage

of every grown up and working generation, more than would replace the dispensations of pauperism.

A third fountain, on which pauperism has set one of its strongest seals, and which would instantly be unlocked on the abolition of the system, is the sympathy of the wealthier for the poorer classes of society. It has transformed the whole character of charity, by turning a matter of love into a matter of litigation. . . . There is a mighty difference of effect between an imperative and an imploring application. The one calls out the jealousy of our nature, and puts us upon the attitude of surly and determined resistance. The other calls out the compassion of our nature, and inclines us to the free and willing movements of generosity. It is in the former attitude, that, under a system of overgrown pauperism, we now, generally speaking, behold the wealthy in reference to the working classes of England. . . . Were this economy simply broken up, and the fountain of human sympathy again left free to be operated upon by its wonted excitements, and to send out its wonted streams . . . we doubt not that from this alone a more abundant, or, at least, a far more efficient and better spread tide of charity would be diffused throughout the habitations of indigence.

But there is still another fountain, that we hold to be greatly more productive even than the last . . . . the sympathy of the poor for one another. In the veriest depths of unmixed and extended plebeianism, and where, for many streets together, not one house is to be seen which indicates more than the rank of a common labourer, are there feelings of mutual kindness, and capabilities of mutual aid, that greatly outstrip the conceptions of a hurried and superficial observer: And, but for pauperism, which has released immediate neighbours from the feeling they would otherwise have had, that in truth the most important benefactors of the poor are the poor themselves—there had been a busy internal operation of charity in these crowded lanes, and densely peopled recesses, that would have proved a more effectual guarantee against the starvation of any individual, than ever can be reared by any of the artifices of human policy. . . . We may be sure, that for the supplies which issued from the store house of public charity, there would be ample compensation, in the breaking out of those manifold lesser charities, that never fail to be evolved, when human suffering is brought into contact with human observation.

XI

THE BEGINNINGS OF
COMMUNITY ORGANIZATION

Griscom had seen the need for some unified plan for the dispensation of the charities of the multitudinous societies in a city. It remained for the Reverend Joseph Tuckerman to demonstrate the practicability of cooperative effort among independent and jealous organizations. The constitution of the Association of Delegates from the Benevolent Societies of Boston,[17] of which he was founder and president, might well have been the model for those of most of the councils of social agencies which flourished in the second quarter of the twentieth century,[18] while his system of registration of cases was the direct ancestor of the social service exchange, developed in Boston a generation later and afterward a universal element in the provision of social services.[19] He instituted regular monthly service reports from the participating societies and thus was able to prepare a factual summary of the total community situation which was much less threatening than unverified supposition had pictured. At the same time, the monthly meetings of the delegates provided an opportunity for a

[17] *First Annual Report.* See R25.
[18] For accounts of the development and organization of councils of social agencies see Homer Borst, "Community Chests and Councils," in Fred B. Hall, ed., *Social Work Yearbook, 1929* (New York: RSF, 1929), and Clarence King, "Councils in Social Work," in Russell H. Kurtz, ed., *Social Work Yearbook, 1939* (New York: RSF, 1939). Further sources are listed in Chap. XXXIV, n. 51.
[19] For the evolution of the social service exchange philosophy see Associated Charities of Boston, *First Annual Report* (1880), p. 5, and *Third Annual Report* (1882), pp. 12–13; Margaret F. Byington, *The Confidential Exchange: a Form of Social Cooperation* (New York: Charity Organization Department, Russell Sage Foundation, 1912); Beatrix R. Simcox, "The Social Service Exchange, Part II: Its Use in Casework," *Journal of Social Casework,* XXVIII (1947), 388–90; Stephen L. Angell and Frank T. Greving, "A New Look at the Social Service Exchange," *Social Work Journal,* XXXVI (1955), 16–17.

stimulating exchange of experience among volunteer workers—the beginnings of on-the-job training for the practice of social work.

Tuckerman himself, a Unitarian missionary to the poor of Boston, was one of the first to make service to the poor a full-time occupation.[20] The Association of Benevolent Societies was an extracurricular activity designed to secure greater uniformity in community efforts for the poor. In his report to this group, Tuckerman tended to stress the negative results of mechanical, unthinking giving of material relief. He emphasized the responsibility of the giver for the unfortunate outcome. He propounded the doctrine of "lesser eligibility" (the condition of the relief recipient should always be "less eligible," that is, less comfortable, than that of the lowest paid independent workman) which had recently been set forth by the English Poor Law Commissioners, but he added qualifications which reflected his experience and his sensitivity for the people with whom he was working.

Tuckerman's attitude toward tax-supported relief hinted at his admiration of Thomas Chalmers (R24) but did not lead him to reject social action; government should do something about the liquor traffic. Following tradition concerning the impotent in his classification of the physically handicapped as persons who could always be regarded as "proper subjects" for relief, he added a new element when he identified widows as "feeble" because of their social handicaps. His concern about children was to be reiterated by many people in support of many projects as the century wore on.

[20] Tuckerman (1778–1840) had been a rural minister before William Ellery Channing persuaded him to undertake the work of city missionary in 1826. Among the activities he initiated in this capacity were a sewing school and two libraries, one for children. In 1830 he won a prize in an essay contest conducted by Mathew Carey (R26) on the problems associated with low pay for female workers. In an 1832 report on poor relief for the Massachusetts legislature he pointed to the inadequacy of wages to meet bare necessities and recommended methods for helping people achieve self-support. His philosophy and his relief and group activities are described in Daniel T. McColgan, *Joseph Tuckerman* (Washington: Catholic University of America Press, 1940).

Tuckerman was far too broad a man to be limited to a negative approach. He was profoundly concerned about the inadequacy and uncertainty of wages; he recognized that people were not altogether responsible for shortcomings arising out of lack of opportunity. His emphasis on the individuality of the person in need, and on the value of personal support and encouragement, is highly suggestive of the charity organization slogan of half a century later: "Not alms, but a friend." In his encouragement of schools, clubs, and recreational activities, though these are not revealed in this item, his ideas were in keeping with those of the settlement movement as it developed at the end of the century (R58–60).

25. We Associate That We May Know

The First Annual Report of the Association of Delegates from the Benevolent Societies of Boston [Joseph Tuckerman, President] (Boston: I. R. Butts, 1835), pp. 3–5, 7–8, 10–15, 24–25, 28–30, 34–39, 41–44

Twenty-six Societies are represented in the Association. . . . Twenty have made reports . . . of the names and residences of the poor whom they have visited and assisted, and generally of the kind and amount of the assistance given, and of the character and claims of those whom they have visited. In a book prepared for the purpose, these names are all entered in an alphabetical order, so that reference may in a moment be had to any name; and in connexion with each name, it may be seen at a glance by what societies any individual, or family, was assisted . . . and, what are the judgements which were formed by the visiters of those who were thus brought under their notice or care. It is indeed much to be regretted, that while we have had full and satisfactory monthly reports from some of the societies, the returns from others have been irregular and defective. This is an error which we trust will not be carried into the future. . . . Our monthly meetings were, however, well attended during the time of the active operations of the Societies, and the most perfect harmony of views and feelings was maintained in them. Much valuable information was given in the monthly reports, and much was imparted in the discussions which grew out of them. The right, indeed, is not recognised by us, of any interference with the objects, or mode of operation, of either of the societies represented in the Association. . . . It is proper, however, to give the information, that we learn from the monthly reports which have been rendered, that from October, 1834, to April, 1835, eleven hundred and thirty-two families, or individuals and families, were assisted by twenty of our benevolent societies. And of those thus assisted, it will be interesting to know, that

765 were assisted but	once
238	twice
64	three times
22	four times
14	five times
11	six times
9	seven times
2	eight times
3	ten times
2	eleven times
2	twelve times

In view of the cases of illness which will be remembered, and of extreme destitution, a more favorable result could hardly have been anticipated. We think we have here the most satisfactory evidence, that, as an Association, we have not labored in vain. . . . Your committee were surprised to find that only sixty-four were assisted three times, and only sixty-five more than three times. We believe also that nearly all those who were most frequently aided, were of a class to require little, if any, short of the aid which they received. Had it not been, however, for the influence of this Association, or, in other words, had the Societies in this connexion acted through the last winter, as they acted in former winters, without any knowledge of each other's operations, we believe, that, by a comparison of the records of the twenty Societies which have reported to us, a very different result might have been shown. . . .

The convictions are now deep . . . that no great and permanent improvement of outward condition is to be looked for, but through an improvement of character; that the best resources for improving the condition of the poor are *within themselves;* that they often need enlightenment respecting these resources more than alms; and that alms may even be a means of perpetuating poverty. . . .

Charity, or alms-giving is abused, whenever it ministers in any way to a neglect of forethought and providence, to idleness, to pride or vanity, or to luxurious or intemperate appetites; when it encroaches in any degree upon the feeling of a healthy self-respect, or a regard to character; when it in any degree lessens in the receiver the feeling that it is disgraceful to depend upon alms-giving, as long as a capacity of self-support is retained. . . . Children are to a very great extent made beggars, through the facilities and excitements which are given to beggary. We say, therefore, that to give to one who begs . . . or in any way to supersede the necessity of industry, of forethought, and of proper self-restraint and self-denial, is at once to do wrong, and to encourage the receivers of our alms to wrong doing; it is to patronise pauperism, and it may even be, great vice. Alms-giving is one of the highest . . . of our duties as Christians. . . . But we believe that a clear perception, and a faithful avoidance of the evils, of an injudicious bestowment of alms, is essential to Christian alms-giving. . . . We are not unnecessarily to do evil by the means by which we may, and should do good.

The history of the Poor Laws, and of the charitable foundations of England, furnishes abundant records of the dreadful abuses which have thus been made of charity or alms. . . .

Human wants are divine provisions for human exertions. . . . Yet many are, and ever have been, disposed to live with as little labor and self-denial as possible. Many are industrious, economical, careful for the future, only as they are compelled to be so by the absolute necessity of their conditions [21]. . . . We say not this in reproach. We do but state facts; and facts, for the evil of which the rich have as much cause to blame themselves, as to blame the

[21] Cf. Chalmers's "first fountain," R24.

poor. Nay, as far as the poor are concerned, there are often great extenuations. . . . Still . . . established provisions for the relief of the poor have never failed to obtain claimants, to any extent to which such provisions have been made. And not only so. The relief thus given has been received, not as alms, but as the proportion due to the receiver from a recognised common stock. As yet we see these results but to a comparatively small extent in our own country. . . . But we have experience enough of these results to make us quite sure that they are not fictions. . . . "I know that you have assisted those who require aid less than I do, and therefore I ought to be assisted," is language which has probably often been addressed to each one of us. And if we . . . take into account the peculiar pressure for aid . . . incidental to seasons of scarcity, and to those fluctuations of commercial and manufacturing interest by which many for a time are thrown out of employment, and the wages of labor are reduced to those who may still be employed, while the price of food may even be considerably enhanced, the whole mystery of the danger of permanent provisions for the relief of want, and of all other than purely moral provisions for these exigencies, will be dispelled. . . . The difficulties, it may be the actual sufferings of the poor, but independent laborer, are often very great. A strong sense of character, it may be a strong sense of duty is then required, for the maintenance of his independence. It may even be his duty to receive temporary assistance, because he may not be able to live without it. But even in this case, are not the principles to be respected . . . by which he would even to the last maintain his independence? . . . Are they respected, when, under the weakness of a temporary necessity, he is aided, not from private sympathy which might stir his heart, and call forth all his energies, but from funds dispensed by others than their owners, and in receiving which he is made to feel himself a pauper? . . .

What has all this to do with the action of Benevolent Societies? . . . We have associated for the purpose of obtaining a knowledge of each others' procedures, of avoiding interference with each others' measures and movements, of profiting by each others' experience, and of gaining all the light we may as well respecting our dangers, as our duties in the dispensation of alms. . . .

Our first principle . . . is, that *every error or mistake in almsgiving, and every misapplication of alms, known to a visiter belonging to any of the Societies here represented, is to be made known to all the visiters.* . . . We would know, and we associate that we may know, and avoid all abuses in this department of charity. . . .

We would state as our second principle, and it is a fundamental one, that *beggary is as far as possible to be broken up—and especially, beggary by children.* . . .

As far as our influence can be extended, *no child that is sent out to beg shall in any case receive alms in the hours in which children who go to school are in the schools of the city.* . . .

Another rule . . . is, *that individuals and families that ask for alms, are to be relieved only at their homes, and after a personal examination of each case; and that relief in these cases, when given, is to be, not in money, but in the necessaries required in the case.* . . . The exceptions to it cannot be too few. . . .

Our third principle respects those who are called the able bodied poor. It is, that *the alms which interfere with the necessity of industry, forethought, economy and a proper self-denial, are not only encouragements, but causes of pauperism.* . . . Except the feeble, the aged, the maimed and the diseased, the number is comparatively small among us, who, by industry, economy and temperance, could not provide for themselves and their families. We feel bound, however, to say, that among the feeble here referred to, we include a very interesting class of females, principally widows, and who have the charge of two, three, four or five children. Their sole dependence, except that of occasional alms, is either upon their needle, with which they can at best earn a dollar, or a dollar and a half a week; or upon employment for a day, or part of a day, whenever they can get it, in any of the coarse work of a family. . . . They are unequivocally proper subjects of alms. But still greater is the number who are able bodied, both women and men, and who yet apply for alms. . . . It is a delicate, and often a very painful office to which we are called, of judging and acting upon applications for aid, where want, and even necessity may at the time be pressing, but where it is not only perceived that this necessity might have been obviated by a proper self-denial and economy on the part of the applicants, but that, through the continued neglect of this econ-omy, there will be a perpetual recurrence of the very necessity which pleads for immediate relief. In respect to these cases we can only say, that if relief must be given—and it sometimes must be—it should never be of a kind, or to a degree, which will make this dependence preferable to a life of labor. It should, however, be remembered—and justice requires us to remember—that many would be economical *if they knew how to be.* But they have been reared in ignorance, and indolence, and thriftlessness. . . . If we cannot remedy these evils in parents, let us at least do what we may for their prevention in children. . . .

Wherever, in our intercourse with the poor, we meet with in-dustry, with frugality, with self-respect, and with a preference of self-denial to dependence upon alms, the proper encouragement and support of an individual of this character is, not alms, or any other form of charity as a substitute for alms, but the simple and true respect and regard for character, which such a one will never fail to know how to appreciate. . . . He . . . will equally pre-fer our simple confidence, our just appreciation of motives, and our respect, expressed not by words, but by treatment and con-duct, to any alms which we could give. . . . No two characters, or cases, are precisely alike. Much must necessarily be left to the judgment of the almoner. But he is not fitted to be an almoner, who does not understand and feel, that sincere respect, sympathy and interest, will do more to improve the whole condition of the poor, than any alms which we can give them. . . .

Where there are relatives of the poor who are able to provide for them, there should be no interference of alms with the duties of such relatives. . . .

The question arises . . . "what *ought* we to do?" or, "what *shall* we do in the cases, in which, but for intemperance, there would be no call for alms?" This question is easily answered by those who have never been visiters of the poor. . . . *Alms should as far as possible be withheld from the intemperate. . . . They should not be given to the drunkard.* But the wife and children of the drunkard . . . may be without food . . . and wholly innocent in respect to the causes of their destitution.[22] . . . Let him who thinks it easy always to act wisely in reference to these classes of application become a visiter of the poor, and give us the light of his counsel and example. . . . *To the intemperate, whether man or woman, money should never be given. Nay, more. Even relief in kind should never be given to the families of the intemperate, beyond the demands of unquestionable necessity.* We would inflict upon them no suffering. . . . Law might do far more than it has ever done for the suppression of pauperism. But while it licenses the dram-shop, and interferes not with the drunkard . . . we must do what we can that our alms may not minister to the drunkard's recklessness. . . .

We cannot close our report, without a distinct expression of the strong interest with which we regard the accession to our Association of the delegations from our Infant School Societies, and from the Societies for the Employment of the Female Poor.[23] The objects of these Societies are, to an important extent, precisely those of our Association. . . .

[22] Here Tuckerman opens up a problem which is recurrent throughout the readings: the relationship between need, personal fault, and relief.
[23] R27 and 28.

XII

THE PROBLEM OF WAGES

Most persons who undertook to deal with relief and the care of the unfortunate accepted prevailing economic doctrines, which harked back to Adam Smith and his followers. Yet in many quarters these doctrines were being subjected to question and challenge. Owen and others, with their socialist utopias, were seeking new arrangements of economic life. Shortly Marx would proclaim a doctrine of combined economic and political revolution. Some writers on the problems of the poor, without seeking the overthrow of the existing order, saw the intimate relationship between the system of low wages, based on the principle of a free market in labor, and the problems in the administration of poor relief.

Matthew Carey, a Philadelphia bookseller and pamphleteer, whose son was the leading American economist of the time, examined essential family expenditures. Following the same kind of method that is used in establishing today's public assistance budget standards, he demonstrated that fully employed workers found it impossible to meet current expenses, let alone save for times of illness or old age. Not being immediately confronted with the problems of the administrator, he was inspired by moral and religious concern, and concluded that the economic theorists were wrong in asserting that employees would invariably receive enough to support themselves and families under a free market in wages. Some of his solutions may seem superficial or outmoded, but his arguments are familiar to the social planner. His forthright statement of the problem and his moral indignation, reminiscent of the Hebrew prophets, remain as challenging as when they were written.

The Boston Seaman's Aid Society, under the leadership of Sarah Josepha Hale, a widow and editor of popular women's magazines, made a practical application of Carey's moral and economic ideas in its sheltered employment program, but in so doing utilized additional significant understanding of human motivations. Not only did these ladies avoid "grinding the faces of the poor," by determining wages in accordance with the normal living needs of the workers, but they recognized and demonstrated the importance of incentive wages and adequate relief which would permit the recipient to be like other people. This is set in sharp contrast with the prevailing concepts of deprivation wages and niggardly relief intended to force rather than encourage people into greater effort.

No twentieth-century organizations trace their direct lineage to Carey or Hale. Their perceptions were too much ahead of the thinking of their time to leave durable institutional monuments, but their ideas became part of the ever-expanding humane and liberal heritage of the nation.

26. An Appeal to the Wealthy of the Land

M[athew] Carey,[24] *Appeal to the Wealthy of the Land . . . on the . . . Situation, and Prospects of Those Whose Sole Dependence for Subsistence Is on the Labour of Their Hands* (Philadelphia: stereotyped by L. Johnson, 1833), pp. 3–34

There is frequently as intense a degree of distress suffered here, as in London or Paris. The principal difference is not in the *intensity*, but in the *extent* of the distress. . . . It is no alleviation of the misery of an unfortunate female in Philadelphia or Boston, who . . . earns from nine to fifteen cents per day, that there are fewer similarly circumstanced here than in those cities.

It is often triumphantly asked . . . What remedy can be applied to such an inveterate evil? Does not the proportion between supply and demand, in this, as in all other cases, regulate prices? . . .

I contend for it, that every principle of honour, justice, and

[24] Born in Dublin in 1760, Carey came to America in 1784 after being imprisoned for his criticisms of England's Irish policies. He became a leading bookseller, publisher, and pamphleteer on political and economic subjects.

generosity, forbids the employer to take advantage of the distress and wretchedness of those he employs, and cut down their wages below the minimum necessary to procure a sufficiency of plain food and of clothes to guard against the inclemency of the weather. Whoever passes this line of demarcation, is guilty of the heinous offence of *"grinding the faces of the poor."* [25] The labour of every human being ought to insure this remumeration at least. . . .

By proper efforts, the oppression of the mass of the sufferers may at least be *mitigated*, and no inconsiderable portion of them may be completely relieved. . . .

I have known a lady to expend a hundred dollars on a party; pay thirty or forty dollars for a bonnet, and fifty for a shawl; and yet make a hard bargain with a seamstress or washerwoman, who had to work at her needle or at the washing-tub for thirteen or fourteen hours a day, to make a bare livelihood for herself and a numerous family of small children! This is "a sore oppression under the sun," and ought to be eschewed by every honourable mind. "Let it be reformed altogether."

Essay I

I propose . . . to refute, certain pernicious errors which too generally prevail respecting the situation, the conduct, the characters, and the prospects of those whose sole dependence is on the labour of their hands. . . .

1. That every man, woman, and grown child, able and willing to work may find employment.

2. That the poor, by industry, prudence, and economy, may at all times support themselves comfortably, without depending on eleemosynary aid—and, as a corollary from these positions,

3. That their sufferings and distresses chiefly, if not wholly, arise from their idleness, their dissipation, and their extravagance.

4. That taxes for the support of the poor, and aid afforded them by charitable individuals, or benevolent societies, are pernicious, as, by encouraging the poor to depend on them, they foster their idleness and improvidence, and thus produce, or at

[25] Isaiah, 3:15.

least increase, the poverty and distress they are intended to relieve.

These opinions . . . have been pernicious to the rich and the poor. They tend to harden the hearts of the former against the sufferings and distresses of the latter [26]—and of course prolong those sufferings and distresses. . . .

Essay II

In the most prosperous times and countries, there are certain occupations, which, by the influence of fashion or other causes, suffer occasional stagnations. There are other occupations, at which employment is at all times precarious—and others, again, which furnish little or no employment at certain seasons of the year.

To the first class belong all those who minister to the fanciful wants of society—wants contracted or expanded by the whim or caprice of fashion. . . .

The custom of cropping the hair threw half of our hairdressers out of employment. The general use of lamps produced a similar effect on the chandlers. . . .

In the second class, the most conspicuous are the shoe-binders, the spoolers, and seamstresses employed on coarse work, who, being far more numerous than the demand for their service requires, a portion of them are at all times but partially employed.

In the third class may be enumerated labourers on canals and turnpike roads, hod-carriers, wood sawyers, wood-pilers, &c. &c. . . .

By the annexed letter from Joseph M'Ilvaine, Esq., formerly secretary of the board of canal commissioners, it appears that the average wages of this class [canal laborers], in common times, are from ten to twelve dollars per month and found; [27] that in winter they may be had for five dollars; and that sometimes, in that season, when labour is scarce, they work for their board alone. . . .

I will therefore assume ten dollars for ten months, and five

[26] Cf. Chalmers (R24) on the hardheartedness of the rich.
[27] I.e., board and lodging.

dollars for two—and take the case of a labourer with a wife and two children. Many of them have three or four.

10 months at 10 dollars	$100.00
2 months at 5 dollars	10.00
Suppose the wife to earn half a dollar per week	26.00
Total	$136.00

I now submit a calculation of the expenses of such a family, every item of which is at a low rate.

Shoes and clothes for self and wife, each 12 dollars	$ 24.00
Washing at the canal, 6¼ cents per week	3.25
Shoes and clothes for two children, each 8 dollars	16.00
Rent 50 cents per week	26.00
Soap, candles, &c. 6 cents per week	3.12
Fuel, at 12 cents per week	6.24
Meat, drink, vegetables, &c. &c. 8 cents per day, each, for wife and children	87.60
	$166.21
Deficit	$ 30.21

This is one of a large class, whom some of our political economists of the new school are not ashamed to stigmatize as worthless and improvident, because they do not, forsooth, save enough out of their miserable wages, to support themselves and families, in times of scarcity, without the aid of benevolent societies; whereas it appears that their wages are inadequate to their support, even when fully employed.

Here let it be observed, there is no allowance for a single day in the whole year, lost by accident, by sickness, or by want of employment—no allowance for expense arising from sickness of wife or children. . . .

Essay III

They must rely, on those occasions, upon the overseers of the poor, or benevolent societies, or charitable individuals, or on such extraordinary aid, as, to the honour of our citizens, the late (1830) distressing scenes called forth. If I succeed in deeply imprinting this important truth on the public mind, so that it may produce the proper effect, by removing the injurious prejudices that prevail on the conduct and character of the labouring poor, on the effects of benevolent societies, and on the claims of those societies for extensive support, I shall regard myself as signally fortunate. . . .

While I freely admit that there are among the poor many worthless, I am fully satisfied, from the most attentive examination of the subject, that the worthless of both sexes bear but a very small proportion to those who are industrious and meritorious. . . .

The industry and virtue of the labouring poor appear undeniable, from the fact, that there is no occupation, however deleterious or disgraceful, at which there is any difficulty in procuring labourers, even at the most inadequate wages. The labour on canals in marshy situations, in atmospheres replete with pestilential miasmata, is full proof on this point. Although the almost certain consequence of labouring in such situations is a prostration of health, and danger of life . . . their places are readily supplied by other victims who offer themselves upon the altars of industry.

This is one of those decisive facts which ought to silence cavil for ever on this important subject.

Essay IV

Let us now turn to the appalling case of seamstresses, employed on coarse work, and to that of spoolers: and here "I will a tale unfold, to harrow up the soul" of all those endowed with feelings of humanity.

Coarse shirts and duck pantaloons are frequently made for 8 and 10 cents. The highest rate . . . is 12½ cents. Women free from the incumbrance of children, in perfect health, and with constant, uninterrupted employment, cannot, by the testimony of ladies of the first respectability, who have fully scrutinized the affair, make more than nine shirts per week, working from twelve to fifteen hours per day, and possessing considerable expertness. . . .

How little attention is paid to the awful denunciation against those that *"grind the faces of the poor."* Allowing nine shirts per week, at 12½ cents, and constant, uninterrupted employment, let us view the appalling result.

9 shirts per week—1.12½ . .Per annum	$58.50
Rent at 50 cents	$26.00
Shoes and clothes, suppose	10.00
Fuel per week, say 15 cents	7.80
Soap, candles, &c., 8 cents	4.16
Remain for food, and drink 20 cents per week, or about 2¾ cents per day!!!!!	10.54
	$58.50

. . . . .

Here is no declamation; no pathetic appeal; no solemn invocation, to arouse the dormant feelings of humanity. It is all a plain statement of harrowing facts, that defy the severest scrutiny. It exhibits a state of suffering which, I had almost said, cries to heaven for vengeance.

In speaking of the effect on some of the unfortunate seamstresses, to drive them to licentious courses, I ought to use the strongest language the subject would admit of. . . . Let those who pass a heavy censure on them, and are ready exultingly to cry out, with the Pharisee in the gospel, "Thank God, we are not like one of these," ponder well what might have been their conduct in similar circumstances. . . . This subject has for five years been pressed on the public attention, in almost every shape and form, without exciting a single efficient effort in Boston, New York, or Philadelphia. . . .

Essay V

But we are gravely told, that some of the seamstresses ought to go to service—that servants are scarce; if they would condescend to fill that station, they might have comfortable homes, abundance of good food, light labour, and high wages. . . .

Some individuals among those oppressed women . . . might

go to service. . . . But on a careful inquiry . . . I am persuaded the number is small, and bears but a slight proportion to the whole number of the seamstresses. There is among them a large proportion of aged widows, who are wholly unfit for service, and many young widows, with two or three small children . . . and whom their wages, as servants, would not support at nurse. . . .

Essay VI

It follows, of course, that the poor rates, the aid of benevolent societies, &c., far from producing the pernicious effects ascribed to them are imperiously necessary, and that without them, numbers would . . . actually perish of want, or would have recourse to medicity; and mendicants impose a far heavier tax on a community than the same number of paupers supported by poor rates. The support of 549 out-door paupers of Philadelphia, in 1830, averaged 46¼ cents per week—or less than 7 cents per day. Some of them received only a quarter of a dollar a week. I submit a statement of the whole number, with the pittance they respectively received:

42	a	25 cents
2	a	$31\frac{1}{4}$
186	a	$37\frac{1}{2}$
259	a	50
17	a	$62\frac{1}{2}$
42	a	75
1	a	100
549		

. . . . .

Those of our fellow-citizens who complain of the oppression of our poor laws, will learn with surprise, that of the 549 out-door paupers, there were no less than 390 above 60 years of age, and 6 above 100. Almost all of these were in a state of superannuation, 50 of them were blind, and 406 of the whole number . . . were widows. I annex a statement of their respective ages.

Between 10 and 20	4	60 and 70	154
20 and 30	26	70 and 80	161
30 and 40	42	80 and 90	60
40 and 50	40	90 and 100	9
50 and 60	47	Upwards of 100	6
	159		390
			549

Of the whole number, 381 had 935 children, of whom 372 were at home with their parents. . . .

Essay X

A cause has been steadily and powerfully operating to increase the poor rates. . . . I mean the rapid and oppressive reduction of wages, consequent on the wonderful improvements in machinery. Manual labour succumbs in the conflict with steam and water power: and . . . every thing that supersedes the demand for that labour must increase competition; lower wages; produce distress; and, to the same extent, increase the poor rates. . . .

Essay XII

What remedy can be found for the enormous and cruel oppression experienced by females employed as seamstresses. . . . I venture to suggest a few palliatives.

1. Public opinion, a powerful instrument, ought to be brought to bear on this subject. . . . The pulpit ought to unite in this crusade. . . .

2. Let the employment of females be multiplied as much as possible. They are admirably calculated for various occupations from which they are at present in a great degree excluded, more especially shop-keeping in retail stores.

3. The poorer class ought to have exclusively the business of white-washing and other low employments, now in a great degree monopolized by men.

4. Let the Provident Societies, intended to furnish employment for women in winter, be munificently supported; and let those Societies give fair and liberal wages, following the laudable

example of the Impartial Humane Society of Baltimore, and the Female Hospitable Society of Philadelphia.

5. Let the ladies have some of the poor women, who are half starved, making coarse shirts at 6, 8, and 10 cents each, taught fine needle-work, mantua-making, millinery, clear starching, quilting, &c. There is always a great want of women in these branches.

6. Let schools be opened for instructing poor women in cooking. Good cooks are always scarce.

7. Schools for young ladies, and infant schools, ought, with few exceptions, to be taught by females, who should be regularly educated for those important branches, which are peculiarly calculated for their sex, and which would afford excellent occupation for the daughters of reduced families.

8. Ladies who can afford it, ought to give out their sewing and washing, and pay fair prices. . . .

9. In the towns in the interior of the state, and in those in the western states, there is generally a want of females as domestics, seamstresses, &c. &c.; and in factories, as spoolers, spinners, and weavers. It would be a most meritorious appropriation of a part of the superfluous wealth of the rich, to provide for sending some of the superabundant poor females of our cities to those places.

10. To crown the whole, let ladies who lead the fashion, take up the cause of these poor women, *con amore*. It is a holy cause.

27. A Charity of Wages

Third Annual Report of the Managers of the Seaman's Aid Society of the City of Boston [Sarah Josepha Hale, President] (Boston: James B. Dow, 1836), pp. 4–13 [28]

It is three years, this day, since our Society was formed. . . .
The first proceeding of the ladies was to get up a Fair, in order to obtain funds. They were successful; and soon more than *one*

[28] The author of this report was the president of the Society, Sarah Josepha Hale, then editor of the *Ladies' Magazine*. In 1822 she had been

thousand dollars were in the hands of the Managers. A question then arose, respecting the manner in which this money should be used, in order to meet that clause in the Constitution, which requires *"improvement in the character and conditions of seamen, and their families."*

There had never been but one method of improvement adopted by benevolent Societies, whose object it was to relieve the poor, namely, that of giving alms. These, to be sure, were distributed in several ways and under various restrictions; but *all*, in the end, came out alike; all gave away their funds, and pauperism increased every year. . . .

Many of the females who applied for charity, were healthy and able to support themselves; but they had little employment, and for what they did obtain, the pay was so inadequate, that they were not incited to industrious habits. And when they had once become pensioners on a benevolent society, they soon seemed to consider that they had a right to the funds; their self-respect was gone; they had been branded as paupers; and all hopes of improvement, in their character and condition, were at an end, till this necessity for charity could be removed.

Yes—ladies left their families, gave up useful occupations, elegant pursuits, or improving studies, to assemble themselves together, and make coarse garments, to be distributed gratuitously; while poor women, who ought to have been employed in needlework, and to whom, probably, these very garments were given, were spending their time in idle gossip, or vicious indulgences! . . .

The feeling among our members became unanimous, that the Seaman's Aid Society should not be instrumental in promoting, in our country, idleness and vagrancy, by offering a premium

---

left a widow with five small children to support, an experience reflected in her attitude toward the women to be aided by the Society. Her ideas for employment of women at a fair wage were set forth in a letter to Mathew Carey in April, 1832, before the organization of the Seaman's Aid Society. Isabelle Webb Entrikin, *Sarah Josepha Hale and Godey's Lady's Book* (Philadelphia: by the author, 1946), p. 39.

in the shape of alms to all who can prove that they are destitute. And yet the poor were to be assisted, in order to their improvement; for it was plain, that, without a place to stand upon, they could no more raise themselves, than the philosopher of old could raise the world. It was seen that the true way, was to give employment, paying such a price for the labor, as would enable those who were industrious and faithful, to provide for their own support. This was the first step in improvement.

Impelled by these motives, the Managers proceeded to make arrangements for opening a Clothing Store. The first appropriation was only *three hundred dollars*—so fearful were we of risking much of the public funds, in what many then believed a visionary experiment. We decided to have our ready-made clothing consist chiefly of Seamen's apparel, and to employ, as workwomen, none but females belonging to the families of Seamen, if these should be found capable of doing the work. . . .

We intended to have our clothing well made, and offered at the usual prices. We would not attempt to undersell the slop-shops.[29] It was no part of our plan to interfere with what is called the market price of goods. Our object was, to correct the evil of insufficient wages to poor females, because, if this could not be done, pauperism must go on increasing. The poor must have a living. If they cannot obtain this by their own earnings, they must solicit alms.

The most delicate part of our duty was to fix the scale of prices for our work. We thought it a righteous principle, that the person who labors steadily and faithfully, shall receive as wages, sufficient, at least, for his or her support. Accordingly, we assumed the sum of three dollars per week, as the rate of wages, which a healthy adult female, who is very industrious, and tolerably handy with her needle, ought to earn; we ascertained what such an one could perform, and graduated the prices we paid for needlework accordingly. We found that we could pay this rate, and still sell our garments at the same price as the

[29] "Slop" was a common term for sailors' clothing.

slop-shops without loss, though we gave, on some garments, nearly double wages to our work-women.

Our store was opened February 26th, 1834. The results of that year are embodied in our Report of last January. . . . We had distributed . . . about *six hundred and fifty dollars*, and had only diminished the original sum entrusted us by the public, *thirty-eight dollars*. . . .

We have now on hand, in goods, garments at cost, and in cash . . . $3,314.23—being only about *two hundred dollars* less than the amount of the funds from the public; though we have distributed over *one thousand dollars*, in wages and charity, during the year, besides paying all the expenses of our establishment. . . .

We have gained—what is better than gold—the confidence and co-operation of the poor themselves, in this plan for their improvement. They feel that this is the true charity—that it does good to the mind, as well as the body. They take pride in the acknowledgment that they are employed by our Society; because it shows that they are receiving good wages, and that they work well.

Some persons have inquired, Where was the charity, though we do pay a higher price for making garments, while we insist on having these so well made? . . .

They know little of human nature, who do not take into account the feelings under which a task is performed. Give a poor woman a shirt to make, for which she is to receive but *ten cents*, and what motive is there to prompt her to diligence and neatness in her work? She knows that, if she strives ever so hard, she cannot maintain herself—if she must beg, it is just as easy to ask for a whole loaf, as a slice. She is discouraged, and she "dawdles about," . . . does little, and nothing well. But offer her *twenty cents*, if she will make the same garment neatly, and see if the stimulus does not quicken her fingers, and awaken her ingenuity and ambition. I am aware, that, to dwell on the influence of a few cents to those who reckon their income by thousands of dollars, may seem preposterous; but to one who is in want of all things, the difference between *ten* and *twenty* cents is a great matter. . . . What money they do earn, they can use as they please. They are not called to account to us about the matter. They may live very meanly, but still are not paupers; their children cannot be taunted with that disgrace.

The charity of Societies that give alms ought to be carefully guarded. I mean no imputation on this watchfulness when I assert, that the scrutiny, instituted into the private history and all the proceedings of the individual who solicits relief, is almost sure to degrade the poor. It thwarts their affections, contemns their judgment, and breaks down their self-respect.

"I think you have spent that half-dollar, which Mr. A—— gave you, very soon," said a dispenser of public charity to a poor woman, who applied for relief. "How did you lay it out? You surely did not want wood."

"No, Sir—but John was quite sick, and I bought an ounce of tea, and a little sugar, and a few crackers."

"And so spent the fifty cents in luxuries," pursued the gentleman.

"No—not all of it: I laid out ninepence for a yard of calico, to make Peggy an apron; the poor girl wanted to go to school, and her gown was not decent, and the children laughed at her."

"It won't do for poor people to think so much about appearances," remarked the gentleman, gravely. "I cannot assist you any more at present."

Think you that poor woman did not go away with deep resentment in her heart, against Benevolent Societies, that she had been told had funds to assist the poor, and yet withold all aid, except the sufferer is in the lowest state of dependence and wretchedness?

Now, we encourage our poor to think about *appearances*. We believe that those who are indifferent about good appearances, will soon be equally so about the reality of goodness. We have a committee of ladies, who visit our workwomen as friends, to encourage their virtuous efforts; their report usually is, that they find these poor women busy and cheerful, "getting along well," as they say of themselves, "since they were favored with work from the Store."

We have, during the past year, employed, more or less, about fifty females—but we have found that, on many accounts, it is better that those who work for us should be wholly in our employ; for the last three months, therefore, we have employed steadily more than twenty women, mostly widowed mothers, or those who have others besides themselves to support.* Surely it is doing no small amount of good, to furnish to twenty poor families the means of comfort and improvement. I have the pleasure of informing you, that scarcely a single family, who take work from our Store, has applied for charity during the year. . . .

To find employment for the poor, paying them a just price for the labor, is the only charity which will permanently improve their condition, and benefit society. . . .

I am aware it is the creed of political economists, that trade must regulate itself; that the market price of labor is the just price. But I insist, that a benevolent society has a right to establish a charity of wages, if that be the proper phrase, when it is found that the honest, faithful laborer cannot subsist by the market rate. . . .

Already our example has had an influence for good. Many of the Slop-shops have raised their rate of wages; on some garments *one-third*. . . . This is the consummation at which we aimed, to secure to our own sex the profits of the needle, that that employment may be to them a resource in the day of adversity.

* These families probably include about eighty individuals. Now the Institution for the Blind was founded at an expense of more than *one hundred thousand dollars*, it receives annually several thousand dollars from the State, besides other large donations; and yet there are not more than fifty or sixty pupils, during the year, who are benefited by that charity. It was a noble philanthropy which founded the Institute for the poor blind children; but will not a system of benevolence, which shall improve the condition and character of Seamen and their families, be equally praiseworthy, and far more beneficial?

28. To Secure the Just Enjoyment of Earnings

Fourth Annual Report . . . Seaman's Aid Society. . . .
[Sarah Josepha Hale, President] (Boston: March, Capan
& Lyon, 1837), pp. 13-15 [30]

Experience and observation have shown us that, to make the
system complete, another principle must be carried out in connexion and harmony with the first, namely, *to secure to the industrious poor the just enjoyment of their own earnings, by taking measures to save them from paying exorbitant prices for the
necessaries of life.*[31]

It is a notorious fact, that the poor now pay from twenty
to a hundred per cent. more for groceries and fuel than the
rich. . . .

Let the benevolent form an association, to purchase fuel when
it is cheapest, and keep a sufficient stock to sell to these poor
laboring people. . . . Before God, human beings are willing to
humble themselves; but in their intercourse with each other, it
is their nature to regard what they consider *justice* far more
complacently than *mercy.* . . .

Those who are endowed with clearer judgment, and better
talents, who have enjoyed the advantages of education, and inherited or acquired large wealth, should consider these advantages
as imposing on them the duty of protectors and benefactors to
those who cannot help themselves; securing to such that justice
which their sex, their ignorance, or their low estate, prevents
them from obtaining in the business of the world.

[30] Shortly after this report was written Mrs. Hale went to Philadelphia,
at the urging of Mathew Carey, to become editor of *Godey's Lady's Book*,
for which she is famous. Although she retained her interest in the Seaman's
Aid Society, the active leadership passed to other hands, and it soon lost
the dynamic quality it had while she was there.
[31] Note that the system whereby wealthy persons provided capital to
enable goods to be sold at low prices is different from the cooperative
movement that came into existence a few years later, in which the members themselves provided the capital.

XIII

THE ENVIRONMENTAL APPROACH

Along with economic reform and individual regeneration, many people in the second quarter of the century saw a third approach to the amelioration of the appalling problems of the masses. This was through the use of the police power of the state to compel the improvement of the environment in which they lived. In England, Edwin Chadwick, the civil servant who had steered the Poor Law reforms to enactment in 1834, was now engaged in sanitary reform, the beginnings of public health work. In America, one of the early leaders in public health and sanitary reform was Dr. John H. Griscom, health officer of New York City, and son of the founder of the Society for the Prevention of Pauperism. His graphic description provides background for the activities of the AICP and the Children's Aid Society, depicted in R30–36. Note that here Griscom shifted the concept of fault away from the unfortunate sufferers and attached it to the landlords and the system under which they operated. Both, in his mind, were subject to regulation by government, in the first instance through city ordinance.

29. A Tainted and Unwholesome Atmosphere

John H. Griscom, M.D., *The Sanitary Condition of the Laboring Population of New York* (New York: Harper, 1845), pp. 2–10, 12–13, 55

The objects of this communication, briefly stated, are these: —1st, to show that there is an immense amount of sickness, physical disability, and premature mortality, among the poorer classes; 2d, that these are, to a large extent, unnecessary, being in a great degree the results of causes which are removable; 3d, that these physical evils are productive of moral evils of great magnitude and number, and which, if considered only in a pecuniary point of view, should arouse the government and individuals to a consideration of the best means for their relief and prevention; and 4th, to suggest the means of alleviating these evils and preventing their recurrence to so great an extent. . . .

There is an amount of sickness and death in this, as in all large cities, far beyond those of less densely peopled, more airy and open places, such as country residences. . . . The congregation of animal and vegetable matters, with their constant effluvia, which has less chance of escape from the premises, in proportion to the absence of free circulation of air, is detrimental to the health of the inhabitants.

These circumstances have never yet been investigated in this city, as they should be. Our people, especially the more destitute, have been allowed to live out their brief lives in tainted and unwholesome atmospheres, and be subject to the silent and invisible encroachments of destructive agencies from every direction, without one warning voice being raised to point to them their danger, and without an effort to rescue them from their impending fate. Fathers are taken from their children, husbands from their wives, "ere they have lived out half their days"—the widows and orphans are thrown upon public or private charity for support, and the money which is expended to save them from starvation, to educate them in the public schools, or, perchance, to maintain them in the work-house or the prison, if judiciously spent in improving the sanitary arrangements of the city, and instilling into the population a knowledge of the means by which their health might be protected, and their lives prolonged and made happy, would have been not only saved, but returned to the treasury in the increased health of the population, a much better state of public morals, and, by consequence, a more easily governed and respectable community. . . .

Sanitary regulations affect the pauper class of the population more directly than any other. . . . They are more crowded, they live more in cellars, their apartments are less ventilated, and more exposed to vapours and other emanations, &c., hence, ventilation, sewerage, and all other sanitary regulations, are more necessary for them, and would produce a greater comparative change in their condition. . . .

The basis of these evils is the subjection of the tenantry, to the merciless inflictions and extortions of the *sub-landlord.* . . .

The tenements, in order to admit a greater number of families, are divided into small apartments, as numerous as decency will admit. Regard to comfort, convenience, and health, is the last motive. . . . These closets, for they deserve no other name, are then rented to the poor, from week to week, or month to month, the rent being almost invariably required in advance, at least for the first few terms. The families moving in first, after the house is built, find it clean, but the lessee has no supervision over their habits, and however filthy the tenement may become, he cares not, so that he receives his rent. . . .

Very often . . . no cleaning other than washing the floor, is ever attempted, and that but seldom. White washing, cleaning of furniture, of bedding, or persons, in many cases is *never* attempted. . . . Every corner of the room, of the cupboards, of the entries and stairways, is piled up with dirt. The walls and ceilings, with the plaster broken off in many places, exposing the lath and beams, and leaving openings for the escape from within of the effluvia of vermin, dead and alive, are smeared with the blood of unmentionable insects, and dirt of all indescribable colours. . . .

By the mode in which the rooms are planned, *ventilation is entirely prevented.* It would seem as if most of these places were built expressly for this purpose. . . . If there is a sleeping apartment, it is placed at the extremity of the room farthest from the windows, is generally but little larger than sufficient to hold a bedstead, and its area is reduced, for air, by the bed furniture, trunks, boxes, &c. and having no windows, fresh air and sun light are entire strangers to its walls. In this dark hole there is, of course, a concentrated accumulation of the effluviae of the bodies and breaths of the persons sleeping in it (frequently the whole family, several in number), and this accumulation goes on from night to night, without relief, until it can easily be believed the smell becomes intolerable, and its atmosphere productive of the most offensive and malignant diseases. . . .

I have had recent occasion to visit several of these pestiferous places, and I pen these paragraphs in the month of August, with their sight and smell fresh upon my senses. . . .

The deficiency of water, and the want of a convenient place for washing, with no other place for drying clothes than the common sitting and bed room, are very serious impediments in the way of their [the tenants] improvement. Without any convenient or safe place to deposit wood, or coal, or food in large quantities, all their purchases are by "the small," from the neighbouring grocer (who is perhaps the landlord) at prices from 10 to 50 per cent. above the rates at which they might be obtained, under better circumstances.[32]

But the most offensive of all places for residence are the *cellars*. It is almost impossible, when contemplating the circumstances and condition of the poor beings who inhabit these holes, to maintain the proper degree of calmness requisite for a thorough inspection, and the exercise of a sound judgment, respecting them. You must descend to them; you must feel the blast of foul air as it meets your face on opening the door; you must grope in the dark, or hesitate until your eye becomes accustomed to the gloomy place, to enable you to find your way through the entry, over a broken floor, the boards of which are protected from your tread by a half inch of hard dirt; you must inhale the suffocating vapor of the sitting and sleeping rooms; and in the dark, damp recess, endeavor to find the inmates by the sound of their voices, or chance to see their figures moving between you and the flickering blaze of a shaving burning on the hearth, or the misty light of a window coated with dirt and festooned with cobwebs—or if in search of an invalid, take care that you do not fall full length upon the bed with her, by stumbling against the bundle of rags and straw, dignified by that name, lying on the floor, under the window, if window there is. . . .

In some courts to which I can point, *the surface is below the*

[32] Cf. R28; also R30, n. 36.

level of the street, and at every rain, the water being unable to run off into the street, is all discharged down into the adjacent areas and cellars, keeping them almost constantly wet. It was but a short time ago I met with the case of a woman, the wife of a tailor living in a noted court. . . . She has lived there six months, four of which she has been sick with rheumatism, and on that account, unable to work. Otherwise she would be able to earn considerable by assisting her husband. They have four children depending upon them, and are obliged to seek assistance from the public, in consequence of this sickness. She attributes her disease to the water in the cellar, which runs in, and obliges her to bale out, and wipe up, at every storm. The money expended upon them in charity, would have rectified all this difficulty, have preserved the health and strength of the family, and saved all parties much trouble and suffering. . . .

It is not a difficult matter for the Dispensary Physician, while receiving applications for medical aid at the office, to distinguish, in a majority of cases, the cellar residents from all others, without asking a question. If the whitened and cadaverous countenance should be an insufficient guide, *the odor of the person* will remove all doubt; a musty smell, which a damp cellar only can impart, pervades every article of dress, the woolens more particularly, as well as the hair and skin.

At No. 50 Pike-street is a cellar about ten feet square, and seven feet high, having only one very small window, and the old fashioned, inclined cellar door. In this small place, were lately residing *two families consisting of ten persons,* of all ages. . . .

Almost every one can recall . . . the effects of nauseous odors . . . or of sleeping in a small confined apartment, upon his own health and feelings. . . . Compare the pale face of the city belle, or matron, after the long confinement of the winter and spring, with the same countenance in the fall, upon her return from a few weeks tour to the Springs and Niagara, and observe whether the return of the long absent rose upon the cheek, is not accompanied with a greater elasticity of frame, and a happier and stronger tone of mind.

Descend a few steps further, from the airy and well-lighted chamber and parlor, to the confined apartments of the pent-up court, and the damp, secluded cellar; draw a contrast between the gay inhabitant of the former, and the attenuated tenant of the latter, and we may then judge of the influences of the air, which they respectively respire. . . .

[According to] the reports of the three medical charities, for the year ending March, 1844, there were prescribed for at the offices, and the homes of the poor, at the

Northern	Dispensary	13,317	Patients
Eastern	"	17,107	"
New York	"	23,858	"
	Total	54,282	

. . . . .

Does it not become the duty of the magistrate and the philanthropist upon the presentation of such a statement as this, of the waste and havoc of the life, health, and strength of the people . . . to use every possible means to alleviate them? . . .

A sanitary police . . . would constitute an efficient corps of *Health Missionaries*. Their time would be principally devoted to the purpose of teaching the poor the rules which should regulate their household operations; and the value of fresh air, ventilation, cleanliness, temperance, &c., would form constant themes for them. The circulation of Tracts of Health, distributed with the same freedom as religious tracts now are, by hands equally interested in the comforts and condition of the poor, would form a powerful addition to their means of usefulness.[33] . . .

A well regulated and efficient Health Police might do much towards correcting the existing evils, but to carry the desired reform to the utmost limit, and with a greater permanency,

[33] By mid-twentieth century governmental and voluntary agencies, insurance companies, and commercial organizations were turning out floods of health tracts.

measures which no police can carry out, are necessary. And as these evils are not confined to the laboring and destitute part of our population, but afflict also the wealthier portion, a more healthy state of public opinion is absolutely necessary, to effect the desired results.

XIV

THE ASSOCIATION FOR IMPROVING THE CONDITION OF THE POOR

Simultaneously with the movement for public health measures came a new wave of apprehension over the sordidness of the lives of great numbers of people and the ineffectiveness of the relief practices of the period. The New York Association for Improving the Condition of the Poor was organized in 1843 with the younger Griscom as a prominent participant. Not only did the new agency achieve permanence, but its example was followed in cities throughout the country, so that there was, in the middle of the century, what might be referred to as an "AICP movement."

The AICP utilized an administrative pattern similar to those recommended by the elder Griscom and Chalmers, with stress on the individual approach through volunteer visitors, each to be responsible for the work in a small locality. The emphasis was to be on reeducation and moral suasion, with relief as a secondary objective.

It was recognized at the outset that for personal influence to be effective, the visitor must maintain a sympathetic and noncritical attitude. As repeatedly happened with similar organizations both before and after the AICP, the urgency of the economic deprivation of those applying for help so taxed the energy and resources of the visitors that counseling tended to give way to relief-giving as their primary activity.

The goal of improving the environment in which the indigent lived early led the Association over into social action activities with respect to general community conditions. It instigated the establishment of the Juvenile Asylum in 1851 to take care of homeless and neglected children (the juvenile delinquents of that time). Research and study were deemed important, and in 1853 a major sanitary survey of the city was published. A venture into the field of housing was the construction in 1855 of a huge "model" tenement house for working people which, with its early experimental plumbing and inadequate ventilation, proved to be anything but a model.[34]

Neither moral suasion nor environmental improvement was sufficient to cope with some of the most deplorable situations that the visitors were observing. Inadequate parental supervision of children and poor school attendance were seen as contributing to future problems of poverty. The leaders felt the need for some form of authority to deal with cases where personal influence was ineffective, and in 1853 they successfully memorialized the legislature to strengthen the right of citizens to bring vagrant and unschooled children to the attention of the courts. This use of the police power for the control of individual behavior differed from its use for the control of property, which Griscom had advocated. The steps in this early example of efforts to develop policy and method involving both individual and group approaches to human problems were: first, observe frequent incidents in the cases that come to direct attention; second, secure legislation to modify conditions of the large group similarly situated; and third, make certain that the legislation is enforced generally and applied in the agency's own cases.

To be effective, an institution must have not only philosophy and goal, but skilled administrative leadership. Central figure in the New York AICP was Robert M. Hartley. Probably the first man in the United States to make a career of the administration of charitable organizations, he served as its secretary from its founding until his retirement in 1876. The Confidential Instructions to visitors, based on twelve years' experience, illustrate the way in which he, like any strong executive, constantly reiterated, reinterpreted, and redefined the purposes of the organization.

Of particular interest are the following ideas, all of which are

[34] For a graphic description, see Robert H. Bremner, "The Big Flat: History of a New York Tenement," *American Historical Review,* LXIV (1958), 54–62.

found in social work practice a hundred years later: (1) There should be selective intake—of only those cases which the organization thinks it is especially equipped to help—with referral of others to appropriate resources in the community (this selectivity is possible because basic public provision is available for everybody, and the voluntary agency is expected to have a different function from that of either public agencies or religious organizations); (2) There is danger of permitting material help to become an end in itself; (3) There is a constructive value in adequate relief; and (4) inadequate public relief provision does not justify a shift in emphasis by the voluntary agency to make up for that deficiency.

30. The Elevation of the Moral and Physical Conditions of the Indigent

First Annual Report of the New York Association for the Improvement of the Condition of the Poor [35] for the year 1845 with the Constitution, Visitor's Manual . . . . (New York: 1845), pp. 8–9, 11, 20, 26

CONSTITUTION

Article II. Its design is the elevation of the moral and physical condition of the indigent; and so far as compatible with these objects, the relief of their necessities. . . .

Article X. The city shall be divided into seventeen Districts, each Ward forming a District; and the Districts be subdivided into Sections. Each District shall have an advisory Committee, to consist of five members; and each Section a Visitor.

Article XI. It shall be the duty of the Members of the Association . . . to give practical effect to its principles; especially to discountenance indiscriminate alms-giving and street-begging; to provide themselves with tickets of reference; and instead of giving aid to unknown applicants . . . to refer such applications to the Visitor of the Section in which the applicants reside, in order

[35] When the Association was incorporated in 1848, the name was changed to New York Association for Improving the Condition of the Poor. In 1938 the Association merged with the New York Charity Organization Society to form the Community Service Society of New York.

that they may be properly inquired into, and, if deserving, relieved.

BY-LAWS

Article III. It shall be the duty of the Sectional Visitors to
confine their labors exclusively to the particular Section assigned
them, so that no individual shall receive relief, excepting in the
Section where he is known and to which he belongs. They shall
carefully investigate all cases referred to them before granting
relief; ascertain their condition, their habits of life, and means of
subsistence; and extend to all such kind services, counsel, and
assistance, as a discriminating and judicious regard for their
present and permanent welfare requires. And in cases of sickness
and want, it will be their duty to inquire whether there is any
medical or other attendance; whether relief is afforded by any
religious or charitable society, and what assistance is needed. To
provide themselves with information respecting the nearest
dispensary, and in all cases, when practicable, to obtain aid from
existing charitable societies. And when no other assistance is
provided or available, then to draw from the resources of this
Association—not money, which is never allowed to be given,
except with the consent of the Advisory Committee or a member thereof—but such articles of food, fuel, clothing, and similar
supplies, as the necessities of the case require. And in all cases of
want coming to the knowledge of the Visitors, they will be
expected to perform the same duties although no application
has been made. It shall be their duty, moreover, to render a report of their labors, and also an account of all their disbursements,
to their respective Committees, on the last Wednesday of every
month.

ANNUAL REPORT, 1845

Some few have . . . objected to the *dietary* system, which
has been observed in giving relief.[36] In this they have overlooked

[36] One of the earliest publications of the Association was *The Economist;
or, Plain Directions about Food and Drink with the Best Modes of Preparation*, published in a number of editions after 1847.

some of the fundamental rules of the Institution, which require the Visitor—

To give what is least susceptible of abuse.

To give even necessary articles in small quantities, in proportion to immediate need.

To give assistance at the right moment; and not to prolong it beyond the duration of the necessity which calls for it; but to extend, restrict, and modify it with that necessity.

VISITOR'S MANUAL

Article III. Without delay . . . visit them at their homes; personally examine every case; ascertain their character and conditions; and carefully inquire into the causes which have brought them into a state of destitution. You will become an important instrument of good to your suffering fellow-creatures, when you aid them to obtain this good within themselves. To effect this, show them the true origin of their sufferings, when these sufferings are the result of imprudence, extravagance, idleness, intemperence, or other moral causes which are within their own control, and endeavor, by all appropriate means, to awaken their self-respect, to direct their exertions, and to strengthen their . . . capacities for self-support. In your intercourse with them, avoid all appearance of harshness, and every manifestation of an obtrusive and a censorious spirit. Study to carry into your work a mind as discriminating and judicious as it is kindly disposed, and a heart ready to sympathize with the sick and the infirm, the widow and the orphan, the tempted and the vicious. . . .

The most effectual encouragement . . . is not *alms chiefly*, or any other form of Charity as a substitute for alms, but that sympathizing counsel which re-enkindles hope, and that expression of respect for character, which such individuals [those reduced to indigence by unavoidable causes] never fail to appreciate.

31. The State Should Assume the Position of Parent

Tenth Annual Report, New York AICP (New York: 1853), pp. 23–24, 69–72

ANNUAL REPORT

Of all the forms . . . which pauperism assumes, that affecting the children of vicious pauper parents, is the most lamentable and unmanageable, and has consequently required the most comprehensive and energetic measures for its correction. Notwithstanding all the effort and influence the Institution had brought to bear upon this evil, it became so alarmingly prevalent, that a special organization, clothed with new legal powers, was deemed indispensable to its suppression. Hence the origin of the "Juvenile Asylum," an offshoot of this Association . . . which has been chartered, and is now in effective operation. But even more than this, in the way of legal provision, was considered necessary to arrest the progress of an evil so widespread and inveterate. The Board being decidedly of the opinion, that it is not only the just right, but the imperative duty of the State, in a matter so vitally affecting the public welfare, to enforce by legal enactment, the proper care, training, and instruction of neglected children, united with others, during the past year, in memorializing the Legislature, for a law to that effect. In accordance with the application, at the recent Extra Session of that Body, a general law was passed, authorizing the arrest of vagrant and truant children, on the complaint of any citizen before a magistrate, to be so disposed of as that the State itself should assume the position and responsibility of parent to such children, in order to be so educated, as to secure their usefulness, and promote the well-being of society.

CIRCULAR TO DISTRICT SECRETARIES AND VISITORS

Gentlemen:—In compliance with the instructions of the Board of Managers, I herewith transmit for your use, a copy of "An

Act to provide for the care and instruction of idle and truant children," passed April 12th, 1853. . . .

The Board of Managers, last winter, solicited your special efforts to induce the attendance at school of the children of suitable age, whose parents applied to this Institution for aid. Now, the foregoing law not only strengthens our hands in this good work, but encourages us to renewed exertions by the assurance that, in the judgment of the Legislature, we have not overrated the importance of the subject. . . .

The Legislature, be it observed, has now done all that it can consistently do. It has framed the machinery, and put it into our hands. But that machinery will be useless lumber, or fail to effect its purpose, except it be put into operation. . . . While this, however, is the duty of every citizen, it is in a peculiar sense obligatory on this Association, because of its relations to the poor and their offspring, and its superior facilities for acting with proper intelligence and efficiency through its numerous Visitors, in respect to all requiring their interference; also, by co-operating with the public officers, whose imperative duty it is to attend to all such children as are described in the foregoing Act.

The Board would therefore respectfully urge on Visitors a faithful enforcement, in all proper cases, of the foregoing law.

32. Confidential Instructions to the Visitors of the AICP [37]

New York, December 1st, 1855

Dear Sir,—The season being at hand when your duties as a Visitor of the Association will become increasingly arduous and difficult, permit a few plain practical suggestions relative thereto.

Notwithstanding the recent abundant harvests, the necessaries of life are high and employment scarce, so that a very large amount of indigence will, probably, have to be provided for, the coming winter. In anticipation of this, it appears important to

[37] A copy of this printed letter is pasted in the bound volume of official board minutes for the period 1850–76.

refresh our memories in regard to the part which it is the design of this Institution to take in the relief of the needy.

You scarcely need be reminded that the objects of this Association are twofold: *First,* The moral and physical elevation of the poor; and *Second,* . . . the relief of their necessities. But this order, unhappily, has been too often reversed, and almsgiving obtained a precedence which does not belong to it. The physical relief of the indigent, rather than their moral and economic wants, have received attention—present need rather than permanent elevation. Nor is it surprising that such has been the case. The poor seek relief, not reform; they ask bread, not counsel. Their poverty and wretchedness pleading in their behalf, it is the besetting temptation of the Visitor to relieve, irrespective of the merit or demerit of the applicants, or of its effects on their character. Yet here the greatest firmness is required, for at this point is found the chief difficulty in judicious relief, and the very point, moreover, where we profess to differ from most other charities. Our principles here are clear as a sunbeam. They show that it is worse to debase by alms than to withhold them; that the physical must be subservient to the moral, and the moral receive the attention its paramount importance demands.

Observe in what respect our principles differ from those which govern Almshouse relief. The Almhouse is a *legal* charity. It has no choice of subjects. It is bound to relieve all not otherwise legally provided for, without regard to character, for the obvious reason, if neglected by it, they might perish. This Association, on the contrary, is a voluntary charity, based on the social and economical wants of the community. It, of course, adapts its action and agencies to those ends. It has a choice of subjects, and has publicly declared what that choice is, viz., *to aid those whom it can physically and morally elevate, and no others.* And this it can safely do, for those it cannot consistently relieve, it can refer to public charity.

Our danger is to regard giving as an end in itself, and not as a means of attaining the higher and nobler objects which our

Constitution sets forth as paramount. To guard against this danger, we should refer to first principles, which in effect say, "Assist only those whose condition can be improved by such aid and attentions as you may be able to bestow." By this it is not meant that any should be left to suffer, but that the unaided be referred to their appropriate relief, when further responsibility in regard to them will cease. As the Association is not designed to supersede all our other almsgiving institutions, it cannot consistently pursue a less discriminating course. It were evidently impracticable for it to relieve all the indigent in the city. There must be a limit somewhere; and that limit, as defined by our principles, expressly excludes those it cannot elevate. If the Institution fails in this discrimination, and has no higher aim than the Almshouse, why should it exist at all? and why should those already heavily taxed for the public poor intrust funds to this charity? No one in this indirect way expects or desires to be taxed twice for the same object. Means, on the contrary, are intrusted to it, because its avowed objects are essentially different from those of legal, public aid. It aims to improve as well as to relieve. It is solely on these grounds that its appeals for patronage are so confidingly responded to. Take away these considerations, and the motives for its support would cease.

The principles of the Association have grown out of the exigencies of its position. Being not less a matter of necessity than choice, they carry with them their own vindication. Their first and most obvious effect would be to exclude from this charity the least manageable and hopeful of the population, whose condition it cannot improve, and thus greatly reduce the number of the relieved. Hence, without an increase of the general fund, the allowance to each proper recipient might be increased, and so employed by judicious almoners, as correspondingly to increase their moral power. If the amount now afforded is often too small to be morally effective, its multiplication two or three-fold would remove this cause of inefficiency. And if but half the former number of the poor should fall to the care of each Visitor, by concentrating his influence on fewer persons, which has hitherto been diffused among many, his efficiency in the same ratio would be augmented. . . .

For unrelieved applicants and to allay the dissatisfaction of donors, if any should thence arise, provision has been made in the arrangement of cards of reference; and these cards, if given to the unrelieved, and shown to donors, will always be satisfactory. Persons unrelieved by this Association, will be cared for by the Almshouse, or Emigration Department,[38] on which they have admitted claims, and which are legally bound to care for all proper cases. As it would be scarcely less absurd than impracticable for this Association to make the delinquency of these institutions the rule of its relief, all that it can do in authenticated cases of neglect, will be to investigate them, and endeavor to obtain such aid for the suffering as the law provides. . . .

If these various practicable provisions . . . are faithfully carried out, there can be no doubt that a new era of augmented efficiency would dawn upon the Association with corresponding moral and social benefits to the poor and to the community.

Respectfully yours, by order of the Board,

James Brown, *President*

R. M. Hartley, *Secretary*

[38] A state-operated relief agency for immigrants who became public charges.

XV

THE "DANGEROUS CLASSES"—
PREVENTION, NOT CURE

Much as in the case of the Society for the Prevention of Pauperism and the AICP, the Children's Aid Society reflected the changing times and the emotional reactions and leadership ability of one man. Charles Loring Brace seems to have been more immediately impelled by a feeling of hopelessness at the total ineffectiveness of current methods—in prisoner reformation, religious mission efforts, and institutional care of children—and by fear of what might happen to the privileged classes, than by the sufferings of the persons he set out to help, although he was not insensitive to their plight. The increase of criminality rather than growing relief needs stirred him. Support for his agency was stimulated by generating popular alarm over the "dangerous classes" as well as by appealing to pity for the helpless.

In words similar to those of the senior Griscom, Brace concluded that remedial efforts with delinquent and neglected children provided the only hope of eventual reduction in adult criminal behavior. Brace, however, relied to a greater extent on personal influence than did proponents of institutional care. The movement thus founded was part of a general trend toward specialization in clientele, begun early in the century with institutional provision for orphans and handicapped groups.

While Griscom had approached the problems of antisocial behavior with the hope of discovering a scientifically validated method, and Hartley developed a complex philosophy as to ultimate goal, Brace was of a pragmatic turn of mind, bent on finding through trial and error what would work. From his intuitive observations, he decided that children responded to individual attention and opportunity for fun and advancement rather than to exhortation. He further believed that advantage could be taken of their influence on each other, a device still used in therapeutic group work.

Brace made use of many kinds of approaches then in current vogue, including industrial education, sheltered workshops, group religious meetings, outings and vacations,[39] but is best known for his development of residences for self-supporting adolescents and for pioneering in foster home placement. In common with many of his predecessors and contemporaries, it seemed to him that removal from society was a likely way to reduce the number of problem children in his own community, but Brace contrived a way to secure their removal and at the same time capitalize on the beneficial influence of home life. This actually was a return to the colonial system of dealing with homeless children rather than a new arrangement, but Brace injected a modern touch with his emphasis on the promise of the expanding West.

The casual, opportunistic way in which Brace developed the services of his agency is illustrated in the selection of the director of the first Newsboys' Home and the first attempt to use Middle Western foster homes. Despite his firm conviction that family life offered the greatest promise for child training and reeducation, in most of his early efforts he bypassed the natural family completely and provided only token effort to make sure of the quality of substitute family care.

33. *The New and Practical Movement*

Charles Loring Brace, *Short Sermons to News Boys*
(New York: Scribner's, 1866), pp. 7, 9, 12–14

At that time [1848–53] a deep and earnest movement had passed over Europe, of sympathy and reform for the lowest classes—"the masses," as they were significantly called. . . . This wave reached this country; and the new and practical movement of religious reform at once took its direction toward the masses. . . .

[39] For a list of the varied activities conducted by the Children's Aid Society about the time of Brace's death, see Charles Loring Brace, *Life, Chiefly Told in His Own Letters*, ed. by his daughter, [Emma Brace] (New York: Scribner's, 1894), pp. 501–3.

Among the various benevolent movements . . . the most prominent peculiarity was their entire breaking away from the old methods of religious influence, and *the adapting themselves to the practical wants* of these classes. This has now become so general a principle . . . that its novelty can hardly be recognized. But at that time it met with great opposition. To give a poor man bread before a tract . . . to urge the entire change of circumstances and the emigration to country homes, as of far more importance to a certain class of vagrant children than any possible influence of Sunday-schools or Chapels, to talk of cleanliness as the first steps to godliness—all this seemed then to have a "humanitarian" tendency, and to belong to European "socialism" and "infidelity." . . .

During an extended tour in Europe, I had been studying the various institutions of charity and reform, and on my return, at once began a series of voluntary labors on Blackwell's Island [40] and in the "Five Points," [41] with the hope of benefiting the unfortunate and criminal population of those localities. After more than a year's trial, I became convinced that no far-reaching and permanent work of reform could succeed among these classes.[42] It was right that those who loved humanity in its lowest forms should labor for the forlorn prostitute, and the mature criminal. But on a broad scale no lasting effects could be expected to society from such efforts. . . . The hopeful field was evidently among the young. There, crime might possibly be checked in its very beginnings, and the seed of future good character and order and virtue be widely sown. . . .

The result . . . was the formation of the CHILDREN'S AID SOCIETY, in 1853, which has been the parent of so many charities for children since.

[40] The city prison.
[41] A crowded section of the Lower East Side, where Brace was associated with a religious mission.
[42] Brace frequently referred to the "dangerous classes," which he defined as "the ignorant, destitute, untrained, and abandoned youth: the outcast street-children grown up to be voters, to be the implements of demagogues, the 'feeders' of the criminals, and the sources of domestic outbreaks and violations of law." Charles Loring Brace, *The Dangerous Classes of New York* (New York: Wynkoop & Hallenbeck, 1872), p. ii.

34. *The Children's Aid Society's First Circular*

Charles Loring Brace, *The Dangerous Classes of New York* (New York: Wynkoop & Hallenbeck, 1872), pp. 90–93

This society has taken its origin in the deeply settled feelings of our citizens, that something must be done to meet the increasing crime and poverty among the destitute children of New York. Its objects are to help this class by opening Sunday Meetings and Industrial Schools, and, gradually as means shall be furnished, by forming Lodging-houses and Reading-rooms for children, and by employing paid agents whose sole business shall be to care for them. . . .

We remember that they have the same capacities, the same need of kind and good influences, and the same Immortality as the little ones in our own homes. . . . Thus far, alms-houses and prisons have done little to affect the evil. But a small part of the vagrant population can be shut up in our asylums, and judges and magistrates are reluctant to convict children so young and ignorant that they hardly seem able to distinguish good and evil. The class increases. Immigration is pouring in its multitude of poor foreigners, who leave these young outcasts everywhere abandoned in our midst. For the most part, the boys grow up utterly by themselves. No one cares for them, and they care for no one. Some live by begging, by petty pilfering, by bold robbery; some earn an honest support by peddling matches, or apples, or newspapers; others gather bones and rags in the street to sell. They sleep on steps, in cellars, in old barns, and in markets, or they hire a bed in filthy and low lodging-houses. They cannot read; they do not go to school or attend a church. . . . And, yet, among themselves they show generous and honest traits. Kindness can always touch them.

The girls, too often, grow up even more pitiable and deserted. Till of late no one has ever cared for them. They are the cross-walk sweepers, the little apple-peddlers, and candy-sellers of our city; or, by more questionable means, they earn their scanty bread. They traverse the low, vile streets alone, and live without mother or friends, or any share in what we should call a *home*. . . .

These boys and girls, it should be remembered, will soon form the great lower class of our city. They will influence elections; they may shape the policy of the city; they will, assuredly, if unreclaimed, poison society all around them. They will help to form the great multitude of robbers, thieves, vagrants, and prostitutes who are now such a burden upon the law-respecting community. . . .

In view of these evils we have formed an Association which shall devote itself entirely to this class of vagrant children. We do not propose in any way to conflict with existing asylums and institutions, but to render them a hearty co-operation, and, at the same time, to fill a gap, which, of necessity, they all have left. . . . We propose to give to these work, and to bring them under religious influence. As means shall come in, it is designed to district the city, so that hereafter every Ward may have its agent, who shall be a friend to the vagrant child. "Boys' Sunday Meetings" have already been formed, which we hope to see extended until every quarter has its place of preaching to boys. With these we intend to connect "Industrial Schools," where the great temptations to this class arising from want of work may be removed, and where they can learn an honest trade. Arrangements have been made with manufacturers, by which, if we have the requisite funds to begin, five hundred boys in different localities can be supplied with paying work. We hope, too, especially to be the means of draining the city of these children, by communicating with farmers, manufacturers, or families in the country, who may have need of such for employment. When homeless boys are found by our agents, we mean to get them homes in the families of respectable, needy persons in the city, and put them in the way of an honest living. . . .

This society, as we propose, shall be a medium through which all can, in their measure, practically help the poor children of the city.

We call upon . . . all who believe that crime is best averted by sowing good influences in childhood; all who are the friends of the helpless, to aid us in our enterprise. . . .
March, 1853

35. *A Simple Experiment—a Lodging House*

Brace, *Short Sermons*, pp. 15–17, 19–22, 44–45, 47

We were forced at every step, to test our means by the practical results on the children. If one method failed, we attempted another. When men meet on such a platform, their technical differences fade away, and there is found less variation between different sects than is commonly supposed. Our objects of labor—the persons whom we would help, were sunk so low, were so ungoverned, ignorant and unfortunate, that even the slightest improvement among them was hailed by us as a great advance. . . .

In 1853–'4, I was pained at the sight of such numbers of news boys and street-boys, sleeping about at nights near the newspaper offices, in boxes or under stairways. . . .

I had resolved . . . to attempt a simple experiment—to open a *Lodging-House* for them, as the entering wedge for good influences. . . .

The especial condition for the success of the movement . . . was the man to carry out the execution of it. Providentially at this time, I chanced upon one of those men who are perhaps peculiar to America—a skillful mechanic, self-educated, of much natural tact, with an unbounded pity for the weak and miserable, and a good deal of sternness toward the lazy and shiftless, and who had been long at work among the children of the Sunday-schools. . . . Much against the advice of his friends, [he] agreed to take charge of the intended Lodging-House. He at once began his search for a house, but few would admit such a set as the news boys then were, within their building. . . .

The first night (March 18th, 1854), the school-room was crowded with a motley congregation of ragged and rough boys

—many having come in only to make a disturbance. Mr. Tracy addressed them simply and kindly, and told them the objects of the plan: that we wanted to prevent them from growing up vagrants, and to save them from exposure to the weather, and consequent disease, and to help them on in the world. But that they were not objects of charity, but each one a lodger in his own hotel, paying his six cents for a bed, and the only rules were that they should keep order among themselves, and use the bath. They cheered him warmly, and a larger boy, a "speculator," created a great impression by paying at once his whole week's lodging in advance. . . .

The great peculiarity of the New York News Boys Lodging-House, as distinguished from similar European institutions, is *the payment demanded from the lodgers.* The object of this is to cultivate the feeling of independence and self-respect in these children, and to aid in the support of the Charity. They value the place more from paying for it, and do not contract the vices of paupers. . . . The Superintendent acquires great tact in discerning who are truly impoverished and unlucky, and who lazy or deceitful. Possibly, the public opinion among the boys themselves, helps him in obtaining pay from so many. . . .

During the twelve years in which the Lodging-House has been at work. . . . at least more than *twenty thousand* different boys have been the subjects of this charity. During that time $42,177.78 have been expended by the Children's Aid Society for this object, of which the great proportion has been the fruit of private liberality.

36. Our First Emigrant Party [1854]

By a Visitor [E. P. Smith] in Brace, *Dangerous Classes,*
pp. 246-54

On Wednesday evening,[43] with emigrant * tickets to Detroit, we started on the *Isaac Newton* for Albany. . . . Forty-six boys

[43] The date of departure from New York was Sept. 20, 1854. Brace, *Life,* p. 492.
* Since this first experience, we have always sent our children by regular trains, in decent style.

and girls from New York, bound westward, and, to them, home-
ward. They were between the ages of seven and fifteen—most of
them from ten to twelve. The majority of them orphans, dressed
in uniform—as bright, sharp, bold, racy a crowd of little fellows
as can be grown nowhere out of the streets of New York. The
other ten were from New York at large—no number or street
in particular. Two of these had slept in nearly all the station-
houses in the city. One, a keen-eyed American boy, was born in
Chicago—an orphan now, and abandoned in New York by an
intemperate brother. Another, a little German Jew, who had been
entirely friendless for four years, and had finally found his way
into the Newsboys' Lodging-house. . . .

Another of the ten, whom the boys call "Liverpool," defies
description. Mr. Gerry found him in the Fourth Ward, a few
hours before we left. Really only twelve years old, but in dress a
seedy loafer of forty. His boots, and coat, and pants would have
held two such boys easily—filthy and ragged to the last thread.
Under Mr. Tracy's hands, at the Lodging-house, "Liverpool"
was soon remodeled into a boy again; and when he came on board
the boat with his new suit, I did not know him. His story interested us all, and was told with a quiet, sad reserve, that made us
believe him truthful. . . .

We had a steerage passage, and after the cracker-box and
ginger-bread had passed around, the boys sat down in the gang-
way and began to sing. Their full chorus attracted the attention
of the passengers, who gathered about, and soon the captain sent
for us to come to the upper saloon. There the boys sang and
talked, each one telling his own story separately, as he was taken
aside, till ten o'clock, when Captain S. gave them all berths in
the cabin; meanwhile, a lady from Rochester had selected a
little boy for her sister, and Mr. B., a merchant from Illinois, had
made arrangements to take "Liverpool" for his store. I afterwards met Mr. B. in Buffalo, and he said he would not part with
the boy for any consideration; and I thought then that to take
such a boy from such a condition, and put him into such hands,
was worth the whole trip.

At Albany we found the emigrant train did not go out till noon. . . . When we were about ready to start, several of them came up bringing a stranger with them. There was no mistaking the long, thick, matted hair, unwashed face, the badger coat, and double pants flowing in the wind—a regular "snoozer." . . .

They didn't know his name even. "Only he's as hard-up as any of us. He's no father or mother, and nobody to live with, and he sleeps out o' nights." The boy pleads for himself. . . .

Our number is full—purse scant—it may be difficult to find him a home. But there is no resisting the appeal of the boys, and the importunate face of the young vagrant. Perhaps he will do well; at any rate, we must try him. If left to float here a few months longer, his end is certain. . . .

So a new volunteer is added to our regiment. . . .

At the depot we worked our way through the Babel of at least one thousand Germans, Irish, Italians, and Norwegians, with whom nothing goes right. . . . The motley mass rush into the cars, and we are finally pushed into one already full—some standing, a part sitting in laps, and some on the floor under the benches—crowded to suffocation, in a freight-car without windows—rough benches for seats, and no back—no ventilation except through the sliding-doors, where the little chaps are in constant danger of falling through. There were scenes that afternoon and night which it would not do to reveal. . . .

We were in Buffalo nine hours . . . but were all on board the boat in season. We went down to our place, the steerage cabin, and no one but an emigrant on a lake-boat can understand the night we spent. . . .

Landed in Detroit at ten o'clock, Saturday night, and took a first-class passenger-car on Mich. C.R.R., and reached . . . a "smart little town," in S. W. Michigan, three o'clock Sunday morning. The depot-master, who seldom receives more than three passengers from a train, was utterly confounded at the crowd of little ones poured out upon the platform, and at first refused to let us stay till morning; but, after a deal of explanation, he consented, with apparent misgiving, and the boys spread themselves on the floor to sleep. At day-break they began to inquire, "Where be we?" and, finding that they were really in Michigan, scattered in all directions. . . .

Several of the boys had had a swim in the creek, though it was a pretty cold morning. At the breakfast-table the question was discussed, how we should spend the Sabbath. The boys evidently wanted to continue their explorations; but when asked if it would not be best to go to church, there were no hands down. . . .

The children had clean and happy faces, but no change of clothes, and those they wore were badly soiled and torn by the emigrant passage. You can imagine the appearance of our "ragged regiment," as we filed into the Presbyterian church (which, by the way, was a school-house), and appropriated our full share of the seats. The "natives" could not be satisfied with staring, as they came to the door and filled up the vacant part of the house. . . .

At the close of the sermon the people were informed of the object of the Children's Aid Society. . . . On returning to the tavern, I found that my smallest boy had been missing since day-break, and that he was last seen upon the high bridge over the creek, a little out of the village. So we spent the afternoon in hunting, instead of going to church. (Not an uncommon practice here, by the way.)

We dove in the creek and searched through the woods, but little George (six years old) was not to be found. . . .

Monday morning the boys held themselves in readiness to receive applications from the farmers. They would watch at all directions, scanning closely every wagon that came in sight, and deciding from the appearance of the driver and horses, more often from the latter, whether they "would go in for *that* farmer." . . .

There was a rivalry among the boys to see which first could get a home in the country, and before Saturday they were all gone. Rev. Mr. O. took several home with him; and nine of the smallest I accompanied to Chicago, and sent to Mr. Townsend,

Iowa City. . . . They are to receive a good common-school education and one hundred dollars when twenty-one. I have great hopes for the majority of them. . . .

Several of the boys came in to see me, and tell their experience in learning to farm. . . .

But I must tell you of the lost boy. No tiding were heard of him up to Monday noon, when the citizens rallied and scoured the woods for miles around; but the search was fruitless, and Peter lay down that night sobbing, and with his arms stretched out, just as he used to throw them round his brother.

About ten o'clock a man knocked at the door, and cried out, "Here is the lost boy!" Peter heard him, and the two brothers met on the stairs, and before we could ask where he had been, Peter had George in his place by his side on the floor. They have gone to live together in Iowa.

On the whole, the first experiment of sending children West is a very happy one, and I am sure there are places enough with good families in Michigan, Illinois, Iowa, and Wisconsin, to give every poor boy and girl in New York a permanent home. The only difficulty is to bring the children *to* the homes.

E. P. Smith

XVI

HUMANE AND CURATIVE CARE— A PUBLIC RESPONSIBILITY

Quincy and many others had firmly declared that all needy persons should be cared for in almshouses, and the public complacently considered that the community's responsibility to its dependents was met if such an institution was available, with almost no regard for the quality of care actually given. The result was that most almshouses held a conglomerate mixture of very young, feeble-minded, insane, handicapped, ill, and aged persons in all stages of deterioration. Where even such an almshouse was lacking, or an inmate proved troublesome, often the local jail was the only custodial resource. The violent emotional reaction that Dorothea Dix experienced when she discovered the degradation to which public wards, particularly insane people, were subjected led her to embark on one of the most extensive and effective reform movements of the century.

Observation of the scattered incidence of insanity early convinced Miss Dix that the prevailing system of local responsibility for the care of the mentally ill, provided in almshouses and jails, made it impossible to secure the understanding, therapeutic care which was needed. Hence she threw her influence, in state after state, in favor of the establishment of state hospitals.

Several methods of research entered into the preparation of her campaign in each state. Wide reading was supplemented by extensive personal surveys of existing crude financial and service records, and by assembling the impressions and opinions of persons close to the work. Throughout, Dorothea Dix was moved by her sympathy for the individuals who were suffering, and her marshaling of effective case illustrations, buttressed by statistics to indicate the appalling extent of the problem, made it difficult for hearers or readers to resist her humanitarian appeal.

In her first attempts to interest local leaders and to memorialize state legislatures she focused primarily on elimination of the extreme cruelties that were frequently practiced,[44] but by the time she succeeded in stirring New Jersey to establish a hospital exclusively for the insane, she was also urging the curative possibilities of such an institution.

Dorothea Dix's preoccupation with the care of the insane, like Brace's concentration on the needs of children (R33-36), was typical of the growing tendency toward specialization in humanitarian efforts in the nineteenth century. One of Miss Dix's lasting contributions was the idea that disability is no respecter of persons and that adequate and appropriate care should be available for everybody. She saw governmental provision as the only means of achieving such total coverage, and regarded its financing in the same light as that of other public facilities.

The obstacle she ran against was the unwillingness, and often the inability, of the states to finance the building of such institutions. Other public improvements such as schools and roads were experiencing similar difficulty, and a familiar pattern was the appropriation by Congress of a portion of the public domain to help pay for them. It was natural, therefore, for Miss Dix to turn to Congress [45] for assistance in a campaign which had now become national in scope, and for Congress, after several rebuffs, to pass a bill appropriating ten million acres of public lands to the states for the establishment of hospitals for the insane.

The vision of an expanded state program stimulated by Federal funds was shattered by a veto from the pen of President Franklin Pierce. The social goals of the measure became enmeshed in the states' rights controversy, which dominated the political scene. Adopting a "strict constructionist" approach to

[44] Dorothea Lynde Dix, "Memorial to the Legislature of Massachusetts, 1843," in *Old South Leaflets*, VI, General Series, No. 148 (1904), 1-31.

[45] "Memorial of D. L. Dix Praying a Grant of Land . . . June 23, 1848" (U.S. Thirtieth Congress, 1st Sess., "Senate Miscel. Document No. 150") in Sophonisba P. Breckinridge, *Public Welfare Administration* (Chicago: University of Chicago Press, 1927), pp. 195-221.

the Constitution, Pierce declared that charitable activities were a state function, and he therefore refused to approve the bill. The dictum became dogma controlling Federal-state relations in this department of public life for two generations. This setback to the concept of the expanding role of government might have been less damaging to social welfare had it not been coupled with an approach to need which called only for the alleviation of present wants, with no regard to either prevention or cure. On the other hand, Pierce did point out the unity of the whole range of human need, as contrasted with the categorical approach of Dix and Brace.

37. *Memorial to the Honorable the Senate and the General Assembly of the State of New Jersey*

[Dorothea Lynde Dix], New Jersey, *Senate Journal* (1845), pp. 175–76, 178–80, 182, 188–89, 191–92, 195, 198, 201–2, 204–7, 214–15

Gentlemen:

I come to solicit your attention to the condition and necessities of Idiots, Epileptics, and the Insane Poor, in the State of New Jersey. . . .

I come to ask *justice* . . . for those who, in the Providence of God, are incapable of pleading their own cause. . . . Be patient with me—it is for your own citizens I plead; it is for helpless, friendless men and women, in your very midst, I ask succour . . . the clanking of whose heavy chains still sounds upon my ear. Have pity upon them! Have pity upon them! . . . their grievous, forlorn estate may be shared by yourselves or your children. . . .

Within the last few months, I have traversed a considerable portion of your state, and have found, in jails and poor-houses, and wandering at will over the country, large numbers of insane and idiotic persons whose irresponsibility and imbecility render them objects of deep commiseration. These, whether the subjects of public bounty or of private charity, are inappropriately treated for recovery . . . they are left to exposures and sufferings, at once pitiable and revolting. . . .

The County Poor-house is several miles from Salem, near *Sharptown.* . . .

In a basement room, which was tolerably decent, but bare enough of comforts, lay, upon a small bed, a feeble aged man, whose few gray locks fell tangled upon his pillow. As we entered, he addressed one present, saying, "I am all broken up, all broken up!" "Do you feel much weaker, then *Judge?*" "*The mind*, the mind is going—almost gone," responded he, in tones of touching sadness: "Yes," he continued, murmuring to himself, "the mind is going." This feeble, depressed old man—a pauper, helpless, lonely . . . who was he? I answer as I was answered—but he is not unknown to many of you. . . . He filled various places of honor and trust among you: his ability as a lawyer, raised him to the bench. As a jurist, he was distinguished for uprightness. . . . He was for many years a member of the legislature. . . . I could learn . . . nothing to his discredit, but much that commends men to honor and respect. The meridian of . . . life was passed; the property . . . on which he relied for comfortable support during his declining years, was lost through some of those fluctuations which so often produce reverses for thousands. He became insane, and his insanity assumed the form of frenzy; he was chained "for safety"; in fine, he was committed to the county jail for greater security! Time wore away, excitement gave place to a more quiet, but not a rational state; he was . . . placed in a private family. When the . . . small remnant of his . . . property was consumed, he was removed to the poor-house—there I saw him: without vice and without crime . . . he is withering away in an obscure room . . . receiving his share of that care and attention that must be divided and subdivided among the hundred feeble, infirm, and disabled inmates. For such men as Judge S., is no hospital needed? or if too late for him, hasten—it may be finished only to open its merciful shelter for yourselves or your children. . . .

Burlington County Poor-house. . . . I found here twenty-two insane—ten of these were occupants of the cells in the cellar, "or low basement." . . . "We have no other place for such as these," replied the master of the house . . . "we need a State Hospital." . . .

In the jail at Newark, I particularly remarked a child, who was charged with a larceny, listening with delight to several adult prisoners, his seniors in crime as well as years; he was committed in *November*, and was to have his trial in *January*. He *had* learned his daily task without urging, and will need, by-and-by, no prompter when he brings the lessons he gets here by theory, into practice. Who is blameworthy if this boy becomes an accomplished rogue? Himself or the community? The whole, or the integral members of society? . . .

The poor of *Essex County*, are sustained in their several townships. . . . *Newark* has a poor-house. . . . It is a small establishment, some . . . of the lodging rooms, were in a miserable and dirty state. Here, in November, were twenty-nine inmates—eleven men, eleven women, and seven children. . . . There was but one person here very insane—this was a woman, who was kept in an out-house in the yard. . . .

It would be necessary to remove the unfortunate maniac to the main building when the cold weather should render a fire absolutely wanted, to prevent suffering from frost. But in the main building, already fully occupied, I could see no apartment either safe or convenient for an insane person subject to high excitement, and having the habits which would convert any place into a nuisance. . . . The children were gathered listening . . . to the impure language of this miserably degraded creature; such were *their* early lessons in morals and manners. . . .

There is no poor-house in *Bergen county*. The poor are placed in those families who agree to receive them at the lowest prices. "Sometimes they fare tolerably well," said a citizen, "oftener, I am afraid, their condition is of the hardest." . . .

There is a poor-house—poor in every sense—in Paterson. . . . The establishment . . . is the most ill-ordered place I have seen. . . . The town . . . once owned the farm; but it had been sold to an individual, who rents it to an Irishman, and who, on his part, takes the poor of the town to board—the adults for a dollar a week each, the children, I think, at a reduced price. The house is old and dilapidated; perhaps it has received a coat of white-wash since it was first built, but this is conjectural. Two or three small apartments were more decent than the others, but the oc-cupied rooms were positively loathsome. The inmates uttered no complaints—perhaps they were satisfied. Several were insane and idiotic. . . .

The cases of insanity in private families, some of which are blessed with affluence . . . are numerous. . . .

Not long since, a young girl froze to death in the cold, wretched garret of her father's house; where abandoned to every neglect, except starvation, she for three years lingered on through sufferings which we can find no language to describe. *Found dead* one severe cold morning, and frozen stiff, amidst heaps of filthy straw, at one end of the remote garret; people contented themselves with saying " 'twas strange she lived so long!" . . .

The establishment of hospitals for the insane has, within the last century, become so general . . . that the neglect of this duty seems to involve aggravated culpability . . . which can find neither justification nor apology. . . . Most of the ancient na-tions received the idea, that insanity was produced by super-natural agencies; that it was a just judgment from Heaven, di-rectly visited upon the individual, or his parents and family. . . . And so men argued "shall those who receive no mercy from the Just One, not also be cast out; and shall we cherish those aban-doned ones whom the Almighty has forsaken?" . . . St. Vincent de Paul, that pious, self-sacrificing Apostle, became "the *provi-dence* of God," to soften the hearts of European nations towards the oppressed maniac, and the neglected idiot. With an un-quenchable zeal, he traversed vast regions . . . teaching men, that to be humane, was to be allied to Deity. . . . But it remained for France to exhibit the first effectual systematic efforts in be-half of the insane. . . . Thousands of maniacs were brought under control by the influence of *firmness* and *kindness;* and manacles and fetters, and the blood-imbrued lash, were banished from hospitals and asylums, where they so long had been the rule of government.

It is to Pinel, the great and good Pinel, a physician attending at the hospital of the Bicêtre, two miles south of Paris, that we owe this first great triumph of humanity and skill, over ferocity and ignorance. . . .

The rapid diffusion of correct principles . . . in the United States, within the last twenty years, is too well known to render any historical detail of our asylums necessary here. New hospitals . . . and old . . . [are] made to keep pace with the rapid improvements of the age. . . . [Skillful physicians] "spend and are spent" in the noble effort to heal or mitigate those diseases which derange the healthful functions of the brain, and thus disturb the reasoning faculties and perceptions. . . .

I have confidence in hospital care for the insane, and in no other care. . . . Insanity is a malady which requires treatment appropriate to its peculiar and varied forms. . . . If this care is needed for the rich, for those whose homes abound in every luxury . . . how much more it is needed for those who are brought low by poverty, and destitute of friends? For those who find refuge under this calamitous disease only in jails and poor-houses, or perchance, in the cells of a State Penitentiary? . . .

If prisons are unfit for the insane, under ordinary circumstances, poor-houses are certainly not less so. . . .

Poor-houses, which have for their object the comfort of the aged, the helpless, and the invalid poor, are often so complex in their arrangements and objects, that the purpose of their establishment is lost sight of. Seldom planned with a view to the proper separation and classification of the inmates, order and morality are with difficulty maintained. When to the care of providing for a large and miscellaneous family, is joined the charge of a farm, on the part of the master, and the most various and burthensome duties on that of the mistress of the house, it is not surprising that the difficult task of managing the insane and the idiots, should soonest be neglected, and soonest produce troubles which few have the patience and skill to sustain. Beside, it should be remembered, that while many are capable of judiciously directing an extensive poor-house establishment, very few have either the tact or experience requisite for rightly managing the insane. . . .

Perhaps one cause for the unwillingness felt by some, to promote the establishment of hospitals for the insane, is a doubt of the curability of the malady, or of the superior advantage of hospital treatment over private practice. Such doubts are fast passing from the public mind. . . . We daily witness the most gratifying results, in the large number of patients restored to their friends, confirmed in bodily and mental health. The twenty third annual report of the M'Lean Asylum, at Sommerville . . . Massachusetts, by Dr. Bell, shows that "the records . . . justify the declaration, that *all cases certainly recent . . . recover under a fair trial.*" . . .

On the ground of a discreet economy alone, it is wise to establish a State Hospital in New Jersey. But I will not dishonor you by urging this suit on the money-saving principle. . . . In provision for the poor and needy, and in care of the distressed: the insane and idiots alone have been too long insufficiently provided for. I speak advisedly in saying, that were a system carefully projected, having for its single object the perpetuity of insanity, by treatment ensuring the incurability of the patient, one more infallible could not be devised than that which consigns to the State Penitentiary, to jails, and alms-houses, the maniac and the demented; the idiot and the epileptic. . . .

Permit me, in conclusion, to urge that the delay to provide suitable asylums for the insane, produces miseries to individuals, and evils to society, inappreciable in their utmost influence, except by those who have given time to the examination of the subject, and who have witnessed the appalling degradation of these wretched sufferers in the poor-houses, and jails, and penitentiaries of our land.

Shall New Jersey be last of "the Thirteen Sisters" to respond
to the claims of humanity, and to acknowledge the demands of
justice? [46]

Respectfully submitted,

D. L. Dix

Trenton, January 23d 1845

38. The Federal Government—
the Great Almoner?

President Franklin Pierce's veto of the bill resulting
from Miss Dix's efforts, *Congressional Globe*, Thirty-
third Congress, 1st. sess. May 3, 1854, pp. 1061–63

My deliberate conviction [is] that a strict adherence to the
terms and purposes of the Federal compact, offers the best, if not
the only, security for the preservation of our blessed inheritance
of representative liberty. . . .

If Congress have power to make provision for the indigent
insane without the limits of this District, it has the same power
to provide for the indigent who are not insane; and thus to
transfer to the Federal Government the charge of all the poor
in all the States. It has the same power to provide hospitals and
other local establishments for the care and cure of every species
of human infirmity, and thus to assume all that duty of either
public philanthropy, or public necessity to the dependent, the
orphan, the sick, or the needy, which is now discharged by the
States themselves, or by corporate institutions, or private endowments existing under the legislation of the States. The whole field
of public beneficence is thrown open to the care and culture of
the Federal Government. Generous impulses no longer encounter
the limitations and control of our imperious fundamental law.
For, however worthy may be the present object in itself, it is
only one of a class. It is not exclusively worthy of benevolent

[46] The New Jersey State Hospital was the first to be established as a
result of Miss Dix's efforts. Miss Dix spent the last years of her life as a
guest of the hospital in recognition of her part in its founding. Helen E.
Marshall, *Dorothea Dix, Forgotten American* (Chapel Hill: University of
North Carolina Press, 1937), p. 105.

regard. Whatever considerations dictate sympathy for this particular object, apply, in like manner, if not in the same degree, to idiocy, to physical disease, to extreme destitution. If Congress may and ought to provide for any one of these objects, it may and ought to provide for them all. . . . The question presented, therefore, clearly is upon the constitutionality and propriety of the Federal Government assuming to enter into a novel and vast field of legislation, namely, that of providing for the care and support of all those, among the people of the United States, who, by any form of calamity, become fit objects of public philanthropy.

I readily, and I trust feelingly, acknowledge the duty incumbent on us all, as men and citizens, and as among the highest and holiest of our duties, to provide for those who, in the mysterious order of Providence, are subject to want and to disease of body or mind, but I cannot find any authority in the Constitution for making the Federal Government the great almoner of public charity throughout the United States. . . . It would, in the end, be prejudicial rather than beneficial to the noble offices of charity, to have the charge of them transferred from the States to the Federal Government. Are we not too prone to forget that the Federal Union is the creature of the States, not they of the Federal Union? . . . When . . . they resolved . . . to confer on the Federal Government more ample authority, they scrupulously measured such of the functions of their cherished sovereignty as they chose to delegate to the General Government. . . .

Can it be controverted that the great mass of the business of Government that involved . . . the relief of the needy, or otherwise unfortunate members of society, did, in practice, remain with the States; that none of these objects of local concern are, by the Constitution, expressly or impliedly prohibited to the States, and that none of them are, by any express language of the Constitution, transferred to the United States? Can it be claimed that any of these functions of local administration and legislation are vested in the Federal Government by any implication? . . .

In my judgment you cannot, by tributes to humanity, make any adequate compensation for the wrong you would inflict by removing the sources of power and political action from those who are to be thereby affected. . . .

If the several States, many of which have already laid the foundation of munificent establishments of local beneficence, and nearly all of which are proceeding to establish them, shall be led to suppose, as they will be, should this bill become a law, that Congress is to make provision for such objects, the fountains of charity [47] will be dried up at home, and the several States, instead of bestowing their own means on the social wants of their own people, may themselves, through the strong temptation, which appeals to States as to individuals, become humble suppliants for the bounty of the Federal Government, reversing their true relation to this Union. . . .

To assume that the public lands are applicable to ordinary State objects, whether of public structures, police, charity, or expenses of State administration, would be to disregard . . . all the limitations of the Constitution, and confound, to that extent, all distinctions between the rights and powers of the States, and those of the United States. For if the public lands may be applied to the support of the poor, whether sane or insane . . . then Congress possesses unqualified power to provide for expenditures in the States by means of the public lands, even to the degree of defraying the salaries of Governors, judges, and all other expenses of the Government, and internal administration within the several States. The conclusion . . . is, to my mind, irresistible, and closes the question, both of right and of expediency, so far as regards the principle of the appropriation proposed in this bill.

[47] Cf. Chalmers, R24.

THE PERIOD OF NATIONAL
EXPANSION
1854 – 1895

INTRODUCTION

The years following the Civil War were a riotous period of phe-
nomenal expansion in all aspects of American life—geographic,
to include most of the continent—scientific—industrial. Wealth
and poverty grew side by side, with flagrant corruption in politics. In keeping with this spirit of rapid growth, philanthropic
organizations proliferated everywhere.

In social welfare, philosophy, administration, and program
were developed within the boundaries defined by the Pierce doctrine. This involved increasing recognition of the limitations and
weaknesses of strictly local administration. While local responsibility for poor relief was not abolished, as specialized programs
of care were developed, the tendency was for these to be placed
under state administration, while in other ways the administrative, investigatory, and supervisory powers of the state with
respect to local administration tended to increase. At the same
time, the recognition of the universality of the problems being
dealt with, which had stimulated Miss Dix to seek Federal support, led to the development of national associations which
brought together individuals and groups with mutual concerns.
Of these, the one representing the widest range of interests was
the National Conference of Charities and Correction, the pre-
cursor of the present-day National Conference on Social Welfare.

While the National Conference was highly practical in its
orientation, many leaders in social welfare were in close touch
with the rapid developments in the physical and social sciences.
For some prominent and highly vocal groups, the passion to
achieve a "scientific" charity became little short of a mania. In
this they found support in the clarity and ordered assurance of
the sociology of Spencer which agreed so well with the biology
of Darwin. All that was needed was to discover and apply im-
mutable law to the formulation of programs for dealing with

human problems. This movement for the rationalization of procedures in the care of those in need was further supported by the success which had attended the earlier application of sanitary measures and by the promise of amelioration held out in the struggle for housing reforms. But thoughtful advocates of scientific charity were destined to disappointment when their theory-based programs were tested in crisis situations. It appeared that the marriage of a mechanistic approach to treatment with a doctrine of personal fault as the basis of poverty was inadequate to meet the challenge of widespread destitution in a time of deep economic depression. Holding fast to the value of the scientific approach, the search for underlying causes of poverty and personal inadequacy received major encouragement.

Despite the influence of science in certain localities and in certain movements, the great bulk of charitable activity, both governmental and voluntary, continued to be carried on in response to motivations which ranged from compassionate care of the unfortunate to the unheeding callousness observed by Dorothea Dix. The earlier development of specialized facilities and programs now became so universal that it was difficult to comprehend the complex structure of services available in a community. Not only were increasingly specialized programs set up for each age, sex, or disability group, but each such group was served by different organizations with competing methodological approaches. In the case of dependent and neglected children, from a wide variety of approaches three are here represented: Charles Loring Brace and the New York Children's Aid Society provided transportation for removal of such children to new homes on farms in the Western states; the Catholic Protectory of New York provided removal to institutions in the near vicinity; and the Massachusetts State Board of Charities developed a program of supervised foster home care for children in or near their home communities.

Brace and others advocated concentration on the problems of one group only as conducive to greater efficiency and effectiveness. The AICP and later the Charity Organization Society stressed a broad and coordinated approach to problems of poverty. Charity organizationists in particular became highly vocal exponents of "scientific charity." Since most of the needy were recipients of help from public poor relief authorities, and for generations the administration of public poor relief had been under fire in England and America, it was easy to develop the proposition that public relief was the cause of "pauperism." From this followed dogmatic assertion that public relief was inherently bad and that the only constructive relief was bestowed privately (according to the principles of the charity organization movement). This idea, repeatedly stated by persons of great intellectual and social authority, became widely accepted while carefully prepared statements by governmental officials went unnoticed or were categorically rejected. Nevertheless, the experience of the depression of 1893–94 forced upon charity organization leaders a degree of humility which made it possible for this movement to survive the tendency to institutional decay and to become the focus for the study and invention of different ways of treating the multiple causes of economic deprivation and personal inadequacy.

The charity organization movement in these scientific efforts became the most energetic element in the emergence of a profession of social work. By the middle of the century the administration of charities was sometimes a full-time job; in the third quarter of the century it began to be a recognized career. Among the first such careers were those of Robert Hartley, Charles Loring Brace, and Franklin Sanborn. These were the outstanding leaders who propounded the philosophy and directed the course of the organizations with which they were associated. But the bulk of the direct service was still provided by volunteers or by paid agents who were widely regarded as undesirable substitutes for volunteers. Where any qualitative basis of selection of staff was applied, it was likely to be either the applicant's religious profession or the employer's intuitive judgment of desirable personal characteristics. It was in the charity organization movement, with its emphasis on method, that toward the end of the century it came to be recognized that the paid agent, with his full-time, continuous experience, might be in a better position than a volunteer to identify the type of problem being dealt with, determine what should be done, and know how to do it. The evolution of the social work profession was to accelerate rapidly after 1895, but by that time it was possible to distinguish a nucleus of the professional group—such persons as Zilpha Smith, Amos Warner, and Philip Ayres—from the volunteer leaders who had given the charity organization movement its start, such as Josephine Shaw Lowell, Charles Bonaparte, and Albert Treat Paine.

By the end of the period three foci of activity are clearly observable: a search for improved methods for governmental assumption of responsibility in the care of special groups; a search for causes of poverty and breakdown in the individual; a search for the causes of poverty and breakdown in the socioeconomic system.

XVII

THE STATES ASSUME RESPONSIBILITY

In the states and local communities, to which the Pierce veto had assigned the responsibility for all types of charitable activities, the extent to which there was concern for the amount and quality of care being given varied greatly. Much of what concern there was focused on the needs of particular groups, but some was directed toward the total system. In a state like Massachusetts, where the settlement laws permitted the towns to shift responsibility for the care of a sizable proportion of the indigents to the state, which operated a system of almshouses and other institutions, it was natural for public concern to be centered on the operation of the state system. The result was that Massachusetts, by establishing its Board of State Charities in 1863, set an example which was quickly followed by a number of states. It provided a means whereby the state could finance care on a scale usually not possible by private means, but citizens could continuously influence methods and effectiveness of services given. State boards saw their function as that of safeguarding the interests of taxpayers, recipients of services, persons in charge of giving services, and the general public that might be endangered (R50).

In the Massachusetts law it is notable that the Board was given authority to reorganize the programs of the several state institutions, and to redistribute the inmates according to a state-wide classification plan, but not to control the business operations of the separate institutions. Four years later the Board was requesting enlarged executive authority over the institutions, foreshadowing a struggle between state boards and institutions over their management which has continued to the present. The authority of the Board to require uniform reports from local officials with respect to poor relief is also a step, but a less drastic one, toward state supervision and control.

One key to the influential role played by the Massachusetts Board is found in the establishment of the position of secretary apart from that of agent, who was responsible for the actual program of care. By thus dividing the executive responsibilities, the state recognized that there was need for two types of leadership—one in the faithful provision of established services, and the other in the analysis of needs and the planning of new or improved methods.

A second key was in the quality of imaginative inquiry which the new secretary brought to his job, taking it out of the ordinary and making it a platform for national leadership. Franklin B. Sanborn, a man of wide interests and great literary ability, had been much influenced in his thinking by Emerson, Theodore Parker, and Samuel Gridley Howe, a member of the Board. Each year Sanborn took advantage of the legal requirement that annual reports be made to the legislature by presenting a careful and extensive treatise on various aspects of poverty, disease, and crime, along with the specified record of transactions and recommendations for legislative action. This early and continuous broad interpretation of the underlying purposes of the program to secure adequate backing was a device adopted by many executives.

39. *The Board Shall Investigate and Supervise*

"An Act in Relation to State Charitable and Correctional Institutions, April 29, 1863," *Acts and Resolves Passed by the General Court of Massachusetts in the Year 1863*, c. 240

Section 1. The governor, with the advice and consent of the council, shall appoint . . . the board of state charities. . . .

Section 2. The governor . . . shall appoint some suitable person as general agent of state charities. . . . He shall be a member of the board of state charities, *ex officio*, and shall, subject to the control and direction of the said board, oversee and conduct its out-door business, especially the examination of paupers and lunatics, to ascertain their places of settlement and means of support, or who may be responsible therefor; the removal of paupers and lunatics to their usual homes; the prosecution of cases of settlement and bastardy. . . .

Section 3. The governor . . . shall appoint some suitable person to be secretary of the board of state charities. . . . He shall keep an accurate record of the proceedings of the board. . . . He shall . . . examine the returns of the several cities and towns in relation to the support of paupers therein, and in relation to births, deaths and marriages, and he shall prepare a series of interrogatories to the several institutions of charity, reform and correction, supported wholly or in part by the Commonwealth, or the several counties thereof, with a view to illustrate in his annual report the causes and best treatment of pauperism, crime, disease and insanity. He shall also arrange and publish in his said report all desirable information concerning the industrial and material interests of the Commonwealth, bearing upon these subjects . . . and he may also propose such general investigations as may be approved by the board. He shall be paid, annually, the sum of two thousand dollars and his actual traveling expenses.

Section 4. . . . [The board] shall investigate and supervise the whole system of the public charitable and correctional institutions of the Commonwealth, and shall recommend such changes and additional provisions as they may deem necessary for their economical and efficient administration. They shall have full power to transfer pauper inmates from one charitable institution or lunatic hospital to another . . . but shall have no power to make purchases for the various institutions. . . .

Section 5. The board . . . shall annually prepare and print for the use of the legislature a full and complete report . . . showing the actual condition of all the state institutions under their control, with such suggestions as they deem necessary and pertinent. . . .

Section 9. The expenses of the lunatic hospitals for the support of lunatics not having known settlements in this state committed thereto, shall be paid by the Commonwealth at the same rates charged for other lunatics residing therein, not exceeding two dollars and twenty-five cents a week for each lunatic.

40. *Coordination and Direction of Public Alms*

Fourth Annual Report of the Board of State Charities of Massachusetts (1868), Board report, pp. lxxiv, xci–xciii, xcvi–xcvii; Secretary's report, pp. 129, 133

REPORT OF THE BOARD

[Schools for Idiots] are founded upon the principle that all human beings are improvable; that each has a right to the means of improvement; and that his right implies a duty on the part of the others to furnish such means. As we improve the ordinary child in order that he may become a better man than he would otherwise be, so we must improve the imbecile child in order that, even if he does not rise above idiocy, he may be better as an idiot. We may not bury even his poor talent in the napkin of sloth. . . .

A deep sense of the importance of . . . a change in the policy of some of the Institutions; a consciousness of our inability to exert any direct influence in such change; and the plain requirement of the law . . . to make recommendations to the Legislature, have determined us to ask, *That additional executive powers be granted to the Board of State Charities.* . . .

There ought to exist somewhere a greater central power to adopt and carry out a uniform policy in the administration of the State Charities.

Decentralization is conformable to the spirit of our political institutions, and to the genius of our people. It is important for the life and efficiency of local charitable institutions; and desirable for the sake of distributing the duties of charity widely among the community, and so bringing them home to the hearths and hearts of the people.

But, on the other hand, centralization of some kind is absolutely necessary for accomplishing the objects aimed at by the establishment of the separate Institutions. . . .

All these establishments have certain general wants and certain common ends; and they should be directed by one general policy. A vague and ill-defined sense of the importance of this was among the influences which created the Board of State Charities. . . . But . . . in no case had the Board full power, and in most cases no power at all, to direct the administration of the special institutions. . . .

All the State Institutions are filled with human beings who, whether old or young, sane or insane, innocent or guilty, sound or infirm, have certain common wants, and require a certain common method in their treatment; and those wants can be better supplied by a certain unity in principles of administration, and by a co-ordination of the forces of the several Institutions, than without them. But no such direct power of co-ordination exists, except in the Governor and Council, who, amid the pressure of other duties, seldom exercise it. . . .

We believe that the great object of Public Charity should be to equalize the condition of men by lifting the lowly and strengthening the weak. . . . We aim to co-ordinate and direct all public charitable institutions and agencies, in such wise as to help improve the physical powers and the outward condition of the poor and the feeble; and thus check the formation of classes of the dependent and the vicious, who will inherit tendencies to pauperism and crime, just as certainly as more fortunate classes inherit tendencies to prosperity and virtue.

We desire, moreover, that this great work may be done, not solely, nor even mainly, by delegating it to special establishments and to agents set apart for it; but, so far as possible, by the people themselves in their families. . . .

SECRETARY'S REPORT

Must there Always be Public Provision for the Poor?

This question has been negatively answered by some theorists who seem to have conceived a state of society in which *either* sickness, old age, emigration, orphanage, and other adjuncts of our present social condition are to cease entirely; *or* the justice and charity of individuals are to act with a constancy, celerity and good judgment which has never yet been witnessed on earth. . . . We must be allowed to doubt the coming of a time when disease will not incapacitate. . . . Until private charity has been taught to relieve distress with the same speed and certainty that is seen in the best forms of public almsgiving, the public alms must be given, and all that we can reasonably hope is to reduce them to a minimum.

The causes of pauperism are, in my opinion, *first*, Physical degradation and inferiority; *second*, Moral perversity; *third*, Mental incapacity; *fourth*, Accidents and infirmities; *fifth* (and often the most powerful of all), unjust and unwise laws, and the customs of society. These may be regarded as general causes, but under these five heads come innumerable minor and proximate causes, such as intemperance, profligacy, insanity, indolence, false education, monopolies, privileges, ignorance, superstition, and, indeed, all the enemies of human advancement; for pauperism is one of the sloughs in which the progress of mankind is stopped.

Some of those which I have called general causes cannot be removed. Accidents and infirmities occurring to individuals, such as result from earthquakes, storms, floods, unwholesome seasons, the maladies of a locality, and the like, cannot be removed by human agency, beyond a certain degree. Moral perversity, in the individual, also, being incident to moral freedom, must always be regarded as one of the few necessary evils of human life. But physical and mental degradation, and the unwise laws, and customs of society, can be reached and removed gradually, and with them would disappear much of the pauperism which now molests and poisons our civilization. Such is my belief. . . .

XVIII
RIVALRIES IN WELL-DOING

While Brace was flooding the Western countryside with children and the reading public with praises of the Children's Aid program, other groups were also putting forward alternative approaches to the care of dependent and neglected children. The founders of the Catholic Protectory attempted to eliminate two features of the Brace program that they considered objectionable.

Rightly or wrongly, Catholics felt that the Children's Aid Society was a device for Protestant proselytizing among the children of Catholic immigrants. Their response was to set up an agency in which the faith of such children might be protected and strengthened rather than lost. Sectarian agencies had not been unknown before that time, but with immigration bringing in streams of persons from many lands and from many religious backgrounds, the next half century was to see a proliferation of specialized religious and nationality agencies. They all sought in one way or another to preserve religious and cultural values of their own groups, but many of them were small and without adequate financial resources. In some states, notably New York, Pennsylvania, and Illinois, the law permitted such agencies to receive financial grants from governmental bodies, and they often did, much to the distress of numerous public administration theorists.

The Catholic Protectory also is representative of a widespread approach to the care of dependent children which sought to keep them within the shelter of the institution rather than to distribute them in homes throughout the community. The Children's Aid operation, involving as it did transportation to another part of the country, was open to additional charges, but the Protectory was by no means alone in its belief that placement in homes should be the exception rather than the rule in the care of children. Throughout the country, orphan asylums and children's homes flourished until about the time of the Second World War. The Protectory pioneered in the belief that children should be prepared for return to their own families while at the same time reformative efforts with parents by parish priests and volunteers made that return feasible. How often such efforts were successful was questioned by the proponents of foster family care, but the germinal idea of simultaneous treatment for parent and child had been introduced into the professional stream of thought.

41. *From the Gutter to the College*

Brace, *Dangerous Classes*, pp. 261–63

Yale College, New Haven, Oct. 11, 1871

Rev. C. L. Brace, Secretary Children's Aid Society:

Dear Sir—I shall endeavor in this letter to give you a brief sketch of my life, as it is your request that I should.

I cannot speak of my parents with any certainty at all. I recollect having an aunt. . . . [She] left me to shift for myself in the streets of your city. I could not have been more than seven or eight years of age at this time. . . .

At this period I became a vagrant, roaming over all parts of the city. I would often pick up a meal at the markets or at the docks, where they were unloading fruit. At a late hour in the night I would find a resting-place in some box or hogshead, or in some dark hole under a staircase. . . .

I have a distinct recollection of stealing up upon houses to tear the lead from around the chimneys, and then take it privily away to some junk-shop, as they call it; with the proceeds I would buy a ticket for the pit in the Chatham-street Theatre, and something to eat with the remainder. This is the manner in which I was drifting out in the stream of life, when some kind person from your Society persuaded me to go to Randall's Island.[1] I remained at this place two years. Sometime in July, 1859,

[1] Randall's Island, in East River, housed the children's department of the New York City Almshouse; the House of Refuge, founded by the Association for the Prevention of Pauperism (R22) for delinquent and

one of your agents came there and asked how many boys who had no parents would love to have nice homes in the West, where they could drive horses and oxen, and have as many apples and melons as they should wish. I happened to be one of the many who responded in the affirmative. . . .

Twenty-one of us had homes procured for us at N——, Ind. A lawyer . . . was at N—— at the time. He desired to take a boy home with him, and I was the one assigned him. He owns a farm of two hundred acres lying close to town. . . . I was always treated as one of the family. . . .

I taught a Public School in a little log cabin. . . .

My pastor presented the claims of the ministry. . . .

I had accumulated some property. . . . At the academy I found kind instructors and sympathizing friends. I remained three years, relying greatly on my own efforts for support. After entering the class of "74" last year, I was enabled to go through with it by the kindness of a few citizens here.

42. The Salvation of Thousands of Destitute Catholic Children

"Appeal," in *The Society for the Protection of Destitute Catholic Children* (New York: Sadlier, 1863), pp. 13–15

Fellow Catholics: . . . The time for action, in behalf of our destitute children, has at length arrived. . . .

We address ourselves to IRISHMEN, who constitute the great body of Catholics in this city, while, as we all know, the children of Irishmen make up by far the largest proportion of sufferers for whom we are called upon to provide. Vast numbers of these defenceless young creatures are daily wandering over the face of this great city, exposed to all the horrors of hopeless poverty— to the allurements of vice and crime in every disgusting and debasing form. . . .

---

predelinquent children; and the institution for feeble-minded children. This boy might have been in either of the first two.

We address you as Catholics. And here the very character of our religion would seem to furnish a sufficient stimulus to our zeal. . . . Our organization is to place within their reach, the salvation of thousands of destitute Catholic children! children who, under their present circumstances, are almost certain to lose their *faith*, and consequently to peril their *souls!* . . .

It is true, we have our orphan asylums, our parochial schools, our society of St. Vincent de Paul; all of which, under your liberal patronage, are giving relief to the utmost extent of their capacity. Yet the amount of Juvenile delinquency and wretchedness is hardly diminished. . . . Let us not be put to shame by the untiring zeal of the religious denominations around us. Believing, as *they* do, they set us, in many respects, a noble example. But believing, as *we* do, their very exertions, in respect to our destitute children, render more urgent the demand upon ourselves. . . .

In respect to a sufficiency of means, we run no risk. If we do what our *own* means afford, we may safely rely, as to further need, upon the bounty of the state. She has never failed to give a helping hand to those benevolent organizations, that are sustained by zealous, individual effort. In so doing her bounty is wisely bestowed; for this is the most efficient and least expensive way to fulfil her obligations to the destitute.

43. *A Thorough Training*

First Annual Report, Society for the Protection of Destitute Catholic Children (New York: Sadlier, 1863), pp. 42–44

Applications in behalf of unprotected children became so numerous and pressing as to compel the Executive Committee, in view of their necessarily limited means and accommodations, to restrict the number of inmates to such boys as might be committed from the courts, or transferred to their care by the "Commissioners of Public Charities and Correction." . . .

The committee were unable to make provision for the reception of girls before the first of October. About that time, however, they succeeded in procuring a building. . . .

The managers have been solicitous to secure to the institution [2] that internal economy which may best suit the purposes of *reformatory discipline* . . . which may do for destitute children something more than merely to rid the city of them, at great expense, for a few months. . . .

The managers have made it their primary care to see that the children committed to them understand and practise their religion. . . .

Next . . . the children are taught to have regard to that which they owe their parents. . . .

In all those cases where children of parents able to support them have been committed for the minor offenses, we insist upon returning them so soon as, in our judgment, it can safely be done. In regard to many of this class of young delinquents, a few weeks of strict, but kind discipline, are found to be as effectual in subduing their tempers and restoring a spirit of filial obedience, as a much longer period. . . .

The benefit of this policy is twofold: it tends to strengthen the family bond, and to promote the essential virtues of industry and economy. For we have not only to avoid the serious evil of weakening the family tie by unnecessarily separating children from their parents, but also to guard against what is hardly less pernicious, the mischief of taking away from these parents that main stimulus to exertion—the necessity of providing for their own households. . . .

The managers have exacted of parents, as they might be able to give it, some small contribution to the support of their children in the institution. Besides the effect of inducing parents to husband their earnings, this requirement saves them from the self-humiliation of total dependence upon others. . . .

The next care of the managers has been to secure to the class

[2] This institution, long known as "The Catholic Protectory," is now Lincoln Hall, Lincolndale, N.Y.

of utterly destitute children a thorough training, before sending them into the world. A comparatively small number . . . have any moral or mental fitness to meet the dangers of a hard and untried life in our new settlements of the West. . . .

Besides, in this unsettled and money-making age, few men can be trusted as masters. . . .

The managers, therefore, have been induced to make the early apprenticing of destitute children the exception; while, as a general rule, they insist upon a long and thorough training of such children before leaving their parental supervision.

XIX

PUBLIC RESPONSIBILITY
FOR CHILDREN

Citizen concern for the dependent child was not limited in its expression to voluntary children's agencies, sectarian and otherwise. Immediately after its organization, the Massachusetts Board of State Charities attacked the dual problem of children in the state almshouses and the lack of supervision for those children who had been indentured out of the almshouses. In both cases the officials recognized the moral and legal obligation of the state to safeguard the well-being of the children under its care, and the system of foster home placement under close surveillance which it worked out became the prototype of later programs of care elsewhere.

This concern for children was common to most state boards, and the report by Hastings Hart of his investigations for the Minnesota Board is illustrative of the way in which these organizations succeeded first in curbing and finally in eliminating unsatisfactory unsupervised child placing.

44. The Indentured Children

First Annual Report, Massachusetts Board of State Charities, 1865; pp. xx–xxii

Connected with the Reform and Industrial Schools are several hundred boys and girls of a suitable age to be indentured,[3] and in the State Almshouses are seven hundred children, a portion of

---

[3] Indenture was a formal contract by which a servant was bound to a master for a specific period of years. While such an arrangement might be advantageous to both parties, a child so placed out might find himself caught in an abusive situation. To allow for escape from an unsatisfactory situation, the New York Children's Aid did not arrange formal indenture for the children it placed, and both child and foster parent were free to terminate the placement without review of the case by court or agency.

whom should also be provided with homes in private families. These persons are now mainly supported by the State; many of them are orphans, and have no relatives or friends that can ever assist them. It will be seen at once what a relief to the State, and what an advantage to them it would prove, if they could be placed in suitable families. The State has already indentured . . . nearly four thousand persons. . . .

The by-laws of these institutions make it obligatory upon their officers to see that the parties applying for boys and girls to indenture, sustain a good moral character; and they are also required to exercise a watchful care over those indentured. But these requirements are very imperfectly carried out. . . . In some cases this watchfulness is continued with some degree of fidelity for months or years, while in others, little or no information whatever is obtained respecting the situation and treatment of the indentured. Besides, this oversight cannot be maintained as it should be, by correspondence; it needs personal inquiry and acquaintance. There are instances, moreover, where the indentured boys and girls are badly treated, and not unfrequently returned to the institution, without any fault on their part. If the State takes the place of a parent or guardian in binding out these poor children, is it not her duty to follow up that parental relation and see that the compact is faithfully adhered to, and that no harm befall the party dependent upon the State? To do justice to this class of boys and girls, there should be a person, possessing the right qualifications, charged with this particular duty. He should visit all these indentured children, ascertain from different sources the character of their masters, and how they are treated, hear and dispose of any complaints on either side, and advise and counsel as a parent would, with these indentured boys and girls. While doing this work, such an agent might readily find homes for others. Thus the number of those well indentured from the State Institutions might be greatly increased, thereby saving to the State every year a sum far greater than the whole expenses of such an agency. We would, therefore, recommend to the Legislature that an agent of this kind be appointed.

45. *Homes for Orphan and Friendless Children*

"Report of the Visiting Agent," *Fourth Annual Report,*
Massachusetts Board of State Charities (1868), pp.
145–58

Since the first of October, 1866, there have been placed out
from the State Primary School and Almshouse 156, making [with
children previously placed] the number supposed to be in their
places 759.

These children have been scattered over the States of Massachusetts, Connecticut, Vermont, New Hampshire and New
York, with here and there one in the Western States. A large
number had not been heard from since leaving the institution.
. . . Children were transferred from family to family, without
authority, and became lost to the knowledge and care of the
State. That neglect and abuses were frequent under this system,
is not surprising. The State had for twelve years been providing
homes for its orphan and friendless children, without causing
them to be looked after, or correcting the wrongs that had grown
up among them. . . .

Four hundred and ninety-five . . . of the children have been
visited or their condition ascertained by visiting the families
where they were placed. This number includes twenty-three
who had left their places or had run away from the Almshouse
and found places for themselves. The condition of the latter
was generally found to be deplorable. . . . To improve their
condition by establishing them in permanent homes, or hiring
them out and looking after their wages, has been one of the
cares of the Agency. . . .

The common neglects from which these children suffer are
insufficient schooling, non-attendance at church upon the Sabbath,
and inadequate clothing. Occasionally a child is overworked and
maltreated. . . .

Cases of injustice and abuse are the exception, not the general
rule. Aside from slight neglects, which are now being corrected,
the majority of the children are doing well, and have pretty

good homes. Some of them take the names of the families in which they live, and are treated in all respects as children of those families.

In visiting the children your Agent has endeavored to make them feel that he is their friend—that he has their interest at heart and desires to benefit them. . . . They have been anxious to learn about their brothers, sisters and other friends, information of whom has been communicated by letter as soon as it could be ascertained. To each of the children visited a book has been presented, at an expense to the Agent of about $100.[4] These little gifts have been kindly received by the children and have aided materially in obtaining their good will. . . .

Another feature of the agency is the finding of homes for children. One hundred and forty-seven families have been found who promised to take children. Many of these have already visited the institution and made their selections. To others, children have been sent. . . .

Too great care cannot be exercised in letting children go out among strangers. It is not enough that the applicant bring the recommendation of the selectmen,[5] for it has been found that almost anybody can get such a recommendation. A careful inquiry should be made of the applicant concerning his family before the child is permitted to go. With this precaution, and an effort to furnish children adapted to families, many troubles will be avoided. . . .

The children will more and more rely upon the Visiting Agent as their friend—looking to him as a protector in times of need, and the pacificator of all their difficulties; and he will find it easier and pleasanter to prevent wrongs and abuses among them than to correct those which have been so long accumulating.

[4] The agent's annual salary was $1,200.
[5] Highest elected town (township) administrative officials.

46. Placing Out Children in the West

Hastings H. Hart,[6] *NCCC*, 1884, pp. 143–50

I am to speak of the work of the most extensive and important children's charity in the United States . . . the Children's Aid Society of New York City. As one branch of its work, it places in homes some 3,500 children annually. . . .

Criticisms of the emigration work of the Children's Aid Society have stated that many vicious and depraved children are sent out by the society; that they are hastily placed in homes without proper inquiry, and are often ill-used; that the society, having disposed of the children, leaves them to shift for themselves without further care; and that a large proportion turn out badly, swelling the ranks of pauperism and crime. . . .

The friends of the society and its critics seemed involved in hopeless contradiction, each party quoting many individual instances in support of their opinions. It did not appear that any comprehensive inquiry had ever been made into the history of the children sent to any one State (at least, of late years). . . . It was thought, however, that, with so small a number as we have in Minnesota (only 340, all received within three years), information might be gathered sufficiently to yield valuable figures. The attempt has been made, with only partial success. . . . Six of the seven counties receiving children were visited by the secretary about a year ago, and four have been revisited within the past few weeks. Lists of the children were obtained, careful inquiry was made as to each case, and a considerable number of the children were visited in their new homes. The results were carefully tabulated, after correspondence with the chairman and most active members of the local committees appointed by the society in the seven counties, and a full correspondence with Secretary Brace and Agent Mathews of the society.

The inquiry will be grouped under four heads:

[6] Hart was then secretary of the State Board of Correction and Charities of Minnesota. In 1891 he succeeded Sanborn as secretary of the NCCC. In 1908 he took charge of the child-helping work of the Russell Sage Foundation, assuming major leadership in the First White House Conference (R87).

First. Is it true that many vicious and depraved children are sent out? A few such were found, but there is no evidence that their selection was intentional. . . .

Second. Are children hastily placed in homes without proper inquiry, and are they often ill-used? Some five or six cases of abuse are reported. . . . To the first count of this indictment, however—namely, the hasty placing of children without proper investigation—we fear that the society must plead guilty. The plan is as follows: A representative of the society first visits the town . . . and secures three leading citizens to act as a volunteer committee, pass upon applications for children, and take general charge of the matter. A notice is published in local newspapers inviting applications and announcing the day of arrival and distribution. I was myself a witness of the distribution of forty children . . . by my honored friend . . . who is a member of this Conference.[7] The children arrived at about half-past three P.M., and were taken directly from the train to the court-house, where a large crowd was gathered. Mr. Mathews set the children, one by one, before the company, and, in his stentorian voice, gave a brief account of each. Applicants for children were then admitted in order behind the railing, and rapidly made their selections. Then, if the child gave assent, the bargain was concluded on the spot. It was a pathetic sight, not soon to be forgotten, to see those children and young people, weary, travel-stained, confused by the excitement and the unwonted surroundings, peering into those strange faces, and trying to choose wisely for themselves. And it was surprising how many happy selections were made under such circumstances. In a little more than three hours, nearly all of those forty children were disposed of. Some who had not previously applied selected children. There was little time for consultation, and refusal would be embarrassing; and I know that the committee consented to some assignments against their better judgment. There was similar speed . . . elsewhere. In Watonwan County, only six days intervened between the published notice and the arrival of

[7] Cf. R36.

the children, leaving no time for investigations by the committee. The committee usually consists of a minister, an editor, and a doctor, a lawyer or a business man. The merchant dislikes to offend a customer, or the doctor a patient; and the minister fears to have it thought that his refusal is because the applicant does not belong to his church. . . . Committee men and officers of the society alike complain of this difficulty. . . . While the younger children are taken from motives of benevolence and uniformly well treated, the older ones are, in the majority of cases, taken from motives of profit, and are expected to earn their way from the start. The farmers in these counties are very poor. I speak within bounds, when I say that not one in five of those who have taken these children is what would be called, in Ohio or Illinois, well-to-do. . . . A boy . . . was taken by a family whose children had been clothed by ladies of my church, so they could go to Sunday-school. I have seen other similar instances. Probably as many failures have resulted from unsuitable homes as from the fault of the children. We believe that the society should employ responsible, paid agents to investigate deliberately all applications before-hand.

Third. Does the society, having disposed of the children, leave them to shift for themselves, without farther care? No, not in Minnesota. The agents of the society have revisited the counties where children are placed—most of them repeatedly. These trips, being hurried, have not permitted visits to all of the children, special attention being given to urgent cases. Cases of incorrigibility reported to the society have received prompt attention —homes being changed or the child removed from the State, as seemed best. . . .

The present system of supervision works well with young children and tractable older ones; but it fails with the restless and intractable, who need supervision. The employer gives no security for redeeming his promises, and may discharge the child without warning, "if found *useless* or otherwise unsatisfactory." . . . On the other hand, "the children are free to leave, if ill-treated or dissatisfied." A bad boy is sure to become dissatisfied, and good boys often do; and most boys feel ill-treated the first time they are punished or even reprimanded. The result is that many boys, from ten to sixteen years old . . . have exercised their privilege, and left. . . . Thirty per cent. of the children . . . have gone from the vicinities where placed; and, of these, at least forty have drifted off and been lost sight of in less than three years, for lack of adequate supervision. The agents are efficient men, but they are not omnipresent. We believe that the society should have responsible, paid local agents, to whom legal guardianship should be given. . . .

Fourth. The crucial question is, Does "a large proportion turn out badly, swelling the ranks of pauperism and crime?" . . .

From our experience, we are positive in the opinion that children above the age of twelve years ought not to be sent west. . . . In this opinion, I understand that the officers of the society concur. . . . If the society would adhere to this wise rule, we should have little cause for complaint.

Our examination shows, with reference to the children under thirteen years old, that nine-tenths remain, four-fifths are doing well, and all incorrigibles are cared for by the society. If properly placed and faithfully supervised, we are willing to take our full share of these younger children in Minnesota.

XX

THE NATIONAL CONFERENCE

Hardly had the Massachusetts Board issued its first annual report in 1865 when it launched a national movement by issuing an invitation to a meeting of a "Social Science League." The object of the organization was to be:

. . . the discussion of those questions relating to the sanitary condition of the people, the relief, employment, and education of the poor, the prevention of crime, the amelioration of the criminal law, the discipline of prisons, the remedial treatment of the insane, and those numerous matters of statistical and philanthropic interest which are included under the general head of "Social Science." [8]

The American Social Science Association, thus founded, was the seedbed for later development in many directions. The scope of its interests is indicated by the departments into which it was divided: education, public health, social economy (from which soon split off a department of trade and finance), and jurisprudence. The Association brought together persons with mutual interests, and there was a tendency for special groups to form, many of which ultimately developed into learned and professional societies while the Social Science Association itself faded out of the picture after the turn of the century.

By 1874 there were nine states with boards of charities, whose members felt the need for intensive study of problems and comparison of methods. They held a meeting of their members and paid administrators in connection with the Association, at which they formed permanent committees on the most urgent study questions. Later in 1874,[9] the paid secretaries of these boards got

[8] Quoted in F[ranklin] B. Sanborn, "The Work of Social Science, Past and Present, a Report by the General Secretary," *Journal of Social Science*, VIII (1876), 25.
[9] F[ranklin] B. Sanborn, *et al*, [reports of] "Committees of the New York Meeting," *ibid.*, VII (1874), 398. Another account of the founding of

together to set up common statistical studies and to plan the second annual Conference of Charities. This may well have been the first national meeting limited to persons who were making a career of charitable activities.

The Conference of Charities continued to meet with the Social Science Association until 1879 when, led by Frederick H. Wines, of Illinois, and Andrew E. Elmore, of Wisconsin, the group representing the boards of charities secured complete separation in order to give more intensive study to the "practical" work. There was considerable overlapping between the two organizations; the Conference opened its doors to others than members of the state boards, especially to persons engaged in private philanthropy, both religious and nonsectarian, while the Association continued to have discussions of problems of "pauperism," other social problems, and philanthropy (R52).

The open-door membership policy of the Conference bore the seeds of change. Already by 1879, only two years after the founding of the first COS in the United States, the Conference had set up a committee on charity organization in cities. The rapid growth of the COS movement during the next decade, with its radically different philosophy concerning the role of the state, and with its violent criticisms of public relief, led to a schism. This found its verbal expression in Mrs. Josephine Shaw Lowell's attack on Sanborn's committee report in 1890 (R64, 63).

The triumph of the COS was symbolized by the election of one of its lay leaders as president of the Conference in 1895. The

---

the Conference stated: "This important institution arose out of a visit of the State Commissioners of Public Charities of Illinois to Madison, Wisconsin, in February, 1872. It was then proposed that a conference of neighboring boards be called; and May 14, 1872, five delegates from Michigan, four from Illinois, five from Wisconsin, met in Chicago for a two days conference. Its success was largely due to the efforts of Frederick H. Wines of Illinois, S. D. Hastings of Wisconsin, and H. H. Giles, president of the board of Wisconsin. Another conference was held at Milwaukee in 1873. In 1874 the Social Science Association invited the State Boards of all States to send delegates to a conference to be held in New York City on May 19. This meeting was known as the First Conference of Charities." "National Conference of Charities and Correction," in *The Encyclopedia of Social Reform*, ed. William D. R. Bliss (New York: Funk and Wagnalls, 1897), p. 914.

distress of the traditional state board leadership of the Conference over this development is reflected in Wines's committee report (R50). Nevertheless, the trend toward the domination of the Conference by private agency interests continued throughout the period covered in this book. The name of the Conference has varied as the prevailing interests of its members have shifted. In 1879, at its first separate meeting, the decision was made to change the name to "Conference of Charities and Correction." In 1884 "National" was added. With the growth of professionalism, in 1917 it became the "National Conference of Social Work." In 1957, the most recent change was made to "National Conference on Social Welfare."

47. Conference of Boards of Public Charities Held at New York, May 20 and 22, 1874

Journal of Social Science, No. VI (1874), pp. 60, 64, 87

In accordance with an invitation extended to the Boards of Public Charities in [nine] States . . . a Conference of these Boards was held. . . . At first, only delegates of these Boards and members of the Executive Committee of the [American Social Science] Association were present; but after the organization . . . the reporters were admitted, and members of the Association or others having experience in the matters discussed were invited to take part. . . .

The first subject considered was, "The Duty of the States toward their Insane Poor." . . .

Dr. Bishop spoke in condemnation of the present costly architecture of establishments for the poor, both the sane and the insane; and, upon his motion, a committee of five was appointed to consider and report upon the subject of Buildings for the Indoor Poor. . . .

The second topic considered . . . [was] *The Laws of Pauper Settlement, and the Best Mode of Administering Poor-law Relief.* . . .

A committee was appointed . . . to report a plan for the

Uniformity of Statistics, and a better co-öperation among the Boards of Charities throughout the United States. At the second session . . . this committee made a preliminary report, to the effect that it was desirable to have the statistics of pauperism, crime, insanity, and the other topics discussed in the boards' reports, made as completely as possible upon a uniform plan. . . . It was also voted that the Chair appoint a committee of five to consider the condition of destitute and delinquent children, and the prevention of pauperism.

48. The Conference Not a Department of the Association

Report of F[ranklin] B. Sanborn, General Secretary of the Association, *Journal of Social Science*, IX (1878), 11

Besides the work strictly belonging to our Association, there is offered again—as in Saratoga last year, in Detroit in 1875, and in New York in 1874—the opportunity to discuss the broad subjects of public charity and the prevention of crime, in the annual meeting known as the Conference of Charities. This body was in its origin an informal organization of official persons from a few of the States, where the tasks of public charity were intrusted to boards of State officers. Still retaining this form, the Conference has become a gathering of many more persons, all of whom are in some way connected with the dispensation of charity, public or private, or else with agencies for the repression of pauperism and crime. Its sessions are open to all members of our Association, and its papers and debates are of much interest to those who give their attention to the very grave topics that will be discussed there. The Conference, however, is not a department or branch of the Association, but an independent convention, which does us the favor to meet conveniently near us.

49. The Conference
an Independent Organization

Address by G[eorge] S. Robinson, President, *Proceedings of the Sixth Annual Conference of Charities, 1879,* pp. 1–2, 143–44

This is the sixth annual meeting of the Conference of Charities. Hitherto its sessions have been held in connection with the American Social Science Association; but to-day, for the first time, it assembles as a separate and independent organization. I regret that on this occasion we shall be deprived of the presence and counsel of several able and distinguished gentlemen of that Association, who have been accustomed to meet with us; but can assure you that, although absent in person, yet in feeling, in sympathy, and in hope for our success, they are with us. I feel confident, however, that those who are present have come here with a determination to do their whole duty in the great work not only engaging our attention, but the attention of thousands of other philanthropic men and women throughout the land, and that our deliberations will result in more active, united, efficient efforts to mitigate the sufferings of humanity. The work in which we are engaged, the subjects we have met to discuss, the plans to be carried out, and the results we hope to accomplish, should command the attention of every good citizen. The administration of our public charities is a subject of vital importance to our people, viewed not only from a humanitarian, but from a financial standpoint as well; an imperative duty, from which we cannot shrink if we would, and would not if we could. How to administer them successfully, wisely, and economically, is a problem not easily solved. How to alleviate the sufferings of our unfortunate classes, to support and maintain them in a proper manner without overburdening our people, thereby causing a reaction in public sentiment detrimental to the wards of the state and the nation; how to attain the best practical results in dealing with the evils of pauperism, crime, and insanity, and especially how to lessen the number of their victims—are questions of paramount importance, which should challenge our earnest and serious consideration. . . .

List of Standing Committees for the Year 1879–80

1. Insanity. . . .
2. Public Buildings for the Dependent Classes. . . .
3. Dependent and Delinquent Children. . . .
4. Penal and Prison Discipline. . . .
5. Statistics. . . .
6. Medical Charities. . . .
7. On the Causes and the Prevention of Pauperism. . . .
8. Committee on Charitable Organization in Cities. . . .
9. Committee on Criminal Law and Its Administration. . . .

50. *The Ideal of Universality*

"Ideal Public Charity," Report of the Standing Committee on State Boards of Public Charities [Frederick Howard Wines, Chairman], *NCCC*, 1895, pp. 28–30

All institutions are the embodiment of ideas. . . .

It is the idea that underlies this Conference, which gives it vitality and influence. The same idea underlies the State Boards of Public Charities. . . .

In its original constitution this Conference is essentially the annual meeting with each other of the American State Boards of Charities, which the representatives of all charitable and correctional institutions and societies in the United States are invited to attend. The motive of the invitation so freely extended is two fold: it includes the desire on the part of the members and officers of these boards to qualify themselves for their work by a wider survey of the field which it is their special duty to cultivate; and also the wish to create a wise public opinion upon all questions connected with the care of the destitute, the unfortunate, and the criminal, as the only medium in which these boards can act so as rightly to discharge their peculiar function of influencing legislation. The aim of the State Boards and of the Conference, in this regard, is identical. More with a view to emphasizing the permanent relations of the boards to the Conference than for any other reason, its President has always, until this year, been chosen from their own number. To keep the Conference alive and to extend its power for good is one of their first and highest obligations, as it is their obvious interest. No other power can do it. If the general direction and control of the work of the Conference should ever be wrested from them, at the suggestion of personal ambition or excessive enthusiasm for the promotion of some special philanthropic interest, by the will of an accidental numerical majority, the organization would, in our judgment, be in peril of going to pieces, and the section which should retain the name, but not the substance which the name implies, would become a fragmentary body. . . .

The first element in the composite ideal for which the State Boards and the Conference stand is universality. . . .

They depend upon no section of the community for support and authority. They sustain no official relation of affiliation to any religious sect. They are or should be above the limitations of partisan fealty.[10] They are under no obligation; and they have no right to reflect, in their sympathies or efforts, the narrow views of any set of social or philanthropic *doctrinaires*. . . . Their work is essentially one of perpetual readjustment—of classification, apportionment, and distribution. It is universal in a double sense. Upon one side it includes all the people, upon the other all who have claims upon the people (including even the deaf and blind). In other words, it includes all who give and all who receive.

[10] Wines, who had been secretary of the Illinois state board from 1869 to 1892, had been dropped by Governor Altgeld because of Wines's political affiliations. Frank J. Bruno, *Trends in Social Work . . . , 1874–1946* (New York: Columbia University Press, 1948), p. 13.

XXI

THE CHARITY ORGANIZATION SOCIETY

By the mid-seventies thoughtful givers began to have doubts about the frenzy of diversified philanthropic activity which was going on, and small, isolated experiments in cooperation and systematization began in many parts of the country. In Boston, a group of volunteers started an exchange of information on relief recipients, more elaborate in plan than Tuckerman's. This became one of two organizations which later formed the Boston Associated Charities.[11] In Denver, a plan for common money-raising emerged which anticipated by a generation the community chest movement [12] and which became the basis for the Associated Charities of Denver. A clergyman in Buffalo was impressed by the philosophy and method of the London Charity Organization Society, and founded the first COS in this country. So many inquiries came to him that he published an account of the Buffalo experience.

The COS movement was not greatly different in its aspirations and practices from those put forward earlier by the AICP. However, in most places, the AICP by 1880 had succumbed to the dangers foreseen by Hartley and was limited to relief-giving with investigations, if any, on a perfunctory basis. Most AICP's and benefit societies devoted little or no attention to the broader problems of charity. The COS was imbued with the idea that planning and a scientific approach along many lines (a "system") should be possible. In most places where a COS was organized, it attempted a threefold approach: provision of new facilities to

[11] See Margaret Rich, "The Modern Spirit of Earlier Days," *The Family*, IV (1923), 216.

[12] Mathew Carey (R26) had undertaken a joint fund-raising project half a century earlier. See his "Address to the Liberal and Humane," May, 1829, reprinted in *Social Service Review*, XXIX (1955), 302-5.

encourage thrift, promote health, and provide better humane care; legislation to control the quality of public services and discourage begging and vice; and perfection of methods of personal treatment. Paid "agents" were used to make investigations for well-to-do contributors; committees of volunteers determined what approach was preferable for each case, and a volunteer "friendly visitor" used personal influence to bring about desired changes in family circumstances.

A large literature grew up which codified for new recruits the successful experiences of volunteers and expressed the grandiose hopes of the sponsors, only a few typical samples of which can be given here. Gurteen and Kellogg set forth two of the earliest philosophical treatments. The Philadelphia Manual described the specific behavior deemed most likely to help the visitor succeed in "reconstruction." The earliest beginnings of established ways in which a helpful relationship could be fostered are evident in admonitions to be tactful, respect the personality and privacy of those being helped, and refrain from direct criticism. Primitive record-keeping reflects the recognition of the need to preserve continuity and evaluate progress. Results of these methods are found in accounts of cases helped in Boston.

Bonaparte's letter to one of the district agents in Baltimore illustrates the way in which volunteers controlled the performance of agents. He was inclined to urge more acceptance of antisocial behavior than was then prevalent, and after fifteen years' trial, in a formal speech, took a critical look at some of the movement's cherished assumptions, seeing help for the recipient rather than protection of the donor as the desirable focus. Bonaparte was one of the first persons to foresee the enabling role of the professional worker in relation to the volunteer, that of making "every one work the more."

51. A Plan for Charity Organization

Rev. S. Humphreys Gurteen, *A Handbook of Charity Organization* (Buffalo: by the author, 1882), pp. 30–32, 120–29

The basic axiom, the cardinal principle of the "Charity Organization Society" is diametrically opposed to all systems, all institutions, all charities, all forms of relief whatsoever, which avowedly or tacitly adopt the creed of Charles Lamb to "give and ask no questions," or which is worse, that system of injudicious questioning at the door, or on the street, which leads the beggar on to invent additional falsehoods. The fundamental law of its operation is expressed in one word, "INVESTIGATE." Its motto is: "No relief (except in the extreme cases of despair or imminent death) without previous and searching examination." It says virtually to the distributors of official relief, "Refrain from giving a single cent until the individual case of each applicant has been thoroughly examined." . . . The Poormasters of England are advised, as a rule, to give no relief to able-bodied men, except in return for work done; and this plan, which has been widely adopted, has been found to work marvels. . . . It has forced many a lazy, shiftless man back to his own field of labor . . . while . . . the work performed . . . has proved a vast saving to the public treasury, being employed, as it has been, on a variety of public works. This work-test is one of the most perfect touchstones for discriminating between the deserving and the undeserving that has ever been devised. . . .

By far the larger percentage of all the confirmed paupers in the country have hung for a time on . . . [the] border-line of involuntary poverty, and only by the sheer neglect, or still oftener through the misdirected charity of benevolent people, have they been dragged down to the lowest depths of confirmed pauperism. If, therefore, pauperism as an institution, a profession, is ever to be broken up, it can only be done by restoring the involuntary poor to a position of self-support, self-respect and honorable ambition. If left to themselves . . . they will inevitably sink lower and lower, till perchance they end their course in suicide or felony. If . . . our charity is not tempered by judgement, they will as inevitably learn to be *dependent*. . . . To avoid these two extremes, both of which are fatal, is the grand object of the Charity Organization Society. It views man as God has made him, with capabilities of manliness and self-respect and holy ambition. . . . Its axiom, accordingly, is, "HELP THE POOR TO HELP THEMSELVES." [13] . . .

CHARITY ORGANIZATION AND THE BUFFALO PLAN

A Charity Organization *Society* is thus a centre of intercommunication between the various charities and charitable agencies of any given city; an intermediary acting on behalf of each and for the welfare of each, and, from its neutral character, making possible a degree of co-operation which would be impossible apart from such organized action.

Now, the principles which the Society lays down in order to effect the full and complete co-operation of which we have spoken, and apart from which no lasting co-operation is possible, are the following:

1. *There must be no exclusion of any person or body of persons on account of religious creed, politics or nationality*. . . .

2. *There must be no attempt at proselytism on the part of the Agents or others employed by the Organization*. . . .

3. *There must be no interference with any existing benevolent societies; each society must retain its autonomy intact; its rules, funds, modes of operation and everything which gives it individuality*. . . .

4. *There must be no relief given by the Organization itself, except in very urgent cases*. . . .

5. *There must be no sentiment in the matter. It must be treated as a business scheme, if success is to attend its operations*. . . .

In every large city the work to be done by an organization of charities may be included under the four following heads:

---

[13] The "self-help" idea was very popular in England, on the Continent, and in America. See Samuel Smiles, *Self-Help; with Illustrations of Character, Conduct, and Perseverance* (rev. ed.; Boston: Lothrop, n.d. [*ca.* 1880]).

1. The detection of fraud—this is its *repressive* work.

2. The adequate relief of the honest poor, and the reclaiming of the pauperized poor—this is its *benevolent* work.

3. The establishment or promotion of various well-proved schemes for the encouragement of thrift and self-help—this is its *provident* work.

4. The suppression of social abuses—this is its *reformatory* work. . . .

The first thing to be done is to show the community, in very plain language, the following facts:

1. That Organization renders most efficient aid to the clergy, benevolent societies, institutions, benevolent individuals and the city almoner, by investigating, *free of charge*, all cases applying for relief. . . .

2. That, wherever Organization has been started, it has, without a single exception, either abolished out-door city relief altogether or has reduced the amount, hitherto annually expended, within comparatively reasonable limits. . . .

3. That beggars and cripples are removed from the streets, and, if able to work, are compelled to do so, if not, they are provided for in some less degrading way. . . .

4. That the poor are gradually but surely led from a state often bordering on pauperization to love self-dependence; while in many cases, actual paupers are reclaimed, and brought to acknowledge the true kindness of the Society's plan, as it rekindles their all but extinct sense of independence. . . .

A public meeting was held, at which a constitution was adopted and the Council of the Society was elected. One point we must mention here. *No clergyman was elected to the Council.* The members were all business or professional men, and the very ablest that the city afforded.

Then, a Central Office was taken, and a Superintendent appointed. Circulars were sent to all church societies, relief societies, benevolent societies and fraternities, and to all asylums and hospitals, asking for particulars as to their modes of operation, the kind of relief given, etc. Then, the books of the Poormaster's office were copied; and shortly after, through the kindness of the Superintendent of Police, blanks were delivered at every house in the city, by the police, asking for full particulars of any relief that any citizen was giving at that time to any poor person or pensioner. These forms were collected by the police twenty-four hours after delivery, and out of some 30,000 issued, some 3,000 were returned filled in.

And thus our first work of registering the names of all in the city in receipt of relief, whether official or private, was begun.[14] . . .

We divided the city into eight Districts, corresponding with the police precincts. We avoided the *ward* divisions, considering that they were the worst that could be adopted, from their political bearings. . . . The first thing that we did was to lay it down as a rule that the District Office should be near the centre of the District, in order to be easy of access to the poor, and that, if practicable, it should be in the dwelling-house of the paid Agent who was to have charge of the district, so that there should be no taint of officialism about our work, but that the poor might come to a real *home*, with home surroundings, and thus be, perhaps unconsciously, bettered by the contact.[15] . . .

The Society, however, *gives no relief*.[16] . . . The case is referred to some citizen or to one of the benevolent societies which co-operate with the Organization, and suggestions are offered as to what it is wise to give and what not to give, so as not to pauperize the recipient. Meantime, a Visitor is appointed, if needful, to act as the poor man's friend, to encourage him and strengthen his resolves; the Agent occasionally visits him for the same purpose; and as soon as possible, he is given employment which the Committee has, in the meantime, obtained for him.

[14] The social service exchange idea was thus incorporated into the first American COS (R25).

[15] At Baltimore and elsewhere the COS adopted this device, which was inspired by the same influence which led to the development of the settlement movement (R58, 59).

[16] This was a moot point in the COS movement. For one clash, see statements by Charles D. Kellogg, of New York, and Zilpha D. Smith, of Boston, quoted in "Almsgiving by Friendly Visitors," *Lend a Hand*, IV (1889), 131–35.

52. *The Principle and Advantage of Association in Charities*

Rev. D. O. Kellogg, *Journal of Social Science*, XII
(1880), 84–90 [17]

The weal of society embraces vastly more than so-called wealth. . . .

When a man ceases to be a machine whose out-put is merchantable, and is esteemed worthy of education and personal improvement for his own sake, then he is an object of solicitude to the humane spirit, rather than of calculation to the economical mind. Of course, this distinction is only approximate and general, for . . . there is a law of economy in beneficence . . . having in its keeping a new age of humanity. . . . Of recent years there has arisen in many minds a new conception of charity. In its lowest degradation, the term meant a class of *actions* done without remuneration, for the relief of suffering or depression. A better sense of the term is a *sentiment* of kindness or benevolence. The higher conception of it is a *law* of love. As a class of external deeds, the value of it lay in the doing of them, without much regard to their motive or effects. The actor might perform the charitable works for his own moral cultivation, for his own reputation, or as deeds of supererogation. . . . Genuine charity must consider well what is the effect of her actions, and that not upon the mover of them, but upon the objects of them. [18]

Charity as a sentiment relegates the deeds thereof to individual impulse, if not caprice. It tends to isolated work, and recognizes no law of self-restraint for the actor. But, if charity is a *law of love*, then it gives rise to a system. . . . Law is the statement of an order or a process, and it is discovered by the human mind through experience. It presupposes observation, classification, generalization. Charity has its laws which can only be detected by a study of past experience. It is, therefore, a science—the

[17] President D. C. Gilman, of Johns Hopkins University, who chanced to hear this paper delivered at Saratoga, was so impressed that he immediately stimulated the organization of a COS in Baltimore. Kellogg was president of the newly organized society in Philadelphia.
[18] Cf. Bonaparte, R57.

science of social therapeutics.[19] Again, as art is the application of science, it follows that there can be no true act of charity until its laws are formulated. Until this is done, benevolence is not much else but quackery, however amiable its motive. Indeed the true impulse of love cannot rest until it has found its science; for it cannot stop short of effective methods and sound principles.

From these premises, it will be easy to see that charity organization is as practicable as industrial association. . . .

There may seem a danger in thus placing benevolent exertion under law. . . . The individual may be in danger of passing from sight, and machine-like processes may take the place of sympathetic action. But were this danger more real than it is, we should have to weigh and determine whether the greater evils were on the side of uninstructed impulse, or of studious, systematic work. It is not true that the best motives of the human heart are deadened or dissipated because they are taught how to be most skilful and efficient. On the contrary, nothing checks generous dispositions so much as disappointment, and the painful discovery that their schemes to cure an evil have only exacerbated it.

We have spoken of social therapeutics as an inductive science. Induction is not an ignoring of individuals and particulars, but the reverse. Its value depends on the accurate, painstaking study of detail, which is essential to improved methods of charitable action. The philanthropist who keeps his own methods and their results out of sight, not only puts himself at a disadvantage, but he abstracts from the general cause the benefit of his successes. On clear general principles it may be held to be desirable that philanthropists should be a community. Instead of a poor sectarianism of charitable effort, where petty societies work in the dark, ignorant of one another's methods, suspicious of each other, rivals for patronage and for advertising statistics, shrinking from criticism, solicitous neither to apply right principles nor to correct mistakes, there should be a community of philanthropists in which the experience of one enriches them all. . . .

There is another important line of thought leading directly

---

[19] Courses in research are justified in the curricula of schools of social work by similar arguments. Cf. Abbott, R78.

to the organization or association of charities. Social evils are whatever things work against the common welfare of men. Society is a unit—a solidarity, of which individuals are a part. The person gains his highest development in that unity. . . . Where persons have become incapable of self-control, or steadiness of effort, or where they are hardened against moral influences, restraint must be invoked. For both these classes, and for the incompetent ones, there must be education. Even where incompetency has arisen from bodily defect, much has been done to overcome it by education, as in the cases of the blind and deaf, and more rarely among persons of feeble intellect.

The kind of education required is not that of the text-book, nor of the industrial school, so much as it is that furnished by the great school of society. . . . The educational power of association is of incalculable strength. These remedial measures require the largest concert of action in the community. . . .

The anarchy of charity gives rise to disorder and encourages evil. . . . Mutual understanding, cooperation and intelligence, based on wide experience, will set the recuperative forces of the commonwealth in effective operation, and the benevolent dispositions of mankind will be increased in proportion as effectiveness and blessing wait upon their efforts, and the disappointments of crude experiments cease.

One further thought remains. The organization of charity must not be regarded as the attempt to set on foot new agencies of relief or of education, but to systematize the institutions now existing, and to promote concord of endeavor. . . . It would be unhistorical and revolutionary to attempt to displace old agencies by new measures.

53. General Suggestions to Those Who Visit the Poor

Rev. R. E. Thompson, *Manual for Visitors among the Poor;* published by the Philadelphia Society for Organizing Charitable Relief and Repressing Mendicancy (Philadelphia: Lippincott, 1879), pp. 14–21

No person of right feeling can live in the same city, and especially in the same neighborhood, with great numbers of poor persons, without having a desire to do something for them. But it is not so easy to find what is the right thing to do; and even kind and well-meaning people manage, at times, to do a great deal more harm than good. The following suggestions have been gathered out of the experience of persons who have been much in this good work, and who seem to have done it at least as well as any others.

1. The best means of doing the poor good is found in friendly intercourse and personal influence. The want of money is not the worst evil with which the poor have to contend; it is in most cases itself but a symptom of other and more important wants. Gifts or alms are, therefore, not the things most needed—but sympathy, encouragement, and hopefulness.

2. Women are, in all ordinary cases, by far the best visitors of the poor. A true woman carries with her an atmosphere of influence which makes itself felt. She can go, without offence, where men would not be welcome. She will see a great many things which ought to be considered, but which would escape men. Women, have, commonly, more tact and skill in suiting themselves to the case before them. . . .

3. A small number of families, from three to five, are enough to exhaust all the time, attention, and friendly care which one visitor has to bestow upon them. The more experience a visitor has, the more certain she is to prefer this to a larger number.

4. The starting-point of all really useful work is a genuine neighborly interest in those whom you seek to serve. They must be approached as beings of the same flesh and blood, and therefore kinsfolk. Any notion of condescension or patronage is not only wrong in itself, but is also sure to do harm, by preventing the visitor from getting into right and natural relations with her poor friends. No eyes are keener of vision than those which have been sharpened by want.

5. The poor man's house or room is his castle, just as much as the rich man's home is his. *Wherever it is possible an introduction to each new household should be had through some neighbor,* who is well acquainted with them. The manner of the visitor should always be respectful. She should avoid calling at

inconvenient hours. She should make her poorer friends feel that she fully recognizes the fact that she has no right to enter their homes, except that given her by their courtesy.

6. The visitor will do well to avoid undertaking the distribution of alms in any case. Nothing will so much interfere with her proper work as to be recognized as a public almoner. It will close against her the doors of poor people who cannot afford to be thought dependent on charity, but to whom she might be of great service. It will destroy her highest influence with those who continue to receive her, by turning their thoughts steadily in the mercenary direction. . . .

7. In cases of urgent need, help may often be obtained at once from poor neighbors.[20] They are the most generous of givers, and to deprive them of such opportunities is to impoverish their own lives. In cases of less urgency, the visitor will refer the person in need of relief to the office of the Ward Superintendent. But it should be understood that nothing can be had through the visitor from any source, which cannot be got without her by direct application to the Ward Office.

8. When the visitor or any of her friends are able and willing to give some personal assistance, it should take the form of employment. Where work is given, it should be paid for at fair, business-like rates.[21] *It is of no use to cover up alms in any other dress,* for the result will be much the same as from direct giving.

9. The visitor will need to make some effort to keep steadily in view the main purpose of her visit in the midst of the many distractions which will occur. Without making up any formal catechism of topics, she should accustom herself to keeping in mind the chief ways in which influence may be brought to bear, and advice or assistance given, and to applying these to the circumstances of the family whose guest she is for the time. She should keep a memorandum-book for the record of each day's work, partly to refresh her own memory, partly for the information of her successor in the work, in case she should be obliged to relinquish it. But it is not best to use a note-book during a

[20] Cf. Chalmers, R24.   [21] Cf. Carey and Hale, R26, 27.

visit, either to prompt questions or to record answers, as this would make the visit seem less friendly.

10. The visitor needs to cultivate the habit of looking below the surface of things, and not judging by first impressions. The poor who have the strongest claim upon our sympathy are generally the silent, sensitive, painfully respectable people, whose clean and tidy rooms conceal to the utmost the evidence of their poverty. They must be sought out with delicacy, and treated with the utmost courtesy.

11. Poverty is very largely associated with disease and a consequent lack of vitality. Our medical profession, through dispensaries and hospitals, have made ample provision for every possible want in that direction. But the sick poor do not always discern their need of medical treatment. . . . Even when they are well aware of their need, they do not always know how to get assistance. The visitor should make herself acquainted with the facts in regard to our medical charities, as given in this manual, so as to be competent to give advice here. At the same time, she should be on her guard to avoid seeing disease where there is none, nor should she send to dispensaries those who are able to pay for medical attendance.

12. The visitor should also make herself acquainted with the location of the nearest Orphan Asylums, Temporary and Permanent Homes, Day Nurseries, and other charities for children, with their rules for admission. While the unnecessary separation of children from their parents is always to be avoided,[22] there are many cases where these institutions can be used to advantage.

13. Every visitor to the poor should have some knowledge of sanitary laws, since the violation of these is the most prolific source of disease. . . . For like reasons, she should inform herself of the nearest parks, squares, and other grounds open to the people, and of the rules which govern their use. In warm weather the health of children, and even adults, is much promoted by passing the morning hours in such places.

14. The poor have legal rights which they often fail to enjoy,

[22] Cf. White House Conference, R87, and Vaile, R88.

through ignorance. They have a right, under our sanitary laws, to have all nuisances abated, and proper precautions taken for their health. They are often imposed upon. . . . Where cases arise which do not come within the purview of the Board of Health, the visitor will do well to call to them [*sic*] the attention of some member of the bar with whom she is acquainted. . . . The redress of such wrongs is one means of keeping the poor in wholesome sympathy with society, by making them feel that laws and courts are for rich and poor alike.

15. Those who have the greatest need to be economical in their purchases are often much less so than other classes. . . . They have not learned the best ways of preparing food. . . . On . . . points of thrift the visitor can give advice which will be worth more than money. But in most cases the subject must be approached with care, to the avoidance of every appearance of censoriousness or meddlesomeness.

16. The poor, as a rule, have never learned "the power of littles." The habit of watching where the pennies go, and of laying up against a rainy day, is generally wanting to them. Our savings-banks and our building associations are patronized by but a very small part of their number. A word in season may be of use to keep spare money out of the whiskey-seller's till, and to get it put to better use.

17. In every case the visitor should seek to foster a spirit of self-respect and independence. Her poor friends should be encouraged to feel how great the gulf between honest *poverty* and the *pauperism* which is willing to rely upon gifts and alms.

18. Although there is abundant provision made for public education, a very large proportion of poor children get little, and some of them none at all. . . . The visitor should awaken and cherish right feeling on this subject, that parents may be induced to make sacrifices for their children's sake.

19. The poorest poor are those who *have no wholesome contacts with society or with each other.* . . . The visitor's first aim should be to strengthen their family ties. . . . She should seek to awaken and cherish their home affections, to cultivate courtesy

of speech and manner, and to prompt the little mutual sacrifices which make life gracious. And she should encourage every effort to make home a pleasant and attractive place.

20. Churches and Sunday-schools, aside from all their other uses, will help in the same direction, since they put the poor in the way of a more orderly home life. There are very few of our people who have no affiliation with some religious body, and where these ties have been sundered for a time, the visitor should seek to have them renewed. But using *her influence to win proselytes will* seriously mar her work, and is in direct contradiction to the principles and rules of this Society.

21. It is wisest to work for the results which come in the long run, to anticipate disappointments, and not to be disheartened by them. The habits of a lifetime are not to be corrected in a day. The most successful visitor will have discouraging experiences, and, perhaps, for a time little else. The greatest patience, the most decided firmness, and an inexhaustible kindness are all needed in this work.

22. In appealing always to the "better self" of her poor friends, the visitor must always make the appeal from her "better self." She should, for instance, discipline herself never to hear from their lips of wrong doing of their neighbors with either exultation at their exposure or any other of the lower emotions.

54. *Reports of the District Conferences*

Fourth Annual Report of the Associated Charities of Boston, 1883, pp. 35–44

We have had our failures. We have not succeeded in reforming the lazy people in our charge, nor in rescuing their children, because such parents will not allow their children to go from home. Several times, we could have put them in good homes, if the parents had consented. . . .

The barriers to friendly influence are increased by a foreign language and different ideas and customs. It is much harder to stop begging, for instance, when the beggars look upon it as a natural and satisfactory way of earning a living. We have one family where the man is an organ-grinder and the wife has so many little children that she cannot go out to work. She seems to be a nice woman, and takes excellent care of her family; but, on pleasant days, she dresses her children in their prettiest clothes, and stations herself and them at some street corner, where they form such an attractive group that people stop to give them cakes and pennies. . . . In such cases, nothing but time and watchfulness on the part of the visitor can change their ideas and prevent them from becoming American vagrants as they lose their . . . picturesqueness. . . .

We need visitors who can speak their language, and, while teaching them the value of reading and writing, regular work, etc., can understand and sympathize. . . . One . . . woman . . . was referred to us in a really suffering condition. Her husband had died, leaving her a widow in a strange city, without money or work and quite ill. Temporary relief was procured for her till she was better, then the visitor [who spoke her language] had her come to her own house, and let her try different kinds of work. She found her to be so good a seamstress that, by getting engagements for her among her friends, she was soon made self-supporting; and, better than all, the kindness with which she has been treated by her visitor and the ladies at whose houses she sews has roused her from the depths of despair and made her courageous and contented. She now has all the work she can do. Of course, she owes this greatly to her own skill; but, as a stranger, it would have been impossible for her to obtain this work or any of a superior kind without the interest of the visitor, who for a month or two gave her constant care and thought. . . .

Another typical case of chronic dependence is that of a widow with six children. When she was referred to us nearly four years ago, her children were very young, and she, though well-meaning, was stupid and inefficient. The problem was *not* whether aid should be given—that was clearly necessary, for the woman could not earn anything with her little children to care for—but if the aid could be given in such a way as to really benefit them. Relief was procured from the proper sources, $20 a quarter from the "Shaw Fund for Mariners' Children," $2 a month in groceries from the city, and at times $1 a week from the St. Vincent de Paul Society. The visitor who first interested himself in the family and who has been their friend and counsellor ever since, received the quarterly $20 for them, paid the rent with $13 of it, and gave the rest to the woman, who knew just what she had to depend upon, and learned to use it properly. As the children grew older, the boy went into a district telegraph office, and the girl, wishing to go into a store, asked the visitor to find her a place. He thought, however, that it was wiser to teach *her* how to find one, and, after suggesting some good establishments at which to apply, told her to get references from her school-teacher and others, and go herself to ask for work. This she did with some difficulty, and got a place; and when, after a time, she gave it up, she knew what to do, and had no difficulty in finding another. The boy refused to be apprenticed to a joiner, as the visitor wished, but is working hard in a place he found himself. The second boy goes to school, and sells papers. In summer, the visitor, with the consent of the Conference, has sent the younger children into the country to board for a month. He has taken pains to have the family live in a healthy tenement, and in many ways has insured their well-being. They are now partially self-supporting; and the older children are respectable and industrious, which we feel is greatly due to the good influence that the visitor has exerted over them and their mother for four years.

Once this year, a woman applied to us, because she had seen in the newspapers that our society *did not give relief.* She would not ask for or receive relief; but she was in great trouble and out of work, and was very thankful for the advice, help, and opportunity to work given her by a visitor.

This suggests the idea that, by being avowedly a society for sending friendly help to people, we may sometimes be of use to those above the ignorant and pauper classes. If our committees should come to be regarded as men and women working together for the sake of assisting in the best way open to them *any friendless people in difficulties,* one important object of our society would be reached. . . .

The benefits of skilled and thorough investigation, that keen and valuable instrument of our work, searching out the causes of evil, probing the wounds to cure them, beneficent, alert, judicial, can be illustrated. . . .

The agent found an old . . . man we had been asked to visit living alone in the midst of much dirt and confusion. He earned but seventy-five cents a week, by carrying an organ for a lame man. His rent was fifty cents a week. Even on this small income, he lived within his means, and although he could not boast any savings, had no debts to worry him. There was an evident scarcity of food; yet he was of good cheer, eager to get work at his trade. . . . The reports from the Provident Association and Overseers of the Poor, through the Registration Office, spoke well of him. The Provident Association and the lady who referred the case gave temporary aid, while we continued the investigation by sending a visitor to become acquainted with the man and his life. "The poor man has had no tailoring for a year," reported the visitor, "and is too feeble to work. His mind is failing. He lives on anything he can pick up during the summer—herbs or fungi or bits of bread and scraps. . . . [He] says he can live on five cents a day. He is getting into debt for rent. A good old man he seems to be. I am much interested in him, and think he would be very unhappy in an institution. What can be done?" . . . Now came the question as to the best way of providing the permanent support required.

A glance back at the agent's investigation showed that there were relatives upon whom he might have a claim, and the Committee advised the visitor to look them up. . . . Upon inquiry through the Charity Organization Society in A., N. Y., the visitor learned that the niece . . . was unable to contribute anything. . . . The brother-in-law . . . wrote that he had not . . . seen our . . . man for twenty-five years; but he promised to send a regular pension of five dollars a month. Besides paying the rent (reduced by request of the visitor to forty cents a week), this pension furnished him with seventy-five cents a week for his living. The brother-in-law also sent comfortable clothing. Improvement has been made in cleanliness; but . . . the visitor is looking for a boarding-place . . . where he can have a home and good care.

If there had been no careful investigation, [he] . . . might have worn out a miserable existence in an almshouse; but, with his dislike for institution life, he would probably have drifted into a worse condition, living on, half-starved and wretched in his filthy abode, begging for the little which would keep him from death. But the long-severed connection with his relatives is once more united, and a continuous support is secured to him. He has grown better and happier by means of investigation.

55. *Let All Work to One End*

Rocky Mountain News [Denver], June 21, 1888

The King's Daughters
Yesterday's Meeting
Combined Charity Advocated
Resolutions Passed

The King's Daughters held a large and enthusiastic meeting in the crypt of St. John's cathedral yesterday afternoon. . . .

Rev. Myron W. Reed was present and spoke to the society, advocating the consolidation of all the relief organizations in Denver. He said he thought it would be a good plan to establish a central office somewhere in the city and appoint at least one good salaried officer, whose duty it would be to control the affairs of the combined societies, sending representatives, who would meet at the office once a month for the purpose of considering such subjects as would materially advance the interest of charity. Charity began at home, and the only way to keep it there is by united effort. He did not believe in abolishing the existing associations; let them preserve their individuality, but let all work to one end, to accomplish the one thing—the uplifting of the poorer classes and elevating as much as possible the standard of civilization. The officer in charge of the central office of the combination thus formed would devote all her time for the interest of the organization.

Rev. Thomas Van Ness being present, championed the cause advocated by Mr. Reed, and urged its adoption by the society. He also impressed upon the ladies the necessity of taking an adjournment at an early date for the summer; it was too hot to do good during the summer months; he believed it to be the wisest and safest plan.

The following resolution was then introduced by Mrs. Appel:

Resolved, That a committee of ten ladies and ten gentlemen be appointed by the president to formulate a plan for a basis of union of the various relief and charity organizations of Denver, and to hold meetings as they in their judgment may deem necessary during the summer months, and report at the first meeting in September, the chairman to be elected by the committee.

Accepted.

It was moved and seconded, to hold the next meeting in the Tabernacle on Blake street. . . .

Carried.

Mrs. Appel then introduced another resolution which read as follows:

Resolved, That the King's Daughters as an organization, being composed of representatives of every church and religious society in Denver, firmly believe that the proper time has arrived when it is necessary to unite with one another and form a strong and compact association, and honestly believe that a better system can be maintained in the distribution of relief and the giving of assistance to the poor and needy, that a great amount of labor and money can be saved in carrying out a plan of united charity. With this object in view the King's Daughters request all the different societies of a philanthropic nature, of whatever race or creed to lend their aid to the furthering of this union of charitable and relief organizations. *Accepted.*

56. *She Needs a Friendly Visitor*

Charles J. Bonaparte[28] to District Agent, Charity Organization Society, Baltimore, Feb. 18, 1892; Charles J. Bonaparte Papers, Library of Congress, Box 138, pp. 237–38

I am duly in receipt of your report in the case of Mrs. ——. I have formed a favorable impression of this young woman from what I saw of her, although I have no doubt you are right in thinking that some of her trouble has been due to high temper on her part and a certain amount of indiscretion, excusable, perhaps, in one so young. I am confident that the reports which you have received from her husband's family are grossly exaggerated, even if not absolutely without foundation. At the trial of the habeas corpus case, testimony of the most disgraceful character, and which I believe to have been utterly devoid of truth, was given by her husband's younger brother. It was evidently disbelieved by the Judge, since he would not hear any testimony on her behalf at all. I think that she particularly needs a friendly visitor, or, at all events, some judicious adviser.

If she reaches the determination to place her elder child in any institution, be good enough to keep me advised of the facts, because I feel under some obligation to have the Judge informed of any change in the child's custody, and to get the Court's sanction to this.

With respect to Mrs. ——'s refusal to be reconciled to her husband, I think she was justified in this course under the circumstances; at least, if she adhered to the determination which she adopted by my advice immediately after the hearing. This was to stipulate, as a condition of such reconciliation, that he should move away from the influence of his family, and to also require

[28] Bonaparte, grandnephew of Napoleon, was prominent in Baltimore society. He was a wealthy, successful attorney, close friend of Cardinal Gibbons, a leader in the national civil service reform movement, and later was Attorney General in the cabinet of Theodore Roosevelt. For many years he was chairman of the board of the Baltimore COS. He had referred Mrs. —— to the agency for service and had apparently received a report from the district agent.

him to avow his disbelief of the testimony given by his brother. Without going into particulars, I may say that the last condition was one which any person with a proper self-respect would have been compelled to exact.

I send these particulars because I think they may be of service in guiding your future action in this case, and remain, as ever,

Yours very respectfully and truly,

[Charles J. Bonaparte]

P.S. In the course of the trial I learned incidentally that the reputation for veracity of the —— family was of the very worst. Mrs. —— in her conversation with me, left upon my mind the impression of a truthful person.

57. *The Ethics of Organized Charity*

Address delivered by Charles J. Bonaparte before the COS of New Haven, Connecticut, April 30, 1893; Bonaparte Papers

. . . . Most persons who hear much and know little about organized charity believe its ends to be principally, if not altogether, the detection and exposure of frauds on the benevolent. This work has its place . . . but if we dwell on its merits . . . to the exclusion of other considerations, we lose sight of . . . "the bigger half" of the problem before us. When one gives alms . . . the beggar may be the worse for it, but . . . the man whose pocket has been lightened feel fifty cents' worth to the good for the loss. . . .

And if we tell him *ad nauseam* that generosity and compassion must wait until the "case" has been duly indexed and the forms have been duly filled and the first visit and the second visit and the preliminary report and the final report have all been made *modo et forma*, we should not be altogether surprised when he pronounces our whole system a scheme to put a nickel . . . in the slot and see so many yards . . . of relief come out automatically at the other end of the machine. . . .

Having been once invited to address an Annual Meeting . . . I took as text for my little "lay sermon" . . . "The Lord loveth a cheerful giver," with the result of convincing myself (I do not answer for the rest of my hearers) that "cheerful giver" is the biblical name for a Charity Organizer. . . .

What "the Lord loveth" is a "giver," not a payer of debts or taxes. There are those who . . . set aside a tenth or more or less of their income to be given in charity. . . . To me this seems no *giving* at all, the claims of charity are not satisfied by ten or ninety or ninety-nine *per centum* of what we have . . . nothing that we can do with any portion will give us the right to do what we please with the rest. Every dollar . . . is spent or hoarded or given at the holder's immediate, personal, terrible risk; he will be no more justified for what he wastes on others than for what he wastes on himself. And if he would show that what he gives is not wasted, that he has sought by his alms . . . to do all the good he could do according to his best lights, he applies the principles of Organized Charity.

But it is not enough that we *give*, we must also give *cheerfully*. . . . No one can feel the true pleasure of giving unless . . . his purpose be to so aid that he who is aided will be more and not less a man. With this aim to his giving he may overlook the sordid aspect, the ignorance, even the vice of its object . . . so the very hideous, loathsome maladies of his sick soul make him precious; they love him because they can do him so much good. Such I believe are the "cheerful givers" whom "the Lord loveth"; and such only do or can apply fully, consistently, practically the principles of Charity Organization. . . .

Applications for relief are often classed as "worthy" and "unworthy"; can *any* man be *unworthy* of real help from other men? He may indeed require help in an unusual form: not infrequently the sound application of a cat-o'-nine-tails would be, to my mind, the most salutary "relief." But . . . my limited experience of the typical "worthy" case of "Mothers' Meetings" and other Church and charitable societies, leaves an impression of obtrusive respectability and piety serving as stock in trade for chronic helplessness and voluntary pauperism.

It is, however, most important of all to consider *what* the text would have us give and give cheerfully. Not, surely, money only or what money will buy. The enlightened benevolence of the present age . . . bids us give the poor "not alms but a friend." I would ask rather for both: alms are needed; but alms, to do real and lasting good, must come, and be known and felt to come, from a friend. Now a friend must be *given*. . . . Money may hire servants for the poor, as for the rich; faithful, zealous, useful servants often, but neither for a king nor for a beggar can you buy or lease a friend. And as it is a friend's service that counts beyond price or measure, it is such service and no other which "the Lord loveth." . . . Whoever thus gives, again adopts practically and consistently the vital principle of Charity Organizations. . . .

No man has the right to give alms unless he . . . has done all he can in reason to assure himself, that his alms will do good, and the most good that, if well given, these might do. . . . But if all gave all their time to intelligently dispensing relief, all would soon come to need relief, and here . . . common-sense dictates a division of labor. Experts are needed in charity as elsewhere, and Charity Organization employs experts, but to supplement, not to supplant, individual effort, not to make any one work the less, but to make every one work the more, since each knows that he works to good purpose. . . .

Everybody would like to do his duty, and would do it if this were not so laborious and unpleasant a proceeding. . . . We all pass most of our lives trying, with greater or less success, to persuade ourselves that we are better men than we know we are. There is always, however, far down in our consciousness a knowledge, carefully covered up under layers of self deception but still there, that this ill earned complacency is merely an elaborately pondered lie, and therefore it is a mortal offence for any hand to strip off the disguise and display us as we are to ourselves. It is said that a certain clergyman . . . persuaded, with much difficulty, those in charge of the charities of his church to obtain from us, as an experiment, reports as to ten of their habitual beneficiaries: nine of the ten . . . figured, with the aid of petty fraud . . . on the relief rolls of other churches or charitable organizations. On learning this, the congregation resolved immediately and unanimously under no circumstances to refer to the Charity Organization Society in the future. . . . The old humbugs we thus exposed were very serviceable to that congregation; they procured its members an amount of self satisfaction which would have been cheap at twice the cost. Coddling them and . . . doling out, in return for . . . outrageous flattery, driblets of material aid, was easy and appeared inexpensive; to study and supply their true needs, to elevate their lives, to discover and correct their vices, to make them better and society better through their betterment, this meant real work with disagreeable incidents, with doubtful immediate results, with perhaps an appreciable first outlay. What was spent on them . . . had been far better thrown into the sea, and they consigned to the almshouse at once, for they were . . . an object lesson of the good living to be gained by mendicancy, flavored with hypocrisy; but the money was meant to serve another purpose and this it served well. . . .

When we, believers in Organized Charity, say that . . . the practices it condemns constitute . . . subterfuges used by indolence and self-love when these would masquerade as charity, we trample on many bulging shoes and the first response is a cry of disgust and pain. This will die away, but the truth will remain: and, within its sphere of human life, the principles of Organized Charity are the truth.

XXII

THE SETTLEMENT MOVEMENT

The major emphasis in nearly every preceding reading has been on methods of dealing with poverty or other forms of particularized need which rendered the individual dependent on aid from outside the family. The following two readings introduce in specific form the concepts that all people, whether or not they are in a state of destitution, have potentials for personal development—social, economic, intellectual; and that society has a responsibility to provide opportunities for all persons to fulfill their potentialities.

The services here described were directed to so-called "normal" people rather than to those who were antisocial or sick. They were based on the beneficiaries' interests and abilities rather than on a pattern of behavior prescribed by the donors. Yet they also reveal a deep cleavage within the settlement movement between the aristocratic ideal of doing for others and the democratic ideal of enabling the beneficiaries to work together for individual, group, and neighborhood self-improvement (R61 and 71 give further indications of these two points of view).

A unique thing about the settlement philosophy was its concentration on the total problems of a single geographical area. It did not lose sight of the economic or social needs of the individual, but it saw him as a member of a group through which joint activity could be conducted. It did not overlook the need for broad social and economic reforms, but it saw these as growing out of the experience, thinking, and action of the whole population of a neighborhood cooperating with similar groups in other neighborhoods.

Methodologically, early settlement workers relied on the stimulation of one participant by another, the enthusiastic response of people to opportunities for learning and experience previously denied them, and on the example and warm interest of persons of education. As with the COS, the original idea of settlements came from England. In 1886 in New York City, Stanton Coit, after seeing London's pioneer settlement, Toynbee Hall, was the first person to attempt an adaptation of Oxfordian aristocratic and scholarly tradition to the democratic American scene. Excerpts are given from his statement of underlying philosophy, as well as from an account by an observer of the early activities of another New York settlement. Here services to underprivileged individuals were stressed in addition to educational projects and neighborly interest in the entire area.

By 1895 the settlement idea was gaining momentum, and people in many cities were considering founding something similar. Probably the best known settlement was Hull House in Chicago, started in 1889 by Jane Addams (see R71–73).

58. The Completest Efficiency of Each Individual

Stanton Coit,[24] *Neighborhood Guilds: an Instrument of Social Reform* (London: Swan Sonnenschein [George Allen & Unwin Ltd., successor], 1891), pp. 1–19, 150

No one has as yet accepted, in the full sense in which he meant it, General Booth's challenge [25] to bring forward a better scheme than his for lifting the fallen classes of society into independence and prosperity. He demanded that over against the Salvation Army and the network of measures he had proposed, any one who refused to support him should not only point out other and better methods, but also another body of

[24] Coit, a disciple of Felix Adler, was one of the leading exponents of the Ethical Culture movement. Although Coit was American by birth and early education, most of his life after 1889 was spent in England as minister of an ethical society. He had great influence with the leading English university teachers of philosophy. He was an ardent supporter of the Labor movement and of women's suffrage.

[25] William Booth was founder of the Salvation Army. He explained and defended his idea in *In Darkest England and the Way Out* (London: Funk and Wagnalls, 1890), esp. p. 281: "If it be that you have some plan that promises more directly to accomplish the deliverance of these multitudes than mine, I implore you at once to bring it out."

workers who were ready and competent to execute them. This
no one of his opponents has done. . . .

In the following pages the Neighborhood Guild will be considered primarily as a scheme for getting the right men. . . .
The first step in social reform, if my psychology be correct,
must be the conscious organization of the intellectual and moral
life of the people for the total improvement of the human lot.
. . . The second step, the enlightenment of the people in social
principles, could [then] be easily made. . . . Whatever be the
final and widest-sweeping reforms—whether the wage system is
simply to be modified or is to be superseded by a better method
of production and distribution—still the immediate line of advance will be through the organization of all labourers, women
as well as men, into trades unions, through a reduction of the
hours of work, through friendly societies, through greater domestic conveniences and healthier surroundings, through better
education in general, and through increased recreation and higher
amusements. With these specific schemes of reform the Neighborhood Guild is already allied. . . .

II

The very name, Neighborhood Guild, suggests the fundamental idea which this new institution embodies: namely, that,
irrespective of religious belief or non-belief, all the people, men,
women, and children, in any one street, or any small number
of streets, in every working-class district in London, shall be
organized into a set of clubs, which are by themselves, or in
alliance with those of other neighborhoods, to carry out, or induce others to carry out, all the reforms—domestic, industrial,
educational, provident, or recreative—which the social ideal demands. . . .

It is an expansion of the family idea of co-operation. In the
family all ages and both sexes meet mentally and morally, and
do not limit their combination of effort to the attainment of any
one special object in life, such as the mere physical comfort, or

the health, or the financial convenience, or the intellectual development, or the sympathetic encouragement of one another; but all of these aims are pursued at once, and any one of them may become supreme as occasion demands, and each member receives the kind of help adapted to his present need.

The bad effects of forming societies of working people for any one object alone, however good in itself, seem (because they are indirect) to escape the notice of many would-be philanthropists. Such a society causes its members to magnify out of all proportion that one side of life or culture which it aims to develop. . . .

In its social reform work the Neighborhood Guild does not even limit its effort . . . to the rescue of those who have already fallen into vice, crime, or pauperism. Equally would it touch and draw to itself the whole class of self-supporting wage-earners, and not only with the object of preventing them from falling into these worst evils, but also of bringing within their reach the thousand higher advantages which their limited means do not at present allow them individually to attain. The supreme aim which it constantly keeps in view is the completest efficiency of each individual, as a worker for the community, in morals, manners, workmanship, civic virtues and intellectual power, and the fullest possible attainment of social and industrial advantages. . . . But in pursuing the loftier aims, it must not be supposed to be quitting the rescue and preventive work; for no hard and fast line can be drawn between the former and these latter. . . .

The first Guild was started about five years ago in one of the poorest and most crowded quarters of New York City.[26] . . . At present it consists of six clubs and a kindergarten, and it has recently been accepted by the newly formed American University Extension Movement[27] as their first settlement and centre

[26] Coit's Guild, founded in 1886, became University Settlement, located on the Lower East Side. He kept in touch by correspondence and visits and participated in the settlement's fiftieth anniversary.

[27] This is the English term. In the United States it became known as the University Settlement Association.

of work. . . . Two years and a half ago, a similar institution was started in London. . . .

It is something . . . in two and a half years . . . to have organized five clubs well, and through them to have founded a circulating library, Sunday afternoon free concerts, Sunday evening lectures, Saturday evening dances for members, a choral society, and fifteen to twenty classes in various branches of technical and literary education, and to have inspired the members of the Guild with the desire to plant new Guilds, and to push forward, as they are doing, at least one specific reform of general interest. . . .

III

Dr. Chalmers appreciated . . . the influence of locality in cities as a charm and attraction to the philanthropic worker, and many have followed out his hints. . . . He also appreciated more than any one else had done, the vast amount of timely help, which in cases of distress and bereavement is constantly being administered with wisdom and tenderness, in the poorest districts, by the neighbors themselves. . . . But Chalmers' scheme of philanthropy was after all aristocratic. While he would organize his rich parishioners into disciplined bodies of workers, he never seemed to think of developing and lifting out of its spasmodic and intermittent state that instinctive philanthropy to be found among the families of the labouring classes in any one street or house. It is just this idea, however, which is the root principle of the Neighborhood Guild. . . .

XXIV

Unlike the many utopian dreams of the earlier communism, the scheme I have been proposing does not seek to isolate a group of families from contact with their surrounding society, or to disregard the present conditions and motives of life. On the contrary, it plants itself in the midst of the modern city, believing that in it there is already room to lay at least the foundations of the New and Perfect City.

59. *University Settlement* [28]

Miss H. F. Freeman, *Lend a Hand*, V (1890), 154–58

In the lower part of the city of New York a group of young women are living in a way that will excite interest and surprise. These young women, all having the advantages and attainments given by a college education, go there voluntarily, and without pecuniary compensation. They have selected their home in the most crowded district in the city, said to be more densely populated than any part of London. . . . One-tenth of all arrests for crime, and one-half of all arrests for gambling, in the city of New York come within the limits of the election precinct in which they live. There is one saloon to every one hundred inhabitants, and but five churches to fifty thousand people. . . . The population is made up of emigrants from Central Europe, largely of Germans, and of Russian and Polish Jews. . . .

This is not a Bureau of Relief. . . . It is a Home, where kind women, in pleasant, clean rooms, live regular, helpful lives, and are always ready to see those who will come to them. It began by the children coming. They were received kindly, entertained by picture-books, games, and music. They went home and told their parents, who became interested, and asked the young women to call on them. This invitation was accepted in a neighborly way, the call usually made on Sunday, when the father could be seen. The result is, their acquaintance has grown larger and larger. The people come to them, they never have to go out to draw people in.

Last May, 1889, a house was hired in this neighborhood. It was put in good sanitary condition, and in October seven young women, one of them a doctor, moved into it. They resolved they would have no servants. They were thus saved many complications, for they were to live on the basis of the people of the neighborhood. They have a housekeeper, for cooking, and do

[28] The official name was College Settlement. Founded in 1889 by Dr. Jane E. Robbins and Miss Jean Fine, graduates of colleges for women, it was located on Rivington Street.

the other household work themselves, in turns. They have a little maid, selected from the district. The first night she came she simply took off her shoes and dress when she went to bed. No severe criticism was made, as that would infer [*sic*] she had not been well brought up, and would reflect upon her parents. But the example was before her. She was imitative, and the third night she hung out her flannels to air, that all "poisonous exhalations" should be removed. After living for two months in decent surroundings, she had so far improved in cleanliness and neatness that a place was obtained for her as housemaid in the upper part of the city, and this work was begun over again by taking another girl.

The people of the neighborhood do not appear as poor as they are, because they are so well dressed. They will suffer every privation: they will go without food, will be cold, but they will have decent clothes—that is, those who go out. It may be the older girls who go to school will be dressed so as to make a good appearance, while the younger ones cannot go out of the house because they have no clothes, no shoes or stockings—perhaps only one garment. The clothes are always bought ready made. The occupation of these people is largely tailoring: shop work, or slop work, as we call it. A garment will pass through a dozen hands before it is finished, one woman stitching, another basting, another making button-holes, and so on. The women thus have their work at home, doing it in odd moments, between baby-tending and house-keeping. They have no time to give to the training of their older children, the girls growing up without knowing how to thread a needle.

It is curious how little these women know of each other, even when living in the same house. . . . But the home of the young university women is a safe ground of meeting, and thus they can succeed in their desire to establish a more neighborly feeling.

Clubs are encouraged among the children; indeed, it is among them that the whole work is largely founded. These college women almost hesitated about the older women, thinking life might have taught the hard-working mothers as much as education had taught them. Indeed, it is felt not much can be done for women over twenty. They can be helped in manual training, but their characters at that age become fixed.

One of the first things done was to put out the sign, "Warm Baths for five cents." Nobody came; the young women were told nobody would come. People were not in the habit of bathing. Indeed, in the crowded quarters in which they live, where no privacy is possible, it is questionable if it is not more decent to remain unwashed, and perhaps the unwashed are doing altogether the proper thing. Besides, how would one like to go into a strange house for a bath? But as the College Settlement (which is the name the young women gave their home) became known, the bathers came of themselves, without being coaxed in. The door-bell rings for one thing or another all day, beginning at breakfast-time and continuing until bed time.

One day is Library Day. Then the children come after school, get their books, hear music, and have games to play, the college residents leading all such entertainments.

But it is asked of these young women, "Does it pay? Could you not as well live in some respectable quarter in the upper part of the city, where you would have some rest and quiet, where you could have some social life, and yet carry on this work just as well?" Yes, and no. The club work could probably be done just as well, and the library and entertainment work as well, but the neighborly feeling, on which this whole work is based, would not then exist. For instance, a woman, with a baby, had sickness in her family. The residents at the Settlement offered to take the baby for a week. The mother assented, for it was so near that she could go in and see the child every night and morning. The baby was returned at the end of the week in a state of health that delighted the mother. Do you think she would have sent it a couple of miles up town, had some kind ladies lived there? Again, in a family well known to them, the husband, in a drunken fit, drove the wife and baby out of doors at night. Tomorrow, when "the drunk" would be passed, he would be a very good husband, but to-night where should she go? Not to one of her neighbors, whom she had known for years, but to these young women, who, for such a short time, had been so friendly. These little incidents, continually happening give many opportunities which could not be, did these young women go down and visit the people, and then return to their own homes.

"Does it pay?" It depends upon what you consider paying. If these young women work for gratitude, it may be thought a failure. The people around them have no idea of what they give up. They have a clean, comfortable house, plenty of warmth, plenty of clothes, plenty of food. Whether there is work or not, their living comes to them just the same. Have they not all that is needed in life? How can they want anything more? What sacrifice can there be when everything is so comfortable around them?

These poor people, on the other hand, live without any system in their lives. They have breakfast or not, as there is anything to eat. They go to work or not, as there is a job. The children get their correction by a blow to-day, a laugh to-morrow. Nothing is regular. The truth is never told. The children lie without any consciousness of what the truth is. They find, indeed, at the Settlement that if anything is promised it comes to pass, and they begin to rely on what is told them, and know there is one place where something is sure.

These college women, who so gravely take this in hand, know that this is not a thing of a year or two. The adults, even the older boys and girls, are beyond much help. This work must be continuous. They dare look forward ten years. A child of ten, whom they begin with to-day, will then be twenty, and will then be a different man or woman because for ten years he or she has seen women for all that time who keep their word, speak the truth, are gentle, kind, and unselfish, and are always ready to help.

Such are the statements made by Miss Fine, who has been in charge of the Settlement since it was established. . . .

One word more as to what is next to be done at this Settlement. A young woman is to go there with her microscope. Through the tube, which so reveals the wonders of creation, she is to open the eyes of these people to some things which have never come into their dull, hard, sordid lives. She will show them that there are some things in this world besides food, clothes, and money. It is doubtful if these children know what sand is more than they know what a diatom is. They are to be shown a handful of sand, and then they are to see a few grains with another eye, more wonderful than that which Nature gives us. The girls work in shops, handle woolen, silk and cotton threads. These threads are to be put under the microscope. They will see why woolen clings, and why silk slips. They will learn there is much outside of what has been the narrow horizon of their lives. If the college women will stay long enough they can, indeed, work the miracles promised.

XXIII

THE BEGINNINGS OF EDUCATION

The COS and the settlement movements were the primary places where an interest in method and education moved workers and the emerging field of social work toward professionalization. While neither of the writers quoted was an official spokesman for all their colleagues, the contrasts between their approaches is suggestive of philosophical differences between the groups which led to much earlier emphasis on specific professional education among caseworkers than among group workers.

The authors were fellow townsmen from Boston. Zilpha Smith, the executive of the Associated Charities, was the one to whom Mary Richmond had gone for her first instruction in COS methods. Afterward she was for many years an influential teacher of casework in the Boston (Harvard-Simmons) school of social work. Robert Woods was head resident of Andover House, afterward long known as the South End House.

While there was some agreement between them on the importance of exchange of information as a means of learning, their ideas show many more elements of contrast. For instance, in the matter of the method of learning, Woods places great emphasis on the value of observation and informal mutual exploration among equals, whereas Miss Smith stresses a more formal guided experience for the new worker, utilizing selected teaching materials.

The differences go deeper, however. Woods tends toward the aloof, observational approach of the person oriented primarily to social science, while Miss Smith talks of the worker learning primarily by experience, and his need to identify with the person being helped. Woods emphasizes the value of the feedback of the learning experience to social science knowledge and to general culture. On the other hand, Miss Smith emphasizes the importance of the development of skill and its impact on the individual beneficiary. Valuable as was the generalized approach, it did not carry with it the impetus for professional education implicit in the search for skill, and when the first schools of social work emerged a few years later they were under the aegis of charity organization societies.

It is of interest to note Woods's use of the terms "social work," "professional," and "visitor," the last two in distinctly different ways from those in which they are now used.

60. The Education of the Friendly Visitor

Zilpha D. Smith,[29] NCCC, 1892, pp. 445-49

Life itself will still be the chief schoolmaster of the friendly visitor; and the part of the society with which he works must be to bring him into relation with new aspects of life, and to help him by contact and conferences with other workers to see them rightly, and to use to the best advantage his opportunities for doing good. . . .

Friendly visiting on any large scale can hardly be successful without conference meetings, without that frequent opportunity of hearing about others' work and of helping each other by bits of suggestion. After experimenting with various intervals, all our fourteen conferences in Boston have found weekly conferences best. While the attendance at each meeting may not be so large, a greater number will have been present in any one month. We cannot expect every visitor to attend every meeting, and we may be fairly satisfied with an average attendance of eight or ten out of fifty visitors. . . .

[29] Zilpha Smith had been a clerical worker and government clerk before joining the Boston Associated Charities to help set up their Registration Bureau. She showed aptitude for friendly visiting and administration of the volunteer program and in four years was promoted to executive. She always declared that volunteers had taught her but she was convinced there should be a better organized way of profiting by the experience of others and shortening the period of personal experimentation. Margaret E. Rich, "Zilpha Drew Smith," *The Family*, XI (1930), 67–69, and unpublished Smith papers, Library of Simmons College School of Social Work.

We have gradually divided the responsibility of the conference. There are three persons who are sure to have more or less to say, the chairman, the secretary, and the member of the committee who has prepared and presents the business for discussion. The more we increase the number who take part, the more likely a new visitor is to gain courage to speak, the more each learns from touch with the thought and experience of others. In the course of the meeting two or three opportunities should be given for any visitor present to ask a question or make a report. . . . No wish to expedite business . . . should crowd out accounts of successes or lead us to make decisions without considering together the principle involved. . . .

A lady who had very high ideas of what should be done, and was often impatient because her poor friends were not so quick as she to see what was right and best, was appointed a member of the committee which prepares the business for the conference and presents it there. In this way she came to know much of the work of other visitors, and of the results they attained by slow and patient service. Her own visiting has been greatly improved thereby. She is less quick to judge harshly, more tender and patient. "Ideals are catching," as one of our visitors says. . . .

Because we can give much time to the work, whether we are paid for it or serve as volunteers, because this gives us opportunity to learn much from others, we have a duty toward them, a duty to "lead them forth," which I believe is the true meaning of education, to help them to learn the lessons that the work itself teaches.

A lady offering to become a visitor said she liked all she had heard about our work except our taking children away from parents. Of that she strongly disapproved. It was explained to her that we tried to take children away only when there was no home worth the name, no proper feeling toward the children, no chance of their growing up to be decent men and women. Going to visit a family to which she was assigned, she returned immediately to say that those children must be taken away, the home was too dreadful. Then she was persuaded to try to make the home fit for them to stay in. As in this instance, the new visitor often needs another's steady hand and head to guide him through the first shocks of finding conditions so strange to his experience that he cannot judge them rightly. . . .

I am always anxious to warn others against making friends only with those members of the family who meet you half-way, because I made that mistake myself and suffered the consequences. If the visitor is a woman, the shy ones in the family are usually the man of the house and the older boys, who, as far as material prosperity goes, are the most important members of the family. A visit on Sunday finds them at home, but even then they may be unwilling to talk, and occasion must be made to see them away from their own family.

Most visitors have some things to unlearn when they begin. One is to give up their faith in the power of relief. . . .

Another thing which many have to unlearn is the notion that, when the crisis is past and the family have become self-supporting, they do not need to see the visitor again, that there is no more work to do. One agent guards against this by giving each new visitor two families, one where there is a definite thing to be done at once, the other where the only possibility for the time is to make their acquaintance, and work along slowly, preparing for an opportunity by and by. The experience in the second family is apt to make one use similar methods with the other, and form ties which will hold after the first emergency has been disposed of.

Another agent thinks it better to watch carefully, and, when the first definite thing is nearly finished, to suggest another, perhaps for another member of the family.

Visitors often wish to give up after but two or three visits, because their advice is not taken. Then some one should help them to see that it was best to give the advice on the chance of its being taken, but that we cannot wonder that it was not accepted. We would not ourselves often act on the advice of a stranger; and there may be considerations the family are yet too shy to mention, influencing their decision. The story of what others have accomplished by keeping on a year, of the great change that appeared at last, though progress seemed slow, encourages a visitor to persevere.

We are apt in beginning to be so occupied with our own attitude toward the poor people that we forget to ask ourselves what their attitude toward us may be. We do personal work among the poor, we say; but do we make the poor people feel that it is personal to them? We can make it so by really giving ourselves, not merely our thought and care in their affairs, but telling them from the first something of our own. "Tell them about yourself and your family," is good advice to a visitor. If some one is sick, the mother or sister will be interested to hear about your friends who have recovered from the same disease. All your affairs will be quite as interesting to them as theirs to you, and any confidence you can give will inspire confidence in return. . . .

The record of a family, though all true, often starts a visitor with a false notion. It is said that a criminal is known by the worst thing he ever did, though none of us would care to be measured in that way; and a poor family is often judged by its worst member. There are two ways of avoiding this difficulty at the outset. One is, while giving the whole record to the visitor, to lay special emphasis on the attractive children, or whatever pleasant thing is known of any member of the family. Another is to ask the visitor if there is any special kind of family he wishes to visit. If not, then to give him only the briefest statement of whom he will find in the family who needs work or hospital care or whatever, not showing the record or telling the worst until he comes back to report, and, with the picture of the family in his mind, can give the worst its proper relative place.

Sometimes, happily not often, the visitor unconsciously patronizes the poor people, forgetting that there is more likeness than difference between him and them. Unwittingly, he does and says little things that hurt and make a barrier. Working much with others who from nature or training never make those mistakes leads such persons to avoid them also. It helps all about us to the right spirit, if we take pains not to say "cases" when we could say "families," never to say "your family" when we might say "the Browns" or the "Greens," to speak of a woman as a friend of ours and not merely of ourselves as friends to her; in short, to speak of them and treat them as persons, and not as beings of another race. You want to help some one to a better, happier, or more prosperous way of living. If you begin by believing that there must be something in him to respect or admire, you will find it, and can meantime win him to trust you. You cannot persuade him to give you his confidence and ask your counsel if you despise his.

61. Study and Experiment

Robert A. Woods,[80] "University Settlements as Laboratories in Social Science," in *Proceedings*, International Congress of Charities, Correction and Philanthropy, Chicago, June, 1893 (Baltimore: Johns Hopkins Press, 1894), I, Sect. II, 23–52

A university settlement, in its deepest meaning, is not a charitable or philanthropic establishment. It is an outpost where certain persons from separated sections of society, who by education or by experience become freed from the prejudices of their class, may meet and confer with one another for the sake of having each side know more about the events and the motives of life of the other side. . . . The usefulness of university settlements as laboratories in social science is considerably affected by this view of their nature and attitude. . . .

Social science includes within its data the constructive and reconstructive energy of the conscious mind. It is the science of social nutrition and hygiene, of social pathology and therapeutics. . . .

The particular territory for study and experiment by the university settlement includes the whole reach and depth of human life in that little world which lies within the narrow limits

[80] A graduate of Andover Theological Seminary, Woods spent some time at Toynbee Hall before returning to Boston to take up his lifework as head of Andover (South End) House.

of the neighborhood of which the residents are part. The representatives of the more favored classes come to the less favored; and therefore, for the present at least, their newer knowledge of the life of the educated and well-to-do members of the community is got by observing the effect of it upon the life of the poor and by observing from the new point of view the effect of the life of the poor upon the more favored. . . .

I do not wish, however, to differentiate the work of the university settlement too strongly from other forms of social work. Its domain for practical investigation and action lies very largely in the life of the poorer classes, and to justify its existence the settlement movement must in due time present some substantial results in the way of understanding and of bettering the conditions of life as regards poverty and labor. . . . In study and experiment with regard to those better lines of social action which need to be introduced into the neighborhood and the local district, the residents are led at once to the investigation of such larger enterprise as is already active in the city, whether it be in the way of charity, philanthropy, popular education, trade organization or religious effort. . . .

This then leads the settlement out into the broad field of social economics as studied and practiced the world over. The practical work and study of the settlement should be carried on in the light of such study and such work . . . in various parts of the world. . . . There is much in the spirit and method of settlement work which as yet finds no direction from the traditions, writings, or experience, of others. . . .

The university settlement resident comes to his study and his work with a stirring belief in the life-giving quality of culture. He believes so deeply in what he has to bring, that he is willing to do his work without seeing the results. He confers upon his neighbors, the working people, the signal honor and respect of trusting them with all those better things which refresh and strengthen his own life. . . .

Social science, if it is to be truly scientific, dealing with human beings, must use the most delicate human apparatus in the way of personal acquaintance and sympathy, in order to gain accurate and delicate results. . . .

The acquaintance which the settlement seeks has to do not only with individuals but with families, and . . . with the different little groups into which families resolve themselves. At the Andover House each of several small localities is the special care of a certain resident. He visits its families from time to time until he becomes on easy and familiar terms with all of them. He avoids absolutely the mechanical and inquisitive methods of the census-taker. He is not a "visitor" in the professional sense of that term, going monotonously and regularly from house to house.[31] He is simply a neighborly caller. He gradually comes to know the things that make up the life of these people just as one friend comes to know about another friend. And so he begins to make out a complete schedule of what life means in the particular street or court where his new found friends live, including the outer conditions of the place and the inner nature of the people . . . the homes in which people live, the size, number, convenience and privacy of rooms, the care that is taken of them; the work they do; the wages which the bread-winners receive; the care with which the family income is spent . . . the pursuits and recreation of the members of the family in common and the effect of the life of the family upon its individual members and upon other families; the general character thus given to the locality as a whole, with particular reference to the improving and degrading influences that exist among this group of families. . . . This is the kind of patient and comprehensive investigation which is beginning to be undertaken at the settlements, requiring pains and effort, but made light all the time by the human interest which it calls out. . . .

A peculiarly important line of social investigation . . . is the discovery of such forms of original organization and cooperation

[31] Woods differentiates between the type of neighborhood study made by a settlement worker and the sort of inquiry conducted by the Surveyors in the Booth study of London. (See R69, 70.)

among the people themselves as exist in the neighboring district; and what is equally important, experiment in the way of participating as a local neighbor on the same plane as the rest in such efforts, for the sake of finding what actual social value there is in them, and how that value may be enhanced by the residents without running too great a risk of destroying the independent incentive of the people themselves; for every germ of original social enterprise on the people's part is to the social student of the same stirring interest as a rare specimen to the naturalist. . . .

It is, after all, in influences that come from without that the hope of progress in most of the poorer quarters of the cities come. The university settlements have no desire to deceive themselves into thinking that they and their work are not, to all intents and purposes, influences from without the neighborhood. . . .

I regard it as one of the most important features of settlement work to bring into the various forms of charity and philanthropy that broader sense of the situation, which is gained by living among those whom you would help, and acting as a medium through which the local agencies of charity and philanthropy may to a great extent run the gamut of the need of the locality and take up into themselves more and more of the social energy existing in the neighborhood and capable of being turned to social account. On the other hand, it is of great value to the settlement worker, particularly to the novice, to learn from the experienced and systematic charity worker. . . .

The university settlement being a scientific laboratory, some workers in this laboratory become experts in their departments. The settlement is, indeed, a group of experts in different lines of social effort; a group of such persons living intimately together constantly stirring each other to fresh interest by the result of new information and discovery. And as a poor and crowded neighborhood is a microcosm of all social problems, the resident by his study and experiment in the microcosm becomes equipped for study and work in the broader sphere. . . .

A university settlement, according to its largest idea, would contain among its residents and its active associate workers men and women who would cover the whole range of productive work whether in the way of manual, commercial or professional skill. . . . And thus we may say at the end that the university settlements stand as laboratories in the greatest of all sciences: (1) by bringing together competent persons of varied tastes and training, who learn from day to day with all their senses, in all the usual experiences and in all the sudden turns of working class life, what that life in its outer substance and in its inner forces is. (2) By testing, tempering, and modifying after a better pattern the varied interacting apparatus, whether in the way of charity or self-help, which is set for the accomplishment of social work. (3) By bringing to the test of positive experiment the varied resources of culture and civilization in order to adapt them for accomplishing, by every sort of process, the enlivening and uplifting of humanity. (4) By training men and women to be fit vehicles of such influence; to develop skilled social workers, and to send them out, not merely into professional charity and philanthropy, but into every kind of human activity, in order that they may broaden every kind of human activity so as to make it a truly social function. (5) By bringing far separated individuals and classes together so that they may all learn to classify themselves, not according to their superficial differences, but according to their deeper and more real unity, to the end that society may become truly homogeneous and organic, with a far stronger vital principle through which to adapt itself to its compelling environment, for filling out the pattern of human life, for accomplishing human destiny.

XXIV

CROSSCURRENTS OF
CHARITABLE OPINION

The late eighties and early nineties, during which the foundations of a profession of social work began to take shape, were a period in which there was a free market in ideas concerning the causes and cures of poverty, misconduct, and personal inadequacy. Some were new versions of older philosophies; some were reflections of new political and social ideas growing out of an industrial, scientific society. A suggestion of the scope of this clash of opinion is found in samples [32] taken from the writings of five articulate and farseeing spokesmen.

James, Cardinal Gibbons, Archbishop of Baltimore, was widely known in Protestant as well as Catholic church and academic circles for his efforts to analyze labor problems in the light of religious philosophy. As a friend of Charles J. Bonaparte, he was familiar with the latest developments in charitable endeavor. Zilpha D. Smith, General Secretary of the Boston Associated Charities, was the leading early exponent in the COS movement of the need for methodological skill and training. We have already seen that for a generation Franklin Sanborn had been a statesmanlike advocate of humane, constructive public welfare. By now many of his advanced suggestions were beginning to prove their effectiveness. Robert Treat Paine, first president of the Boston Associated Charities, had been an active lay participant in the National Conference. He was a strong defender of close cooperation between public and private agencies, but with a clear separation of relief-giving and treatment functions. Josephine Shaw

[32] For an extended discussion of the charitable literature of the period, see Muriel W. Pumphrey, "The 'First Step'—Mary Richmond's Earliest Professional Reading, 1889–91," *Social Service Review*, XXXI (1957), 144–63.

Lowell, the patrician organizer and president of the New York COS, had long been identified with a wide variety of charitable organizations. As the first woman commissioner of the New York State Board of Charities and an active worker in the State Charities Aid Association, a citizen group devoted to improved public charitable endeavors, she was much concerned about public as well as privately sponsored philanthropy. Of this group of papers, those by Gibbons, Sanborn, and Mrs. Lowell were originally presented at the 1890 National Conference, considered by some to have been the most stimulating of all the annual meetings.

Gibbons's Conference Sermon was expanded and published the following year in the form of a review of current controversy; it received wide attention and comment. He appears to have been much influenced in his own thinking by Andrew Carnegie's classic declaration that rather than distribute the product of industry through wages, where it would be used for personal desires, a large portion should go to the well-to-do who could more wisely use such a reserve to advance the well-being of all.

The wide divergence of views is seen in the assumptions regarding causation. Gibbons believed that poverty and class distinctions were supernaturally ordained and inaccessible to cure; the religious man was obligated to share his abundance with the unfortunate to mitigate the severest suffering. Paine thought that much misery grew out of inadequate preparation of children for modern industrial competition and lack of any neighborhood facilities or housing restrictions. Mrs. Lowell believed that the poor must be forced to endure deprivation in order to keep them at work; pauperism was the result of indulgence through public or private alms.[33] Miss Smith thought that the poor were no different inherently from others; all human beings craved and could benefit from intimate family living and "steadfast friend-

[33] Despite the extremely doctrinaire approach taken by Mrs. Lowell in this speech, she was sensitive to individual need, and when the depression of 1893 convinced her that wages were often inadequate or impossible to obtain through no fault of the individual worker, she became one of the founders of the Consumers League, an organization devoted to securing adequate wages and good working conditions.

ships." Their limitations were often due to lack of friendly interest and family experience.

There was increasing recognition of the importance of preserving family life, but difference over how this could be accomplished. Sanborn advocated financial assistance in the family's own home to keep it together as the "initial point" of public charity. Mrs. Lowell thought that all relief in homes should be given by private agencies. Paine preferred outdoor relief through private agencies, but believed that public outdoor relief was preferable to breaking up the family. Miss Smith emphasized the value of substitute homes for persons of all ages rather than institutionalization when separation from the family was necessary.

There were faint glimmerings that the distinctions between the givers and the receivers of aid were breaking down. Mrs. Lowell struggled with herself to show how dependence upon an inherited income was different from dependence on relief. Miss Smith was farsighted enough to see that the use of personal relationship might be helpful to persons not in need of relief.

Withal, unresolved issues were beginning to take shape: governmental as against sectarian or nonsectarian private sponsorship and administration; general environmental improvement, compulsory reeducation in an institution, or individualized reeducation within a family; paid versus voluntary staffing of services.

62. *Country Help for City Charities*

Address by Zilpha D. Smith, General Secretary of the Associated Charities of Boston, Worcester, Massachusetts, October, 1888, *Lend a Hand*, III (1888), 640–46

The best result of charity is the uplifting and strengthening of character—and this is accomplished only by individual work, work by one man with another. Philanthropy is no longer satisfied with relief of distress, or punishment of evil—it seeks real cure, it must make the man or woman whole again, must save and educate the child. . . .

The idea is not new . . . but not until our generation has there been a general movement to inspire and foster individual work while giving the separate workers the advantage of an organization behind them, and opportunities for conference and cooperation. . . .

The Associated Charities in Boston, and kindred societies in other parts of New England, organize bodies of volunteer visitors, who consult together, each making himself the special friend of but two or three families. . . .

Many persons who need no relief, and who have committed no misdeed to bring them into public care, would also be the better for the steadfast friendship of good men or women—and we need to remember, in dealing with those who do come to us, that their dependence or their fault does not prove them worse than the rest of the world. These give us our opportunity, and we must not be slow to take advantage of it.

How can the country and suburban towns help in this individual work? . . .

We in the cities must deal with the families. So long as the father and mother live, and the home is decent, and each member keeps in a reasonably straight path, that is the best place for all to be, and family affection, love of home, work with us in helping to make it better and better.

But when the home must be broken up, or one of its members taken away, then the country has many advantages. . . .

Country people can give employment, friendship, membership in the family, hospitality.

For a large proportion, the first step towards the country is the step into an institution. There regular habits take the place of irregular ones, bad associations are forgotten, diseases cured, and a study of character made. The institution can do little more than this. In children especially the routine life necessary to so large a household deadens the energies. More and more it is felt that the institution, even the small and homelike one, can only prepare for life under natural conditions. Such a life must be the test of each individual, as it is also the best means of training him. . . .

Employment. In giving employment, self-interest is naturally uppermost in the employer's mind, but we would add the motive of philanthropy. Speaking broadly, there are three classes of persons needing work, and needing it in the country:

1. Children who have fallen out of family care through orphanage, poverty, neglect, or some misdeed—which was perhaps induced by neglect or bad surroundings.

2. Discharged prisoners.

3. Women burdened with the care of infants, each needing a place at service where she can take her child with her. . . .

A human soul needs more than work, good as work is, and some provision must be made for pleasures, for an occasional hour of freedom, and for society. . . . In some good homes, as they are called, with many comforts, a servant finds no one from one week's end to another, who does not constantly treat her as an inferior. How can she feel it is home? Why wonder that she seeks a freer, more social life? If this is true of ordinary servants, who have friends in the neighborhood, how much more is it true of the girl sent from [the State Industrial School at Lancaster] who is entirely dependent upon the family with whom she is placed and the introductions it may give for her social interests.

All this is true also of the boys who are placed out from the Lyman School at Westboro', another state school, when from twelve to sixteen years of age. Employment in trades for those who dislike farm work would be very welcome. . . .

The secretary of the Prison Commission is always glad of opportunities of employment for prisoners. . . .

A few ladies in Boston carry on an admirable work in the care of destitute mothers and infants, keeping mother and child together when that is possible, and always fostering the mother's love and helping her to support her child. They do not refuse to aid an unmarried mother, if she is not a depraved woman. . . .

Now you may ask what charity there can be in giving employment, since the service is needed, and it is in the employer's interest to pay for it. There is no charity in it, in the old, degraded sense of almsgiving. But in the better sense of love for one's neighbor, one can put as much charity into his duty as employer as he pleases—care and thought and pains for the education of the boy or girl in all the details of home life, in the care of his clothing, the spending of money, the enjoyment of wholesome pleasures, in helpfulness for others, and skill in any work he undertakes.

It may be necessary also to inspire charity in others toward the discharged prisoner—if the fact that he is such leaks out—to help them to regard him as a man not altogether bad and hopeless, but one who in the Reformatory has started on the path of right living, and needs to be guided along it—not frowned upon and forbidden till he seems forced to turn back.

Friendship. It has already been hinted that not all the men and boys are fitted for farm work. They must earn their living at trades or in factories, and board near by. Here is opportunity for friendly service of another kind. The superintendent of In-door Poor at the State House would gladly enlist ladies or gentlemen as friends for these boys. Each should undertake but two or three such friendships, at the most—and enter the work with consecration and earnestness. . . . If you are firm and kind, and in earnest in your wish to help the boy by a steadfast friendship, he will presently learn to look to you as the one person in the world who takes a deep interest in his welfare, one always ready to hear his confidences—to bear with his faults, while striving to correct them, and to help him into a good and happy life. . . .

Membership in the Household. The work which at the outset has the fewest difficulties, and, if well done, bears the best fruit, so far as our eyes can see, is the taking of a child into a family. Legal adoption, giving rights of inheritance and support, is not necessary, though the family usually prefer this if the child is very young—and all children legally adopted are first taken on trial for a few months or more. . . .

All these Homes, voluntary or supported by taxes, need to know of what persons the family consists, and require that it shall be well recommended as of good character, able to maintain the child, and to rear it under good influences, and most of them make personal inquiries to confirm any testimonials the family may offer. This means delay, but it is a necessary safeguard. Except in cases of legal adoption, the Home keeps a knowledge of the child by sending a visitor at irregular intervals.[34]

The Homes do not place a child without wages where it is evident that the chief object is to get work out of the child, and that the time necessarily spent at school will be begrudged. . . .

The Country Week of the Young Men's Christian Union receives already many invitations for children to spend ten days or more in the country, but not enough. . . .

Those who prefer the companionship of adults can give pleasure and renewed strength to a working-girl, who otherwise would get no vacation. . . .

Perhaps invitations do the most good when given to convalescents. . . . Often a patient is retained after he has ceased to need the nursing and care of the hospital, just because he has no fit place to go. . . . An invitation therefore helps two—the convalescent himself and the patient who would take his place in the hospital. . . .

In all this work there will surely be difficulties, and first of all delay. . . . So send the offer early if possible. Then, the guest may be afraid in the unwonted silence of the country, there may be the most unreasoning and persistent home-sickness, even a longing to return to the Reform School, the worker may be slow to learn, and if none of these difficulties appear, others will, that have been unthought of. But the difficulties are there to be overcome, not to overcome us. Even an entire failure—a girl gone wrong, a boy turned thief—should not discourage one from trying again, nor make one believe that all the children in the schools whence these came will turn out badly.

[34] Cf. the program initiated by Sanborn (R44, 45) twenty years earlier.

63. *The Family the Focus of Public Charity*

"Indoor and Outdoor Relief," Report of the Standing
Committee, Franklin B. Sanborn, Chairman, NCCC,
1890, pp. 71–80 [35]

In Massachusetts during the ten years ending April 1, 1889,
the average number of persons partially supported, by what is
commonly called outdoor relief, was at least 16,000; while the
average number fully supported (mostly by indoor relief) has
been less than 8,000. . . . The average annual cost of each outdoor pauper . . . was less than $40 . . . while the average
yearly cost of each indoor pauper was . . . $180 at least, or four
and one-half times as much as the cost of the outdoor poor.

Here we see one reason why outdoor relief is everywhere and
always more common than indoor relief—for the same sum of
money a much greater number of the poor can be aided. But
another cogent reason is that there never has been anywhere,
and perhaps never will be, almshouses, workhouses, hospitals, and
other places of indoor relief in sufficient number to contain all
the poor at any season, or half of them in seasons of special
destitution. . . .

The "workhouse test," . . . cannot be applied in these modern
times very strictly for another reason. . . . There are whole
classes for whom it would be a bad place. It would be bad for
children, for the insane in general, for idiotic women, for the
sick who require nourishing and stimulating treatment, for the
blind and the deaf, for the epileptics, and so on. Establishments
for these special classes, and many more, have sprung up, where
a hundred years ago only the workhouse or almshouse could be
found. . . .

That mythical class, the "able-bodied poor," are scarcely found
in this country in public establishments, except for a few months
in the cold season, when the number of employments, both for
men and women, is considerably reduced by Nature herself. . . .

[35] Sanborn was absent in Europe when his written report was presented,
and tabled without reading. Most of the audience was unfamiliar with
the contents when it was criticized by Mrs. Lowell (R64).

In making the broad, general distinction between two main classes of the public poor, it would seem to be natural and proper to begin with that class which has not been withdrawn from . . . the family. There are persons . . . who need public relief at their own homes, and who can receive it there with greater advantage both to themselves and to the public than anywhere else. Often times these are persons who have a little property, which would be sacrificed or diminished in value if they were removed, even for six weeks, to an almshouse, hospital, or insane asylum. . . . The younger Pitt, said in Parliament, in 1796:

The law which prohibits giving relief where any visible property remains should be abolished. . . . No temporary occasion should force a British subject to part with the last shilling of his little capital, and to descend to a state of wretchedness from which he could never recover, merely that he might be entitled to a casual supply. . . .

[This] is none the less true when applied to free American citizens. Great care should be taken, in relieving their distresses, not to throw them into the great class of vagrant and homeless poor, to which belong many of the inmates of our public establishments, when they go forth from an almshouse, a hospital, an insane asylum, or a prison, into the general community.

Let us . . . adopt as the starting-point of our system of public charities what the French call *Secours à Domicile*, and what we have termed "Family" or "Household Aid." The family in question may be that of the poor person himself, or it may be some family into which he has been adopted as child or boarder. Make the number of these family cases as small as you please, but let it be . . . the initial point of public charity.

Starting, then, from this focus of the family, let the scheme of indoor relief . . . be a scheme capable . . . of indefinite expansion, as civilization advances. By the old "workhouse test," a dozen classes of the public poor were thrown together, higgledy-piggledy, in the great wards of the old-fashioned poorhouse. . . . One reason why family aid has been carried, especially in cities, to such an extent as to prove an abuse—and sometimes a very great abuse—was the desire to prevent the breaking up of families, the corruption of the young, and the unspeakable distress of the old and the virtuous, by throwing them into forced association with the dregs of mankind, in what was ironically termed a charitable establishment. Indoor relief can never be what it should be until separate provision, on a reasonable scale, is made for all the main classes of the distressed, helpless, and vicious poor.

The ancient fallacy . . . was to suppose that the workhouse and its immediate adjuncts could be made, under ordinary circumstances, to receive all the cases of poverty which might otherwise be provided for in families. The modern fallacy is not to take notice of the obvious fact that indoor relief, as we now practise it, is an indefinite extension, in a much better mode, of the old workhouse facilities for restraining, disciplining, and aiding the poor. . . . Experience . . . teaches us that both indoor relief (in its extended form) and family aid, or outdoor relief, as properly practised, are both indispensable in any comprehensive plan of public charity. Wherever and whenever one of these methods has been wholly given up, accidentally or purposely, evils have followed which only the introduction of the omitted method could wholly remove. Where to draw the line between the practical use of the two methods, for individual cases of poverty, is a matter only to be determined by wise discretion on the part of the officers who administer public relief.

64. *The Economic and Moral Effects of Public Outdoor Relief*

Mrs. Charles Russell [Josephine Shaw] Lowell, *NCCC*, 1890, pp. 81–91

I have not been able to assent to the report of the Chairman of the Committee on Indoor and Outdoor Relief, only because, as it seems to me, he does not draw the distinction which is necessary between public and private relief.

I admit, of course, that there are persons who need relief (that is, *help*) in their own homes, and that both Pitt's argument and Mr. Sanborn's argument apply to such: "Great care should be taken, in relieving their distresses, not to throw them into the great class of vagrant and homeless poor." Such people however, are, to my mind, not proper subjects for public relief at all; for what is public relief, and upon what grounds is it to be justified? Public relief is money paid by the bulk of the community (every community is of course composed mainly of those who are working hard to obtain a livelihood) to certain members of the community, not, however, paid voluntarily or spontaneously by those interested in the individuals receiving it, but paid by public officers from money raised by taxation. The only justification for the expenditure of public money (money raised by taxation) is that it is necessary for the public good. That certain persons need certain things is no reason for supplying them with these things from the public funds. Before this can be rightly done, it is necessary to prove that it is good for the community at large that it should be done. . . .

Every dollar raised by taxation comes out of the pocket of some individual, usually a poor individual, and makes him so much the poorer, and therefore the question is between the man who earned the dollar by hard work, and needs it to buy himself and his family a day's food, and the man who, however worthy and suffering, did not earn it, but wants it to be given to him to buy himself and his family a day's food. If the man who earned it wishes to divide it with the other man, it is usually a desirable thing that he should do so, and at any rate it is more or less his own business; but that the law, by the hand of a public officer, should take it from him and hand it over to the other man, seems to be an act of gross tyranny and injustice, which, if carried far enough and repeated often enough, leads to a condition of things where there is not sufficient produced for everybody, and therefore all suffer—the men who earn the dollars as well as those who do not earn them.

It is good for the community that no one should be allowed to starve: therefore, it is a legitimate thing that the public money should be used to prevent such a possibility, and this justifies the giving of public relief in extreme cases of distress, when starvation is imminent. Where, however, shall be found the proof that starvation is imminent? Only by putting such conditions upon the giving of public relief that, presumably, persons not in danger of starvation will not consent to receive it. The less that is given, the better for every one, the giver and the receiver; and, therefore, the conditions must be hard, although never degrading. On the contrary, they must be elevating, and this is by no means incompatible with severity. . . .

There is a stigma attached to public relief, arising from the fact that the money received is actually the property of individuals taken from them against their will and not belonging to the public; and it is necessary to overcome a sense of shame before any one is content to become a pauper, and the loss of this sense of shame in itself constitutes a distinct moral degradation, and leads to still further deterioration of character.

If the advocates of public relief contend that there should be no stigma attached to its receipt, the answer is that, in that case, the tendency would be toward the condition where the whole people would be ready to accept an income from so-called public funds, and that the resulting loss of energy and industry would be sufficient to plunge any nation into a greater poverty than any now suffers. . . . It is not because paupers are primarily more lazy than other people that they will not work for a living if they can be supported without working. If you will consider, you will find that you do not know any one (or, if you do, you regard him or her as a most extraordinary individual) who *works for a living* when it is not necessary, when the living is supplied from some source without any conditions which are dishonorable or irksome. The whole difference between a pauper and any of the rest of us who do not earn our own living is that he wants and gets *very* little, while we want and get a great deal, and that our views of what are honorable and dishonorable conditions differ materially from his.

Of course, to be logical, I ought to go on to the position which Dr. Chalmers took [see R24], that it would be better for the community that there should be no public relief . . . but I

am not prepared to go quite so far as this, for I do think . . .
that the community should acknowledge an obligation to succor,
and even to support, those of its members who are absolutely
unable to fight the battle of life, and that there should be a sure
refuge from starvation. So far as this refuge is furnished from the
funds raised by taxation, however . . . the only safe way to
provide it is under such stringent conditions that no one shall be
tempted to accept it except in an extremity, and under such
conditions, also, as will as soon as possible make the recipient of
help able to support himself again and do his part in supporting
others. I mean that public relief should be indoor relief, inside
the doors of an institution, where cure and education should be
the primary objects aimed at—*cure* of disease, moral, mental,
and physical, and *education* in self-control and self-dependence.
The community may well say to any of its members: "If you
cannot support yourself by your own work, it is a pity. We will
support you by our work; but we will not make it so pleasant
for you that you will desire to continue the condition, and we
will train your mind and body so that you will be able soon
to undertake the care of yourself." . . .

I shall therefore turn now to the effect on individual men and
women of presenting to them the temptations of relief. You will
observe that I no longer say public relief; for I do not wish here
to discriminate between public and private relief, the evil effects
upon the individual man or woman receiving any relief (as distinguished from the help of friends) being about equal. . . .

As it is now given, relief seems to have all the disadvantages
it possibly can have, and none of the advantages. It serves to
weaken the character, to excite the gambling spirit, the recklessness and extravagance which come of chance gains; but it does
not give the quiet and peace, the power to live for worthier objects than mere physical support, which an assured income supplies, while it also destroys all the incentives to activity, energy,
and industry which are usually supplied by the struggle to "make
a living." . . .

The temptation is potent enough to decoy its thousands within the baleful influence of "relief" getting, and, once under the spell, the salvation of the victim seems impossible, for the rewards are too great on that side and the struggle too severe on this. Imagine a poor, sickly woman, with little children to support. By hard work, which makes her back and head ache to the limit of endurance, she may earn a dollar a day, and keep her children from starvation. By asking for relief, by begging from door to door, she can make more in one day than a week's work will bring. Except for her pride, except for her self-respect, what can weigh with her in favor of the badly paid work as against the well-paid begging? Has any human being the right, instead of going to her assistance in her extremity, so to tempt her to degradation? . . . You see, these people are not in comfortable circumstances. They cannot have what they want, often not what they need, even by making all the exertion of which they are capable. . . . Is it possible that any one with a heart and a conscience and an imagination can be willing to stand as the tempter where the temptation is so dire and the results of giving way mean moral ruin? . . .

As to what may and ought to be done . . . by those persons who . . . are called upon to help those who have less, I can only say that I think there are many poor, feeble, suffering women, now struggling for their daily bread, whom it would be a very desirable thing to supply with an income sufficient to keep them in comfort to the end of their lives, and that the injury to their characters would be no more and no other than the injury of resting in comfort to the characters of the many strong and happy women who now live on incomes which they do not earn.

Finally, the real condemnation of relief-giving is that it is material, that it seeks material ends by material means, and therefore must fail, in the nature of things, even to attain its own ends. For man is a spiritual being, and, if he is to be helped, it must be by spiritual means. . . .

Those who claim that relief must be given, even though it does destroy the character, because without it they fear that there may be physical suffering, besides forgetting the fact that it makes more suffering than it cures, forget also the awful question: "What shall it profit a man if he gain the whole world and lose his own soul? Or what shall a man give in exchange for his soul?"

65. *Wealth and Its Obligations*

James, Cardinal Gibbons, in *North American Review*, CLII (1891), 385–95 [36]

I . . . undertake . . . [to state] the Catholic view of wealth and its administration. . . .

The church claims to be the fulfillment . . . of the Judaic dispensation. . . . The Rev. Hermann Adler . . . shows, the law of charity assumed the form of tithes. . . . The individual Christian or the body of Christians who cannot stand this test may well seriously doubt of the sincerity of his or their professions of faith.

Those familiar with the daily lives and sentiments of the laboring classes know what a stumbling-block to their faith is pious penuriousness, the charity that begins and ends at home. They cannot reconcile godliness and greed. For most other forms of human weakness there is tolerance, even at times compassion; but for the man who acknowledges our common fatherhood and brotherhood, with his hands tightly closed upon his purse-string, there is a fierce contempt. . . . One sanctimonious miserly millionaire in a community works more deadly harm to Christianity than a dozen isolated cases of burglary or drunkenness. . . .

In this view it is most melancholy to consider the estimates of such thoroughly informed public men as Mr. Gladstone and Cardinal Manning upon the shrinkage of private charity going on contemporaneously with the enormous increase of wealth in England. . . .

In the United States this condition of things does not, in my

[36] An international debate on philanthropic philosophy had been in progress, involving, among others, Andrew Carnegie, "Wealth," *North American Review*, CXXXXVIII (1889), 654–64; William E. Gladstone, "Mr. Carnegie's Gospel of Wealth," *Nineteenth Century*, XXVIII (1890), 677–93; "Irresponsible Wealth," a symposium by Henry Edward, Cardinal Manning, Rev. Hermann Adler, and Rev. Hugh Price Hughes, *Nineteenth Century*, XXVIII (1890), 876–900. Cardinal Gibbons refers to these in his remarks.

judgment, exist to the same alarming extent. Among Catholics
. . . taking them as a body, I make no doubt they fulfil the whole
law in the broad Christian manner so eloquently expounded by
the Cardinal Archbishop of Westminster. Those who give more
than is required of them by any law far outnumber those who
give less. . . . The law of charity still standing on the divine
statute-book has not been by them rendered obsolete. . . .

The church provides homes for those yet on the threshold of
life and furnishes retreats for those on the threshold of death.
. . . She rocks her children in the cradle of infancy; she soothes
them to rest on the couch of death. . . .

In the State of Maryland and the District of Columbia—I
speak of these because I happen to be officially connected with
them—there are under Catholic auspices, and in a total Catholic
population of a quarter of a million, two foundling asylums, two
asylums for colored children, and ten for white orphans, housing
and educating fifteen hundred little ones, all of whom are admitted regardless of creed, together with six hospitals and a large
number of reformatory institutions. In the more populous centres
. . . the statistics of Catholic benevolence swell in the ratio of the
population. . . .

And here a number of objections may be urged. Mr. Carnegie
boldly asserts the probability that nineteen-twentieths of the so-
called charity of to-day is unwisely spent—"so spent, indeed, as
to produce the very evils which it proposes to mitigate or cure."
Surely this is a statement which he will, upon fuller experience
and reflection, cheerfully retract. No matter what efforts may be
made by philanthropists and social economists for the removal of
poverty, we must make up our minds that poverty in one shape
or another will always exist among us. The words of Christ will
be ever verified—"The poor ye have always with you." As well
attempt to legislate vice out of existence as to legislate poverty
and suffering out of the world. . . . It is in accordance with
the economy of Divine Providence that men should exist in un-
equal conditions in society, in order to the exercise of benevolent
virtues. Moreover, sickness and death will come upon the bread-
winner, and wife and child have their whole support suddenly

snatched away. Disasters like those of Johnstown and the recent shocking losses of life in Pennsylvania mines will leave hundreds of widows and orphans no alternative but charity. . . .

In the olden days of strife and bloodshed women moved between opposing lines of battle, endeavoring to bring about peace. Ofttimes they were allied by blood and interest to the combatants on either side. If we may believe those who stand upon the watch-towers and scan the signs of the times, a tempest of war, to which all former wars were holiday tournaments, looms big upon the horizon and threatens to whelm the world in horrors. Wealth and poverty, they say, stand more and more apart and glare across the widening chasm more fiercely. . . . Capital and labor, after severe skirmishes with varying success, are arming for the supreme conflict. . . .

[The religious orders], with the credentials of self-renunciation, pass between the lines, averring on one side that superfluous wealth is a curse and a snare, that honest labor has its rights; on the other, that some in the providence of God must labor, that toil is honorable and consecrated by Christ's example; and to both sides crying out that Christ's reign, if they acknowledge his leadership, is primarily and essentially a reign of peace. How imminent the struggle may be no man can affirm precisely, but signs there are which may well fill us with disquiet. The rich are daily becoming richer, the poor poorer; luxury, high living, and the pride of life are on the increase. The thirst for wealth becomes daily more insatiable; the cries of the distressed more sharp and loud and poignant.

The economic conditions in the United States are fast approaching those of England. . . . The well-being of the car-horse is more solicitously watched than that of the driver. Small wonder that strong men, maddened by the tears of wife and cries of starving children, band themselves together, and sometimes resort to deeds of violence. . . .

Gladstone, Manning, and Hughes, in England . . . review the situation and sound a note of warning. Most opportunely, here, does a millionaire like Mr. Carnegie declare it to be the duty of a man of wealth, first, to set an example of modest, unostentatious living, shunning display or extravagance; to provide moderately for the legitimate wants of those dependent upon him; and, after doing so, to consider all surplus revenues which come to him simply as trust funds which he is called upon to administer; the man of wealth thus becoming the mere agent and trustee for his poorer brethren. . . .

Let employers and employed come together in amity, with a view to mutual understanding. Let them state their mutual grievances and ascertain their mutual demands, and, temperate Christian counsels reigning, the result will be lasting peace.

66. Pauperism in Great Cities: Its Four Chief Causes

Robert Treat Paine, *Proceedings*, International Congress of Charities . . . Chicago, 1893; I, Sect. II, 23–52

The extremes of society grow more pronounced, so that from the increasing numbers of the very poor . . . Charles Booth's Submerged Tenth,[37] Charles Loring Brace's Dangerous Classes,[38] reach such proportions that they can no longer be dealt with in detail and hopefully as individuals. . . .

What hope for boys and girls growing up in such atmosphere of sin, in overcrowded cities from which playgrounds have been excluded by rising rents; playgrounds for the innocent outpouring of the boys' animal spirits which will have some vent,[39] if not in hockey and football, then in breaking into empty buildings, stealing lead pipes, and stoning dispensary doctors or police with even-handed delight. . . .

The methods of dealing with pauperism hitherto applied are impotent against this swelling tide of brutal, degraded pauperism. . . .

[37] Charles Booth, *Labor and Life of the People* (London: Williams and Norgate, 1889–91; 2 vols. in 3).
[38] See R33, n. 42.
[39] Paine was much interested in, and influenced by, the work of Joseph Lee, a pioneer in the playground movement and a member of the Associated Charities Board.

Has not the principle of repression miserably failed, when its effort . . . hardens tramps into such brutal degradation that in their game with society they seem just now to hold in their hands the winning cards, and yet on the other hand the worthy poor of England are in such straits that a great pension scheme throws its baleful shadow across the land? . . .

Has not the new charity organization movement too long been content to aim at a system to relieve or even uplift judiciously single cases without asking if there are not prolific causes permanently at work to create want, vice, crime, disease and death; and whether these causes may not be wholly or in large degree eradicated? [40]

If such causes of pauperism exist, how vain to waste our energies on single cases of relief, when society should rather aim at removing the prolific sources of all the woe.

The four great causes [41] of pauperism and of degraded city life have long seemed to me to be these:

1. Foul homes.
2. Intoxicating drink.
3. Neglect of child life.
4. Indiscriminate almsgiving. . . .

All of them are remediable in different ways and to different degrees. . . .

The agency which must be invoked to rescue the very poor, whether virtuous and struggling, or degraded and indifferent, is *the municipal power to destroy utterly unfit abodes of habitations.*[42]

Sad, indeed, is the fact that when charity aids some wretched family to move out of a vile basement or dark and nasty slum, presently some other like family moves in. . . .

All that is needed is *aroused public interest* to learn the unspeakable horrors of the homes of the wretched poor to-day, and then to insist on a *higher standard of habitability.* . . .

[40] For hope of improvement through mass reforms, cf. Griscom and the AICP, R29–32.
[41] For lists of causes, cf. R22, 40, 51, 69.
[42] Griscom had earlier identified and indicted housing as the source of other ills (R29).

It is a cause of surprise and regret to find in the reports of charity organization or relieving societies of different cities so little attention paid to this supreme yet eradicable cause of pauperism and crime. . . .

Absence of playgrounds almost compels [a boy] to choose, in a great city, between stupidity and crime. Absence of manual training forces him to live by his wits or by commonest forms of labor. But I wish especially to draw attention to the need of a great development of charity in the treatment of widows with young children. . . .

England very largely refuses out-relief to the widow with children, breaks up the family, and sends one or more of the children into the district school or into that department of the almshouse called the industrial school, usually a vast institution where children are gathered by hundreds. The mother is left with only one or two children whom she may be able to support. . . .

The New York system has no provision of outdoor relief for such a family of children, and resembles the English method in that the family must be broken up, but the children instead of being sent to great public institutions, are distributed among private institutions which receive a per capita allowance from the State; tempting them to promote this destruction of family life.[43] . . .

The Massachusetts system aims to keep families together where there is a not totally unfit home, and if relief is not obtained from some other source, the overseers of the poor give, and continue, needed relief to a widow until the children grow to an age when their labor added to their mother's earnings can support the home. . . .

The poisonous influence of our outdoor pauper relief must be felt upon the child's character in many cases, yet the family is kept together, and the children are brought up under the loving care and influence of their mother, free from the injurious influence of any institution, and especially escaping the almshouse brand. . . .

Here is a better method which I believe to be the best. Aid the

[43] Cf. the attitude of the Catholic Protectory regarding state subsidy (R₄₃).

mother to maintain her home, provide adequate relief, but free from any pauper poison. Let it go from her church, from some private society, from some benevolent individual. . . . Shame on the charity of any city which shrinks from this duty. . . .

This is the class of cases which has always been used most effectively by our overseers of the poor in advocating the necessity of outdoor relief. Taking from the overseers this class of cases would greatly facilitate its total abolition, or great reduction. . . .

The . . . grand reform aims to recreate the inefficient, always in great cities a numerous class, into self-support by skill and cheer, and to save them from gratuitous relief as deadly poison. I cannot learn what New York, Chicago or London do with this class except to leave them to struggle with the law that the unfit must perish. . . .

We who want to solve the problem of our cities' poverty can . . . resolve that the boys and the girls as they grow up, shall have, besides such training of the brain in books as they can get and hold, such training also of all the rest of the body, the various senses, especially the eye and the finger, as will fill the land with artistic and skilled mechanics, and so increase the earning powers of labor and open a brighter future for workingmen. . . .

The whole standard of manual skill and of cultivated taste must be raised and widely disseminated, so that the children of the working classes shall have a fair chance in the race of life, and not start under such heavy handicap that they soon fail and despair.

XXV
MASS MEASURES TO MEET
ECONOMIC RISKS

While some philanthropic leaders were philosophizing about the causes of poverty and methods of dealing with its bad effects, others were wrestling with concrete solutions to the economic problems faced by great numbers of people. Not so closely identified with the spreading waves of socialism as were the suggestions of Stanton Coit (R58), these two readings clearly reflect the impact both of socialism and of the newer economic thinking of the period, especially with respect to the possibility of ameliorating the effects of cyclical unemployment and superannuation. It is interesting to note that the professional charity organizationist is more conservative in his economic, political, and social outlook (e.g., his restatement of the doctrine of lesser eligibility) than the renowned minister and orator.

67. Universal Life Endowments

Editorial by Edward Everett Hale,[a] *Lend a Hand,* V
(1890), 521–24

Life insurance is a magnificent instance of the growth and sway of the Christian principle that each man must bear his brother's burden. The long-lived man agrees to take potluck with the man who dies young, by whatever accident. So far—well. But, as the matter stands, the people who thus unite in insurance, only agree and unite with those who appear to be in good health. . . .

But it has been proved . . . that rates of insurance can be made for people whose symptoms of health are not such as would pass a medical examiner. . . .

[a] Hale, a Boston Unitarian minister, was interested in a variety of social reforms and editor of the philanthropic magazine *Lend a Hand*. He was on the organizing committee of the Boston Associated Charities.

It seems desirable to increase systematically the insurance, or the endowment, of such lives. We might cite Dr. Holmes's interesting suggestion, among his aids to longevity, that one way of living to be eighty is to have a physician tell you that you have a hidden fatal disease. . . .

The United States is preparing, at a large cost, to undertake a health insurance, as it may be called, for the survivors of the soldiers who fought in the Civil War. The establishment of a pension list for disabled soldiers who served is to be looked upon as a health insurance which applies, not to all the people, but to a very considerable part of the men who are more than fifty years of age. . . .

Such a proposal enlists the undefined sympathies of every one, whatever his views as to the true national policy.

Those sympathies are quickened by the central truth that the one disease which no one escapes, except by early death, is old age. . . .

It happens, therefore—and for a very good reason—that where nations or communities look askance at other schemes for compulsory life insurance or endowment, systems for general pensioning of the aged have been much more cordially received. A well-considered plan for a general system of pensions for all the aged has been under discussion in England for several years, apparently with the favor of some important leaders of opinion. But in England there is a difficulty readily perceived. The plan proposes a new tax—virtually a poll-tax imposed on all English men and women after they are eighteen years of age. With the proceeds of this tax pensions are to be paid eventually to all persons, say over the age of seventy. Now it might be possible to persuade Hodge and Lucy at eighteen that they would be glad to stow away two pounds every year, for ten or twenty years, to be sure fifty years hence to receive a competent little income in old age. But it is not so easy to persuade Hodge and Lucy to give this money to the state now, and let the state use it now to pension old Gaffer Diggory, or the Widow Dogberry, who never paid any two pounds a year for any such service. The proposal, therefore, of a pension for the aged to begin now is unpopular in England. And any plan for one to begin fifty years hence, meets the "manana" disposition of all politicians, and is deferred to the next session.

68. Depression a Trial to Charity Organization Principles

Philip W. Ayres,[45] "Is Emergency Relief by Work Wise?" *NCCC*, 1895, pp. 96–100

Is relief by work wise in time of long-continued emergencies, such as industrial depressions? We have just come through such a period, which has taxed all charitable agencies to the utmost. Many large cities, both in England and America, have tried the experiment of relief by work. What are the results of this experience? . . . This is a timely question, since the frequency and comparative regularity of past depressions hardly lead us to suppose that we shall escape similar trouble in future.

In hard times the burden appears to fall heaviest upon the very poor; and who can measure the privation that the poor in our cities have recently undergone? Those of us who have been able to watch the forces at work among the people during the last two years appear to have discovered this law,—that in times of industrial depression the burden of curtailed expenses, like the incidence of taxation, tends to fall heaviest upon those least able to resist.

I have in mind a colored woman with a blind son and a little grandson to support. She did washing for a family of which the man worked in a railroad freight office. When the railway handled less freight, it dropped this man from its pay-roll. After a few weeks, when he obtained no other work, his wife herself did the washing. Thus my friend, the colored woman, with her blind son, was without resources, but could shift the burden no further.

While the great body of the poor, who earn a small and sometimes precarious living, bear the burden, there appear mixed with

[45] Ayres received the degree of Doctor of Philosophy from Johns Hopkins University in 1888 and had been a friendly visitor in the Baltimore COS. During the depression of 1893 he was executive of the Cincinnati COS.

them the criminal, the idle, and the vicious, ever ready to take advantage. These, though relatively few in number, complicate the question greatly, since humanity decrees that they also shall not be permitted to starve in hard times.

When an accident occurs to the human frame, a wise physician will seek to keep the body in a condition as nearly normal as possible until the bad results have disappeared. We who, as members of the Charity Organization Society, come to be social physicians in spite of ourselves, need to bear the analogy in mind. To keep the social condition as nearly normal as we can in time of depression, to improve it incidentally if we may, but to keep it normal until the depression is over, to make no residuum of paupers who shall prey upon the community, an affliction to themselves and to others, when more nearly normal conditions again prevail—this is our task.

With the great body of the poor to deal with, both men and women, with their great diversity of character, with the need of comparative haste, with *work* as the normal condition before the emergency and after, is it possible for us to maintain the social equilibrium through a period of several pressing months or a year without work? Has it not been the universal experience in large cities that work has been provided because it has been necessary and vital to two main factors in the situation, namely, the equable distribution of material and the maintenance of moral independence?

But this is only half. As, in all relief, intelligence is more important than amount, so in emergency relief by work, the employment given may be wise or unwise exactly in proportion to the intelligence of its administration. It is important to note that private may differ from public work in being better administered. Public relief by work, like public alms, may create immense mischief, and for the same reasons. Indeed, of the two, alleged work hastily given and badly managed is likely to be more harmful, in that it may degenerate character the more rapidly.

In how many of our cities has the cry gone out, "We have had relief work, but for the sake of the poor we hope we may never have to resort to it again"! On the other hand, workers in several cities are fairly satisfied with results of relief by work, and feel that no very bad conditions remain from it. May we not believe that this difference in result arises from difference in administration?

Looking at our experiences, good and bad, what do we find to guide us through the next industrial emergency? The following several points may serve as a summary:

1. Public relief by work administered by unwise officials is harmful, because it stimulates an excessive number of applicants, more than it is possible to investigate well. It usually lacks skillful foremen, so that the work is done in a slovenly manner. It appeals strongly to the politician to use this large number of places to reward his followers.

2. Private relief by work is likely to be inadequate from insufficient funds. Money enough is not always subscribed to guarantee that no suffering occurs. This form appears to yield better results when applied to women than to men, as in the preparation of fur for hats through the Brooklyn Bureau of Charities.

3. A combination of public and private efforts can be made to eliminate some of the evils arising from the use of either separately, so that the funds of the State and the knowledge of local societies, especially of the Charity Organization Society's registry, can both be brought to bear.

4. The work must be given to local bread-winners who are heads of families, and to no others. Unless the tramp and the loafer are dealt with through some form of labor still less attractive, such as the stone-yard or the wood-pile, they will swamp the best-laid plan of relief by work. The effect of their presence upon laborers is fatal.

5. Old persons or weak or youths should be referred to private relief societies, since the presence of these will deter stronger workers from earnest efforts.

6. The work given must be adequate in amount to prevent families from suffering either hunger or cold; but at the same time it must be really hard work in order to prevent dabbling, and it

must be decidedly underpaid in order not to attract those who already have work at half-time or who have otherwise disagreeable work. The whole must be so unattractive as to guarantee that, when other work can be had, the laborer will seek it.

7. Some form of public improvement, as work on parks or roads, grading or light quarrying, can best be undertaken, since it is simple, easily learned, adaptable to different grades of strength, and does not interfere with the market of other laborers.

One proposition stands out strong and clear. It is that, if the municipal or other local authorities have work that must be done at some time, such as park improvement or road-making or public building, it is especially well that this be given through regular contractors or otherwise at the period of hard time. Such work at such times will tend to preserve the normal condition without interfering with the regular course of labor, and where it has been tried, as in Cincinnati, has greatly improved the situation. This is by no means a concession to the cry of the socialists that the State should supply work to all who need it. Far from it. This is but using the State to aid in preserving social equilibrium, so that the highest individualism, which includes the individual well-being of the poor as well as of the rich, may have free play.

The past depression came upon us unawares, and has been a great trial to the principles and methods of charity organization societies. They have stood the trial nobly. Let us take courage. When the next emergency arrives, we shall be better able to meet it.

XXVI

THE APPLICATION OF
SCIENTIFIC ANALYSIS

Although there was constant reference to the need to draw on the social sciences and make philanthropy into an applied science, only a few leaders actually tried to do so. Amos Warner's efforts showed advanced reasoning and meticulous use of the research tools so far developed. He possessed both theoretical knowledge and practical experience, for he had been general agent of the Baltimore COS while getting a doctorate in history and political science at Johns Hopkins University and later he had reorganized the public charities in Washington, D.C.[46]

Warner's essays give a picture of the kind of studies then being made and the early fumbling for ways in which research techniques could be applied to the complexities of human situations. He saw the many limitations in simple statistics, and yet tried to use factual material to appraise some of the preconceptions of his day, such as the doctrine that poverty is certain indication of personal fault, and the prevailing belief that most relief recipients were alcoholic. These extracts, with only a few samples of his numerous tables, do not do justice to Warner's wide reading and elaborate tabulations. The student of research history should go to the originals and read them in full.

Warner was a true trail blazer in his conviction that there were multiple, interrelated causes of need and personal inadequacy; the profession of social work is still struggling with the relation of "inner" and "outer" factors. Figures on the high incidence of need in certain recent immigrant groups are similar to

[46] Warner alternated academic appointments with responsibilities as executive of private and public agencies. See Biographical Preface by George Elliott Howard in Amos Warner, *American Charities*, rev. by Susan Coolidge (New York: Crowell, 1908).

those found in present-day studies that stress high incidence among Puerto Rican and nonwhite peoples.

Warner's work did much to promote a more discriminating use of counting procedures and stimulated a questioning attitude whenever conclusions were drawn from unsystematically assembled data.

69. Notes on the Statistical Determination of the Causes of Poverty

Amos G. Warner, *Publications*, American Statistical Association, New Series, I, No. 5 (1889), 183–201

The analysis given below was worked out by non-statistical methods, but yet represents something more than a philosophical study of the subject. It was elaborated while the author was General Agent of the Charity Organization Society of Baltimore, and its adequacy tested by continued reference to concrete cases of destitution. The analysis . . . gives a bird's-eye view of a large and ill-mapped field which statisticians are only beginning to explore.

Most of those who have definitely undertaken a statistical search for the causes of poverty have merely employed some system of case-counting. They have considered a large number of cases, one by one, and assigned to each whatever cause of poverty seemed to be of most importance. A glance at our analysis of causes will show that such a method would be likely to exaggerate the importance of the subjective as compared with the objective influences. In dealing with individuals their character is more studied than their environment. Even when environment is the primary cause of poverty, the immediate cause, or a co-ordinate result, is often deterioration of character. Sickness is more obvious than bad sanitation, laziness than a malarial atmosphere, inefficiency than a defective educational system. The one who attempts the analysis of cases is also confused by the fact that under the operation of exactly similar general causes some families are destitute and some are not. One man is able to secure an adequate income under the most adverse circumstances—bad climate, bad housing, bad taxing, no opportunities for education, etc. Another man, under exactly the same conditions, will become destitute, and the observer concludes that the final and determining cause must be something in the physique or character of the latter person. The ministers and charity agents who come most intimately in contact with the poor are very prone to take short-sighted views of the causes of poverty.

Analysis of the Causes of Poverty

SUBJECTIVE
Characteristics
  1. Undervitalization and indolence
  2. Lubricity
  3. Specific disease
  4. Lack of judgment
  5. Unhealthy appetites
Habits producing and produced by the above
  1. Shiftlessness
  2. Self-abuse and sexual excess
  3. Abuse of stimulants and narcotics
  4. Unhealthy diet
  5. Disregard of family ties

OBJECTIVE
  1. Inadequate natural resources
  2. Bad climatic conditions
  3. Defective sanitation, etc.
  4. Evil associations and surroundings
  5. Defective legislation and defective judicial and punitive machinery
  6. Misdirected or inadequate education
  7. Bad industrial conditions
     a. Variations in value of money
     b. Changes in trade
     c. Excessive or ill-managed taxation
     d. Emergencies unprovided for
     e. Undue power of class over class
     f. Immobility of labor
  8. Unwise philanthropy

We premise, then, that a statistical analysis of a concrete mass of poverty or pauperism will probably give more light concerning the subjective causes of poverty than the objective. Such we will find to be the case as we review the work that has been done in this line. It is useful, and need not be misleading, if its limitations are remembered. We must recollect that we are enumerating immediate and not primary causes. On the other hand, it may be said that those who study the question from a philosophical standpoint are apt to lay too much stress on the influence of institutions and of our surroundings. Thus, Mr. George [47] thinks that a modification of the tax system would abolish poverty, and the socialists generally think that a change of institutional environment is the one thing needful. . . . In the statistical work which this paper reviews the method almost exclusively used is that of case-counting; and the results, for the most part, bear only indirectly upon the great primary questions of environment. . . .

The first question in considering tables of this sort is as to the class of families whose cases have been examined. We will consider five collections of figures gleaned from the study of as many different classes of people.[48] First, 528,257 cases of those receiving public relief in Prussia; second, some of the results reached by Mr. Charles Booth in studying the entire population of East London, numbering about 1,000,000 souls; third, 27,970 cases of those who asked for relief, and were investigated by the Charity Organization Societies of this country; fourth, 6,197 cases relieved by either public or private agencies of Buffalo, N.Y., and investigated by the Charity Organization Society of that city; and, fifth, the facts gathered by O. C. McCulloch, of Indiana, and R. L. Dugdale, of New York, regarding certain large and persistently pauper families. . . .

[47] Henry George started the single-tax movement, the theory of which he expanded in his most famous book, *Progress and Poverty* (New York: Appleton, 1880).

[48] As each was quoted and analyzed in elaborate detail Warner gave exact citations of his sources as follows: "Statistisches Handbuch für den preussischen Staat," 1888; Charles Booth, "Condition and Occupation of the People of East London and Hackney," *Journal of the Royal Statistical Society*, Vols. L and LI; Charles D. Kellogg, *NCCC*, 1887; Buffalo COS, *Tenth Annual Report;* Oscar McCulloch, "The Tribe of Ishmael," *NCCC*, 1888; Richard L. Dugdale, *The Jukes* (3d ed.; New York: G. P. Putnam's, 1877).

A very cursory examination of the causes here tabulated will show how doubtful must often be the decision between them. Is a man so indolent that no one will employ him, or are there causes, external to himself, that render him idle? While under the influence of liquor he breaks his leg—is the cause to be given as intemperance or accident? A man is not very strong, and has a rather large family—shall the cause be given as infirmity or large number of children? The personal equation is necessarily large. A radical "prohibitionist" would get very different results than would a "moderate drinker." Under similar difficulties Mr. Booth expresses the hope that the prejudices of different observers will cancel each other; but where possible error is so large a factor in the amount involved, the results can only be reasoned from with extreme caution. . . .

[He] has made an heroic attempt to draw a statistical picture of industrial society in East London. . . .

Mr. Booth wrestles manfully with the lack-of-employment problem. . . .

Neither class B [persons with casual earnings] nor class C [persons with intermittent earnings] work much more than half of their time. Also . . . most of the work done by class B is inefficiently done. . . . If the whole of class B were swept out of existence, all the work they do could be done, together with their own work, by the men, women, and children of classes C and D [regular minimum earnings] . . . [He concludes:] The poverty of the poor is mainly the result of the competition of the very poor. The entire removal of this class out of the daily struggle for existence I believe to be the only solution of the problem of poverty. . . .

He further speaks of improving this class off the face of the planet. The conclusion is novel and somewhat startling. . . . To crowd all who drop into this class mercilessly out of existence is not possible in the present state of public opinion. If, however, the key to the whole situation lies in the word "improve," we have a very sound conclusion, but a very old one. But, whatever may be the solution of the problem, the terms of the problem itself stand out with new and helpful distinctness in consequence of Mr. Booth's ingenious and faithful work. . . .

[Mr. Charles D. Kellogg's] figures were gleaned from the reports of about forty Charity Organization Societies. . . .

[He] comments as follows:

. . . There is a notable unity of opinion that only from thirty-one to thirty-seven per cent, or say one third of the cases actually treated, were in need of that material assistance for which no offices of friendly counsel or restraint could compensate. The logical application of this generalization to the whole country is that two thirds of its real or simulated destitution could be wiped out by a more perfect adjustment of the supply and demand for labor, and a more vigorous and enlightened police administration. . . .

The moral that Mr. McCulloch draws is that public out-door relief, as administered by American political officials, "sends the pauper out with the benediction 'be fruitful and multiply' "; and "that private indiscriminate giving joins public relief in producing still-born children, raising prostitutes, and educating criminals." This, it will be seen, bears upon the last cause given in the analysis with which this paper began, viz., Unwise philanthropy. . . .

Dugdale's "Tentative generalizations on heredity and environment" conclude as follows: "The logical induction seems to be that environment is the ultimate controlling factor in determining careers, placing heredity itself as an organized result of invariable environment."

We have thus worked our way back to the conclusion at first reached, that the study of individuals leads us to dwell upon character as a factor in causing poverty, but that if we search far enough we find that the primary cause is environment. In investigating the causes of poverty classed as "objective" nearly all the social and some of the natural sciences must be required to furnish conclusions, and statistics, as the bond servant of them all, will have its share of work.

70. *The Causes of Poverty Further Considered*

Warner, *Publications*, American Statistical Association, New Series, IV, No. 27 (1894), 49–68

Since [the 1889] paper appeared much new material has been collected. . . .

The question commonly in the minds of those who undertake to investigate the causes of poverty by a system of case counting is this: Is poverty a misfortune or a fault? No full answer to the question can probably be worked out by scientific methods, but the question is so frequently asked that it seems worth while to ascertain what light a case-counting investigation of poverty can throw upon it. With this end in view, I have arranged a table giving a comparison of the results reached by German investigators, by Mr. Charles Booth, and by the American Charity Organization societies, grouping the specified causes of poverty under three main heads: first, those indicating misconduct; second, those indicating misfortune; and, third, those not classified or unknown.

The first duty of one presenting such a table as this is to indicate clearly what it does not show. It deals, as already indicated, only with the exciting causes of poverty, and yet this fact is not kept clearly in mind even by careful workers. Mr. Booth, for instance, includes "pauper association and heredity" in this list of causes, and the American societies include "nature and location of abode." Both of these are by their nature predisposing causes rather than immediate or exciting causes, and it is confusing to mix the two kinds. Secondly, many of the persons whose cases are here tabulated have been, as Mr. Booth says, the foot-ball of all the causes in the list. Under such circumstances to pick out one cause and call it the most important is a purely arbitrary proceeding. Any one of the causes might have been inadequate to produce pauperism had not others co-operated with it. . . .

The writer was so thoroughly convinced of this that at the Conference of Charities at Buffalo, when the first of the cause schedules was adopted, he tried to have the societies directed to consider the influences resulting in destitution in each case as making up ten units, and indicate the relative force of each by a proportionate number of units. This would serve to show the grouping of the causes. The chief cause could be indicated in each case, and also the contributory causes. The system was rejected as too complicated, and after I had tried to have the agents of a single society, that of Baltimore, use it in making their reports to the central office, I concluded that possibly the objection was valid. Yet if the requisite amount of skill and care were used it would give valuable results. . . .

The impossibility of giving an accurate statistical description of the facts is still clearer when we try to separate the causes indicating misconduct from those indicating misfortune. Back of disease may be either misconduct or misfortune. The imprisonment of the bread-winner indicates misconduct on his part, but may only indicate misfortune on the part of wife and children. The same is true in the case of abandoned children and neglect by relatives. This particular classification is made in deference to popular inquiry only. In my own opinion its chief value consists in showing how little it is worth.

But after all possible allowance has been made for the "personal equation" of the investigator, and for all the inevitable inconclusiveness of the figures, there is a residuum of information to be got from the tables. They give, as well as such statistics can, the conclusions reached by those who are studying pauperism at first hand. If the figures furnished by all the investigators were added together into one great total, and this only were put before me, I should indeed hesitate to base any conclusions whatever upon it. But when it is found that different investigators, at different times, in different places, reach conclusions which, while varying in many and often inexplainable ways, are yet in agreement as regards certain important facts, we can but think that the figures to some extent reflect actual conditions. . . .

Considering at present only the figures for American cities . . . we notice first that the percentages for all causes indicating misconduct vary only between ten and thirty-two. The most important of the individual causes here grouped is "drink," which averages about 10 per cent. . . .

The causes grouped under the heading "matters of employment" account for somewhat more than a third of the destitution dealt with by the American societies. . . . No one well acquainted with the cases with which the Charity Organization Societies deal can at all doubt that most of those whose poverty is said to result from lack of employment are somehow and to some extent incapable or unreliable. If one wanted thoroughly efficient help, male or female, he would hardly expect to find it among the "out-of-works" with whom the charitable societies deal. Back of the cause "lack of work" ordinarily, and in ordinary times, will be found some perversion of character, or some limitation of capacity.

Under "matters of personal capacity," "accident," and "physical defect" exert a minor but quite constant influence, the former somewhat greater than the latter. . . .

So far as these tables show, the most constant cause of poverty everywhere, at all times, and according to all investigators, is "sickness." In both American and English experience the percentage attributable to this cause sinks but once slightly below 15, and never quite reaches 30. The average is between 20 and 25. To my mind this is one of the most significant facts brought out by these tables. It was not one which I anticipated when the collection of statistics began, and yet it has been confirmed and reconfirmed in so many ways that the conclusion seems inevitable that the figures set forth real and important facts. Personal acquaintance with the destitute classes has further convinced me that most of the causes of poverty result from, or result in, a weakened physical and mental constitution, often merging into actual disease. . . .

Two facts are brought out prominently . . . one is the tendency of statistics based on case counting to degenerate into mere description of the personal characteristics or condition of dependents, and the other is the tendency of drink as a cause of pauperism to disappear when we study chiefly chronic cases of long standing. . . .

As the first question popularly asked regarding the causes of poverty would probably be whether poverty indicates misconduct or misfortune, so the second would probably be, What are the indications as to the tendency of different nationalities or races to become poor? For the purpose of finding what answer could be obtained to this question Table V was prepared, giving the facts regarding 7225 American cases. They are classified, horizontally according to the causes of poverty . . . and vertically according to nationality.

CAUSES OF POVERTY IN AMERICAN CITIES BY NATIONALITY

		American		German		Colored	
		No.	Per Cent	No.	Per Cent	No.	Per Cent
Indicating Misconduct	Drink	409	15.14	66	7.83	34	6.1
	Immorality	17	.63	1	.11	5	.91
	Shiftlessness and Inefficiency	248	9.19	63	7.48	31	5.6
	Crime and Dishonesty	20	.74	4	.47	4	.7
	Roving Disposition	44	1.63	8	.95	1	.1
Indicating Misfortune — Lack of Normal Support	Imprisonment of breadwinner	18	.66	1	.11	2	.3
	Orphans and abandoned children	10	.37	---	----	2	.3
	Neglect by relatives	24	.88	7	.83	7	1.2
	No male support	111	4.11	36	4.27	16	2.9
Matters of Employment	Lack of employment	663	24.57	242	28.62	95	17.4
	Insufficient employment	179	6.63	64	7.60	47	8.6
	Poorly paid employment	56	2.07	22	2.61	5	.9
	Unhealthy and dangerous employment	3	.11	2	.23	1	.1
Matters of Personal Capacity	Ignorance of English	----	----	4	.47	---	---
	Accident	72	2.66	30	3.56	8	1.4
	Sickness or death in family	548	20.31	193	22.92	216	39.6
	Physical defects	92	3.40	40	4.73	30	5.4
	Insanity	25	.92	6	.71	---	---
	Old age	76	2.81	23	2.73	25	4.5
Not Classified	Large family	14	.51	10	1.18	3	.5
	Nature of abode	2	.07	1	.11	1	.1
	Other, or unknown	67	2.58	29	3.44	12	2.1
Total		2,698	----	842	----	545	---

Irish		English		French		Russian Polish		Spanish		Italian		Scandinavian		Other Countries		TOTAL	
No.	Per Cent	No.	Per Cent	No.	Per Cent	No.	Per Cent	No.	Per Cent	No.	Per Cent	No.	Per Cent	No.	Per Cent	No.	Per Cent
83	23.62	107	16.93	11	9.25	5	3.24	---	----	6	5.60	3	9.09	30	14.21	1,104	15.28
5	.27	2	.31	---	----	---	----	---	----	---	----	---	----	2	.94	32	.44
06	5.78	45	7.12	7	5.88	11	7.09	4	10.00	9	8.41	2	6.06	17	8.05	543	7.51
7	.38	7	1.10	3	2.52	---	----	1	2.50	3	2.80	---	----	---	----	49	.68
7	.38	16	2.53	1	.84	2	1.29	---	----	1	.93	---	----	6	2.84	86	1.19
22	1.20	8	1.26	1	.84	---	----	---	----	1	.93	1	3.03	1	.47	55	.76
7	.38	4	.63	---	----	2	1.29	---	----	---	----	---	----	---	----	25	.34
7	.38	8	1.26	1	.84	10	6.45	1	2.50	1	.93	---	----	---	----	66	.91
03	5.07	20	3.16	6	5.05	10	6.45	2	5.00	7	6.54	2	6.06	8	3.79	311	4.80
46	18.87	156	24.68	32	26.89	37	23.87	5	12.50	33	30.85	14	42.42	51	24.17	1,674	23.16
7	6.38	30	4.74	12	10.08	7	4.51	---	----	6	5.60	3	9.09	6	2.84	471	6.51
5	.81	9	1.42	3	2.52	3	1.93	6	15.00	5	4.67	---	----	7	3.31	131	1.81
1	.05	---	----	---	----	---	----	---	----	---	----	---	----	---	----	7	.09
1	.05	---	----	2	1.68	6	3.87	5	12.50	4	3.75	---	----	8	3.79	30	.41
7	3.10	17	2.69	3	2.52	6	3.87	---	----	4	3.75	1	3.03	9	4.26	207	2.86
3	19.80	145	22.94	21	17.65	39	25.16	13	32.50	18	16.82	4	12.12	49	23.22	1,608	22.27
4	3.49	11	1.74	9	7.58	10	6.45	1	2.50	3	2.80	2	6.06	5	2.37	267	3.69
7	.91	8	1.26	1	.84	1	.64	---	----	---	----	---	----	4	1.89	62	.85
8	6.97	23	3.63	4	3.36	1	.64	1	2.50	3	2.80	1	3.03	4	1.89	289	4.00
6	.87	5	.79	---	----	3	1.93	1	2.50	1	.93	---	----	---	----	53	.73
1	.05	3	.47	1	.84	---	----	---	----	---	----	---	----	---	----	9	.12
0	1.09	8	1.26	1	.84	2	1.29	2	----	2	1.87	---	----	4	1.89	145	2.00
3	----	632	----	119	----	155	----	40	----	107	----	33	----	211	----	7,225	----

Of the Americans, Germans, Colored, Irish, and English there are enough cases in each column to make the percentages tolerably trustworthy, while of the French, Polish, Spanish, Italian, Scandinavian, and "other countries" the numbers are too small to make the relative figures of much value. . . .

Those who know the Colored people only casually, or by hearsay, may be surprised to find the misconduct causes running so low among them, while sickness as a cause is of greater relative importance than in any other nationality. But to one who has worked in Baltimore or Washington it seems a natural result, and, indeed, a confirmation of the reliability of the statistics. The Colored people are weak physically, become sick easily, and often die almost without visible resistance to disease. At the same time they have a dread of taking relief, especially when they think an institution will be recommended, and this, together with a certain apathy, will often induce them to endure great privations rather than ask for help. . . .

But one must hesitate to put much weight upon a general average of this kind, and I have therefore given separately the constituent elements of the table, that is, have made out for each city a table like this one for all four cities. . . .

Table X shows for the four cities the percentages of Native White, Colored, and Foreign born among the population as a whole, and among those who applied to the charity organization societies in these cities. It will be noted that the proportion of applicants who are foreign born is considerably larger than of the population as a whole. . . .

A matter which is not brought out by the tables thus far given, but which is well shown by the collateral investigations of the different agencies, is the large number of children either dragged into pauperism by the destitution of their parents, or entirely abandoned by the latter. In the investigations of almshouse pauperism of course this is not brought out, as the children have been put in other institutions and are beyond the view of the investigator. But in the American experience, where the cases are studied as they cross the pauper line, the large number of children is striking.

Out of . . . persons dealt with by the New York Charity Organization Society in 1891 over 40 . . . per cent . . . were under 14. In Boston . . . 42 per cent. . . . In Buffalo . . . over 48 . . . per cent. . . . In Baltimore the percentage . . . drops to a little less than 16. It thus appears that while "large families" is not assigned as a cause of poverty in many cases, and while, as a rule, the families are not relatively large, yet those applying for relief are weighted with a considerable amount of the weakness that comes from immaturity. The burden of child raising is among the very considerable burdens which they bear.

Our general conclusion must be the same as that reached in the previous paper—that the commonest cause of the poverty that approaches pauperism is incapacity, resulting in most chronic cases from sickness or other degenerate and degenerating conditions. Weakness of some sort is the most typical characteristic of the destitute classes. Manifestly, our analysis of causes is only preliminary. It has hardly more value than that of a physician who should try to determine the causes of disease by examining carefully the persons of a large number of patients; by recording temperatures and respirations and pulsations, and by studying the other characteristics of those who were sick. To get at the remote causes of illness he would have to inquire, first, regarding the habits and heredity of the individuals, and, second, regarding the climatic, sanitary, and other conditions of their life and work. So also the remote causes of the weakness that begets poverty must be learned by wider investigations than any here attempted.

THE PERIOD OF
PROFESSIONALIZATION
1895 – 1937

INTRODUCTION

In the forty years between the panic of the nineties and the depression of the thirties, social work became a recognized profession, perhaps not fully developed in all particulars, but meeting most of the usual criteria.

One main issue, continuously debated but never fully settled, was whether its primary obligation was to serve individuals or to promote the good of society in general, thereby providing a better environment for every person. The great period of preoccupation with services to individuals was between the First World War and the great depression. The haphazard, intuitive approach of earlier days had been superseded by a highly developed systematic process of investigation before the insights of psychiatry brought an exciting burst of inquiry into, and refinement of, treatment processes. The individual approach was in partial eclipse during two great waves of reform, each directed toward change in the social structure. Prior to the First World War emphasis was on such matters as housing, child labor, wages, and the income tax; during the depression the New Deal culminated, so far as social welfare was concerned, with the Society Security Act. Social workers forthrightly expressed opinions, agitated for public support, and helped draft proposals. Toward the end of each wave, social workers received general recognition and acceptance as specialists. Much of the Bull Moose platform in 1912 was an almost exact replica of a program which had been put forward by social work leaders at the National Conference of Social Work that year.[1] Harry Hopkins and Frances Perkins rose to positions of great authority during the period of the New Deal, and many other social workers participated in research, political action, and governmental administration.

[1] Report of Committee on Standards of Living and Labor, *NCCC*, 1912, pp. 376–94; Paul U. Kellogg, "The Industrial Platform of the New Party," *The Survey*, XXVIII (Aug. 24, 1912), 668–70.

The prevailing emphasis governed the selection of methods for development at any one time—social action, neighborhood organization, public interpretation, community research; or therapeutic techniques, enhancement through group experience, giving of personal opportunity. Efforts for prevention took the form either of removal of harmful conditions or of provision for early care and training.

A persistent theme was that the paid, full-time careerist, with background knowledge, training, and experience, was best fitted to give service. Ideas on the role of the volunteer ranged from a belief that he could provide the most individualized personal service to the opinion that his most useful contribution would be the kind of expert business experience which Chamber of Commerce members could donate to ensure efficiency in administration and financing.

Schools for professional training were organized and expanded. At the start of the period, paid workers were beginning to get together on local, state, and national levels to promote common concerns, prevent duplication, and learn from each other. Most early associations and conferences included interested leaders from the public at large, but by 1918 exclusively professional membership bodies were beginning to form.

Concern with methods and techniques became more pronounced in each professional specialty. Casework was the first to emerge as an organized grouping of skills for helping people, followed by social group work, social work research, and community organization. Only a hint of the steps in the evolution of each method can be given in these readings.

As the range of professional specialties indicates, social work was not a unified profession. Divisiveness arose out of many circumstances: public, private, and sectarian sponsorship; the type of clientele served, such as adults, children, handicapped, and the foreign-born; or the kind of problem to be dealt with, such as unemployment, ill-health, emotional instability, and slum neighborhoods. A low financial and social status traditionally had characterized the person who sought the help of the social worker, but by the time of the depression, it was becoming clear that these were not the only criteria which might apply. Group work agencies were concerned with the social development of the so-called "normal" child; mental hygiene workers, with the good adjustment of every child, whatever the family income. The insurance and other aspects of Social Security were set up to include a large segment of the population which did not ordinarily regard itself as in need, nor turn to social agencies for help.

For the person who wishes to see in capsule the state of the profession just before the passage of the Social Security Act, the Hartford Survey (R104) and the articles by Reed (R107) and Grace Coyle (R108) show both practice and philosophy. For the hopes and doubts of professionals after the passage of the Act, see Hopkins (R110) and Bruno (R111).

With a new system of economic provision for aid established, many members of the social work profession concentrated on technical developments. However, in this the profession was to find itself again divided. On the one hand were those who accepted Bruno's challenge to develop the administrative relationships, regulations, and procedures which would make the new governmental system of economic aid function effectively and remain sensitive to the needs of individuals. On the other hand were those who followed the lead of Virginia Robinson (R95), Newstetter (R97), and others in the development of more refined methods of working directly with people. Shortly after the period covered by this book several authors produced treatises dealing with specific treatment techniques.

The daily tasks and immediate objectives of social workers were, for a time, to diverge so widely as to make it difficult for them to see themselves as members of a common profession. The hope of professional unity rested in the homogeneity of their ultimate goals.

XXVII
LOOKING ASKANCE

By 1899 the charity organization movement and the settlement movement had become rivals for the allegiance, financial support, and voluntary service of the philanthropic public. During the preceding ten years, each group had produced an eloquent professional spokesman, and these two were to continue to be the accepted rival leaders for the next quarter of a century. Born only a few months apart, Mary Richmond and Jane Addams had entered charitable activities at almost the same time. Now, after a decade of service, they had come to know and respect each other, and each had had opportunities to observe the strengths and weaknesses of the movement which the other represented. Within a few months of each other, they set their appraisals down on paper.

The two documents speak for themselves, but we may perhaps call attention to a few points of similarity and difference. Both were aware of possibilities of helpfulness on the part of sincerely motivated persons of privilege. Both recognized the danger of unnaturalness and superficiality in paid neighborliness. Miss Addams and the settlement movement generally doubted the wisdom and efficacy of the formal methodology and especially the meticulous investigations of the charity organization movement. Miss Richmond and the charity organizationists were suspicious of what appeared to them to be the fuzzy and opportunistic thinking of settlement workers in their efforts to become genuine parts of the neighborhoods in which they were working and to adjust their methods and activities to the particular individuals and organizations with which they were associated. Leaders in each group were well aware of the limitations in the work of their colleagues, pointed out by the other, but tended to regard such shortcomings as individual failings, whereas they regarded the questionable aspects they saw in the other approach as being basic to its operation.

71. *Good Spirit and Earnestness*

Mary E. Richmond[2] to "Florence"; Personal Correspondence, Mary E. Richmond Archives, Library, New York School of Social Work, Columbia University

Baltimore, June 3, 1899

My dear Florence.[3] . . .

On Monday afternoon the subject was "The Relation of the Settlement to Ward and City Politics."

Mr. Woods[4] opened the discussion with a fifteen minute talk in which he questioned the wisdom of settlement workers trying to become political leaders in the settlement ward. The expression "he is our kind" describes the ward's sense of kinship with the ward leader in a way that it could never describe the settlement

[2] Mary Ellen Richmond (1861–1928) was then general secretary of the Baltimore COS, and gaining national recognition. On the invitation of Jane Addams, Miss Richmond attended the Conference of American Settlements held at Hull House, May 16–18, 1899. She was accompanied by two board members of the Baltimore COS, each a future president of the NCCC: Jeffrey Brackett, then president of the Baltimore Board of Public Charities; and Mary Willcox Brown, afterward Mrs. John M. Glenn, then secretary of the Henry Watson Children's Aid in Baltimore. The complete program and a summary of major speeches from the point of view of the settlements were published in *The Commons*, in April and June, 1899 (III, No. 33 [1899], 27; IV, No. 2 [1899], 23, 25–29). For a contemporary description and identification of local leaders see John Palmer Gavit, *Bibliography of College, Social and University Settlements* (3d ed.; Cambridge, Mass.: Co-operative Press for the College Settlements Association, 1897). This conference was the first of national scope held under the independent auspices of the settlements. Previous meetings had been held at Plymouth, Mass. under leadership of the Ethical Society, in theological conventions and university departments of political economy.

[3] Florence Converse (1871–), appears to have been the intended recipient of this letter which, from unquoted content, was obviously directed to a Bostonian. Miss Converse graduated from Wellesley College and had been a resident of Dension House (College Settlement) since 1897. Her name appears as a mutual friend in the correspondence of Zilpha Smith with Mary Richmond. A novelist of social causes, she was then on the editorial staff of *The Churchman*, and, 1908–30, of the *Atlantic Monthly*. She was associate editor of a questionnaire study of later experiences of former settlement residents, "After Twenty-five Years," in the College Settlements Association *Anniversary Report, 1889–1914*, which includes recollections of the period described in this letter.

[4] Robert A Woods (R60) was the settlement leader with whom Mary Richmond maintained closest association over the years.

worker, who is at best an ambassador of one kind of people to another kind. The relation is a diplomatic one, using that word in its highest and best sense. (I am not sure that Miss Addams would accept this way of stating it, but I notice that in her last article in the May number of the "Annals of the American Academy of Political and Social Science," she speaks of the settlement worker as an interpreter. The relation between the best sort of an interpreter and an ambassador is close.) Mr. Woods seemed to think that the settlement's best chance of political influence was with its particular following of people throughout the city. These and not the neighbors would be ready to increase the independent vote and push for a larger municipal programme, including parks, playgrounds, public baths, municipal gymnasia, etc. With these definite results, serving as object lessons to the people, the administration would touch them in other tangible ways beside the only one now evident to them—the securing of jobs.

Mr. McCord of the Union Seminary Settlement of New York, took issue with this view, contending that settlement workers can furnish leadership to the more decent element in poor neighborhoods, and can encourage these to commend and support the political party that did the most for the people.

Graham Taylor [5] thought the Settlements ought to work to get the balance of political power in their districts and so force upon both parties a municipal programme.

Mr. Rosenthal,[6] head worker of Maxwell House, gave a lurid picture of politics in his ward, and declared that no settlement worker could keep himself clean who mixed in such matters at all. He gave an amusing account of three local campaigns in which he was decidedly worsted.

[5] Graham Taylor (1851–1938), professor of social economy at Chicago Theological Seminary, was founder and resident warden of Chicago Commons. He was president of the Chicago School of Civics and Philanthropy, 1903–20.
[6] Rosenthal had been candidate for alderman from the 7th ward, Chicago, in 1896 (*Chicago Commons*, I, No. 1 [1896], 8). It seems probable that he was the Lessing Rosenthal (1867–1949) who was "for many years a militant fighter for election reforms" (New York *Times*, Dec. 21, 1949).

After a good deal of talk in which, as Mr. Woods said after-ward, it was evident that each speaker's views had been moulded by the political conditions in his own neighborhood, Miss Addams said that she found it impossible to keep aloof from the political interests of the 19th ward, and that she had not noticed there the tradition that Mr. Woods referred to, requiring absolute like-mindedness in the poor and their leaders. A business man's policy, that overemphasised honesty and economy in government, might appeal to the smug people in poorer neighborhoods, but left out the idealists. There were those among the poorest that were ready to follow a good leader who could appeal to their imaginations and stir their feelings. Politics, after all, was the most vital inter-est of the neighborhood, not even excepting religion, and to keep aloof from it must be to lose by so much the opportunity of shar-ing the life of the neighborhood. Miss Addams said afterwards that she had not said at all what she intended to say, and had not made her point clear; that, frankly, she was still divided in her mind between the longing to go in and share all the difficulties, and the sense of helplessness where the ward boss is concerned. To turn over to the ward boss all these new municipal activities of which Mr. Woods spoke, seemed to her to give him only so many more means of debauching the people. The difference between them seemed to be that Mr. Woods trusted in the long run to using the boss for his own destruction, and Miss Addams still feared his further entrenchment. . . .

Mr. Gavit [7] of Chicago Commons . . . gave us the sensation of the Conference. He said the time had come for settlements to look the situation squarely in the face, that he had sometimes resented it when the settlements were regarded as charities, but

[7] John P. Gavit was editor of *The Commons*, published by Chicago Commons, which purported to be the voice of the settlement movement. In 1900 he went into journalism, became chief representative of the Asso-ciated Press in Washington and managing editor of the New York *Eve-ning Post*. In the thirties he joined the staff of *The Survey*, successor to *The Commons*. Mrs. Gavit was listed as instructor in homemaking and occupations for the 1899–1900 term of the Pestalozzi-Froebel Kindergarten Training School at Chicago Commons. *The Commons* had published an

that, after seeing the charity of his poor neighbors to each other, he felt that "charity" was too sacred and high a word to describe their position. They claimed to come down and live the life of the people, to share their difficulties, when, as a matter of fact, they did no such thing. His family lived at the settlement of the Commons and he had a five months' old baby. On the day that it was born a child was born in the family living across the street from the settlement. The two mothers had exchanged messages and afterward had become quite well acquainted, finding their motherhood a strong interest in common. When he and his wife noticed, however, that the other baby was not kept nearly so clean as their baby, they had to remind themselves that the mother across the street did all her own work and had a hard struggle to get on. Then it was difficult to get good milk in their neighborhood; even with a refrigerator and other conveniences the milk spoiled, and when the mother across the way asked how they fed their baby, and they replied that they used ——, she said, with a sigh, "yes, but that costs too much." It did cost. . . . Here at one blow was cut away all common ground between them. How could they advise, how could they confer, how could they pretend to help the family across the way when the conditions under which they were living were so different, when they were not on the same economic basis at all? For his part, the matter had given him sleepless nights, his heart torn by the thought that their pretence of being helpful in the neighborhood was a mere sham, that until economic conditions were changed they were utterly helpless. Groping about in what was for him a crossing of the ways, and a crisis in his life, he could only suggest what he knew was no solution, but still a possible help, and that was that the settlement, by establishing some cooperative scheme in the neighborhood, put itself in part at least, on a common eco-

anonymous review of Mary Richmond's book, *Friendly Visiting among the Poor* (probably by Gavit), (IV, No. 1 [1899], 14), which said: "It waives the question of social remedies and presupposes conditions as they are." Gavit's attitudes toward the COS were highly critical.

nomic basis, that it have an industrial foothold instead of being nothing but a high-flown "ambassador" among these suffering swarms.[8] . . .

Tuesday morning was devoted to educational methods . . . [Mr. Gavit] was again on his feet demanding that we should "look the situation squarely in the face," and I was told afterward that he was always insisting upon this. He wanted to know whether the educational classes of the settlements really reached the poorest people in their immediate neighborhoods. Miss Addams stated that there were many in every such neighborhood who, in the industrial struggle, had had all ambition for education crushed out of them; whereupon Mr. Gavit said that that was what he wanted them to consider; their educational classes failed of their mission unless they reached just such people. This, of course, was nonsense, and brought several people to their feet, including the head of a Laundress' Union in Cincinnati, a working woman, who felt that these "good ladies and gentlemen" were being abominably abused and that it was high time she came to their rescue. She felt that people who were giving their lives to help the workers should not be spoken of in the disrespectful terms that Mr. Gavit used. She felt that the gentleman had "misbalanced" himself, which seemed to me to describe very accurately his situation. A number of good points were made at the meeting. Miss McDowell [9] urged the need of a vocabulary on the part of students who came to them from the Universities. Even one of the settlement workers who came to lecture to a club of women at Miss McDowell's own settlement had drawn out the remark from them, "she is a *fine* lady, but her language is too high." Mr.

[8] *The Commons*, IV, No. 2 (1899), 26, made no mention of Gavit's speech, but reported that "Abraham Bisno, a socialist of Chicago, who took part in the warm discussion which ensued, scored a close hit in warning the settlements against being nothing better than 'paid neighbors.' "

[9] Mary E. McDowell was head resident of the University of Chicago Settlement, stockyards district. She was subsequently a member of the faculty of the University and, in 1923, Commissioner of Public Welfare of Chicago.

Rosenthal described how on summer nights he was accustomed to sit on the high steps of Maxwell House and soon fifteen or twenty of the neighbors would gather about; during these evenings stories of the Iliad and Odyssey, of the Bible and of the causes that led up to the late war had all been told. During the winter the social gathering had really developed into a geography class, although the words "class" and "geography" had never been introduced. Miss Starr,[10] whose attitude is somewhat of a "chip on the shoulder" one, objected to this as patronizing. It was unfair to inveigle people into being instructed without letting them know what you were about.

Tuesday afternoon was given over to the subject of "Institutional versus Personal Ideals of the Settlement." Mr. Zeublin [11] had a paper on the "Dangers of Institutionalism" and Miss Williams of Rivington St.[12] spoke on "Personal Relations." Miss Williams' talk sounded a little theoretical. It might easily have been compiled from our charity organization publications, but her theories were sound enough, and of course she has been at the helm only a very little while. Mr. Zeublin's chief objection to institutionalism was that it made the settlement another defender of capitalism. It took money to run the institution and the institution gathered about it an affection which was soon transferred in part to the source of its financial support. He did not seem to object to the settlements' receiving money from capitalists, but he desired that they should maintain an attitude of disapproval while doing it. Perhaps this does not state him fairly. I hope the "Commons" will publish his paper, but I am just giving you my offhand impressions, you see. It seemed to me that there were a

[10] Ellen Gates Starr (1859-1940) co-founder of Hull House, was in charge of literary and cultural work there. In 1915-16 she played a leading role in garment strikes and was an unsuccessful candidate for alderman.
[11] Charles Zeublin, a graduate of Yale Divinity School, had founded the Northwestern University Settlement in 1891. Later he became professor of sociology at the University of Chicago. His presence in a settlement is an indication of the close tie between the settlement movement and the then emerging institutional church movement.
[12] Elizabeth Sprague Williams was head worker of the College Settlement, Rivington Street, New York, from 1898 to 1919 (R59).

number of arguments against institutionalism which he did not go into at all. It was at this session that Miss Lathrop [13] called me out to say something. Whether it was my fault or someone's else, the discussion degenerated very much, and the last hour was given over to several gushing clergymen who shocked Miss Addams not a little by calling her "a nineteenth century saint." At this point of the Conference I believe the leaders were rather depressed, feeling that there had been a great deal of scattered talk and no advance made.

Tuesday night there was a rousing public meeting at Steinway Hall, with Mayor Jones of Toledo on "Principle before Party." After he had finished, a song of his entitled "Industrial Freedom," which averaged an economic fallacy to each line, was distributed in the audience, and someone was asked to play on the piano the tune of "Marching Through Georgia." In the simplest and most attractive way the Mayor stood on the platform, raised the tune and led the singing with both hands. Everybody joined in with a will. Some of our party were depressed by the meeting. It seemed to me a very hopeful sign. Mayor Jones has been elected in Toledo by a good big majority on a strictly workingman's platform. He has abandoned both parties, and, on the strength of his success, is inclined to believe that municipal state and national affairs can be better managed without party organization. This is an unwarrantable conclusion, I believe, but so far as municipal affairs are concerned he is probably right, and he is so evidently an honest man that one has faith in him to say that he is wrong when he finds that some of his theories won't work. Mr. Woods, in a very short speech, after Mayor Jones had finished, made it clear that the difference between Boston's recent reforms and those in Toledo, was that Boston's Mayor had not been doing the work he was elected to do, but had carried out a number of reforms without taking the people very much into his confidence

[13] Julia Lathrop (1858–1932), a resident at Hull House, was currently a member of the Illinois State Board of Charities and active in setting up the first juvenile court in the United States at Chicago. She was the first head of the U. S. Children's Bureau, 1912–21.

and rather in spite of the party that elected him. The danger of
this method always was that the city was likely to drift back at
any time, though never altogether, to a less enlightened policy.
He did not say, though very likely meant, that Mayor Jones was
stronger because he was one of the people and honestly represented them. It seems to me that if our American people are to
be saved it must be by this kind of man—one of their own kind.
Men like Seth Low [14] and Mayor Quincy [15] can help, but they
are relatively inefficient instruments. . . .

Wednesday afternoon was the last meeting and the subject was
"The Trend of Trade Unionism." . . .

[Mr. Noyes, of Henry Booth House] begged his fellow workers
to believe that if he had done so little, it had been because he felt
helpless until he could work out some theory of the ultimate end
of social service. He did not see how we could go on gathering
children into day nurseries, and doing in common the hundred
things that formerly were done in the home without realizing
the goal toward which all this tended. . . . [He] was evidently
made quite helpless by the sight of the suffering around him and
the sense of industrial wrong. . . .

Through this discussion particularly . . . I was not a little
amused to find that many of the settlement workers were put on
the defensive and forced to see what we charity workers are
often forced to see; namely, that it is impossible for the world to
stop until everything starts over and starts right, and that, though
Trade Unions and educational classes may be "palliatives" and
"alleviatives," even extending for a time the hold of the present
order, yet we must do the next best thing, pushing on always,
yet never leaving our palliative or alleviation until some better thing
seems practicable.

[14] Seth Low (1850–1916), then president of Columbia University, had
been a reform mayor of Brooklyn, 1882–86, and in 1901 was elected as a
reform candidate for mayor of Greater New York. In both instances his
reform activities contributed to his subsequent defeat.

[15] Josiah Quincy, mayor of Boston, 1895–99, was great-grandson of
Josiah Quincy (R21, 23), who also was a mayor of Boston, 1823–28.

Now for my general conclusions. First of all I was enormously impressed with the good spirit and the earnestness of all the meetings. There was no boasting, no swaggering. In our great National Conference meetings [16] we always have both. The best of the spirit at the settlement meetings was no better than the best at the Conference, probably, but the worst at the Conference is pretty bad, and it was delightful to attend three meetings a day for three days where there was so much sincerity and earnestness. They are inclined to be unduly depressed about their own work, sometimes; I have given you some of Mr. Gavit's characteristic sayings to show you this side, and it is only fair to add that he has his delightful moments of rebound, and often contradicts himself. . . . Miss Addams . . . showed the most delightful tact and good feeling throughout all the meetings. There must have been many undercurrents of which we were oblivious, many local differences and complications around which she steered with consummate skill—not through the kind of managing skill that a woman's club woman usually develops, but through the straightforwardness that is tempered by an exquisite courtesy and good feeling.

I shall always feel more sympathetic toward the settlements for having attended these meetings. . . . Miss Addams made one very good point; namely, that institutionalism was a matter of spirit. . . . If every institution connected with a settlement grows out of the social needs of the neighborhood . . . and is carefully adapted to these needs, institutionalism will probably be avoided. . . .

If I had any criticism to make as to the psychological effect of settlement work upon the workers, it would be that they seem, in an effort to keep their minds open to every sort of influence, to balance arguments "for" and "against" a little too much, and to show a certain inability to make up their minds. . . . The one advantage of the National Conference, going to it fresh from all

[16] Miss Richmond and her associates went from the Settlement Conference to the NCCC. Note the propriety attitude of the charity organizationist toward the NCCC, an attitude dating from Josephine Shaw Lowell's speech in 1890 (R64, cf. R50).

this, was to see how clearly most of the people there knew what they wanted to do next, and were alert to discuss the practical details of the next step. . . .

We have a great deal to learn from each other. Their political economy is rather crude—as much a "pseudo science" as our organized charity is. But I must not let my last word be an unsympathetic one. . . . They have got a great idea, and they mustn't lose their heads or else they will lose the idea too.

72. *The Subtle Problems of Charity*

Jane Addams, *Atlantic Monthly*, LXXXIII (1899),
163–78

Formerly when it was believed that poverty was synonymous with vice and laziness . . . charity was administered harshly with a good conscience. . . . Since then we have learned to measure by other standards. . . .

Of the various struggles which a decade of residence in a settlement implies, none have made a more definite impression on my mind than the incredibly painful difficulties which involve both giver and recipient when one persons asks charitable aid of another. . . .

One of the root difficulties . . . lies in the fact that the only families who apply for aid to the charitable agencies are those who have to come to grief on the industrial side [17] . . . they are industrially ailing, and must be bolstered and helped into industrial health. The charity visitor, let us assume, is a young college woman, well-bred and open-minded. When she visits the family assigned to her, she is embarrassed to find herself obliged to lay all the stress of her teaching and advice upon the industrial virtues. . . . The members of her assigned family may have charms and virtues . . . but it is her business to stick to the industrial side. . . . It often occurs to the mind of the sensitive visitor . . . that she herself has never been self-supporting. . . .

The grandmother of the charity visitor could have done the

[17] Addams and other theorists of this period were using "industrial" in the sense of "thrifty" or "financial," and sometimes of "industrious" or "energetic," rather than to refer to manufacturing and capitalist enterprise.

industrial preaching very well, because she did have the industrial virtues. . . . The charity visitor . . . is perplexed by recognitions and suggestions which the situation forces upon her. . . .

Added to this is a consciousness . . . of a genuine misunderstanding of her motives by the recipients of her charity and by their neighbors. . . . A most striking incongruity, at once apparent, is the difference between the emotional kindness with which relief is given by one poor neighbor to another poor neighbor, and the guarded care with which relief is given by a charity visitor to a charity recipient. The neighborhood mind is immediately confronted not only by the difference of method, but also by an absolute clashing of two ethical standards. . . .

An Irish family . . . struggling to eke out the scanty savings . . . will take in a widow and her five children who have been turned into the street, without a moment's reflection. . . .

The impulse to aid his fellows, served man at a very early period as a rude rule of right and wrong. . . . This rude rule still holds among many people . . . and . . . their ideas of right and wrong are quite honestly outraged by . . . [charitable] agencies. . . . The delay and caution with which relief is given . . . appear . . . the cold and calculating action of the selfish man. . . . They do not understand why the impulse which drives people to be good to the poor should be so severely supervised. . . . In the minds of the poor success does not ordinarily go with charity and kind-heartedness, but rather with the opposite qualities. The rich landlord is he who collects with sternness; who accepts no excuse, and will have his own. There are moments of irritation and of real bitterness against him, but there is admiration, because he is rich and successful. . . . The poor are accustomed to help one another, and to respond according to their kindliness; but when it comes to worldly judgment, they are still in that stage where they use industrial success as the sole standard. In the case of the charity visitor, they are deprived of both standards; she has neither natural kindness nor dazzling riches; and they find it of course utterly impossible to judge of the motive of organized charity. . . .

The poor man who has fallen into distress, when he first asks

aid, instinctively expects tenderness, consideration, and forgive-
ness. . . . He comes somewhat bruised and battered, and . . .
he is at once chilled by an investigation and an intimation that he
ought to work. . . . The only really popular charity is that
of visiting nurses, who carry about with them a professional
training, which may easily be interpreted into sympathy and
kindness, in their ministration to obvious needs without investigation. . . .

When the agent or visitor appears among the poor, and they
discover that under certain conditions food and rent and medical
aid are dispensed from some unknown source, every man, woman,
and child is quick to learn what the conditions may be, and to
follow them. . . . To the visitor they gravely laud temperance
and cleanliness and thrift and religious observance. The deception
doubtless arises from a wondering inability to understand the
ethical ideals which can require such impossible virtues, combined
with a tradition that charity visitors do require them, and from
an innocent desire to please. . . .

The most serious effect . . . comes when dependence upon the
charitable society is substituted for . . . love and sympathy. . . .
The spontaneous impulse to sit up all night with a neighbor's sick
child is turned into righteous indignation against the district nurse
because she goes home at six o'clock. . . .

When the charity visitor comes in, all the neighbors are baffled
as to what her circumstances may be. . . . They imagine untold
stores which they may call upon, and her most generous gift is
considered niggardly, compared with what she might do. . . .
The charity visitor has broken through the natural rule of giving,
which, in a primitive society, is bounded only by the need of the
recipient and the resources of the giver; and she gets herself into
untold trouble when she is judged by the ethics of that primitive
society. . . .

The visitor is continually surprised to find that the safest plati-
tudes may be challenged. She refers quite naturally to the "horrors
of the saloon," and discovers that the head of her visited family,
who knows the saloons very well, does not connect them with

"horrors" at all. He remembers all the kindnesses he has received there. . . .

[She may] say that "every American man can find work and is bound to support his family." She soon discovers that the workingman, in the city at least, is utterly dependent for the tenure of his position upon the good will of his foreman, upon the business prosperity of the firm, or the good health of the head of it; and that, once work is lost, it may take months to secure another place. . . .

The charity visitor may blame the women for lack of gentleness toward their children, for being hasty and rude to them, until she learns to reflect that the standard of breeding is not that of gentleness toward the children so much as the observance of certain conventions, such as the punctilious wearing of mourning garments after the death of a child. The standard of gentleness each mother has to work out largely by herself, assisted only by the occasional shamefaced remark of a neighbor, that "they do better when you are not too hard on them"; but the wearing of mourning garments is sustained by the definitely expressed sentiment of every woman in the street. . . .

The subject of clothes, indeed, perplexes the visitor constantly. . . . [The working girl's] income goes into her clothing out of all proportion to that which she spends upon other things. But if social advancement is her aim, it is the most sensible thing which she can do. She is judged largely by her clothes. . . . Girls' clubs succeed best in the business part of a town, where "working girls" and "young ladies" meet upon an equal footing, and where the clothes superficially look very much alike. Bright and ambitious girls will come to these down-town clubs to eat lunch and rest at noon, to study all sorts of subjects and listen to lectures, when they might hesitate a long time about joining a club identified with their own neighborhood. . . . Every one who has had to do with down-town girls' clubs has had the experience of going into the home of some bright, well-dressed girl, to discover it uncomfortable and perhaps wretched, and to find the girl afterwards carefully avoiding her. . . . In some very successful down-town clubs the home address is not given at all, and only the "business address" is required. Have we worked out our democracy in regard to clothes farther than in regard to anything else? . . .

Every one who goes shopping at the same time with the richest woman in town may see her clothes, but only those invited to her reception see the Corot on her walls or the bindings in her library. . . .

The charity visitor is still more perplexed when she comes to consider such problems as those of early marriage and child labor. . . . A business man, if he is on the road to success, is . . . wise . . . not to marry in the twenties. But this does not apply to the workingman. In many trades he is laid upon the shelf at thirty-five, and in nearly all trades he receives the largest wages of his life between twenty and thirty. . . .

He naturally regards his children as his savings-bank; he expects them to care for him when he gets old, and in some trades old age comes very early. . . .

This economic pressure also accounts for the tendency to put children to work over-young, and thus cripple their chances for individual development and usefulness. . . . It has long been a common error for the charity visitor, who is strongly urging her family toward self-support, to suggest, or at least connive, that the children be put to work early. . . . It is so easy, after one has been taking the industrial view for a long time, to forget the larger and more social claim. . . . The visitor does not realize what a cruel advantage the person who distributes charity has, when she gives advice. The manager in a huge mercantile establishment employing many children was able to show, during a child-labor investigation, that the only children under fourteen years of age in his employ were protégés, urged upon him by philanthropic ladies. . . . The boy who attempts prematurely to support his widowed mother may lower wages, add an illiterate member to the community, and arrest the development of a capable workingman. . . . Is it too much to hope that the insight which the contemporary visitor is gaining may save the administration of charity from certain reproaches which it has well deserved? . . .

The struggle for existence . . . sometimes leaves ugly marks on character, and the charity visitor finds the indirect results most mystifying. Parents who work hard and anticipate an old age when they can no longer earn, take care that their children shall expect to divide their wages with them from the very first. . . .

The writer knows one daughter of twenty-five who for six years has received two cents a week from the constantly falling wages which she earns in a large factory. Is it habit or virtue which holds her steady in this course? If love and tenderness had been substituted for parental despotism, would the mother have had enough affection, enough power of expression, to hold her daughter's sense of money obligation through all these years? . . .

The head of a family . . . has become blacklisted in a strike. He is not a very good workman, and this, added to his reputation as an agitator, keeps him out of work for a long time. The fatal result of being long out of work follows. He becomes less and less eager for it, and "gets a job" less and less frequently. In order to keep up his self-respect, and still more to keep up his wife's respect for him, he yields to the little self-deception that this prolonged idleness is due to his having been blacklisted, and he gradually becomes a martyr. . . . [The charity visitor] cannot, however, call him lazy and good-for-nothing, and denounce him as worthless. . . . She sees other workmen come to him for shrewd advice; she knows that he spends many more hours in the public library, reading good books, than the average workman has time to do. He has formed no bad habits, and has yielded only to those subtle temptations toward a life of leisure which come to the intellectual man. . . . He contributes a kind of intellectuality to his friends, and he has undoubted social value.

[The charity visitor] is reminded of a college friend of hers, who . . . was not going to allow her literary husband to write unworthy pot-boilers, for the sake of earning a living. "I insist that we shall live within my own income; that he shall not publish until he is ready, and can give his genuine message." . . . The action . . . had seemed noble to her, but . . . the workingman's wife . . . faced living on no income at all, or on the precarious income which she might be able to get together. . . . [The charity visitor] is utterly unwilling to condemn her while praising the friends of her own social position. . . . To be sure, she could give up visiting the family altogether, but she has become much interested in the progress of the crippled child, who eagerly anticipates her visits, and she also suspects that she will never know many finer women than the mother. She . . . goes on, bearing her perplexities as best she may.

The first impulse of our charity visitor is to be somewhat severe with her shiftless family for spending money on pleasures and indulging their children out of all proportion to their means. . . . But as the growth of juvenile crime becomes gradually understood, and as the danger of giving no legitimate and organized pleasure to the child becomes clearer, we remember that primitive man had games long before he cared for a house or for regular meals. There are certain boys in many city neighborhoods who form themselves into little gangs with leaders somewhat more intrepid than the rest. . . .

The excitement of a chase, the chances of competition, and the love of a fight are all centred in the outward display of crime. The parent who receives charitable aid, and yet provides pleasures for his child and is willing to indulge him in his play, is blindly doing one of the wisest things possible; and no one is more eager for playgrounds and vacation schools than the charity visitor whose experience has brought her to this point of view. . . .

[An elderly alcoholic] now lives a better life than she did, but she is still far from being a model old woman. Her neighbors are constantly shocked by the fact that she is supported and comforted by "a charity lady," while at the same time she occasionally "rushes the growler," scolding at the boys lest they jar her in her tottering walk. . . . The old lady herself is conscious of this criticism. . . . She tells them . . . that it is in order to prevent the divulgence of [a scandal] that the ministrations are continued.

Some of her perplexed neighbors accept this explanation. . . .
Doubtless many of them have a glimpse of the real state of affairs,
of the love and patience which minister to need irrespective of
worth. But the standard is too high for most of them, and it sometimes seems unfortunate to break down the second standard,
which holds that people who "rush the growler" are not worthy
of charity, and that there is a certain justice attained when they
go to the poorhouse. . . .

Just when our affection becomes large and real enough to care
for the unworthy among the poor as we would care for the unworthy among our own kin, is a perplexing question. To say that
it should never be so is a comment upon our democratic relations
to them which few of us would be willing to make. . . .

We sometimes say that our charity is too scientific, but we
should doubtless be much more correct in our estimate if we said
that it is not scientific enough. . . . Human motives have been
so long a matter of dogmatism that to act upon the assumption
that they are the result of growth, and to study their status with
an open mind and a scientific conscience, seems well-nigh impossible to us. A man who would hesitate to pronounce an opinion upon the stones lying by the wayside . . . will, without a
moment's hesitation, dogmatize about the delicate problems of
human conduct. . . .

In our charitable efforts, we think much more of what a man
ought to be than of what he is or of what he may become. . . .

We have learned to condemn unthinking, ill-regulated kind-
heartedness, and we take great pride in mere repression, much as
the stern parent tells the visitor below how admirably he is rearing
the child who is hysterically crying upstairs, and laying the foundation for future nervous disorders. The pseudo-scientific spirit,
or rather the undeveloped stage of our philanthropy, is, perhaps,
most clearly revealed in this tendency to lay stress on negative
action. . . .

For most of the years during a decade of residence in a settlement, my mind was sore and depressed over the difficulties of

the charitable relationship. The incessant clashing of ethical standards . . . made it seem reasonable to say that nothing could be
done until industrial conditions were made absolutely democratic.
The position of a settlement, which attempts at one and the same
time to declare its belief in this eventual, industrial democracy,
and to labor toward that end, to maintain a standard of living,
and to deal humanely and simply with those in actual want, often
seems utterly untenable and preposterous. Recently, however,
there has come to my mind the suggestion of a principle, that
while the painful condition of administering charity is the inevitable discomfort of a transition into a more democratic relation,
the perplexing experiences of the actual administration have a
genuine value of their own. . . . The social reformers who avoid
the charitable relationship with any of their fellow men take a
certain outside attitude toward this movement. They may analyze
it and formulate it; they may be most valuable and necessary, but
they are not essentially within it. The mass of men seldom move
together without an emotional incentive, and the doctrinaire, in
his effort to keep his mind free from the emotional quality, inevitably stands aside. He avoids the perplexity, and at the same
time loses the vitality.

The Hebrew prophet made three requirements from those who
would join the great forward-moving procession led by Jehovah.
"To love mercy," and at the same time "to do justly," is the difficult task. To fulfill the first requirement alone is to fall into the
error of indiscriminate giving, with all its disastrous results; to
fulfill the second exclusively is to obtain the stern policy of with-
holding, and it results in such a dreary lack of sympathy and
understanding that the establishment of justice is impossible.[18] It
may be that the combination of the two can never be attained save

[18] Many charity organization leaders felt similarly. John Glenn was
chairman of the Executive Committee of the Baltimore COS when he
declared, in referring to Amos Warner (R69, 70), general agent: "In
1887, we were very fortunate in getting an able man who had the two
qualities of the sympathetic and the detective, two qualities absolutely
necessary in anyone connected with charity. If the detective is superior,
the poor get too little help, if the sympathetic is in exuberance, it is de-
moralizing." *NCCC*, 1889, p. 239.

as we fulfill still the third requirement, "to walk humbly with God," which may mean to walk for many dreary miles beside the lowliest of his creatures . . . with the pangs and misgivings to which the poor human understanding is subjected whenever it attempts to comprehend the meaning of life.

XXVIII

THE SOCIAL WORKER AS EXPERT WITNESS

From their observations as settlement neighbors and charity visitors, social workers were becoming more and more aware that many social customs and practices in the economic structure were insuperable obstacles to individual self-sufficiency and maximum personal development, and hence to community well-being and progress. It was difficult to translate such convictions into permanent social change, but many reform movements were initiated or supported by social workers, who soon learned that their firsthand information was a most powerful weapon in social action. Of all efforts, none were more closely allied to the goals social workers were beginning to see than limitation of child labor, compulsory school attendance, and limitation of working hours. Their efforts were made much more effective when the Supreme Court ruled that social observation was as pertinent as previous legal ruling in determining constitutionality. The principle that individual freedom could be curbed to achieve the common good made social reform efforts feasible. *Muller* v. *Oregon* was a landmark, after which social case material was frequently accepted as pertinent evidence, and the social worker's special knowledge, the burdens of people, became recognized as one type of expert testimony.

73. Child Labor and Pauperism

Jane Addams, NCCC, 1903, pp. 114–21

Each age has of course its own temptations, and above all its own peculiar industrial temptations. . . . We are tempted as never before to use the labor of little children. . . .

It is a test of moral insight to be able to see that an affair of familiar intercourse and daily living may also be wrong. I have taken a Chicago street car on a winter's night in December at ten o'clock when dozens of little girls who have worked in the department stores all day are also boarding the cars. I know as many others do that these children will not get into their beds much before midnight, and that they will have to be up again early in the morning to go to their daily work. And yet I take my car almost placidly—I am happy to say not quite placidly—because I have seen it many times. Almost every day at six o'clock I see certain factories pouring out a stream of men and women and boys and girls. The boys and girls have a peculiar hue, a color so distinctive that any one meeting them on the street even on Sunday in their best clothes and mixed up with other children who go to school and play out of doors, can distinguish almost in an instant the children working in factories. There is also on their faces a something indescribable, a premature anxiety and sense of responsibility which we should declare pathetic if we were not used to it. . . .

It is said that the labor of these little children is needed for the support of widowed mothers. Some of us are sure that the widowed mother argument has been seriously overworked. . . .

In a certain manufacturing town it was discovered that 3,600 children on the school census roll were not to be found in the schools. . . . Out of the 3,600 children it was found that 1,100 were legitimately out of the public schools. . . . That left 2,500 to be accounted for, and . . . exactly 66 were the children of widows. . . . Only 23 [of the mothers] were in any way absolutely dependent on the wages of those children, which wages could be only supplementary at best. It was certainly a great deal better for the community, for the widows and the children, that grown up, vigorous people should take care of those 23 widows for a few years, until the children were old enough to go out to work and bring in a decent wage with which to support the family, and that the children should be saved from the breakdown, which premature labor so often implies. . . .

The men who first lose their places . . . in an industrial crisis, those who are the last to be taken on in times of industrial prosperity, who are inefficient and not very strong, men . . . whom the foreman is glad to get rid of in any way, are those who have never had sufficient training, and who curiously lack strength and vigor. How far is child labor responsible for this? . . . We have a municipal lodging house in Chicago largely filled with tramps. . . . We have been trying to see what connection can be genuinely established between premature labor and worn out men. It is surprising to find how many of them are tired to death of monotonous labor and begin to tramp in order to get away from it, just as a business man goes into the woods because he is worn out with the monotony of business life. This inordinate desire to get away from work seems to be connected with the fact that the men have started to work very early, before they had the physique to stand up to it, or the mental vigor with which to overcome its difficulties, or the moral stamina which makes a man stick to his work whether he likes it or not. But we cannot demand any of these things from a growing boy. A boy grows restless, his determination breaks down and he runs away. At least this seems to be true of many of the men who come to the lodging house. . . .

The hospitals are beginning to . . . trace certain diseases to the breakdown of the organs which were subjected to abnormal uses, before they were ready to bear it. I recall a tailor for whom the residents of Hull-House tried to get medical assistance. He died at the age of 33, and his death certificate bore the record of "premature senility" due to the fact that he had run a sewing machine since he was six years old. . . . No horse trainer would permit his colts to be so broken down.

Take the pauperizing effects of child labor on the parents. . . . It is difficult for a man who has grown up in out door life to adapt himself to the factory. . . .

So the parents drop out, and the children make the adaptation and remain, and you get the curious result of the parent of the household being more or less dependent on the earnings of the child. You will hear a child say, "My mother can't say nothing to me; I pay the rent:" or, "I can do what I please because I bring home the biggest wages." All this tends to break down the normal relation between parents and children. . . . That breaking down of normal relation of parent and child and the tendency to pauperize the parent is something to which we have no right to subject him. We ought to hold the parent up to the obligations which he would have fulfilled, had he remained in his early environment.

But the pauperization of society itself is the most serious charge. . . . [Industry] takes those boys and girls at the time when they ought to be at school. . . . The wages which are paid to these children of the poor are . . . wages of mere subsistence, so that the boy and girl take home barely what is necessary to eat and wear. The manufacturer gives him no real instruction and teaches him nothing beyond the habits of promptness and obedience. . . . The work at which the children are employed leads to no trade. By the time they are old enough to receive adult wages they are often sick of the whole business. Such an industry is parasitic on the future of the community. . . .

There is of course the argument that the effect on the wages of the normal adult is such as to point toward pauperism. . . .

Child labor . . . pauperizes the consumers. If I wear a garment which has been made in a sweat shop or a garment for which the maker has not been paid a living wage—a wage so small that her earnings had to be supplemented by the earnings of her husband and children, then I am in debt to the woman who made my cloak. I am a pauper and I permit myself to accept charity from the poorest people of the community. All that can be said against the parasitic character of sweating industries can be said against the parasitic character of child labor, with this difference that the latter robs the assets of the community, it uses up those resources which should have kept industry going on for many years. . . .

It pauperizes the community itself. . . . It debauches our moral sentiment, it confuses our sense of values, so that we learn to think that a bale of cheap cotton is more to be prized than a child properly nourished, educated and prepared to take his place in life.

74. *Limitations Imposed for the Benefit of All*

Muller v. *The State of Oregon*, 208 U.S., 416, 418–23
(U.S. Supreme Court Decision, 1908) [19]

Mr. Justice Brewer delivered the opinion of the court. . . .

We held in *Lochner* v. *New York*, 198 U.S. 45, that a law providing that no laborer shall be required or permitted to work in a bakery more than sixty hours in a week or ten hours in a day was not as to men a legitimate exercise of the police power of the State, but an unreasonable, unnecessary and arbitrary interference with the right and liberty of the individual to contract in relation to his labor, and as such was in conflict with, and void under, the Federal Constitution. That decision is invoked by plaintiff in error as decisive of the question before us. But this assumes that the difference between the sexes does not justify a different rule respecting a restriction of the hours of labor.

In patent cases counsel are apt to open the argument with a discussion of the state of the art. It may not be amiss, in the present case. . . . In the brief filed by Mr. Louis D. Brandeis . . . is a very copious collection of all these matters, an epitome of which is found in the margin.* . . .

The legislation and opinions referred to in the margin may not be, technically speaking, authorities, and in them is little or no discussion of the constitutional question . . . yet they are sig-

---

[19] The decision supported the constitutionality of an Oregon law limiting the hours of labor of women in laundries. The brief by Louis D. Brandeis and the decision in full were reprinted by the National Consumers League under title of *Women in Industry* (n.d.).

* The following legislation of the States impose restrictions . . . upon the hours of labor that may be required of women. . . .

In foreign legislation Mr. Brandeis calls attention to these statutes. . . .

Then follow extracts from over ninety reports . . . to the effect that long hours of labor are dangerous for women. . . . In many of these reports individual instances are given, tending to support the general conclusion. Perhaps the general scope and character of all these reports may be summed up in what an inspector for Hanover says: "The reasons for the reduction of the working day to ten hours—(*a*) the physical organization of women, (*b*) her maternal functions, (*c*) the rearing and the education of the children, (*d*) the maintenance of the home—are all so important and so far reaching that the need for such reduction need hardly be discussed."

nificant of a widespread belief that woman's physical structure, and the functions she performs in consequence thereof, justify special legislation restricting or qualifying the conditions under which she should be permitted to toil. Constitutional questions, it is true, are not settled by even a consensus of present public opinion. . . . At the same time, when a question of fact is debated and debatable, and the extent to which a special constitutional limitation goes is affected by the truth in respect to that fact, a widespread and long continued belief concerning it is worthy of consideration. We take judicial cognizance of all matters of general knowledge. . . .

That woman's physical structure and the performance of maternal functions place her at a disadvantage in the struggle for subsistence is obvious. . . . As healthy mothers are essential to vigorous offspring, the physical well-being of woman becomes an object of public interest and care in order to preserve the strength and vigor of the race. . . .

The limitations which this statute places upon her contractual powers . . . are not imposed solely for her benefit, but also largely for the benefit of all. Many words cannot make this plainer. The two sexes differ in structure of body . . . functions . . . physical strength . . . capacity for long-continued labor. . . . This difference justifies a difference in legislation and upholds that which is designed to compensate for some of the burdens which rest upon her. . . .

Affirmed

XXIX

EDUCATION FOR THE NEW PROFESSION

Increasingly systematic procedures for inducting new workers, both volunteer and paid, characterized both charity organization societies and settlements after 1895. There was less haphazardness and gullibility about the search for plausible theories which might be applied to improve the daily work. New workers were made to feel the value of reading the rapidly growing literature of the field.

For teaching, settlements continued to rely mainly on group staff discussions under experienced leadership, while COS leaders cast about for ways in which successful experience could be imparted to new apprentices through individual conference or formal lecture. The settlements tended to center their academic interests in the labor movement, and in wage, hour, and other economic reforms, while the COS and children's agencies concentrated on perfecting relief investigation, child removal and placement methods, and in securing better housing and compulsory education. Still, there was a great deal of overlapping; COS visitors often were residents in settlements, and settlement workers volunteered to take a few charity cases as friendly visitors. When any concerted reform campaign was under way, young enthusiasts from both movements could be counted upon to assist in arousing the active interests of their staffs and financial backers.

Thoughtful leaders who had had to educate themselves began to feel that more formal education would be needed if a rounded profession were to emerge. Of these, Mary Richmond was one of the most persistent and vocal. She foresaw many of the difficulties which still plague social work education: the diverse settings and specialties which may obscure basic common knowledge and goals; the danger of concentration on presently developed methodology, thereby depriving the worker of the breadth of knowledge which would equip him to meet unforeseen situations with thoughtful analysis and social inventiveness; the proper weighting of the program between practical experience and theoretical knowledge; the constant danger that technicians rather than truly professional people would emerge in the learning process; whether the administrative responsibility for the content of practical work should be lodged in a university or an agency.

Diversity in the origin of schools is illustrated by the experiences of New York, Boston, and Chicago.[20] In New York, by 1898, the COS was convinced that its occasional classes for friendly visitors were not adequate for persons who aspired to be fulltime staff members. Enthusiastically encouraged by Robert deForest, president, and Edward T. Devine, general secretary, the agency instituted a six weeks' summer course for university graduates and young practitioners. By 1904 experience with the summer course stimulated the Society to attempt a full-fledged school of philanthropy with a one-year course, to which a second year was added in 1911. There was no formal university affiliation until 1940, and the agency retained financial control of the school until 1950. In 1904, also mainly inspired by COS leaders, another full-time school was started in Boston with affiliations with both Simmons College and Harvard University. Meanwhile, a cooperative extension course, sponsored by the University of Chicago and the Chicago Commons settlement, had been started in 1901. In 1907 an independent institution, the Chicago School of Civics and Philanthropy, was established. This continued until 1920, when it became a graduate school of the University of Chicago.

[20] Elizabeth G. Meier, *A History of the New York School of Social Work* (New York: Columbia University Press, 1954), pp. 1–26; Alice Channing, "The Early Years of a Pioneer School," *Social Service Review*, XXVIII (1958), 430–40; Edith Abbott, "Twenty-one Years of University Education for the Social Services, 1920–41," *Social Service Review*, XV (1941), 670–72; Ernest V. Hollis and Alice L. Taylor, *Social Work Education in the United States* (New York: Columbia University Press, 1951), pp. 5–11.

At first, schools included economic and social reform theory and methods, but gradually they became preoccupied with teaching the principles and techniques of casework, particularly as it was practiced in private agencies. The Chicago School took leadership in stressing that administrative problems, especially in governmental social work, also should be included in the academic curriculum and field practice.

Naming and defining the profession, and locating its boundaries, were problems both to Mary Richmond and to Edith Abbott three decades later. However, both saw the need for experimental research and for stress on philosophical goals. Both also saw the need for practical experience or field instruction. How to make this most meaningful was the subject for much thought by both educators and agency personnel, and resulted in the development of the concept of educational supervision.

It was customary for social work students to get their practical experience in the usual work of an agency while they were going to school. Miss Abbott, however, envisioned the practice part of the curriculum as being under the direction of clinical instructors who could perfect educational methods in field practice. This represented a major step in distinguishing professional education in social work from apprentice training. The profession laid continuing stress on the importance of "learning while doing" after the completion of formal training, and this gave support to the efforts to perfect the unique tutorial program of supervision, in which the individual emotional and intellectual strengths of the student or staff worker were amplified and weaknesses overcome. Miss Hutchinson pointed out some of the problems in achieving individual progress toward mature professional responsibility and distinguished between what part of the supervisor's task might be educational, what therapeutic, and what administrative. (Some indication of the fact that the casework branch of the profession had become nearly monopolized by women is reflected in Miss Hutchinson's use of feminine pronouns to refer collectively to social workers.) The relationship between worker and supervisor was coming to be viewed as a crucial aspect in the development of a professional worker, by the end of the period covered by this book, and supervision was considered to be another specialized skill.

75. *The Need of a Training School in Applied Philanthropy*

Mary E. Richmond, *NCCC*, 1897, pp. 181–88

It is just twenty years since certain new ideas about the administration of charities came to have currency among us in the United States, and led to the founding of voluntary associations known as charity organization societies. The question now is how to get educated young men and women to make a life vocation of charity organization work. We must educate them. . . . Having created the demand . . . we should strive to supply it.

Moreover, we owe it to those who come after us that they be spared the groping and blundering by which we have acquired our own stock of experience. In these days of specialization . . . we have yet to establish our first training school for charity workers, or, as I prefer to call it, "Training School in Applied Philanthropy."

It is only gradually that the need of such a school has made itself apparent. . . . We have known for a long while that we wanted young people of high character and unusual attainments to devote themselves to a cause which has seemed to us of the first importance; but we are just beginning to understand that these young people have a right to demand something of us in return. Surely, they have a right to demand from the profession of applied philanthropy (we really have not even a name for it) that which they have a right to demand from any other profession—further opportunities for education and development, and, incidentally, the opportunity to earn a living.

Now the opportunities for education and development must always be extremely limited in any calling which has not established a professional standard, a certain fairly definite outline of what the practitioner in that field is expected to know and to be. We are all agreed, I think, that such a standard is desirable. But the matter about which we are likely to differ is this: Some of us will think that a training school is impracticable until we have acquired a professional standard, and others will think that we can never acquire a professional standard until we have the school. This latter is my own view, though I would avoid, if possible, the clamorous solicitude about it of a hen who has only one chick. It may be that we are not quite ready for the school, that such a plan is premature. If so, I urge that we should begin to move without delay in the direction, at least, of some definite system of training. . . .

An experienced worker has written to me that a difficulty in the way of a school of applied philanthropy on a sufficiently broad and inclusive basis would be the fact that our charity work has become so highly specialized. This is true, but our specialization is often essentially false. It is still as erratic as the specialization of the barber who pulls teeth. In the division of modern medicine into many special departments we find few such anomalies. We find, moreover, a broad field of knowledge which is common ground. If, for instance, a neurologist has occasion to confer with a surgeon, each can take it for granted that the other has mastered the elements of anatomy and physiology. But what can we take for granted in a similar case? If an agent of a relief society has occasion to confer with the head of a foundling asylum, is it not likely that the ends they have in view, that the principles underlying their work, that the very meanings which they attach to our technical terms, will prove to be quite at variance? What an incalculable gain to humanity when those who are doctoring social diseases in many departments of charitable work shall have found a common ground of agreement, and be forced to recognize certain established principles as underlying all effective service! Not immediately, of course, but slowly and steadily, such a common ground could be established, I believe, by a training school for our professional workers.

This question presents itself in different ways, according as one looks at it with reference to the needs of small or large towns, of public or private charities, of institutions or societies. Miss Anna L. Dawes who was the first one to suggest the need of a training school for our new profession,[21] conceived the idea after unavailing efforts to find a suitable superintendent for the charitable society of a small city. . . .

Working, as I do, in the charity organization society of a large city, the matter has presented itself to me in a somewhat different way. Like some other charity organization societies, we give our agents a preliminary training in charitable theory and practice; but this training specializes too soon, and our leaders have felt the need of a more intimate and sympathetic acquaintance on the part of our agents with child-saving work, almshouse work, reformatory work, care of defectives, and all the other branches of work represented at this Conference. We feel, of course, that every form of charity could be improved by a better knowledge of charity organization principles; but it seems to us of the first importance, also, that our agents should have a better all-round knowledge of other forms of charity. The school that is to be most helpful to our charity organization agents, therefore, must be established on a broad basis, and be prepared to train relief agents, child-saving agents, institution officials, and other charitable specialists. An important part of their training would be in that shoulder-to-shoulder contact which makes co-operation natural and inevitable.

I recognize that all this is very vague. Let me venture a step further. Before anything is settled about our training school in applied philanthropy save the bare fact that such a school is needed, we should search the country over for the right man to organize it. We need a university-trained man who is now

[21] Anna L. Dawes, "The Need of Training Schools for a New Profession," in *Proceedings of the International Congress of Charities, Correction and Philanthropy, Chicago, 1893* (Baltimore: Johns Hopkins University Press, 1893), Sec. VII, pp. 14–20. For the professional experiences which had led Mary Richmond to her conclusions, see "Mary Richmond 1861–1928," *The Family*, IX (1929), esp. 323–28; and Margaret E. Rich, "Mary E. Richmond: Social Worker," *Social Casework*, XXXIII (1952), 363–65.

engaged in charitable work, and who has had wide, practical experience in it. There are a few such men. . . . To succeed, he must believe that a training school for charity workers is necessary and practicable, and he must be guaranteed time, money, and entire freedom of action, together with the hearty support of our leading charitable specialists.

You will observe that, having found one man, it will become immediately necessary to find another, to furnish the money for this experiment. And this, to some, is like to be the rock on which our new craft might go to pieces. But consider the things that people do spend money for. . . . Why should our school go a-begging if we can once heartily agree that it is practicable?

Given the money and the head master, I can imagine that the latter's first care would be to make a detailed inquiry into the paid service demanded by our charities. His next would be to determine the school's location and affiliations. Probably he would choose a large city—the larger, the better; and it may be that he would seek connection with some institution of learning, though it should never be forgotten that emphasis is to be put on practical work rather than on academic requirements. Vital connection, therefore, would of necessity be made with the public and private charities of the city. Here students could observe the actual work of charity, and take part in it under the daily supervision of their instructors. Theory and practice would go hand in hand, and our best specialists would be engaged to deliver courses of lectures during the less busy months of the year. A two years' course would probably begin with general principles, and would specialize later, so that all regular students would take some of the courses together. Nor would the needs of special students, such as those who could spare only a few months, be overlooked; and probably volunteers who are interested in some particular charity would be glad to avail themselves of the school's opportunities.

I offer this plan in all its crudity, without attempting any elaboration, because I feel that it needs, and I trust will receive, the frankest criticism. . . . More important than any training in detail is the opportunity which a good school would offer for the development of higher ideals of charitable service. "Ideals are catching," someone has said. How important, then, to send our young people, our future workers, where ideals can be "caught"! A friend of mine is in the habit of saying, in praise of a certain college, that its graduates are never ashamed to acknowledge their ignorance, that the school has given all its pupils a certain candid habit of thought. To give our professional charity workers better habits of thought and higher ideals, this should be the chief aim of our School of Applied Philanthropy.

76. A Training Class in Applied Philanthropy

COS of New York City, *16th Annual Report*, 1898, p. 22

A training class in applied philanthropy, consisting of 27 members, mainly college graduates, was organized under the immediate direction of the assistant secretary,[22] and with the oversight of a special committee of the Central Council. No charge for tuition was made, but members of the class were required to enter the service of the Society for a period of six weeks (June 20–July 30, 1898), performing such duties as might be assigned, which were, however, selected in all instances for their educational value. At 8:30 each morning the class met for reports by members and a discussion of such reports. At 9 A.M. there was usually an address by some specialist, frequently the chief executive of an important charitable society or institution from New York City and vicinity, of [sic] from more distant cities. Among those from a distance who gave generous support to this enterprise were Mrs. Glendower Evans, of Boston, who spoke upon the reformation of boys, describing especially the plans of the Lyman school; Mr. Frank B. Sanborn, of Concord, Mass., on the curability of the insane; Mrs. J. H. Johnston, of Sherburn, Mass., Superintendent of the Woman's Prison and Reformatory; and Professor Samuel McCune Lindsay, of the University of Pennsylvania. Dr. Lindsay

[22] Philip Ayres (R68, n. 45). Ayres met Mary Richmond's specifications of a university man with practical experience. Edward T. Devine, made director in 1904, had received the degree of Doctor of Philosophy from the University of Pennsylvania and was general secretary of the COS.

spoke of the difficulties and advantages of unity in philanthropic work.

Many of the progressive and instructive institutions in New York were visited, with careful observations of their method. At Sing Sing prison a careful explanation was given by the warden. The institutions on Blackwell's and Randall's islands were visited, beside several of the public and private homes for children and other dependents. Several of the addresses and of the reports presented by members are of such permanent value as to justify publication in scientific journals or as separate leaflets. A portion of each day was occupied in the assigned office duties, including investigations for the major and minor reports required from each student, and ordinary work of the Society for families. The immediate results of this experimental course are all that was anticipated. Permanent positions have been secured by some, others have gained valuable material for the university classroom, while still others have entered upon special lines of inquiry, which will be prosecuted in the future. It is hoped that from this beginning a plan of professional training in applied philanthropy may be developed which will raise the standard of qualification and of usefulness throughout the entire field of charitable work. The Society cherishes the conviction that important results to the philanthropic work not only of New York and vicinity, but also of the country at large, would follow the endowment of a school to which the best minds would be attracted, and from which specialists in the various forms of charitable and correctional work could be entered successfully upon their respective careers in life.

77. *To Help Suffering Humanity Rightly*

COS of New York City, *20th Annual Report*, 1902,
pp. 39–50

The Committee on Philanthropic Education, having conducted for five years the Summer School in Philanthropic Work, feel that the time has come for a more extended course. The Summer School has become a general meeting place for experienced workers from different cities who share their knowledge with the young men and women just starting out in their life work, who come from different charitable socites in the several States and cities, and from the universities. It has made for itself a distinct place and will be continued; but within the short space of six weeks it cannot give adequate training to those who would engage in charitable work and undertake the task of adjusting unfortunate families more perfectly to their complex environment.

The committee has therefore issued an appeal for $100,000, with which to establish a training school for charitable work, similar in some respects to the schools that prepare for other professions, by which under experienced guides new workers may touch the poor helpfully from the start, and not gain their experience by their blunders in trying to help the sick and the needy.

Aside from the necessity to help suffering humanity rightly, there is an important financial aspect to this subject. The New York State Board of Charities has called attention to the fact that the societies and institutions of the State reporting to it expend twenty million dollars annually, and that probably ten million dollars more are expended through the purses of private individuals, churches, etc., not reported, making a total of thirty million dollars in one State. The expenditures in Massachusetts, Ohio, Michigan, and other States are probably nearly as large, while the sum for the whole country has never been estimated. Charity is a vast social engine, and should have competent and trained people to work it. A well equipped School of Philanthropy has become a necessity. . . .

The following two years' course has been worked out by the committee, and will be established as soon as means can be secured for the purpose. By resolution of the Central Council of the Charity Organization Society in New York City, it will receive funds for the establishment of a Training School in Philanthropy and use them exclusively for it.[23]

[23] The full-time school was launched with special donations for the year 1904, but in November John S. Kennedy provided securities yielding an income of $10,000 yearly and in 1911 willed $1,000,000 to the school. Meier, *History*, pp. 21, 41.

Proposed Two Years' Course in Philanthropic Work

During the first year, three months each to the following:

I. The Care and Treatment of Needy Families in their Homes.

II. Child-saving, including the Care of Destitute or Neglected, Delinquent and Defective Children.

III. Medical Charities; the Institutional Care of Adults; and Neighborhood Improvement, such as Tenement Reform and Social Settlement Work.

During the second year [24] a special study of some branch of philanthropic work, with a view to entering it as a life work, as Charity Organization, Relief Work, Placing-out of Children, Church Work, Care of the Feebleminded, Care for Prisoners.

The purpose of the course is to ground the student in the teachings of experience and in the principles of helpfulness in order that he may be ready with keen sympathy and uncrystallized mind to deal with every case of need.

78. The University and Social Welfare

Edith Abbott,[25] *Social Welfare and Professional Education* (Chicago: University of Chicago Press, 1931), pp. 12–17

The work of a good professional school in this field falls into three divisions: (1) the academic curriculum; (2) the clinical social work or field work; and (3) social research—all three of which can be strengthened chiefly by university help.

The academic curriculum of most of the professional schools is now poor and slight and covers in many schools only the various aspects of a single field—case work. None of us will deny the importance of case work. It is as necessary to the social worker

---

[24] The second year was not established until 1911. Other schools were also moving to a second year about that time.

[25] Edith Abbott was dean of the Graduate School of Social Service Administration, University of Chicago. This address was given at the 161st Convocation of the University. For Miss Abbott's place in the total development of social work education, see Elizabeth Wisner, "Edith Abbott's Contributions to Social Work Education," *Social Service Review,* XXXII (1958), 1–10.

as, for example, the study of contracts is to the law student. But case work is very far from being the whole story. There are great reaches of territory, some of them as yet unexplored and stretching out to a kind of no man's land—the great fields of public charitable organization, of law and government in relation to social work, of social economics, of social insurance, and modern social politics—all of which are required if the social worker is to be an efficient servant of the state. In these fields the independent schools will always be limited. It is in the university where there is well-organized graduate work not merely in one, but in all, of the social sciences and where there are co-operative relations with the law and medical schools that the great schools of social welfare will ultimately be developed. At the present time, particularly in the non-university schools, the student too often becomes a routine technician—sometimes a clever technician—but still a technician and not a scientific person "with the love of knowledge and the use of the tools of learning."

The second division of the work of the schools, which is clinical social work or field work, is very imperfectly understood and used at the present time. Social service field work is in many respects like the bedside study of medicine for, like modern medical students, our future social workers must be prepared to assume the grave responsibilities of interfering with the lives of human beings. For the practice of social welfare demands character as well as education; and proper service can be given only by those who are trained for the responsibilities of action. . . . [The] power of making or breaking a family is like the physician's power over life and death and calls for the same disciplined understanding and the same capacity for competent observation, keen scientific judgment, courage for swift decisions and effective action. The educational use of field work possibilities and responsibilities will not be realized until this work is directed by social workers who are full-time members of university faculties as the hospitals are conducted by the university medical faculties today.

The third division of the work of the professional schools should be social research but most of the schools have had neither the funds nor the staff to make any provision for this important method of instructing professional students and advancing the knowledge of social welfare. Scientific data are needed in many unexplored social fields in which preventive methods must be found of meeting and dealing with the social evils that now lie before us. The faculty and the students of a professional school of social work should be together engaged in using the great method of experimental research which we are just beginning to discover in our professional educational program and which should be as closely knit into the work of the good school of social welfare as research has been embodied in the program of the modern medical school. . . .

It is clear that the modern university has a great opportunity before her. On all sides the chronicle points to the state's need of help in the social welfare services. Only with university leadership will the professional schools of social welfare come to see that their field of service lies not merely in meeting the immediate personnel needs of the social agencies but in devoting themselves to the larger task of developing and defining the profession itself.

79. *Supervision in Social Casework*

Dorothy Hutchinson, *The Family*, XVI (1935), 44–47

Supervision in its performance and in its demands is neither dull nor shop-worn. . . . Its quality has the power to determine self-development and, indirectly, the kind of service secured to our communities. . . . As a teaching process it has grown up out of common practice. . . .

We have heard a good deal about the worker-client relationship —of the client's right and freedom to keep his own problem rather than having it taken out of his hand, and of his right to participate. The philosophy behind this represents an advance over the old one in which we as case workers took full responsibility for our clients and assumed we had all the answers to life. The relationship between supervisor and worker has perhaps shown the same trend. We, as supervisors, used to take full responsibility for our workers and for their case work. We were not clear about anything except that the responsibility fell heavily upon our shoulders. Many of us still feel this responsibility and because it becomes such a weight we are not free to give what we have of other and more essential qualities—such as teaching ability, leadership, and increased knowledge.

What is this relationship between supervisor and worker? . . . It would seem that the most important and outstanding factor is responsibility for the worker's growth. Of course some workers will never grow . . . they will never make any creative contribution—with or without supervisors. Perhaps this class of workers will disappear as we become more skilled in selecting staff members and as the community in general becomes more aware of the value of training in social work.

The supervisor-worker relationship should be a growing dynamic one in which each is free. The supervisor is essentially a leader and a teacher of workers and does not impose herself or her ideas on the worker. She assumes responsibility for the worker in that it is her job to know and find out what is going on in the worker's mind, what the worker really thinks and feels. It is her responsibility to understand the worker well enough to know why she does certain things and why she is blocked on others. . . .

If we assume responsibility for a worker's growth we automatically assume a teaching responsibility toward her. And this function is closely allied with and built upon a free relationship with the worker. Being teachers implies that we know more than those we are teaching and also that we have a capacity to impart what we know.

Our teaching of workers is achieved largely through association. . . . Through a wider knowledge and enlarged experience the worker learns to think and feel about clients . . . as the supervisor does. . . . She begins, often, with a judgmental attitude toward people; she grows into an attitude of understanding. This is a big responsibility for supervisors. It means that, despite pressures, we need to find time to read, to think, to take courses, and to discuss problems among ourselves. Supervisors need to grow even more than their workers and herein, it would seem, lies their greatest responsibility. . . .

Just how much supervisors should go into the personal lives of their workers is a question for discussion. Just how much they can keep from doing this is another. . . .

Within the supervisor-worker relationship there are two particular dangers for supervisors: the danger of over-protection, and the danger of authority. . . .

Supervision cannot be made a stereotyped affair applicable to all supervisors and all workers. . . . It will . . . always be an individual adjustment between one certain supervisor and one certain worker.

XXX
PROFESSIONAL ORGANIZATION

There had been difference of opinion whether development of professional methods, standards of competence, and formal professional organization should precede or follow the establishment of academic training. As it turned out, it was chiefly the teachers and graduates of the new schools who felt the need for a different kind of occupational association than the National Conference of Social Work provided. The desire for concerted action on the part of career workers centered in two areas: efforts to recruit able college graduates to the rapidly growing occupation; and efforts to define the role of social work in relation to other professions.

The desire to be "professional" received a tremendous impetus when the famed authority on graduate education, Dr. Abraham Flexner, questioned the status of social work. Not all social work leaders accepted his criteria, but enough did that moves to form a professional brotherhood and to perfect a transmissible technique gained momentum.

In 1912 the Intercollegiate Bureau of Occupations, an employment service for college graduates, established a special department to place volunteer and paid social workers. Agencies found it so helpful that when, in 1917, there was question as to its future financial stability, it was converted into a membership body of practicing social workers and employing agencies. This National Social Workers' Exchange provided a nucleus of people interested in discussing such problems as working conditions, standards of preparation, and salaries.

Social workers in hospitals and clinics, constantly aware of the contribution a professional society made to doctors and to medical advance, organized the American Association of Medical Social Workers in 1918. Other social work groups began to wish for something similar. The issue seemed to be whether professional organization would be based on the peculiar problems of each special segment, or on the common interests of all parts of the rapidly expanding, sprawling, profession.

After a year of study, the National Social Workers Exchange decided to become an all-embracing organization which would direct its attention to such common problems as recruitment, ethics, professional standards, levels of remuneration, and means for securing better communication between branches of the profession. In another year the name of the Exchange was changed to American Association of Social Workers.

There was much uncertainty as to who would be included, whether breadth or specificity was to be sought, whether active practice or training should be the criterion of membership. We give here an account of the first membership meeting as it was published in a small mimeographed bulletin, only a few copies of which are known to have been preserved. Organizational meetings throughout the country debated some of the crucial decisions.

The first general publication of the new professional brotherhood was a descriptive booklet on the profession designed for recruitment; something similar has been available ever since. Progress of the group in thinking of itself as a professional body during the first year is indicated by differences in the forewords (R83, 84); and through the years changes in the way the profession hopes it appears to the public have continued to be so reflected.

Almost immediately, questions concerning ethical obligations and proper professional etiquette arose. One institute group had attempted to formulate how a social caseworker should conduct himself, while officers of the Association contributed an analysis of social work for an interprofessional symposium.[26]

Many perplexing questions remained. One of the most baffling concerned who was to make the ultimate decisions in practice: Did the practitioner directly in contact with the recipient of

[26] Graham Romeyn Taylor and Mary van Kleeck, "The Professional Organization of Social Work," *Annals* of the American Academy of Political and Social Science, CI (1922), 158–68.

service assume final responsibility, or was he still to carry out instructions of an executive or board? Were social workers to be "agents" of the well-to-do, "mediators" to summon other professions, or "social engineers" to build independently and creatively in the field of human relationships?

80. Is Social Work a Profession?

Abraham Flexner,[27] *NCCC*, 1915, pp. 576-90

The word *profession* or *professional* may be loosely or strictly used. In its broadest significance it is simply the opposite of the word *amateur*. . . . Social work is from this point of view a profession for those who make a full-time job of it; it is not a profession for those who incidentally contribute part of themselves to active philanthropy. . . .

The question put to me is a more technical one. The term profession, strictly used, as opposed to business or handicraft, is a title of peculiar distinction, coveted by many activities. Thus far it has been pretty indiscriminately used. . . .

To make a profession in the genuine sense, something more than a mere claim or an academic degree is needed. There are certain objective standards that can be formulated. . . . In this narrower and eulogistic sense, what are the earmarks of a profession? . . .

Would it not be fair to mention as the first mark of a profession that the activities involved are essentially intellectual in character? Manual work is not necessarily excluded; the use of tools is not necessarily excluded. . . . But in neither of these instances does the activity derive its essential character from its instruments. . . . The real character of the activity is the thinking process. . . .

The responsibility of the practitioner is at once large and personal. The problems to be dealt with are complicated; the facilities at hand, more or less abundant and various; the agent—physician,

[27] Abraham Flexner, then assistant secretary, General Education Board, New York City, had made a penetrating study of medical education in 1910 which already had brought about major changes. For the paper on social work he had read extensively in *NCCC* and in social work school catalogues and had interviewed leading social workers.

engineer, or preacher—exercises a very large discretion as to what he shall do. He is not under order; though he be coöperating with others, though the work be team work, rather than individual work, his responsibility is not less complete and not less personal. This quality of responsibility follows from the fact that . . . the thinker takes upon himself a risk. . . .

Professions would fall short of attaining intellectuality if they employed mainly or even largely knowledge and experience that is generally accessible—if they drew, that is, only on the usually available sources of information. They need to resort to the laboratory and the seminar for a constantly fresh supply of facts; and it is the steady stream of ideas, emanating from these sources, which keeps professions from degenerating into mere routine, from losing their intellectual and responsible character. The second criterion of the profession is therefore its learned character, and this characteristic is so essential that the adjective *learned* really adds nothing to the noun profession.

Professions . . . are in the next place definitely practical. [The professional man's] processes are essentially intellectual; his raw material is derived from the world of learning; thereupon he must do with it a clean-cut, concrete task. . . .

Each of the unmistakable professions . . . possesses a technique capable of communication through an orderly and highly specialized educational discipline. . . .

A profession is a brotherhood—almost, if the word could be purified of its invidious implications, a caste. Professional activities are so definite, so absorbing in interest, so rich in duties and responsibilities, that they completely engage their votaries. The social and personal lives of professional men and of their families thus tend to organize around a professional nucleus. A strong class consciousness soon develops. . . .

Under the pressure of public opinion, professional groups have more and more tended to view themselves as organs contrived for the achievement of social ends rather than as bodies formed to stand together for the assertion of rights or the protection of interests and principles. . . . Devotion to well-doing is thus more and more likely to become an accepted mark of professional activity; and as this development proceeds, the pecuniary interest of the individual practitioner of a given profession is apt to yield gradually before an increasing realization of responsibility to a larger end.

Let me now review briefly the six criteria which we have mentioned; professions involve essentially intellectual operations with large individual responsibility; they derive their raw material from science and learning; this material they work up to a practical and definite end; they possess an educationally communicable technique; they tend to self-organization; they are becoming increasingly altruistic in motivation. . . .

The trained nurse is making a praiseworthy and important effort to improve the status of her vocation. . . . It is to be observed, however, that the responsibility of the trained nurse is neither original nor final. . . . Her function is instrumental, though not, indeed, just mechanically instrumental. In certain relations she is perhaps almost a collaborator. Yet, when all is said, it is the physician who observes, reflects, and decides. . . . Can an activity of this secondary nature be deemed a profession? . . .

With medicine, law, engineering, literature, painting, music, we emerge from all clouds of doubt into the unmistakable professions. Without exception, these callings involve personally responsible intellectual activity; they derive their material immediately from learning and science; they possess an organized and educationally communicable technique; they have evolved into definite status, social and professional, and they tend to become, more and more clearly, organs for the achievement of large social ends. . . .

Is social work a profession in the technical and strict sense of the term? . . .

The activities . . . are obviously intellectual, not mechanical, not routine in character. The worker must possess fine powers of analysis and discrimination, breadth and flexibility of sympathy, sound judgment, skill in utilizing whatever resources are available, facility in devising new combinations. These operations are assuredly of intellectual quality.

I confess I am not clear, however, as to whether this responsibility is not rather that of a mediating than an original agency. . . . The social worker takes hold of a case, that of a disintegrating family, a wrecked individual, or an unsocialized industry. Having localized his problem, having decided on its particular nature, is he not usually driven to invoke the specialized agency, professional or other, best equipped to handle it? There is illness to be dealt with—the doctor is needed; ignorance requires the school; poverty calls for the legislator, organized charity, and so on. To the extent that the social worker mediates the intervention of the particular agent or agency best fitted to deal with the specific emergency which he has encountered, is the social worker himself a professional or is he the intelligence that brings this or that profession or other activity into action? The responsibility for specific action thus rests upon the power he has invoked. The very variety of the situations he encounters compels him to be not a professional agent so much as the mediator invoking this or that professional agency. . . .

The collaboration of different professions in the doing of specific tasks is a characteristic feature of latter-day organization. Architects, engineers, sanitarians, lawyers, and educators coöperate in the building of a school or a tenement. But it is to be noted that this is a division of labor among equals, each party bearing, subject to general consent, primary responsibility for his particular function, the definiteness of that function and the completeness of the responsibility differing, I take it, from the function and responsibility of the social worker under similar conditions.

Consideration of the objects of social work leads to the same conclusion. . . . It appears not so much a definite field as an aspect of work in many fields. An aspect of medicine belongs to social work, as do certain aspects of law, education, architecture, etc. . . . The scope of interest . . . [includes] the improvement of living and working conditions in the community, the relief or prevention of distress whether individual or social in origin. . . . We observed that professions need to be limited and definite in scope, in order that practitioners may themselves act; but the high degree of specialized competency required for action and conditioned on limitation of area cannot possibly go with the width of scope characteristic of social work. A certain superficiality of attainment, a certain lack of practical ability, necessarily characterize such breadth of endeavor. If, however, we conceive the social worker, not so much as the agent grappling with this or that situation, but rather as controlling the keyboard that summons, coöperates with and coördinates various professional specialists, this breadth of attainment is very far from being a matter for reproach. It imposes upon the social worker the necessity of extreme caution, of considerable modesty, because in these days a considerable measure of certainty is possible to any one person only within a restricted field. Would it not be at least suggestive therefore to view social work as in touch with many professions rather than as a profession in and by itself? . . .

Lack of specificity in aim affects seriously the problem of training social workers. Professions that are able to define their objects precisely can work out educational procedures capable of accomplishing a desired result. But the occupations of social workers are so numerous and diverse that no compact, purposefully organized educational discipline is feasible. . . .

Let me add, however, that what I have just said does not imply that schools of philanthropy are superfluous. Looking at them as educational ventures, I suspect that they are as yet feeling about for their proper place and function. There is an obvious convenience, however, in having an institution which focuses as far as possible the main lines of social activity; an obvious advantage in having an institution that emphasizes the practical side of what might otherwise be more or less academic instruction in many branches. But instruction of this kind is not exactly professional in character; it supplements and brings to bear what good students might well acquire in the course of their previous higher education.

If social work fails to conform to some professional criteria, it very readily satisfies others. No question can be raised as to the source from which the social worker derives his material—it comes obviously from science and learning, from economics, ethics, religion and medicine; nor is there any doubt on the score of the rapid evolution of a professional self-consciousness, as these annual conferences abundantly testify. Finally, in the one respect in which most professions still fall short, social work is fairly on the same level as education, for the rewards of the social worker are in his own conscience and in heaven. His life is marked by devotion to impersonal ends and his own satisfaction is largely through the satisfactions procured by his efforts for others.

There is, however, another side even to this aspect of professional activity. Professions may not be cultivated for mere profit. Neither, let me add, can they develop on the basis of volunteer or underpaid service. . . .

A profession must find a dignified and critical means of expressing itself in the form of a periodical which shall describe in careful terms whatever work is in progress; and it must from time to time register its more impressive performances in a literature of growing solidity and variety. To some extent the evolution of social work towards the professional status can be measured by the quality of publication put forth in its name. . . .

At the moment, therefore, it may be—observe that I am not endeavoring to be very positive—it may be that social work will gain if it becomes uncomfortably conscious that it is not a profession in the sense in which medicine and engineering are professions; that if medicine and engineering have cause to proceed with critical care, social work has even more. . . .

But, after all, what matters most is professional spirit. All activities may be prosecuted in the genuine professional spirit. . . . The unselfish devotion of those who have chosen to give themselves to making the world a fitter place to live in can fill social work with the professional spirit and thus to some extent lift it above all the distinctions which I have been at such pains to make. In the long run, the first, main and indispensable criterion of a profession will be the possession of professional spirit, and that test social work may, if it will, fully satisfy.

81. First Constitution of the American Association of Social Workers

New York: The Association, 1921 [28]

Article II. Purpose

Its purpose shall be to serve as an organization whose members, acting together, shall endeavor through investigation and conference to develop professional standards in social work; (2) to encourage adequate preparation and professional training; (3) to recruit new workers; and (4) to develop a better adjustment between workers and positions in social work. To this end it may maintain a central employment exchange for men and women in social work, and such other departments as are necessary for its purpose. No department shall be conducted for financial profit.

Article III. Membership

Membership in the American Association of Social Workers shall consist of persons professionally engaged in social work, either on a salaried or volunteer basis, such membership to continue as long as annual dues are paid. Membership shall be of three kinds:

1. Active membership: Any individual who is eligible for membership may become an active member on the payment of annual dues of $3.00.

2. Sustaining membership: Any individual who is eligible for membership may become a sustaining member on the payment of annual dues of $5.00–$10.00.

3. Institutional membership: A social agency may be admitted

[28] The antecedent of this constitution was a similar one adopted by the Social Workers' Exchange in their reorganization meeting Nov. 6, 1920 (R82). This version was adopted by the First Annual Meeting of the reorganized Exchange at Milwaukee, June 27, 1921, when the official name was changed to American Association of Social Workers. Both constitutions are now in the archives of the NASW, New York City.

to institutional membership on payment of a minimum annual contribution of $10.00, with higher rates in accordance with service as directed by the executive committee. Each institution or organization subscribing to institutional membership may name one person to represent it in the Association, who shall have one vote and all other privileges as a member. Institutional membership entitles subscribing agencies to the use of the employment service and such other share in the activities of the Association as shall be prescribed by the Executive Committee.

82. A Professional Association Is Launched

The Compass, bulletin of the National Social Workers' Exchange (after June, 1921, the American Association of Social Workers) I, No. 1 [1920; mimeo.], 1–2; I, No. 4 [1921], 3; I, No. 5 [1921], 3; I, No. 6 [1921], 3

THE NEW EXCHANGE

Two years ago the National Social Workers' Exchange became in spirit a cooperative guild of social workers. Within the past month it has changed its Constitution and expanded its program in order to make that spirit an increasingly accomplished fact. For it has become evident that the shortage of social workers, and their aspirations for their profession together with the lack of popular appreciation of their function, were making pressingly necessary the translation of their cooperative spirit into cooperative action. . . .

THE NOV. 6TH MEETING. . . .

Perhaps you felt as did one prominent social worker, "that it marked a milestone in the progress of social work." Two hundred people heard the plans which had been formulated, discussed them and finally amended the Constitution and adopted a program of activity which it is hoped will make for a larger vision and a closer unity.

NEW FUNCTIONS PLANNED

Under the new plans for 1920–21, the Placement Department

of the Exchange will retire from the center of the stage and join hands co-equally with three other departments. . . .

Recruiting Service . . . The piece-meal method of getting new blood into social work from the colleges and other fields, has shown itself inadequate. . . .

Job Analysis . . . An essential one to an organization that is going to work for progress and expansion. . . .

Information Service . . . Collect, compile and distribute vocational information regarding the whole field of social work. . . .

A NEW KIND OF CONFERENCE. . . .

A conference on "The professional outlook for social workers" . . . is to give social workers themselves an opportunity to take stock of their present status and get a glimpse of the direction in which they are going. . . .

Speakers will be Mr. George W. Alger, a prominent member of the New York Bar, Mr. W. Frank Persons, Vice-Chairman of the American Red Cross and Miss Frances Perkins, a member of the New York State Industrial Commission. Mr. Alger will tell something about the legal profession, its development and organization, in order that social workers may compare their own status to that of the other professions. Both Miss Perkins and Mr. Persons will tell of developments within social work, the opportunities, standards and requirements which give the group claim to recognition. . . .

Simultaneous group conferences will be held. . . . The Committee is grouping social workers on the basis of function. There will be four groups. 1. Case Work, Porter R. Lee, Chairman. . . . Those in the Child Helping field, Family Social Work, Social Psychiatry, etc. 2. Group work, Joseph K. Hart, Chairman. . . . Settlements, Community Organization, Recreation, etc. 3. Civic Betterment, Raymond V. Ingersoll, Chairman. . . . Municipal Reform, Public Health, Housing, etc. 4. Industry, Frances Perkins, Chairman. . . . Industrial Investigators, Personnel Managers, Public Officials.

HIGH LIGHTS FROM THE NEW YORK CONFERENCE

Have we, as social workers, any common purpose? Can we meet together and set standards for ourselves, the qualifications which are requisite to practice what is called social work? Does there exist any public opinion concerning social work and social workers which is safe, which is constant, which is uplifting, with our own group? Are we social engineers or are we just hired men and women whose ideals and standards are outside our own keeping?   W. FRANK PERSONS [29]

The time has come when, if the work of the social worker is to be done well and to be permanent and if the personnel is to be maintained without constantly changing, there must be professional standards which are made not by the people who employ social workers but by the social workers themselves. I think the organization should not be an organization of executives but should be an organization which very definitely takes in every last rank and file of social workers. There has been a good deal of handing down in social work. I believe that organization would be extraordinarily helpful in promoting the work which we hope to see accomplished in this generation and the next. . . .

Personally, I feel that in professionalized social work there will be a certain loss, but there will be a much larger gain and we must face the loss for the sake of the gain. The time will, I think, never come when social work will become commercialized.   FRANCES PERKINS [30]

It is not reasonable to expect the public to have a better opinion of us and our standards than we have of ourselves. We have to respect our standards and ourselves before the public will do so. In no sentimental way, but just with the hardest kind of hard work, we have to hammer out our standards. We need a terminology; our terms are not well understood even amongst ourselves. We need a code of ethics; something to abide by, or else we will lose social standing.

MARY RICHMOND [31]

[29] W. Frank Persons had just been appointed vice chairman of the American Red Cross in charge of domestic operations. During the war he had been director general of civilian relief for the Red Cross. Previously he had been director of general work in the New York COS.

[30] Frances Perkins had been in the Bureau of Research in the New York School, 1909–10; executive secretary, Consumers League, New York; and in 1921 was commissioner of the New York State Industrial Commission. She was Secretary of Labor, 1933–45.

[31] Mary Richmond had been director of the Charity Organization Department, Russell Sage Foundation, since 1909 (R71, 75, 91, 92).

I think there is a growing and alarming tendency on the part of increasingly powerful groups of people to treat social workers with a certain kind of contempt, as though they were begging for themselves, and have the poor as an excuse. Unless there is a practical application of the discussion tonight, there is likely to be a life and death struggle for the more difficult kinds of social work.   MRS. FLORENCE KELLEY [32]

How can you describe a social worker so that he can be distinguished from some one else? What does a social worker know? What are the particulars in which a social worker is especially proficient? What does he know that the ordinary run of educated men and women, either in or out of other professions, do not know? We have talked about standards and qualifications. Those standards and qualifications are ours to work on.   PORTER R. LEE [33]

PHILADELPHIA HOLDS A CONFERENCE. . . .

Dr. Watson Defines Social Work . . . Dr. Frank Watson of the Pennsylvania School for Social Service [34] put squarely up to the audience the question which Mr. de Schweinitz [35] raised at the outset, "What are we and where are we going." After giving a number of definitions, some which were broad and sweeping in their scope, and others which were quite the opposite in the narrowness of their interpretation, and summarizing the results of a thesis on the subject prepared by Miss Alice S. Cheney, of the Pennsylvania School, Dr. Watson suggested the following definition which had been worked out by a group in Philadelphia:

Social work is the science and art of increasing social welfare by adjusting individuals to their physical and social environment and this environment to their needs, i.e., it aims to raise the standard of individual development and of social organization in order to secure

[32] Florence Kelley had been general secretary of the National Consumers League since 1899. A graduate of Northwestern University Law School, she had been a resident of Hull House and of Henry Street Settlement and had taken leadership in many campaigns on behalf of labor reform (R73).

[33] Porter Lee had been teaching at the New York School since 1907 and had been director since 1917.

[34] Frank D. Watson was director of the school, and professor of sociology and social work at Haverford College. He had formerly been on the faculty of the New York School.

[35] Karl de Schweinitz, then general secretary of the Family Society of Philadelphia, presided at the Philadelphia meeting.

greater joy and freedom for all. It is based on applied science, requires technical training and skill and like most other professions depends on personality, character and love or religion in its broadest sense.

83. The Profession of Social Work: I

Foreword, *The Profession of Social Work* (New York: National Social Workers' Exchange Committee on Vocational Information; No. I, 1921), p. 2

The importance of social work has been stressed too spectacularly in the last decade to seem to require further emphasis. Confronted by their greatest trial, the peoples of the earth have been fervently roused to the significance of the work of this embryonic profession. Freely and devotedly, they have subscribed thousands of hours of their time and millions of dollars of their resources to be spent under the guidance of social workers and for the accomplishment of tasks which social workers had ever held at heart.

Such recognition constitutes a challenge! Simply told, it is this.

So long as there remain in the world people who have complicated social relationships—to say nothing of inadequate advantages for the elementary pursuit of happiness—so long should social work summon to its task the elite of the army of young men and young women now moving forward into the professions.

Thus only can it keep the faith with which the last decade has endowed it.

84. The Profession of Social Work: II

Foreword by Paul T. Beisser, *Social Work: an Outline of Its Professional Aspects* (New York: AASW.; No. II, 1922), p. 2

Out of a ferment of activities, ideals and traditions, the profession of social work is gradually emerging. From the simple conceptions of half a century ago, through the later "reform" period, to the present threshold of scientific method and professional practice, social work has developed with ever broadening viewpoints and increasingly effective service.

To sketch briefly the fundamental outlines of this emergence is the purpose of this pamphlet. Confusion we still have, but even now the essential characteristics, the opportunities and the problems of this, the newest profession, increasingly lend themselves to analysis and exposition.

This pamphlet marks a step forward, we believe, from "The Profession of Social Work," published by the Association last year. Similarly, we may expect that next year and the years following will give us new material, new ideas around which to develop a still clearer conception of social work, its technical divisions, its vocational attributes, its professional opportunities for trained men and women.

85. A Code of Ethics

"Experimental Draft of a Code of Ethics for Social Case Workers" (unpublished; prepared for discussion at the NCSW, 1923, by the COS Department, RSF), pp. 1–13 [36]

DUTIES TOWARD CLIENTS

Section 1. The social case worker's first duty is toward his clients, unless the performance of this duty jeopardizes the welfare of the community.

The decision as to whether the best interests of the community are likely to be sacrificed to a client's individual interests is often difficult, but in general it will be found on last analysis that the best interests of the individual and those of the community are reconcilable. The task of making the two compatible is a challenge which the resourceful case worker will have to meet.

Examples. Mrs. Jackson, a widow afflicted with a venereal disease, left the housekeeping position in a family similarly affected for one in a widower's family, where she had been offered wages in addition to a home. The widower had a 13 year old daughter with whom she

---

[36] This code was first formulated in a COS institute sponsored by the RSF in 1920. Each of the statements was followed by an explanation of how it should be interpreted, some with several case examples. Copies are in the COS Department files in the archives of the New York School of Social Work. The early efforts of the profession to examine its ethics are described in Lulu Jean Elliott, *Social Work Ethics* (New York: AASW, 1931), Chap. II.

would be closely associated. Her refusal to submit to an examination and her insistence upon carrying out her own plan made it necessary to reveal her physical condition to the court. The subsequent examination showed her to be in an infectious stage. She is receiving medical attention and when her condition warrants, a home will be found for her.

Mr. Armstrong's family took the downward trail when he began to drink. The mother's ill health, the inadequate income, and the gradual disintegration of the family followed. Long and patient work on the part of the visitor of a family welfare society was needed before any response was apparent, but eventually Mr. Armstrong stopped drinking and began to work regularly. During this period he told the visitor that he had deserted from the Navy 12 years before. In this case the visitor felt that the man's obligation to support his family outweighed his duty to give himself up to the authorities as a deserter, and that her responsibility was concerned with his and his family's best interests.

In general, however, it is found that the enforcement of law is for the client's ultimate good. A correspondent of this Committee illustrates the premise that the ultimate interest of the community is reconcilable to that of the client in this respect, as follows:

A new and beneficent community measure which is still on trial, like the prohibition of sewing trades work in tenement rooms, for instance, finds its most ardent champions among our present day social workers. During the first months or years of the enforcement of such a law there are often hardships for the individual. By instinct and training, however, the social case worker who deserves to be called trained at all regards himself as pledged to defend the public welfare and to bear his full share of the brunt of difficulty in all such adjustments. Fair dealing is not easy anywhere; it is made doubly hard for the social case worker just after a new housing statute or a new industrial law has been enacted, when, as almost invariably happens, the more backward members of the community adjust themselves to the new measure with painful slowness. When, however, a good law is no longer on trial and is in no danger of repeal, the social case worker may well, in dealings with its administrators and with its violators, seek to further that flexibility and essential justice in its enforcement which make for better administration in the long run.

Sometimes the enforcement of the law is advisable because of the moral deterioration which would follow if the violation of the law were ignored or overlooked.

A girl deported because of dependency and immorality returned to this country under an assumed name. She had a position and would probably have been self-maintaining. She was recognized by the social worker to whom she had applied for help before her deportation. The worker reported her to the immigration authorities and she was again returned to Scotland.

In adopting the principle that one's first duty is toward one's client, it is well to define one's client. "When two human beings prove, after inquiry, to bear to one another the relation of oppressor and oppressed, which is the case worker's client—the one who first applies or the one who is found to stand more in need of his services?"

Example. Instances similar to the case of John Clark are not so very unusual. Clark applied to a family welfare society for employment and for payment of his room-rent. He had an elderly mother with whom he lived, but did not wish her interviewed, seeking to "withdraw his application" when he learned that she too must be seen. Meanwhile, outside inquiry had revealed that Clark had used up all his mother's money, had estranged her from her people, was a drug addict himself, and was accused of giving cocaine to his mother. Which of these two was in more immediate need of the society's services? Both needed them, but should Clark be permitted to keep the society and his mother apart because he was the first to make application? Should the society risk offending him by seeking to know and befriend his mother?

Section 2. The worker must have humanity, delicacy and patience in dealing with clients.

This involves the realization that a client is not a "problem" but a "person with a problem." . . .

Section 3. The sacredness of confidences imposed by clients must be inviolate.

The best understanding of an individual problem depends upon knowing as fully as possible all the factors in the life of the individual. The illuminating intimate details which permit the making of wise plans are obtained only for the purpose of making such plans possible.

The principle that confidences are inviolate does not imply that such confidences are not to be incorporated into case records. . . .

Talking over clients' affairs, retailing incidents about clients, discussing their problems either in public places or in the privacy of the case worker's home, are frequent violations of the principle that all of the social case worker's dealings are confidential. Social case work in this regard has not reached the high plane of the medical profession, where it would be deemed highly unprofessional for a doctor to use the affairs of his patients as a general topic of conversation. . . .

Section 4. Honesty, frankness and wisdom are three necessary attributes. Promises should be made only when there is a certainty of fulfilment. . . .

Section 5. In view of the tremendous responsibility assumed in making plans with and for a family, it is necessary that the counsel given should never be casual or hurried. It should be sincere, thoughtful, and based upon an adequate knowledge of causal factors. . . .

Section 6. Punctuality in keeping appointments is an obligation. . . .

Section 7. The tool of encouragement should be used freely but with discrimination. . . .

Section 8. An obligation of the case worker is either to render, or else to procure, the particular aid or service needed by a client when the need of such aid or service is made apparent. . . .

Section 9. The same intelligent and painstaking attention should be given to so-called "hopeless" cases as is given to the ones which seem more hopeful and promising. . . .

DUTIES IN RELATION TO CO-WORKERS AND TO THE
PROFESSION OF SOCIAL WORK

Section 10. The worker is under personal obligation to keep informed of current movements through study, through reading, and through alliance with organizations of social workers, city, state, and national. . . .

Section 11. The duty of upholding the honor of the profession is also personal in application. . . .

DUTIES TO OTHER SOCIAL AGENCIES AND TO OTHER PROFESSIONS

Section 25. Independent steps should not be taken by any social agency without first consultation with the agency primarily interested. . . .

Section 26. The work of another agency should not be disparaged. . . .

THE DUTY OF THE SOCIAL CASE WORKER TO THE COMMUNITY

A lawyer's conception of his duty as that of a citizen plus the duty of upholding the law suggests the idea that the social case worker adds to his duties of citizenship the obligation of promoting the social betterment of the community.

Section 35. It is the duty of the social case worker to do preventive and educational work in connection with service to individuals.

Section 36. Social case workers should report reportable diseases or see that they are reported.

Example. Mr. Briggs had become incapacitated with a venereal disease. He was under medical care and the family were being supported by a family welfare society. The doctor treating Mr. Briggs had not reported the case to the State Board of Health as required by state law. When the social worker pointed out the oversight tactfully it was speedily remedied. Shortly afterwards, the family left for a small town in the same state to make their home with Mr. Briggs' parents. A State Board of Health worker was sent to the town to see that he continued his treatments and to see that the other members in the home were protected.

Section 37. It is the privilege as well as the obligation of the social case worker to bear truthful witness to social needs and to social conditions needing remedy. . . .

XXXI

HOW MUCH SHOULD GOVERNMENT
DO ABOUT LIFE'S HAZARDS?

The wave of reform in the first decade of the century which resulted, under varying circumstances, in the prohibition, limitation, or regulation of the labor of women and children (R73, 74), brought out a wide range of other economic and social proposals and innovations. Of particular significance in the development of social work were some of those involving provision for persons in need who were too young or too old to be part of the normal labor market.

Various social insurance schemes based on, or suggested by, European plans had received considerable academic and some political consideration since the days of Hale's proposals (R67). Workmen's compensation laws were being enacted, and Massachusetts, which had just introduced savings bank life insurance, conducted a substantial legislative inquiry into the feasibility of some form of old age insurance or pension plan. Here, as in other states, the proposals were so diverse, the economic hazards of separate state action so great, and the popular political pressure so weak that the whole matter was dropped.

With respect to dependent children, however, more interest and support could be aroused, and the First White House Conference, followed by the establishment of the United States Children's Bureau, represented a major break in the concept that the Federal government had no responsibility in social welfare matters.

The White House Conference itself provided a summary of what was considered good practice in child care at the time, and of the steps in research and action which needed to be taken to bring child welfare up to desirable standards. On the one hand, the presence of thousands of children in almshouses was decried;

on the other, the desirability of measures, including social insurance, which would provide the family with sufficient economic
backing to keep the child in his own home was strongly advocated.
The care of children was thought of, not as an isolated program
entity, but as a part of a total charitable plan in which the state
had responsibility for inspection, for enforcement of standards,
and for the provision of direct service in which the child received
individualized attention and treatment. An indication of developing techniques is the emphasis placed on careful record keeping
with respect to children under care.

One movement which received impetus from the White House
Conference was that for mothers' pensions or mothers' allowances.
The idea that widows should not have to give up their children
solely because they did not have the means to support them was
not new, and the COS movement had come to regard regular
allowances to such families which showed particular stamina as a
very special exception to the dogma that assured relief inevitably
resulted in pauperization (R66), but the lead for the development
of this as a governmental program came from the new juvenile
court movement. It was fought earnestly, and at times bitterly,
by most COS leaders, including Mary Richmond, who held to
the belief that sound relief practices could not be achieved under
governmental auspices. While a considerable number of states
enacted some form of mothers' pensions legislation, many simply
permitted local governments to set up plans if they desired, while
most of the others were so limited in scope as to make little dent
in the total problem. Nevertheless, the pioneering experience of
Denver gives a foretaste of goals to be achieved and the problems
to be overcome in setting up a national program of public assistance three decades later.

Gertrude Vaile was a product of the COS movement, a student
and respected friend of Mary Richmond, so that in her reports
we see the struggles which a trained professional worker experienced in trying to put into practice in a local community the
noble aspirations of the White House Conference report. There
were the problems of differentiating the citizen's right to a pen-

sion from the stigma of relief when both were based on a poverty test; of making inadequate appropriations stretch to meet the exigencies of even a very small operation, let alone the crying needs of others after the appropriation was exhausted; of carrying on an efficient operation in the face of rapid changes in city administration, accompanied by spoils system raids on the welfare office. There was recognition that only as public welfare made itself known and understood, and secured the hearty support of the public, could it expect to be more than the inadequate, inefficient, even destructive, instrument which the COS saw in it.

86. Old Age Pensions, Annuities, and Insurance

Mass. House No. 1400, Report of the Commission . . .
Jan., 1910 (Boston, 1910), pp. 227–29, 300–302, 310–11,
313–15, 322–23 [87]

FUNDAMENTAL QUESTIONS OF PRINCIPLE INVOLVED

IN OLD AGE PENSION PROBLEM

The admitted need of some system of provision for the support of old age through pensions, insurance or annuities, public or private, is conceded by all persons who have made a serious study of this question. . . .

There is the distressing spectacle of pauperism in old age. It was this that first gave rise to the agitation for pensions in England a generation ago. The men who first agitated the pension idea in that country were shocked by the alarming extent of destitution among the aged. In the second place, there is the problem of industrial superannuation. The changed conditions of industrial life have forced this problem to the foreground. . . . At the same time, the average duration of human life has been lengthened by

[87] The commission was appointed by the governor in June, 1907. The study involved a partial census of the nondependent population over sixty-five; a review of the number institutionalized; description and analysis of existing systems in Germany, England, Belgium, Denmark, France, Italy, New Zealand, New South Wales and Victoria, Australia, Canada, and Austria; analysis of the success of military, fraternal, and industrial pensions in the U.S.; analysis of various plans proposed in the Massachusetts legislature 1903–09. These extracts are part of the analysis of existing and proposed plans.

scientific hygiene and improved sanitation. Thus, the period of non-productive existence at the end of life has been extended from both ends, through the earlier retirement of workers and through the lengthening of human life itself. . . . The problem is destined to become increasingly urgent. . . .

The various plans for the solution of the problem of old age support which have been tried or proposed involve widely different principles and methods. The first issue . . . is, Should the plan be contributory or non-contributory? That is, should the expense be borne in whole or in part by the beneficiaries, in the form of contributions to pension or insurance funds, or should the cost be defrayed entirely by the State, through general taxation? If the contributory principle be chosen, then the further question arises, Should participation in the plan be compulsory or voluntary? That is, should individuals be left entirely free to take advantage of the system of pensions or insurance provided, or should they be compelled to take part in the scheme? If, however, the non-contributory principle be chosen, the matter of compulsion does not call for consideration, because it is evident that every one who really needed such aid would apply for a pension under any non-contributory system. Finally, whether the plan be contributory or non-contributory, this further question comes up for consideration, Should the insurance or pension scheme be universal or partial? That is, should the benefits be extended to all without restriction, or should they be confined to certain persons who meet specified conditions of eligibility? . . .

GENERAL CONCLUSIONS CONCERNING NON-CONTRIBUTORY
PENSIONS, COMPULSORY INSURANCE, AND UNIVERSAL SCHEMES

(*a*) *Non-contributory pensions.* The adoption of any scheme of non-contributory pensions in Massachusetts, or any other American State, seems inadvisable and impracticable. The main reason for rejecting pension schemes of a non-contributory character are, in brief:

1. The heavy expense. Under the British act, out of a total population 70 years of age and over of approximately 1,270,000, about

667,000, in round numbers, have already qualified for pensions. . . . The amount of the pension granted could hardly, if adequate for American standards of living, be less than $200 per year, or $4 per week. To provide pensions of that amount for half the population 70 years of age and over would cost not less than $10,000,000 per year. . . . This would increase the State tax by about 400 per cent.

2. The enervating influence on character, especially the inevitable discouragement of saving. The thrift habit is extremely hard to build up, and very easy to break down. A non-contributory pension system would weaken the motive to individual saving, and would react unfavorably on character, by lessening the sense of personal responsibility and independence.

3. The disintegrating effect on the family. A non-contributory pension system would take away, in part, the filial obligation for the support of aged parents, which is a main bond of family solidarity. It would strike at one of the forces that have created the self-supporting, self-respecting American family. . . .

4. The unfavorable effect on wages. While imposing a heavy tax burden on the industries of the State for the supposed benefit of the working population, a non-contributory pension scheme would, at the same time, exert a depressing effect on wages. . . . The establishment of a non-contributory pension system would operate to the economic disadvantage of the wage earners; what they received in the form of a pension would, in the long run, be taken from them in reduced wages.

In this connection it should be emphasized that no argument for non-contributory pensions can be built up on the contention that wage earners as a class do not receive a living wage. It has been shown that the controversy over this subject cannot be settled conclusively by available statistics. What actually constitutes a living wage, expressed in dollars and cents, and what proportion of the working class really get a living wage, must remain matters of opinion. Even if it were true, however, that the majority of wage earners are not paid enough to make adequate provision for old age, this fact would constitute no reason for the establishment of non-contributory pensions. Indeed, this condition would be rather an argument against the grant of non-contributory pensions, than in favor of such action. The grant of subsidiaries in aid of wages by the State would not create a genuine living wage. On the contrary, the effect of that policy must be, at the worst, to depress wages still further; at the best, to prevent the advance of wages to an adequate living basis. In short, the problem of the living wage is not to be solved by any short-cut device of supplementing wages by doles from the State treasury. Such a policy, in the long run, would make the economic condition of the working class far worse than under a regime of absolute non-interference on the part of the State. . . .

A non-contributory pension system is simply a counsel of despair. If such a scheme be defensible or excusable in this country, then the whole economic and social system is a failure. The adoption of such a policy would be a confession of its breakdown. To contend that it is necessary to take this course is to assume that members of the working class either cannot earn enough, or cannot save enough, to take care of themselves in old age. If that be true, then American democracy is in a state of decay which no system of public doles could possibly arrest, but would rather hasten.

The investigation carried on by this commission has not revealed the existence of any general demand for the establishment of non-contributory pensions. . . . In the absence of an effective demand for legislation of this character, it is at least premature to consider any scheme of non-contributory pensions.

(b) *Compulsory insurance.* The adoption of any scheme of compulsory insurance in this State appears to be inexpedient at the present time. The practical objections to the principle of compulsion are weighty. The idea itself is essentially distasteful to Americans. In England it was abandoned as quite out of the question, in view of the prejudice against compulsion. In this Commonwealth this practical objection is reinforced by constitutional difficulties that stand in the way of any workable scheme of compulsory insurance. In view of these conditions, it would be futile to recommend any compulsory insurance system at this time. Whatever the outcome of American experiments with social insurance may be, whether in the direction of the final establishment of compulsory systems, or the extension of voluntary schemes, the introduction of the former can hardly be seriously considered now. In any event, long training in the development of voluntary insurance agencies seems desirable, to furnish the preparation and foundation for any scheme of State insurance, if such should be found ultimately necessary and desirable.

It is conceivable, however, that the final solution of the problem of old age insurance may be found in some system of obligatory State insurance. That is the conclusion to which many impartial students of this subject have come. . . .

It should be pointed out that the compulsion contemplated by these writers, and by others who hold similar opinions regarding the ultimate solution of this problem, consists in enforcement upon the individual of the obligation of self-support; that is, the obligation to provide for old age is recognized as resting upon the individual, and not upon the State. It may be that eventually the State will undertake to enforce this obligation upon the individual by law. The State may, in the interest of all, say to the individual: "You shall provide for your old age through saving made easy by a system of insurance established by government, in order that the general welfare may not be disturbed by your coming to the State for support in your old age." The principle of compulsory education has been adopted and widely extended. The principle of compulsory sanitation has been applied in various directions. The principle of compulsory insurance might be defended as a needful measure of further State interference for the protection of society against the burden of old age pauperism, precisely as compulsory education and compulsory sanitation have been instituted to protect society against ignorance and disease. A system of State insurance thus grounded would be based on the principle of enforced obligation on the part of the individual to insure himself, and not on that of recognized duty on the part of the State to pension all worthy citizens. The British and

Australian pension systems are based on the latter principle, involving the doctrine that a citizen may claim a pension from the State as a civil right. That doctrine is distinctly un-American. The opposite principle of obligatory insurance, as here interpreted, is the only one that could possibly be harmonized with the American condition, traditions and ideals of to-day.

(c) *Universal schemes.* The question whether any pension system that might be adopted should be universal or partial need not be discussed at length. The commission has reached the conclusion that if any new pension scheme were to be instituted in this State at the present time it should be contributory and voluntary. . . . It is obvious that the benefits of any voluntary contributory system should be extended to all persons who may be able and willing to take advantage of its permissive provisions, especially wage earners. Therefore, so far as the conditions of participation are concerned, the scheme should be universal in scope, in the sense that all persons in need of the opportunities for providing against old age thus offered may be allowed to take advantage of its provisions. Whether in practice the scheme would become universal must, of course, depend upon the degree to which wage earners could be induced to avail themselves of its benefits. As a matter of fact, experience with voluntary contributory schemes points to the inevitable conclusion that such a system never could become universal in its application.

FINAL CONCLUSIONS AND RECOMMENDATIONS

We find that serious practical difficulties stand in the way of the establishment of any general system of old age pensions by this Commonwealth or any single State. Such action would place a heavy burden of taxation on the industries of the State, and thus put them at a disadvantage in competition with the industries of neighboring States unburdened by a pension system. It would also tend to attract workers into the pensioning State, and thus to depress the rate of wages. In view of these and other considerations, it is the opinion of the commission that if any general system of old age pensions is to be established in this country, this action should be taken by the national Congress, and not through State legislation. This course of action was suggested by His Excellency Governor Eben S. Draper, in his inaugural address of 1909, as follows:

I would suggest for your consideration whether, if any general old age pension scheme were ever to be enacted, it would not be wise to have this a national proposition, rather than something to be done by an individual State. We are all citizens of one country, and if our State should take up this matter for consideration, and some States do nothing, and others adopt one scheme, and still others a different one, it would produce a situation which, to my mind, would not be practical or wise. . . .

It seems desirable, furthermore, that the problem of sickness and accident insurance should be dealt with before enacting any additional measures of general legislation concerning old age pensions or insurance. In particular, the present provisions of law relating to compensation of workingmen for industrial accidents are admittedly unsatisfactory in Massachusetts and other American States. . . .

Finally, there is no considerable demand in this State for the establishment of a general scheme of old age pensions or insurance. The hearings held by this commission in various cities of the State have not revealed any active interest in this question on the part of the citizens. The attendance at these hearings was small, and the expressions of opinion in the main were of a general character. There is no alarming amount of old age destitution in this State, such as existed in England and other countries of Europe at the time of the adoption of old age pension systems.

87. *The First White House Conference*

Proceedings of the Conference on the Care of Dependent Children, held at Washington, D.C., January 25, 26, 1909 (Washington, D.C.: Government Printing Office, 1909), pp. 9–14 [38]

Hon. Theodore Roosevelt, President of the United States
  Sir: Having been invited by you to participate in a conference

[38] For a description of events leading up to the Conference see Harold

on the care of dependent children . . . we desire to express the very great satisfaction felt by each member of this conference in the deep interest you have taken in the well-being of dependent children. The proper care of destitute children has indeed an important bearing upon the welfare of the nation. We now know so little about them as not even to know their number, but we know that there are in institutions about 93,000, and that many additional thousands are in foster or boarding homes. As a step, therefore, in the conservation of the productive capacity of the people, and the preservation of high standards of citizenship, and also because each of these children is entitled to receive humane treatment, adequate care, and proper education, your action . . . will have, we believe, a profound effect upon the well-being of many thousands of children, and upon the nation as a whole. . . .

Our conclusions are as follows:

HOME CARE

1. Home life is the highest and finest product of civilization. It is the great molding force of mind and of character. Children should not be deprived of it except for urgent and compelling reasons. Children of parents of worthy character, suffering from temporary misfortune and children of reasonably efficient and deserving mothers who are without the support of the normal breadwinner, should, as a rule, be kept with their parents, such aid being given as may be necessary to maintain suitable homes for the rearing of the children. This aid should be given by such methods and from such sources as may be determined by the general relief policy of each community, preferably in the form of private charity, rather than of public relief. Except in unusual circumstances, the home should not be broken up for reasons of poverty, but only for considerations of inefficiency or immorality.

Jambor, "Theodore Dreiser, the *Delineator Magazine*, and Dependent Children: a Background Note on the Calling of the 1909 White House Conference," *Social Service Review*, XXXII (1958), 33–40; Ephraim R. Gomberg, "Decade of Progress," news release, Golden Anniversary White House Conference, Washington, D.C., 1960; Frank J. Bruno, *Trends in Social Work . . . 1874–1946* (New York: Columbia University Press, 1948), p. 152.

PREVENTIVE WORK

2. The most important and valuable philanthropic work is not the curative, but the preventive. . . . We urge upon all friends of children the promotion of effective measures, including legislation, to prevent blindness; to check tuberculosis and other diseases in dwellings and work places, and injuries in hazardous occupations; to secure compensation or insurance so as to provide a family income in case of sickness, accident, death, or invalidism of the breadwinner; to promote child-labor reforms, and, generally, to improve the conditions surrounding child life. To secure these ends we urge efficient cooperation with all other agencies for social betterment.

HOME FINDING

3. As to the children who for sufficient reasons must be removed from their own homes, or who have no homes, it is desirable that, if normal in mind and body and not requiring special training, they should be cared for in families whenever practicable. . . . Such homes should be selected by a most careful process of investigation, carried on by skilled agents through personal investigation and with due regard to the religious faith of the child. After children are placed in homes, adequate visitation, with careful consideration of the physical, mental, moral, and spiritual training and development of each child on the part of the responsible home-finding agency is essential.

It is recognized that for many children foster homes without payment for board are not practicable immediately after the children become dependent and that for children requiring temporary care only the free home is not available. . . . Contact with family life is preferable for these children, as well as for other normal children. It is necessary, however, that a large number of carefully selected boarding homes be found if these children are to be cared for in families. . . . Unless and until such homes are found, the use of institutions is necessary.

COTTAGE SYSTEM

4. So far as it may be found necessary temporarily or permanently to care for certain classes of children in institutions, these institutions should be conducted on the cottage plan, in order that routine and impersonal care may not unduly suppress individuality and initiative. . . . It secures for the children a larger degree of association with adults and a nearer approach to the conditions of family life, which are required for the proper molding of childhood. These results more than justify the increased outlay and are truly economical. . . . Cheap care of children is ultimately enormously expensive, and is unworthy of a strong community. Existing congregate institutions should so classify their inmates and segregate them into groups as to secure as many of the benefits of the cottage system as possible, and should look forward to the adoption of the cottage type when new buildings are constructed.

The sending of children of any age or class to almshouses is an unqualified evil, and should be forbidden everywhere by law, with suitable penalty for its violation.

INCORPORATION

5. To engage in the work of caring for needy children is to assume a most serious responsibility, and should, therefore, be permitted only to those who are definitely organized for the purpose, who are of suitable character, and possess, or have reasonable assurance of securing, the funds needed for their support. The only practicable plan of securing this end is to require the approval, by a state board of charities or other body exercising similar powers, of the incorporation of all child-caring agencies. . . .

STATE INSPECTION

6. The proper training of destitute children being essential to the well-being of the State, it is a sound public policy that the State, through its duly authorized representative, should inspect the work of all agencies which care for dependent children. . . .

7. Destitute children at best labor under many disadvantages. . . . It is desirable that the education of children in orphan asylums and other similar institutions or placed in families should be under the supervision of the educational authorities of the State.

FACTS AND RECORDS

8. . . . One unfortunate feature of child-caring work hitherto is the scanty information available as to the actual careers of children who have been reared under the care of charitable agencies. . . .

We believe, therefore, that every child-caring agency should—

(*a*) Secure full information concerning the character and circumstances of the parents and near relatives of each child in whose behalf application is made. . . .

(*b*) Inform itself by personal investigation at least once each year of the circumstances of the parents of children in its charge, unless the parents have been legally deprived of guardianship, and unless this information is supplied by some other responsible agency.

(*c*) Exercise supervision over children under their care until such children are legally adopted, are returned to their parents, attain their majority, or are clearly beyond the need of further supervision.

(*d*) Make a permanent record of all information thus secured.

PHYSICAL CARE

9. . . . Each child . . . should be carefully examined by a competent physician, especially for the purpose of ascertaining whether such peculiarities, if any, as the child presents may be due to any defect of the sense organs or other physical defect. Both institutions and placing-out agencies should take every precaution to secure proper medical and surgical care of their children and should see that suitable instruction is given them in matters of health and hygiene.

COOPERATION

10. Great benefit can be derived from a close cooperation between the various child-caring agencies, institutional and otherwise, in each locality. . . . The establishment of a joint bureau of investigation and information by all the child-caring agencies of each locality is highly commended, in the absence of any other suitable central agency through which they may cooperate.

UNDESIRABLE LEGISLATION

11. We greatly deprecate the tendency of legislation in some States to place unnecessary obstacles in the way of placing children in family homes in such States by agencies whose headquarters are elsewhere, in view of the fact that we favor the care of destitute children, normal in mind and body, in families, whenever practicable. . . .

The people of the more prosperous and less congested districts owe a debt of hospitality to the older communities from which many of them came. . . .

PERMANENT ORGANIZATION

12. The care of dependent children is a subject about which nearly every session of the legislature of every State in the Union concerns itself; it is a work in which State and local authorities in many States are engaged, and in which private agencies are active in every State. Important decisions are being made constantly. . . . Each of these decisions should be made with full knowledge of the experience of other States and agencies, and of the trend of opinion among those . . . able to speak from wide experience and careful observation. One effective means of securing this result would be the establishment of a permanent organization to undertake, in this field, work comparable to that carried on by . . . similar organizations in their respective fields. It is our judgment that the establishment of such a permanent voluntary organization, under auspices which would insure a careful consideration of all points of view, broad mindedness and tolerance, would be

desirable and helpful, if reasonably assured of adequate financial support.

FEDERAL CHILDREN'S BUREAU

13. A bill is pending in Congress for the establishment of a federal children's bureau to collect and disseminate information affecting the welfare of children. In our judgment the establishment of such a bureau is desirable, and we earnestly recommend the enactment of the pending measure.

Summary

14. The preceding suggestions may be almost completely summarized in this—that the particular condition and needs of each destitute child should be carefully studied and that he should receive that care and treatment which his individual needs require, and which should be as nearly as possible like the life of the other children of the community.

15. We respectfully recommend that you send to Congress a message urging favorable action upon the bill for a federal children's bureau and the enactment of such legislation as will bring the laws and the public administration of the District of Columbia and other federal territory into harmony with the principles and conclusions herein stated, and we further recommend that you cause to be transmitted to the governor of each State of the Union a copy of the proceedings of this conference for the information of the state board of charities or other body exercising similar powers. . . .

> Hastings H. Hart
> Edmond J. Butler
> Julian W. Mack
> Homer Folks
> James E. West
> *Committee on Resolutions*

88. The Democratic Thing to Do

Gertrude Vaile,[89] "Administering Mothers' Pensions in
Denver," *The Survey*, XXXI (1914), 673–75

The results of the pension have on the whole been exceedingly
gratifying in the improvement of conditions in the families pensioned. It is a temptation to give numbers and illustrations, but they
would prove little. Any good Charity Organization Society could
match the story in families pensioned from private funds. It did
not require the public pensions to prove the value of an assured
and regular income sufficient to meet the family's necessities.

On the other hand, to prove, as has been done, that public pensions have been granted on insufficient investigation or that families have failed to prosper even though pensioned, means as little.
It only proves how well or ill the work has been done in the
place under discussion, and nothing as to the ultimate advantages
or disadvantages of public pensions as compared with relief given
by private societies.

The argument as to those ultimate advantages and disadvantages, I believe, will still have to rest upon theory even when
there are many more facts available for study than now. The
state has long declared in many ways its responsibility for the

[89] Gertrude Vaile was a graduate of the Chicago School of Civics and
Philanthropy. She had been a resident of Chicago Commons and a district
superintendent of the Chicago United Charities. She had participated in
Russell Sage Foundation Charity Organization institutes and conferences,
and was regarded as a highly promising younger worker by Mary Richmond. In 1913 she returned to her home in Denver, volunteered as a home
visitor for the Denver Department of Charities, and later was hired by
them as supervisor, continuing on when a commission form of government
revamped the department as the Department of Social Welfare under a
new head. She resolved to apply COS principles and methods of individual help to the public relief case load, an attempt regarded as dubious
if not highly revolutionary by most casework experts. Her department gave
relief to many types of cases, of which the new widows assistance plan
was a relatively small group.

Later, Miss Vaile was on the staff of the National Red Cross during the
First World War, associate field director of the American Association for
Organizing Family Work, executive director of the Colorado State Department of Charities and Correction, president of the NCSW, 1926, and
associate director of the University of Minnesota School of Social Work,
1930–46.

training and rearing of children, if the parents, for any reason, do not do it satisfactorily. If then a mother is personally well fitted to give that care and training but is prevented by a condition of poverty impossible for the family itself to change, it would seem properly and logically the duty of the state to take cognizance of that condition, and to provide necessary means for the care of the children.

Moreover, it is the democratic thing to do. When the father dies why should a good mother have to depend upon the alms of her more fortunate neighbor for the opportunity to perform her natural and civic duty of bringing up her children—even if her more fortunate neighbors are willing and able to give such alms? And the question will persist in rising whether, after all, they are quite willing and able, even with all the magnificent work the private societies have done. . . .

There is our Mrs. B., unknown to private charity, so far as the confidential exchange shows, though known on the city relief books for very small amounts at long intervals, and not in the year preceding the pension application. When she applied for the pension last spring, she was supporting her three little children by cleaning and laundry work. She boarded the youngest child at five dollars a month, took the second child with her to her work, and the nine year old boy pretty much took care of himself after school. She asked the pension on the ground that she wanted her baby with her and understood that that was what the pension was for. It was clear that she was making a very plucky and a very hard struggle—too hard—but the little pension fund was then exhausted.

We told her we were very sorry. We warned her to take care of her own health, and if she found her work too heavy, to let us help her until more pension fund was available. We hoped she would come in and let us know how she was getting along. But she did not come.

Five months later a neighbor sent us word that the oldest boy was very sick and Mrs. B. in a state of nervous prostration. Then we hurried out to pick up the wrecks. Some pension money being released by the marriage of a pensioner, a pension was granted to her. She is improving, but it will be a long time before she is strong again.

Mrs. B. and others like her, most indeed of our best women, will not give the charities a chance to help until after the catastrophe, but they feel that they can ask with dignity for a public pension as the proper provision made by the state for their children. It is a public pension alone that can do far-reaching preventive and protective work.

89. Statutory Requirements and Local Expediency

Gertrude Vaile to Mary E. Richmond, n.d., enclosing copy of a letter, Feb. 18, 1915, to Dr. Carl E. McCombs, New York Bureau of Municipal Research; Gertrude Vaile Archives, Library of the New York School of Social Work, Columbia University

Dear Miss Richmond:

Here is that copy of my letter. . . . It is about the most daring thing I ever did. But I simply have to come squarely into the open on this pension business or suffocate.

My dear Dr. McCombs: . . .

In regard to your report on the Mothers' Pensions[40] . . . I believe you have not been fully and correctly informed of all the facts involved and that you have failed to distinguish between those conditions which are determined by statute and those which a local community can alter according to expediency. . . .

First, please notice that under the statute appropriation must be made, not to the Juvenile Court, but to the County authorities in charge of the relief of the poor, and must be paid out by the Poor Relief Authorities. Your recommendation [that the Court should be charged with the administration of those funds] upon that subject is then impracticable without amendment of the law.

[40] The government of Denver was being studied by the Bureau of Municipal Research, and the Department of Social Welfare was coming under scrutiny as part of the comprehensive review. Miss Vaile describes the administrative functions of her department and the new law for widows' assistance in unquoted parts of her *Survey* article (R88) and in "Principles and Methods of Outdoor Relief," *NCCC*, 1915, pp. 479–84.

Next, as to duplication of work, if the appropriation must be made to the Poor Relief Authorities and be paid out by them, then they have the right and duty of knowing for what their funds are paid, in other words, the right and duty of investigation. But the law provides that: "The Court shall appoint proper persons for the investigation, supervision, etc." Duplication of work is then inherent in the law at the outset. Such duplication, exceedingly expensive and often cruelly hard upon the applicant, did exist in practice in Chicago under exactly similar conditions.

In Denver a conference between the Court and the Relief Department came to the conclusion that such duplication was nonsense, and it was all promptly and completely eliminated by the good sense of the Judge, who appointed the Relief Department to make the investigation, and have supervision for the Court. So the Relief Department investigates officially on its own behalf and officially by appointment on behalf of the Court. All the results of the investigation and supervision are subject to the review of the Court and are submitted at any time, and in any detail the Court desires.

You report that, "The Juvenile Court conducts its own investigations and exercises supervision through the Probation Officers of the Court." In this you have a misunderstanding. The Relief Department has investigated every case. If the Court has ever investigated one, I have never heard of it. . . . In [one] instance an officer from the Court has very properly visited a number of times, and between us all the problem is working out well. . . . Regarding other than pensioned families, the Relief Department and the Juvenile Court are constantly in such co-operation, the Relief Department taking care of one phase of the problem and the Court of another. But if the Court has ever definitely entered upon the investigation or the supervision of any except the one case cited, in its capacity as a pension case, I have never heard of it. If they had done so I am very sure they would have informed us of their findings. The fact is that the Probation Officers, too few for their own heavy tasks, are already so overwhelmed with work that they have no time for any unnecessary pension visiting, and the Judge has seemed to consider such visiting unnecessary. . . .

You say that the "duplication of service doubles the cost of the city." I have yet to discover a single instance or point of duplication except a small clerical duplication in making up the annual reports, and that is practically unavoidable under the statute. Even that was carefully gone over some months ago to make it as small as possible. In fact the Mothers' Pension work has been one great and shining example of how a common sense agreement and a spirit of co-operation have cut out duplication that must otherwise have existed.

You recommend that the probation officers should make the investigation and that the administration remain wholly with Court. Do you not see, Dr. McCombs, that that would immediately make inevitable that very duplication of work to which you object? Even if we waived our right of investigation for the pension, in all probability we have already investigated and struggled with the family as a relief problem. The test of eligibility for the pension is *poverty*, "if the parent or parents are poor and unable properly to provide for their children but are otherwise suitable guardians." But if they are really so poor that they are unable to provide for their children do you not realize that nine chances out of ten—or let us be exact, in 43 cases out of 47 who have been granted pensions—the family were already known to the Relief Department. And again if the pension for any reason is not granted and yet any need really exists it becomes again a problem for the Relief Department who ought to be in possession of all available facts concerning it.

Let me discuss for a moment the general subject of mothers' pensions. The movement started in a Juvenile Court and swept other communities into the same line before any one had time to think. That it did start in the Juvenile Court is in my opinion to the glory of the spirit of the Juvenile Court and to the everlasting disgrace of the Relief Authorities. The Public Relief Authorities were not dealing adequately or considerately with their dependent families and Juvenile Courts were being called upon to dispose of dependent children who ought never to have been brought to them. There came a time when certain Juvenile Judges, especially in Chicago and Denver, could not stand it. Hence the form which the pension legislation took.

But now all over the country the question is being raised whether, after all, relief administration is a proper function of the court. I dare discuss this boldly for I have already talked about it to Judge Lindsey to whom I shall send a copy of this letter. Before I occupied my present position or any arrangement had been made regarding our Denver pensions I had quoted to Judge Lindsey the opinion of Judge Baker of the Boston Juvenile Court, who arose in the National Conference of Charities in Cleveland two years and a half ago, to warn all communities thinking of trying such legislation not to put it in the hands of the Juvenile Court, saying that the Court had its own very great and delicate task which could only be made the more difficult by having injected into it the administration of relief problems. . . .

If you are . . . interested you can doubtless secure from our State Board of Charities copies of some letters they have from outlying counties in Colorado showing the sharp antagonism that has already developed between the County Judges and the County Commissioners under our Mothers' Compensation Act. Here in Denver both the Court and the Relief Department earnestly and absolutely believe in the main principle of the Mothers' Compensation Act and have tried to administer it in a way to avoid all pitfalls. . . .

Two things I think I do see clearly—first, that the mothers' pension is a relief problem and we cannot if we would wholly separate it from other relief problems, nor separate the individual case from the treatment it may receive as a relief problem before or after the pension application. Second, that we have the law as it stands and it embodies a great principle, and absolutely and solely upon the relation existing between the Court and the Relief Department depends the issue whether there shall be all sorts of confusion and duplication and woe, or whether all the weaknesses shall be corrected and all the splendid possibilities retained.

As it has been carried out in Denver I do not know how any pension law could be better. You criticise the law as giving too unlimited power to the Judge. What check can you suggest that could be better than a careful investigation of each case by another well qualified department? On the other hand if heavy and long continued relief is to be given to individual families from Public Funds it seems to me imperative that there should be some sort of court of review, already existing or specially created, to which the persons administering such relief should be responsible. Both of these ends are secured in the present Denver method. In fact I supposed that in our Denver administration of pensions we had achieved a masterpiece in avoiding inherent difficulties and duplications and finding a way that would keep the work simple, economical and well guarded, and that all that remained necessary was to have enough time and enough well trained workers to do a really good job along the lines laid down. . . .

P.S. [handwritten, in ink]

Miss Richmond,—I wonder if those figures . . . will surprise you in view of my main contention usually made that women do ask with dignity for the pension who would not ask ordinary charity until they break. I suppose we must take it as axiomatic that if the distress is great enough and long enough continued it is bound eventually to come to the notice of some charity. The greatest illustrations of my contention have not been the women who have *never* had help, but those who have had it at some previous time at some particular crisis of sickness or misfortune, but the moment the crisis was past rose up in their independence and worked and suffered and their children suffered to a degree that should never be permitted, rather than turn to charity until the next catastrophe laid them low. It is those women who have had charity at some time, and yet for a year or more before making the pension application have managed to make ends meet without help but at too great sacrifice who have been the significant cases to me. It is in those cases that the changed attitude (and a just & proper change in my opinion) is most marked. Of course our fund has always been so small that allowances could be granted only to the most needy families.

90. Unshaken Belief in Public Outdoor Relief

> Gertrude Vaile to Porter Lee, Dean of the New York School of Philanthropy, who had asked information about Denver's experience. The portion here follows a lengthy recounting of many shifts in policy and administrative arrangements during readjustments to "commission" and then "federal" forms of local government (handwritten, Sept. 27, 1916; carbon copy in Gertrude Vaile Archives).

We have now five district visitors, four new since October but of my own choosing and all splendid people and we have again more clerical help and more room. . . . The attitude of respect at City Hall has noticeably increased. . . . All the newspapers are exceedingly friendly and really helpful. I believe we are getting a stronger and stronger backing and sympathy from the general public, and since [an experienced charity organization worker] has come in [as assistant] we are making good use of excellent volunteers that come to us unsought. (During the winter I hardly had time even to speak to them politely, although I believe our hope is in them.) . . .

I presume I have added many an argument to your distrust of public administration. And yet I am willing to tell the whole story because after working with such troubles by day and thrashing them over by night until I was fairly sick, I am still unshaken in my belief . . . in public outdoor relief. Of course I do perceive that it behooves a public official in time of prosperity to be humble and make the most of his opportunities, for the time may be short, but at least he may take courage in time of adversity for that too may be short and can with effort be shortened. It has been no little comfort to me to feel that if we can make it go pretty well here in Denver with four political administrations in four years and all the harassing consequences they have brought, there is probably no place in the country where they cannot do it well if somebody cares enough to stick to it.

But one thing that I have said from the start grows clearer every day—that we shall build on drifting sand unless we can get our foundations down to the solid rock of intimate under-standing and sympathetic backing on the part of responsible peo-ple of the general community. Friendly visitors, volunteer com-mittees, case conferences, parlor meetings, newspaper items, co-operation with other agencies that shall be so hearty and effective that they simply can't get along without us, so that all the social work in town would just have to rise up in self-defense if any-thing happened to us—in these things lies our only hope of stability in public O.D.R. [outdoor relief] administration. . . .

You are probably thinking—suppose I had been dismissed . . . last October, what then? I can only reply that so much of public support I believe we have already won. I do not believe the political powers would care to do anything to us that would *appear* to make a very radical change in the work. The task ahead is to make that support broader and more intelligently in-formed.

XXXII

EMERGENCE OF METHOD: CASEWORK

Literature on the methodology of social work was largely a twentieth-century product. Before that, there had been generalized accounts of intuitively devised experiences and fumbling experiments with the first crude technique of "advice-giving," written long after the event. In 1905 charity organization societies began a regular exchange of current running case records with some explanation of the worker's advance reasoning about what she had planned to do. When the Russell Sage Foundation set up a Charity Organization Department in 1909 for research and extension in that field, Mary Richmond, the director, at once started a systematic analysis of records from a number of specialties (family, child-placing, child-protection, probation, medical, public relief, and so forth). She concentrated on the step-by-step process of securing pertinent and valid information about each client's past social experiences and of appraising their significance as a basis for determining what was wrong, what were the chances that something could be done, and how improvement could be effected. She conceived study, diagnosis, prognosis, and treatment planning as separate entities in a chainlike series. *Social Diagnosis*, the product of this analysis, with its orderly detailed instructions, was hailed as social work's first technical treatise.

A projected companion volume on treatment techniques was never written. Caseworkers striving for the perfect investigation still had to depend largely on intuition and self-discovery to guide them in treatment, then conceived as a process of mobilizing community institutions and the client's own special abilities in his behalf.

A few years later, in *What Is Social Case Work?* Miss Richmond attempted to define casework philosophically, as part of a wider social work approach to human problems—a process of helping an individual adjust to the social demands impinging upon him, while concurrently so shifting the environment that his adjustment was made easier and his relation to other people more effective and happier. This conception of the worker's role continued to use his familiarity with community services as the chief tool, but hinted at the importance of the client's reaction to the caseworker as a person.

Developments in psychiatry had begun to turn caseworkers' attention after 1917 to personality factors, and within ten years the main focus was on creating a better emotional climate for their clients. The child guidance movement led the way, supported by growing conviction in many quarters that personality deviations and social failures had their roots in unhappy childhood experiences. Case records, such as those edited by Mary Sayles, placed chief emphasis on details of treatment process and only incidentally described how factual information was obtained, though elaborate personal histories were still considered essential before effective treatment could be carried out, and efforts were being made to determine what new kinds of facts were required for the psychiatric approach. In child guidance, casework stood forth as a professional service that people could find helpful regardless of their economic status; deprivations could be emotional as well as economic.

Stimulated by the AASW's expressed aim to study and crystallize method, a varied group of casework specialists met together as a study group for several years. Their codification emphasized that despite adaptations to fit the requirements of each specialty, all casework stemmed from a common base of knowledge and demonstrably useful techniques. All branches of the profession could work together in identifying, articulating, and perfecting them.

Virginia Robinson and her colleagues at the University of Pennsylvania were chiefly responsible for the next stage in casework development. To them, the most significant tool at the caseworker's command was the relationship between himself and his client, a much enlarged view of the old idea of personal influence, of a "steadfast friend," now founded on scientific hypotheses concerning the nature of responses to consciously controlled behavior of a therapist. It was not now important to ascertain every detail in the client's past, but rather to concentrate on ways of stimulating the client to discover and deal with hindering emotional reactions to his current perplexities.

Caseworkers borrowed from the many emerging psychological and psychiatric theories, varying the detail of their own technical procedures according to which school of thought seemed most complete and sound. While sociological and economic theories comprised part of the scientific knowledge base in education, hypotheses concerning personality formation and classification of abnormalities usurped primary attention. Caseworkers were groping for the distinction between the psychiatrist's approach and their own, and seeking ways in which the two disciplines could supplement each other, when the depression of the thirties forced most of them back to a preoccupation with the handling of economic need. But by 1935 the nature of the casework relationship and how it could be made more effective had been identified as the central objectives for next exploration and clarification.

91. Assets and Obstacles

Mary E. Richmond, *Social Diagnosis* (New York: RSF, 1917), pp. 357-60 [41]

1. *Diagnosis redefined.* Social diagnosis, then, may be described as the attempt to make as exact a definition as possible of the situation and personality of a human being in some social need—of his situation and personality, that is, in relation to the other human beings upon whom he in any way depends or who depend upon

[41] Social diagnosis, here delineated, was the concluding stage in a long, involved process of investigation. The bulk of the book deals with ways of securing data, why they are basic, what weight should be given each item in determining final diagnosis, and variants in procedure according to the type of problem to be dealt with. Publication came after five years of part-time exploration and six years of intensive research. Data consisted of a large collection of case histories, correspondence, and institute discussions with expert caseworkers, and treatises on data analysis from other professions.

him, and in relation also to the social institutions of his community. . . .

2. *Diagnostic content.* A poor social diagnosis errs by being too general, by being too detailed and therefore confused, or by overlooking some of the important factors in a case though clear on the main disability; whereas good social diagnosis includes all the principal factors standing in the way of social reconstruction, with emphasis placed upon the features which indicate the treatment to be followed. This emphasis the worker should allow no predisposition toward some favorite causal factor to disturb.

A diagnosis may be mistaken. It is humiliating to find that a case of mental disease or of tuberculosis can still be diagnosed by a social agency as a case of unemployment due to laziness or inefficiency. On the other hand, it is exasperating to find that a tuberculosis nurse can still tell a patient, upon her first visit, that his is the worst case of overwork she has ever encountered, when the facts are notorious that he has never supported himself and his family, and that he has undermined his health by years of dissipation. This absorption of the worker in the superficial aspects of a case is responsible for many mistaken diagnoses.

A diagnosis may be a mere classification. It may be no better than pigeon-holing. The one-word diagnosis, even when it names the general type of difficulty with correctness, is not social. In the days of disorganized social dosing, a woman with children and no male head in her household might be recorded by different agencies as a widow, a deserted wife, or an unmarried mother without any of them having verified her civil condition. Although the affixing of the correct label is an advance, no such label standing by itself has a practical bearing upon prognosis and treatment. . . .

A diagnosis may be too detailed. As the purpose of diagnosis is to throw into high light the factors most influential in bringing a client to his present pass, it follows that the including of details is apt to spoil the perspective and so give either a distorted or a confused picture of the situation. In other words, the defining of a client's need calls upon the worker to distinguish in the evidence collected what is relatively important for successful treatment from what is relatively unimportant. A worker may have gathered the evidence in a case with care; he may have had his perceptions awakened in many directions by the ablest books on the causes of poverty; yet he may have failed to recognize the factors working most mischief in the case under consideration. In short, his work may be painstaking but without penetration. The remedy lies in experience under skilful supervision, where this is possible, as well as in a deepened sense of fellowship with one's clients.

A diagnosis may be partial, although clear on the main difficulty. . . . It is true today of much of the work of case workers with method and experience above the average. The saving strength in their work is that they are testing diagnosis continually by that knowledge of the consequences of a given treatment as applied to a given diagnosis which comes only from long familiarity with social practice. The weakness in their work is that they are apt to note and to treat merely some one conspicuous need in a number of cases too large to allow of more thorough work. True as it is that the results of treatment must be the usual test of a diagnosis, practical experience in observing these results will not save a worker who is under the pressure of too many cases from getting but a partial view of their complexities and possibilities.

A diagnosis can be full without loss of clearness. It is wasteful to gather ample evidence and then, in our eagerness for quick results in dealing with some urgent need, lose sight of the facts significant for a more searching treatment. A fuller diagnosis would bring these into the picture of the case without obscuring any immediate issue.

Thus far, emphasis has been placed upon the defining of the difficulty in the client's situation. We must, however, remember that, while making a comprehensive diagnosis which is to be followed by treatment, we must keep the clues to possible remedies in view. The diagnosis itself should bring together those elements in the situation which may become obstacles or aids in the treatment. We have no word for this summing up of assets and liabilities. Its inclusion in diagnosis is justified only on the ground that the diagnostician, who must have had social treatment in view from the very beginning, has been measuring at every stage of his work the treatment value of each circumstance, each human relation, and each personal characteristic. . . .

Not only the assets but the special obstacles to be overcome and guarded against in treatment should be included. All of this must be dated and must stand, like a bill of lading, "errors and omissions excepted."

92. *Processes Which Develop Personality*

Mary E. Richmond, *What Is Social Case Work?* (New
York: RSF, 1922), pp. 97–99

It is true that social case work has dealt and will continue to deal with questions of restoration to self-support, with matters of health and personal hygiene, as well as with the intricacies of mental hygiene, and that each of these things has a direct relation to personality. But, in so far as each is a specialty (some are specialties demanding quite other forms of professional skill), social case work will be found to be coterminous with none of them, but to have, in addition to its supplementary value in these other tasks, a field all its own. That field is the development of personality through the conscious and comprehensive adjustment of social relationships, and within that field the worker is no more occupied with abnormalities in the individual than in the environment, is no more able to neglect the one than the other. The distinctive approach of the case worker, in fact, is back to the individual by way of his social environment, and wherever adjustment must be effected in this manner, individual by individual, instead of in the mass, there some form of social case work is and will continue to be needed. So long as human beings are human and their environment is the world, it is difficult to imagine a state of affairs in which both they and the world they live in will be in no need of these adjustments and readjustments of a detailed sort.

To state this in a more formal way is to arrive at my tentative definition:

Social case work consists of those processes which develop personality through adjustments consciously effected, individual by individual, between men and their social environment.

What do we mean by "social environment"? The [Century] dictionary defines environment as "the aggregate of surrounding things and conditions," but when we put "social" in front of it, it becomes evident at once that many persons and things have been excluded and many substitutes included; the environment ceases to be environment in space merely—it widens to the horizon of man's thought, to the boundaries of his capacity for maintaining relationships, and it narrows to the exclusion of all those things which have no real influence upon his emotional, mental, and spiritual life.

93. The Technique of Understanding and Adjusting Individual Lives

Mary B. Sayles,[42] ed., *Three Problem Children: Narratives from the Case Records of a Child Guidance Clinic* (New York: Joint Committee on Methods of Preventing Delinquency, 1924), pp. 145, 10, 5–9

THE COMMONWEALTH FUND PROGRAM FOR THE
PREVENTION OF DELINQUENCY

The Commonwealth Fund initiated in 1921 a five-year Program for the Prevention of Delinquency. The purpose of this Program is to demonstrate and promote the wider application of modern psychiatric science and visiting teacher service to the study and guidance of children presenting problems of conduct and maladjustment in school and society.

Problem children, it is recognized, do not all become delinquent in subsequent life, but there is growing evidence that adult criminality has its roots in childhood in the same factors which cause

[42] Mary B. Sayles, editor and presumed author of the Introduction, was on the staff of the Joint Committee on Methods of Preventing Delinquency. Records were of cases in the Bureau of Children's Guidance clinic maintained by the New York School of Social Work. The order of excerpts given here has been changed so that a description of auspices and general program might precede the specific explanation of the nature of this volume.

early disorders of behavior. The understanding and adjustment of children whose conduct suggests underlying mental or physical difficulties should, therefore, make for the prevention not only of juvenile delinquency but of later and more serious criminal tendencies. Even when delinquency is not involved, such study and treatment of problem children should remove the cause of much unhappiness both at the time and throughout life.

The Program consists of a group of related activities made possible by grants from the Fund to four cooperating agencies each of which administers independently a division of the undertaking. . . .

The Joint Committee on Methods of Preventing Delinquency offers this publication in the hope that it may promote acquaintance with a fundamentally important point of view and method in modern social and educational effort. . . .

INTRODUCTION

These narratives . . . are published in order to give some indication of the resources which modern science offers for the assistance of those who seek to understand such troubled young lives and to guide them into the channels of normal social growth. Increasing numbers of social workers, school teachers, probation officers, public health nurses and parents are already aware that psychiatry affords a new approach to the handling of children who are delinquent, or maladjusted, or unhappy. . . .

It is not difficult to identify some of the methods and processes here described as well-established elements in the skill of many a good social worker, teacher and parent. Nor is it intended to imply that expert knowledge from other fields has not been utilized in the practice of social case work. . . . Psychiatry, however, stands in an entirely different relation to social case work. Through its interpretation of the processes of mental life revealed by a close study of all the aspects of personality as well as environment, this branch of science is bringing a new and fundamental contribution to the technique of understanding and adjusting individual lives.

The essential end to be sought is the development of such a rounded technique rather than a definition of the precise share of psychiatry and of social case work in creating and applying it. . . .

Emphasis is laid not upon effort to classify these problem children according to types, but upon the fact that each one exhibits a special combination of physical, mental and social disabilities and assets, making up his or her own distinct personality problem. Attention is thus directed to understanding and helping each child as an individual. . . .

Behavior is now seen not as a problem in itself, but as the result of causes often complex and hidden. It is coming to be understood as the external manifestation of an interplay between great instinctive forces in the individual and the effort of society to shape these forces to serve its own ends. . . .

Under the revealing light of psychiatric study the conduct of many a child which has appeared to parent or teacher to present solely a moral issue is found actually to have its origin not in the child but in circumstances over which he has no control. . . . Traced back to its ultimate source the trouble not infrequently lies in the failure of the responsible adults to understand and successfully manage some of their own problems. . . .

A vital point emphasized by psychiatry . . . is the importance of an objective, unbiased attitude on the part of the worker. The child who feels this attitude gives his confidence with a sense of relief and gladness, and may then by gradual steps be led to discover his own errors, and realize his true situation—a result rarely achieved through the old methods of admonition and discipline. . . .

The psychiatric clinic brings to a focus the resources of physical, psychological, psychiatric and social examination and treatment, utilizing the skilled services of staff members trained in different fields and making possible a complete study and understanding of the child's personality.

94. *Social Casework Generic and Specific*

Reprinted with permission of the National Association
of Social Workers, *Social Case Work—Generic and
Specific; a Report of the Milford Conference;* [48] Studies
in the Practice of Social Work, No. 2 (New York:
AASW, 1929), pp. 3, 11–12, 28–29, 35, 64–72

At the first meeting of the Milford Conference an attempt was
made to define the several fields of social case work. The discussion made it clear that the group were not able at that time to
define social case work itself so as to distinguish it sharply from
other forms of professional work nor the separate fields of social
case work so as to differentiate them sharply from each other. . . .

While these discussions led to no formulations of practical value,
they served to clarify some of the problems facing social case
workers. Their most important result, perhaps, was the emergence
of a strong conviction unanimously held by the members of the
Conference that a fundamental conception which had come to be
spoken of as "generic social case work" was much more substantial in content and much more significant in its implications for
all forms of social case work than were any of the specific em-
phases of the different case work fields. . . .

The Committee's Conclusions

The Committee's conclusions after three years of work on this
assignment are embodied in the report itself. It wishes, however,
to emphasize the following:

1. Social case work is a definite entity. It has a field increasingly well defined, it has all of the aspects of the beginnings
of a science in its practice and it has conscious professional standards for its practitioners. The various separate designations . . .
by which its practitioners are known tend to have no more than

[48] The Milford Conference was an informal discussion group of leaders
from six national agencies who met together for several years in Milford,
Pa. The committee which drafted this final report of the results of the
deliberations was chaired by Porter Lee. *Social Case Work—Generic and
Specific* (New York: AASW, 1929), pp. 3–5; Margaret E. Rich, *A Belief
in People* (New York: Family Service Association of America, 1956), pp.
102–3.

a descriptive significance in terms of the type of problem with which they respectively deal. . . . The outstanding fact is that the problems of social case work and the equipment of the social case worker are fundamentally the same for all fields. In other words, in any discussion of problems, concepts, scientific knowledge or methods, generic social case work is the common field to which the specific forms of social case work are merely incidental.

2. At the present time the practice of social case work is more precise than the formulations of philosophy, knowledge, methods and experience. . . .

3. The remedy for the situation in the judgment of the Committee is clear. Social case workers must become more energetic in pursuing penetrating study and research in their professional subject matter. We believe that this report outlines a content for social case work sufficiently substantiated in the implications to justify the claim that social case work is potentially both scientific in character and professonal in its practice. Scientific and Professional, however, are terms which can at the present time justifiably be applied to social case work chiefly because of its potentialities. . . .

The conclusion of the Committee on this point is that there is no greater responsibility facing social case work at the present time than the responsibility of organizing continuous research into the concepts, problems and methods of its field. . . . Social case workers cannot leave the responsibility for research to foundations and universities. They must do it themselves and participation by social case workers in such research must be widespread. . . .

PHILOSOPHY

Inherent in the practice of social case work is a philosophy of individual and social responsibility and of the ethical obligations of the social case worker to his client and to the community. Such concepts of responsibility must direct the use of all methods . . . and influence the relationships with community resources. . . . We can perceive social values, plus and minus, in certain situations, and by these values justify our objectives in social case work.

The social case worker has need of a thought-out system of social values not only to clarify his general purpose and orient him in relation to theories of social progress, but also to guide him in every professional contact. Such practical questions as the following illustrate the need of a philosophy:

What are the client's rights as an individual?

What are his obligations to his family?

Under what circumstances is it good to try to maintain a family as such unbroken?

Under what circumstances is it good to try to break up a family? (i.e., What values are involved for individual, group, society?)

Is coercion justified in any given case?

How far and when is individual dependency a public responsibility, how far and when a private responsibility?

What individual social needs other than subsistence are public responsibility: education; health examination; mental test; vocational guidance; recreation; etc.?

How far should social environment be altered in the interest of the sick or unadjusted person?

In what circumstances, if any, should the client's confidence be violated by the social case worker?

Is the social case worker responsible for law enforcement?

Thus far the philosophy of social case work has been comparatively little discussed and hardly at all defined. . . . We suggest . . . that discussion and formulation of the philosophy of social case work is a pressing obligation upon the members of the profession.

SOCIAL CASE TREATMENT

The social case worker comes into the life of the client when his deviations from normal social standards have reached a point where he cannot effectively organize certain of his own activities. The measure of the skill of the social case worker is not only the body of knowledge and method he has acquired but his ability to utilize these creatively in social case treatment which has as its objectives the social well being of the client.

The goals of social case treatment are both ultimate and proximate. The ultimate goal is to develop in the individual the fullest possible capacity for self-maintenance in a social group. In attaining both immediate and ultimate goals three fundamental processes interplay at every point: (1) the use by the social case worker of resources—educational, medical, religious, industrial—all of which have a part in the adjustment of the individual to social living; (2) assisting the client to understand his needs and possibilities; and (3) helping him to develop the ability to work out his own social program through the use of available resources.

Proximate goals may involve such things as restoration of health; reestablishment of kinship ties; removal of educational handicaps; improvement of economic condition; overcoming of delinquent tendencies. The attainment of these goals, however, must be in such a way as to further not only the immediate but the ultimate well being of the client. . . .

STANDARDS OF SOCIAL CASE WORK PRACTICE

Application of the subject matter of generic social case work in a specific setting means chiefly the adaptation of the various concepts, facts and methods which we have discussed as generic social case work to the requirements of the specific field. It means in part also certain other subject matter supplementary to the content of generic social case work. The nature of both adaptations and supplementations will be determined by the peculiar and distinctive requirements of the specific fields. If we try to state these peculiar and distinctive requirements for any one field, they would seem to be in part a more intensive development of some aspect of generic social case work than is necessary in other fields and in part quite distinctive equipment, for which other fields have little use. . . . Complete equipment for a specific field would include the following:

1. The full content of generic social case work.

2. The intensive development of appropriate aspects of generic social case work.

3. Distinctive subject matter for which other specific fields have little or no use. . . .

SOME PRINCIPLES GOVERNING THE DIVISION OF LABOR IN
SOCIAL CASE WORK

A. *A social case work agency should do a complete social case work job with its cases and should transfer a case only when the services of another agency are clearly needed.* . . .

B. *There should be no diagnostic authority without treatment responsibility and no treatment responsibility without diagnostic authority.* . . .

C. *A transfer of a case from one organization to another should be made only when there is good reason to believe that better service will result from such transfer.* . . .

D. *The larger the organization the more remote is its management from the needs which it serves.* . . . Social agencies, as they grow in size and complexity, suffer not only the general difficulties attendant upon such growth, but also special disadvantages due to the nature of their work.

The combination of various social case work services in one agency and the development of large agencies in any one field of social case work may go so far as to be incompatible with the most effectual service to clients. . . .

Administratively . . . all social work is specific. Experience clearly shows the difficulty of expanding the number of social case work functions carried by one agency without fostering some of them at the expense of others. This is largely because in these days of complex resources, diversified problems and rapidly expanding knowledge, the executive at the head of a big organization can hardly be equally a leader in several fields of work. Good social case work, moreover, demands that a high degree of freedom and initiative be given the social case worker, because factual material, philosophy and methods are in a rapidly evolving stage, and because social case work is a creative activity. . . .

E. *Social case work organized as a supplementary service within other programs (mural social case work) will be determined, as to scope and tenure on the cases treated, by the requirements of these other programs.* . . .

F. *A community's social equipment should include social case work under both public and private auspices.* . . .

G. *Relief work should be administered by the case work agency having responsibility for treatment.* . . .

H. *Co-operative treatment involving on a single case the simultaneous work of two or more agencies is not only a normal aspect of the division of labor, but may be expected to increase.*

95. Emerging Awareness of Relationship

Virginia P. Robinson,[a] *A Changing Psychology in Social Case Work* (Chapel Hill: University of North Carolina Press, 1930), pp. xi–xiv, 33–58, 95, 143

The social case work movement in the past fifty years presents a picture almost kaleidoscopic in its shifting emphasis. . . . One is struck by the rapid changes in point of view and method which put an interpretation out of date before it can be formulated; and again by the confusing differences in point of view, philosophy, and method in use at the same time in different sections of the country and in different agencies.

Awareness of these differences operates as a source of disturbing insecurity to case workers today. . . . Certainty cannot be found in the social order or in any conceivable reconstruction of it, and behavior has become, with increasing study and understanding, too complex in its forms and conditionings to be forced under any laws of control. In the days of Josephine Shaw Lowell, Zilpha Smith, and Octavia Hill, the social case worker could proceed upon the safe and satisfying guarantee of principle and rule

[a] Virginia Robinson had been professor of casework and assistant director of the University of Pennsylvania School of Social Work since 1918.

behind her. The worker today can only envy the assurance of Miss [*sic*] Lowell in 1884 when she writes on "Methods of Charity." . . .

Social workers are no longer dealing with the same concepts, the same values, or even with the same facts that they were occupied with in 1880. . . . They have, in the process of working, discovered new facts and created new values. The case work relationship between worker and client is essentially different from what it was in 1880, or 1900, or 1920, because personality has grown in these years not only in understanding but in capacity for relationship. The increasing consciousness of personality facts in the past five years, through all fields of science and knowledge and the overwhelming popularization of this knowledge through literature, education, and social work, have brought about a new level of personality development, a greater degree of self-consciousness, a greater capacity for seeing the other person as a different individual. . . .

[The new] values . . . are psychological in contrast to economic, religious, moral, or sociological values. To articulate these values, to define them clearly in relation to other values, to conceive the goals of treatment in terms which will relate these values organically; here is a task which social case work might do well to accomplish within another fifty years. . . .

The first contact with the founder of this [psychoanalytic] movement we owe to G. Stanley Hall since he brought Freud to this country to speak in 1910. . . . Translations of Freud's writings began to appear shortly after. . . .

William A. White [made an] enthusiastic and brilliant presentation of the Freudian psychology in 1916. . . .

Three points particularly were seized upon from the psychoanalytic psychology and made a permanent part of the case worker's psychology. All of these it will be recognized have other origins in other fields than psychoanalysis. . . . However . . . psychoanalysis had a more direct influence at this point through the interpretations of such men as Dr. White and Dr. Glueck. . . . The first, which it has taken case work some years to assimilate, is the concept of determinism in psychic life. Generalized and philosophic recognition of the application of this principle in psychology may have been granted by many sociologists and psychologists but it is Freud's distinction to have shown for the first time a concrete working out of this principle in experience. . . .

A second revolutionary concept which case work seized upon from Freudian psychology was an emphasis on the need basis of behavior as opposed to the intellectual factor. . . . Here was the clue to an understanding of much that had been obscure in the reactions and behavior of patients and clients. Case work now began a search for the individual's needs as a first step in diagnosis, not from the old sociologic approach which accepted the need of all human beings for food, shelter, clothing and certain human associations but with a much more painstaking effort to find the concrete symbols in which these needs had expressed themselves in each individual. . . . Sex was thrown open to exploration as a human need and the case worker's treatment of sex behavior grew increasingly tolerant and understanding. . . .

The third contribution . . . lay in the light thrown upon the knowledge of family relationships and their effect on individual development. . . . Economic and sociological thinking . . . had emphasized community factors in individual and family life. The emphasis from the new psychology pointed out the small family group as the first and most important pressure in conditioning attitudes. Here attitudes, behavior patterns, and the personality of the child were primarily determined. From this point of view, later environmental pressures and obstacles became less and less significant and important. The problem of family relationships and their effect on the development of the child proved to be stimulating to study and research in many fields so that the accumulation of knowledge now at the disposal of students in technical and popular literature has gone far beyond its psychoanalytic origins. . . .

It is the sociological rather than the psychological basis which organizes and gives unity to [Mary Richmond's] . . . *Social Diagnosis*. . . . It represents the assimilation of many years of experience . . . and six years of actual research work. More than this, as the work of a scholar, and a deliberative able mind, it reflects the finest thinking of the period. Law, Medicine, Psychology, History, Philosophy, Sociology, and Social Work each contributed a vital part in the synthesis which this book presents.

Representing as it does, an assimilation and organization going on over a period of fifteen years, its central focus of interpretation is to be found in a point of view antedating 1916, its publication date. . . .

The concepts on which we are working today are no where as yet formulated with sufficient definiteness to afford comparison with the concepts of *Social Diagnosis*. The formulation of the psychological basis on which case work practice rests today will no doubt be met with as much criticism and divergence of opinion as is the formulation of the sociological basis of case work of 1917 which Miss Richmond expressed. However much we have departed from the social point of view of *Social Diagnosis* we have not yet achieved any articulation comparable to this work in unity and organization which we may venture to believe was truly inclusive and expressive of the best thinking and practice of social case work of that period. . . .

Miss Richmond makes an effort to put the diagnosis of the social situation on a more scientific and logical basis in the diagnostic summary. . . . This type of analysis could not go far in its usefulness until there was greater development in the science of "characterology." . . .

Of the social case work relationship, of "contact," little is said directly in *Social Diagnosis*. . . . Enough of Miss Richmond's attitude however can be inferred to give us a sense of a very real and rare human kindliness entering into her conception of this relationship. . . . Critically examined, the relationship between case worker and client is on a friendly, naïve, unanalyzed basis. . . .

The hope held out of finding a logical sequence in the elusive material of everyday human experience . . . proved enormously stimulating to the case work field. . . . It was Miss Richmond herself who . . . pointed out the psychological task of case work in such a way as to stimulate a new interest in getting beneath the purely situational aspects of an individual's problem —"the criterion of the social, its indispensable element, always is the influence of mind upon mind." How to get at "the central core of difficulty" in the social relationships by which "a given personality had been shaped" remained the alluring task which Miss Richmond set for her followers—unsolved but possible of solution. . . .

The entrance of the United States into the war in 1918 brought new and upsetting influences to bear on a philosophy and procedures which might otherwise have crystallized around the organization and point of departure which *Social Diagnosis* offered. The sudden appearance of a new group of clients, the families of the soldiers and sailors, not previously known to any social agency, not accustomed to asking or receiving assistance . . . raised new problems of approach, of contact, of training.[45] . . .

To the war experience was due also the close contact with modern psychiatry. . . . By the time of the Atlantic City [National] Conference in 1919, psychiatric social work commanded the center of attention. . . . At that meeting the famous issue, a bone of contention at many succeeding meetings, was raised as to whether this work is to be emphasized as a specialty with specialized training or as the essential approach to any case work with individuals. . . .

Southard contributed to this interest in the psychological by pleading . . . for the individual rather than the family as the unit of case work. . . . Mr. Lee answered this argument in 1919 in his paper on "The Fabric of the Family." . . . But in spite of the effort on the part of the family workers to keep a well balanced point of view of the family unit, the emphasis on the individual gained steadily. . . .

[45] The Red Cross Home Service developed casework with families of the armed forces, ran training institutes, and wrote a manual of instructions for visitors. There was much discussion as to which procedures of COS were appropriate; particularly, how much information visitors should demand.

With the change . . . from emphasis on sociologic to psychologic fact, from environmental circumstances per se to their value and meaning as individual experiences, the entire organization of the social history is altered. A family case history becomes rather an analysis of the individual members in their interaction to each other and in their social setting rather than a history of a social situation. The unit of study has shifted to the individual although in family case work the family is still assumed to be the treatment unit.

History [46] will not be needed to bulwark our uncertainty or to substitute for our ignorance of present reactions. History will take its place in the relationship not in terms of the case worker's need but as one of the client's reactions. It will come into the record at whatever time and place the client needs to make use of it and his uses of it will be many and various as the relationship proceeds. It will usually be offered in the early contacts as the client's first gift of himself in return for the help he seeks, his first breaking down of the boundaries of separation between himself and another. But equally well it may be withheld at this time by the client who in that one move to take help, to include another, withdraws at the same time defensively to protect himself from invasion. In both cases it is not the facts of the history but the immediate present reality of the client's reaction to the worker which is important for her to recognize in the treatment relationship.

[46] Miss Robinson uses "history" to refer to "case history," or all collected material about the client's past.

XXXIII
EMERGENCE OF METHOD:
GROUP WORK

Activities in agencies interested in helping people collectively in neighborhood and interest groups multiplied during the first two decades of the new century. Youth organizations, settlements, and institutional churches continuously initiated new programs and broadened former ones. Most group workers considered that one of their fundamental purposes was to acquaint new immigrants and underprivileged children and adolescents with the best aspects of American ideals and customs. Agencies also hoped to provide constructive ways in which wage earners might use the new leisure to enhance their political and social position. In so doing, it was hoped that delinquent tendencies and poor living standards would gradually be overcome and the whole society improved.

There was uncertainty whether there was greater value in mass recreation in playgrounds and gymnasia or in small group activity. Settlement and "Y" leaders had to defend hobby clubs and self-help political action organizations which served a few people at a time. They were convinced that something positive happened when people had opportunity to get together but they had a hard time identifying what it was.

When Mary P. Follett described what she saw as the kernel of democratic process—the formation of opinion and organization for action as it occurred in small groups—"character-building" agencies and community organization specialists eagerly seized upon it. At long last they saw the basis for analysis of process in what they had been doing in an opportunistic way. At about the same time, the progressive education movement was pointing out the values of free association and the leadership rather than authoritarian role of the good teacher. This was easily translated to apply to the approach of a "good" leader.

Workers in agencies serving groups began to speculate on what actually happened when an experienced person led a group, in an effort to pinpoint skills and techniques and develop some principles concerning how they could be used selectively and in combination. Wilber Newstetter, after systematic observation and experiments at a summer camp, was one of the first to set down method in an ordered way.

Within the child guidance movement, it soon became apparent to caseworkers that in many children obstreperous or withdrawn behavior was only a symptom of their failure to relate to their peers and work cooperatively with others. Referral to interest groups usually was unsuccessful, as also frequently was casework. Efforts were then made to develop relationship ability by specially designed group experience. From beginnings such as Slavson's, group therapy, based on psychiatric knowledge, became a recognized type of social work.

From that period on, group work agencies have debated whether their central function is to provide a preventive service by giving opportunity for needed association with others to normally developing children, an outlet for self-development through democratic social action to normal adults, or an avenue for personality change through groups geared to take account of individual needs and deviations.

During the depression (R108) group work was just beginning to be seen as a set of skills in social work with which every social worker needed to have some familiarity, and which specialists should work together to improve.

In 1935 a division of the National Conference was formed, comparable to that for caseworkers, and in 1936 the National Association for the Study of Group Work was organized. (This later became the American Association of Group Workers.) The publication of articles describing methodology and philosophy accelerated. Interest turned from describing the ideal institutional structure and *what* should be done with groups, to *how* it should be done.[47]

[47] For a sampling of group work thinking toward the end of this period see a collection of contemporary papers, *New Trends in Group Work*, published under the auspices of the National Association for the Study of

96. The Group Process: the Collective Idea

M[ary] P. Follett,[48] *The New State* (New York: Longmans, Green and Co., 1918), pp. 24–27, 29–30, 33

Let us begin at once to consider the group process. Perhaps the
most familiar example of the evolving of a group idea is a committee meeting. The object of a committee meeting is first of all to
create a common idea. I do not go to a committee meeting merely
to give my own ideas. . . . Neither do I go to learn other people's
ideas. . . . I go to a committee meeting in order that all together
we may create a group idea, an idea which will be better than any
one of our ideas alone, moreover which will be better than all of
our ideas added together. For this group idea will not be produced
by any process of addition, but by the interpenetration of us all.
This subtle psychic process by which the resulting idea shapes itself is the process we want to study. . . .

A has one idea, B another, C's idea is something different from
either, and so on, but we cannot add all these ideas to find the
group idea. . . . But we gradually find that our problem can be
solved, not indeed by mechanical aggregation, but by the subtle
process of the intermingling of all the different ideas of the group.
A says something. Thereupon a thought arises in B's mind. Is it
B's idea or A's? Neither. It is a mingling of the two. . . .

We find in the end that it is not a question of my idea being
supplemented by yours, but that there has been evolved a composite idea. . . .

Group Work, ed. Joshua Lieberman (New York: Association Press, 1938);
and Gaynell Hawkins, *Educational Experiments in Social Settlements*
(New York: American Association for Adult Education, 1937). Stages in
philosophical development are listed in Margaret E. Hartford, "Social
Group Work 1930 to 1960; the Search for a Definition" (New York:
NASW, 1960; mimeographed).

[48] Mary Follett started leading clubs in Roxbury Neighborhood House,
Boston, in 1900 and was instrumental in getting schoolhouses opened for
evening recreation. She was also active in vocational guidance. Her experiences in trying to stimulate interest to attain these ends led her to
consider the psychological aspects of political behavior, which she developed in this work. Henry C. Metcalf, Introduction, in H. C. Metcalf
and L. Urwick, eds., *Dynamic Administration; the Collected Papers of
Mary P. Follett* (New York: Harper, 1942).

Let us consider what is required of the individual in order that the group idea shall be produced. First and foremost each is to do his part. But just here we have to get rid of some rather antiquated notions. The individual is not to facilitate agreement by courteously (!) waiving his own point of view. . . . There are probably many present at the conference who could make wiser plans than I alone, but that is not the point, we have come together each to give something. I must not subordinate myself, I must affirm myself and give my full positive value to that meeting.

And as the psychic coherence of the group can be obtained only by the full contribution of every member, so we see that a readiness to compromise must be no part of the individual's attitude. Just so far as people think that the basis of working together is compromise or concession, just so far they do not understand the first principles of working together. . . .

At the same time that we offer fully what we have to give, we must be eager for what all others have to give. If I ought not to go to my group feeling that I must give up my own ideas in order to accept the opinions of others, neither ought I to go to force my ideas upon others. The "harmony" that comes from the domination of one man is not the kind we want. . . .

To take our full share in the synthesis is all that is legitimate. . . .

It is clear then that we do not go to our group—trade-union, city council, college faculty—to be passive and learn, and we do not go to push through something we have already decided we want. Each must discover and contribute that which distinguishes him from others, his difference. The only use for my difference is to join it with other differences. The unifying of opposites is the eternal process. We must have an imagination which will leap from the particular to the universal. Our joy, our satisfaction, must always be in the more inclusive aspect of our problem.

We can test our group in this way: do we come together to register the results of individual thought, to compare the results of individual thought in order to make selections therefrom, or do we come together to create a common idea? Whenever we have a real group something new *is* actually created. . . .

What then is the essence of the group process by which are evolved the collective thought and the collective will? It is an acting and reacting, a single and identical process which brings out differences and integrates them into a unity. The complex reciprocal action, the intricate interweavings of the members of the group, is the social process.

97. *What Is Social Group Work?*

W[ilber] I. Newstetter,[49] *NCCC*, 1935, pp. 291-99

It is necessary . . . to distinguish between group work as a field, group work as a process, and group work techniques. . . .

The group-work process. Group work may be defined as an educational process emphasizing (1) the development and social adjustment of an individual through voluntary group association; and (2) the use of this association as a means of furthering other socially desirable ends. It is concerned therefore with both individual growth and social results. . . .

Let us visualize our group-worker. He makes a certain conscious effort, called a technique, toward [the] group. Let us call this technique No. 1. And let us assume this is an effort to discover interest. As a result of this conscious effort, or technique, the social process in the group becomes slightly modified. This conscious effort, we may assume, is made in line with the general objectives or aims of group work mentioned above. Now the situation in the group represented by the modified social process determines to a large extent what the next conscious effort or technique of the worker shall be. Obviously this requires observation on the part of the worker. It also requires a scheme for the interpretation of human behavior. So the next technique, number two, is determined not by prearranged sequence, but by the worker on the basis, primarily, of the modified social process in the group. Other considerations, to be mentioned

[49] Wilber Newstetter was on the faculty of Western Reserve School of Applied Social Sciences, director of University Neighborhood Centers and Wawokye Camp. He was currently in the process of developing a theory concerning group adjustment and devising research methods for group work.

below, also enter into this determination. Then technique number two is applied by the worker. This, in turn, further modifies the social process in the group. And this provides the basis, primarily, for the selection of the next technique. It is this reciprocal procedure just described that we may call the group-work process. The nature of this procedure or process is determined by (1) the objectives of the worker; (2) the adjustive efforts within the group itself; (3) the worker's observation and interpretation of the adjustive efforts within the group; (4) the skill of the worker in the selection and application of technique. . . .

What are some of the guiding principles for this educational procedure? First I should mention particularization, i.e., individualization of group members as to backgrounds, capacities, needs, interests, not only on the basis of what is observed in the group itself, but also on the basis of all other information obtainable. Next I should mention self-direction, i.e., promotion of the assumption of maximum responsibility on the part of the group for determining and interpreting its own acts through practice.

Next I should mention indirection, i.e., guidance and stimulation primarily through influence on the social and physical setting of the group rather than through the direct personal influence or authority of the worker. Then I should mention repetition, i.e., the promotion of habitual responses to a variety of life situations. And finally I should suggest integration. This has two aspects: first, guidance in the adjustive efforts of the group in its acceptance of each individual member, and the acceptance by each individual member of the group; second, guidance in the unifying of objectives of individual growth and social results. Generally speaking, stress is placed on the guidance, not the manipulation, of the adjustive efforts being made by members of the group and the group as a whole, rather than on the authoritative direction of these adjustive efforts. Spontaneity, self-direction, and determination are the *sine qua non* of group work. The program is not the thing. It must take a second place. The detailed superimposed leisure-time program and the authoritative leader have little or no place in the process. The group-worker's rôle is largely that of understanding the needs of individual members, of helping to set the stage, of helping to provide the suitable environment for learning, expression, adjustment, and social action. . . .

The school of thought, as well as practice, defining group work as process maintains that unless there is the combined and consistent pursuit of both objectives, the efforts do not fall entirely within this concept of group work. The underlying social-philosophical assumption is that individualized growth and social ends are interwoven and interdependent; that individuals and their social environment are equally important. . . .

The group-work field. If group work is defined as a process as described above, it may be said that much of what is labeled group work today falls considerably short of this particular variety. As we have pointed out, some organizations aim primarily at the development and social adjustment of individuals in a general way but not on an individualized basis. This is indeed a desirable procedure, and is, and probably always will be, a definite part of our work. But we should frankly recognize that work with large leisure-time groups, many having little or no stability of enrolment or attendance; work with groups whether large or small in which the primary objective is a program to fill leisure time, to "prevent delinquency," to "keep them out of mischief," or to "build citizenship," is often making only partial application of the group-work process and that it is a different, though desirable thing, just as mass relief is different from case work. . . . For the time being the group-work field might be defined as including all leisure-time agencies to which the development of the group-work process is centrally important.

Group-work techniques. . . .

The techniques employed in the group-work process are being developed in practice around the means utilized by leaders to deal with a series of very practical problems. Some of these are the following: (*a*) how groups may most effectively be formed and with what types of organization; (*b*) how mutually satisfactory relationships may be established between the worker and the group; (*c*) how individual interests, capacities, differences, attitudes, backgrounds, and needs may be discovered; (*d*) how a tentative program of group activities may be developed on this basis; (*e*) how the group status of each member may be determined and modified; (*f*) how conflicts resulting from different norms or standards, objectives, and personalities may be adjusted; (*g*) how the relationships between members within the group may be improved, and how the relationships of the group itself to other groups may be developed; (*h*) how to provide for the personal guidance of individual members, when necessary; (*i*) how the group process can be made to serve individual and social ends simultaneously.

The technique of recording group experience is also being developed in some quarters. . . .

Relation of group work to other processes. The acceptance of group-workers into the fraternity of social workers bears testimony to the broadening base of social work and an emphasis on generic concepts.

98. *Meaningful Personal Relations*

S[amuel] R. Slavson,[50] *Creative Group Education* (New York: Association Press, 1938), pp. 17–23, 227–28

[Voluntary groups] meet the requirements of the native social, ego, or creative tendencies, or . . . respond to any other kind of deep-seated, wholehearted interest. . . .

The ends of education are best served by the voluntary group: it makes a direct appeal to the basic nature of man. . . .

Voluntary association offers opportunities for a multiplicity of contacts and more meaningful personal relations. It is through these relations that character is shaped. . . . The free group offers opportunities for the true face-to-face experiences: it allows social experimentation and, because it has no specific pro-

[50] Samuel Slavson was lecturer in education at New York University and conducting group therapy for the Jewish Board of Guardians, New York City.

gram to follow, makes direct interplay of personalities possible. . . .

Types of voluntary groups [are]: (1) the socially or culturally homogeneous, (2) the activity, (3) the special-interest or interest-homogeneous, and (4) the therapy group. . . .

The *socially or culturally homogeneous* groups are the easiest to work with if they accept a leader. Often, however, such groups are dominated by a gang spirit. . . .

Many group practitioners consider homogeneous groups educationally most fruitful. . . . Social education aims to develop adaptibility, tolerance, and acceptance of others. . . . The socially homogeneous group must therefore be viewed as only one step in the educational process. . . . New members should be introduced from time to time. . . .

The meetings of [*multi-activity*] groups consist almost entirely of informal individual occupations or small group projects, each member pursuing his own interest, but serving as a stimulus for all the others in the group. . . . The program . . . includes a minimum of rote business and discussion. . . . Members make contacts with one another as the needs arise. . . . Out of these contacts on the job, friendships are slowly established. Members carry over these friendships outside of the group. . . .

[The *therapy group*] calls for a high degree of skill and insight on the part of the leader. Its purpose is to reduce mental stress in disturbed children or youth by supplying their psychological needs on an individual basis. In the practice of the present writer, the general setting of such a group is similar to that of a multi-activity group: materials and tools, and freedom to use them at will. There is, however, greater latitude allowed in this group. Materials, situations, and relations among the members can be destructive as well as constructive. The members can break and destroy and fight with one another. The final objective in this work is not to teach the members social behavior, but rather to eliminate the inner needs for hostile, destructive acts. The general plan in the conduct of a therapy group is to simulate as closely as possible family relationships with the members as siblings and the worker as a substitute parent. The technique also is similar to that employed in the multi-activity group, but it aims rather at discharge of emotion than at achievement of external results.

The aim is recuperation from severe emotional stress. This type of group work falls within the realm of psychiatry. . . .

Enlightened group workers find that most groups pass through stages in their existence that correspond fully or in part to the four types of groups described, and that they employ multiple technique and programs suitable to meet these varying needs. . . .

All the positive elements of family life that the members have missed in their childhood, and that are still denied to them, are emphasized in a therapy group.

The creative activity at the meetings is therefore incidental. Its chief purpose is to bring the members together, to stimulate contact, conversation, co-operation and mutual admiration, and, above all, real love for an adult. The family pattern is simulated to an extent that each group has its own . . . utensils necessary for preparing refreshments in the meeting room. . . . There is no formal organization of any kind. . . .

The girls in both groups [whose records are published] did not know each other previous to joining the "club" . . . they are all problem children, all of whom were receiving psychiatric guidance . . . they were all referred for treatment by schools, the police department, or by parents. Most of these girls did not fit into any organized groups: family, school, street, or neighborhood center. Many of them were rejected by their neighborhood centers and settlements as too difficult and troublesome, and all of them could not fit into the ordinary club, and dropped out or were rejected. Both of these groups joined regular centers after two and one half years of Group Therapy.

XXXIV

EMERGENCE OF METHOD: COMMUNITY ORGANIZATION

While casework methodology was becoming a recognizable entity, and group work was coming to be recognized as something different from work with groups, attention was also being directed to ways of working with the larger community to achieve desirable ends.[51] Such efforts were not new in the twentieth century, and two major approaches, already tried, were pursued in this period. The approach advocated by most settlement workers of developing grass-roots democratic activity on the part of the constituency itself was modified and adapted by many other movements. Sometimes political measures were used to achieve social welfare objectives; sometimes social or health activities seemed to be means to political goals. During the period covered by this book few of these grass-roots movements outside the settlements received wide acceptance among social workers, or made any permanent contribution to professional development.[52]

On the other hand, earlier efforts by the COS and others to get already established organizations to work together more effectively were revived, elaborated, and greatly expanded. Their impact on the profession was profound.

[51] The editors are indebted to United Community Funds and Councils of America, New York City, for access to unpublished, unsigned materials in their historical files. Of special help were notes on interviews with founders of the Cleveland Community Chest; "Concerning Organization of Cleveland Community Fund," 1938; reprints of news items throughout the country; and the memorandum "History of Federated Philanthropic Planning and Fund-Raising," ca. 1953.

[52] E.g., Jessie Frederick Steiner, "The Cincinnati Social Unit Experiment," in Ernest B. Harper and Arthur Dunham, eds., *Community Organization in Action* (New York: Association Press, 1959), pp. 117–26. For further readings on the historical development of community organization consult *ibid.*, pp. 113–41.

The increasing complexity of organized services in cities again led thoughtful people to seek ways to bring order out of what often seemed little short of chaos. The incentives were twofold: persons working in agencies needed some way to work out operational problems caused by gaps or overlaps in their programs; givers felt the need for protection against repeated demands on a relatively few people from many agencies. These incentives tended to merge. Professional workers who were concerned about gaps in service had to consider ways of securing more adequate financial support for all services. Givers who were concerned about the multiplicity of appeals had to find ways of evaluating those appeals on the basis of community need and effectiveness of service.

Shortly after the turn of the century, in various cities, social work leaders got together, first informally, and then more formally, to consider their mutual problems. These councils of social agencies represented efforts on the part of those responsible for the development of the budding profession to improve the quality and effectiveness of their work. To achieve consistency and continuity, however, these councils needed staff persons who could devote full time to the work, and usually this was possible only by allying themselves with the new joint fund-raising efforts.

The Denver experiment in joint fund-raising (R55) had never captured wide support, but when the Cleveland Chamber of Commerce promoted a well-thought-out plan, the results were different. Despite widespread skepticism in the COS and other national organizations and active opposition by notable leaders (Mary Richmond's failure to secure election as president of the National Conference in 1922 was probably partly related to her bitter opposition to the chest movement), community chests increased rapidly in number and strength. Through these it was possible to secure specialized personnel to help communities straighten out the confused tangle of agency structure and function.

It is hard for a later generation to appreciate the cloud of uncertainty, lack of information, prejudice, and dogmatism in which this work was carried on. Much of the effort had to be directed to fund-raising—the development of methods of educating the public to the needs and services of voluntary agencies and of effectively canvassing an ever-widening portion of the potential givers. Another sizable portion of the effort of these specialists was to promote mutual understanding and cooperation among the agencies which were performing the actual services. Still a third aspect was the development of the budgeting process for distributing the funds raised in the chest campaigns in order that the needs of the community as a whole might be best served. If these were not to be haphazard activities, procedures had to be devised, and above all, reliable data were needed. Hence it was natural that great emphasis should be placed on developing the fact-finding techniques illustrated in the next chapter (R103, 104).

99. To Promote Social Work

Social Service Conference of St. Louis, 1909–1910 (Program announcement, St. Louis, 1909), starred paragraphs are from the 1911–12 announcement [58]

The Social Service Conference was organized in January, 1907, to provide a means for bringing active social workers together for the exchange of opinion and information and co-operation in matters of common interest.

The meetings, since its beginning, have been held bi-weekly downtown at luncheon, from October to June, and at less frequent intervals during the summer.

[58] In form this organization combined membership and representation. The status of those who had only a general interest in social work was distinctly different from that of practitioners, and their different levels of competence for decision-making were recognized. When the Central Council of Social Agencies was set up in 1911 it took over planning and co-ordinating functions while the common interests of social workers as employees continued in the Conference, which became a luncheon club. Both were interested in social legislation. *Handbook of the Central Council of Social Agencies, 1912* (St. Louis); Judith Levy, "Historical Analysis of the Evolution of the Community Fund of St. Louis," unpublished Master's essay, Washington University, 1928. Figures in parentheses after the names of committees apparently referred to the number of members.

*The Conference has had an active membership of between sixty and eighty each year, about half of whom have been representative of various philanthropic associations. The associates, those with a general rather than a professional interest in social work, have numbered about seventy-five to eighty.

*While the Conference has devoted its efforts mainly to discussion and exchange of information, it has organized or chiefly assisted in several important movements, among which have been —(1) the experiment in the use of the Patrick Henry School as a recreation center (1908); (2) the Committee for Social Legislation (1909–11); (3) the Association for the Blind; (4) the Central Council of Social Agencies; and (5) the Committee for Social Service among Colored People.

Constitution

ARTICLE II

The purpose of this organization shall be to promote social work.

By-Laws

ARTICLE II. . . .

The membership of this association shall consist of:

First: One representative from each of such organizations active in social work as shall be elected in the manner hereinafter provided. Each organization so elected shall appoint its own representative.

Second: Such other persons, active in social work, as shall be elected in the manner hereinafter provided; but the number of such persons so elected shall not exceed the number of organizations represented in the Conference.

In addition to the members provided for herein, who shall be known as active members, there shall also be a class of associate members, composed of persons with a general rather than a special or professional interest in social service, elected in the same manner as active members. Associate members shall pay the same dues as active members [one dollar a year] and shall be entitled to the same privileges, with exception of attendance at the bi-weekly meetings unless invited as guests. . . .

The Committee on Membership shall investigate the qualifications of the organizations, applicants for representation and of the persons, applicants for membership in the Conference, and shall make reports as early as practicable to the Executive Committee. The adverse votes of a majority of the Committee on Membership shall be sufficient to reject any application; provided that any applicant may appeal from such adverse report to the Executive Committee. . . .

Executive Committee Regulations

Failure on the part of any active member to attend three successive bi-weekly meetings will be considered equivalent to a transfer to associate membership. . . .

Failure to acknowledge two consecutive notices will be equivalent to a resignation.

The Functions of the Various Committees

1. *Outdoor Relief* (5)—To investigate and report to the conference on (*a*) the administration and principles of relief in homes on the part of charitable and religious associations; (*b*) relief to beggars and tramps; (*c*) the relation of outdoor relief as practiced in St. Louis to institutional care.

2. *Schools, Libraries and Recreation* (9)—To investigate and report on (*a*) the social service opportunities and work of both public and parochial schools; (*b*) the social service work of the library and its relation to the schools; (*c*) the extension of organized recreation facilities; (*d*) the suppression of harmful recreation as evidenced in numerous summer gardens, dance halls, nickelodeons, cheap theatres and steamboat excursions.

3. *Health and Sanitation* (9)—To investigate and report on (*a*) the enforcement of health regulations and the need for

further regulation; (*b*) the conduct of hospitals and institutions for the sick (with special attention to social service); (*c*) the practice of midwifery; (*d*) the preventive work of pure milk for babies, the inspection of foodstuffs and places in which foods are made and offered for sale.

4. *Neglected and Delinquent Children* (9)—To investigate and report on (*a*) the care of neglected and delinquent children in institutions and in the care of the Juvenile Court; (*b*) the preventive work in delinquency on the part of the schools and recreation agencies; (*c*) the cooperation of all agencies dealing with children; (*d*) the enforcement of child-labor laws and the laws punishing employers and parents for offenses against the rights of children.

5. *Adult Offenders* (9)—To investigate and report on (*a*) the system of the arrest and treatment of adult offenders in police and criminal courts, (*b*) the jail and workhouse care of offenders, (*c*) the parole and conditional release systems and the after-care of discharged prisoners.

6. *City Plan for Social Betterment* (5)—To draw up and report to the Conference by April, 1910, a plan for the social betterment of the city from the point of view of present needs, as to (1) institutions, (2) laws and regulations governing buildings, streets and health, (3) care of dependents, defectives, and delinquents by the state and city, (4) changes in the relation of private associations, (5) state or city laws affecting social relations and social institutions.

7. *Social Legislation* (9)—To be constantly informed and to report from time to time on the needs in state or city legislation regarding social conditions.

8. *Committee on Industrial Relations* (9)—To investigate and report on (*a*) the general industrial situation—especially wages and unemployment, (*b*) trades-unions and employees' benefit associations, (*c*) social service movements on the part of employers, (*d*) industrial education and trade training, (*e*) the operation of labor laws.

100. Charitable Giving

"The Cleveland Federation for Charity and Philanthropy as Proposed by the Committee on Benevolent Societies of the Cleveland Chamber of Commerce January 7, 1913" (Cleveland: Chamber of Commerce, 1913), pp. 3–9 [54]

In May, 1900, it was found that fifty-one institutions had been created to express in one form or another the good will of Cleveland. In order to be of service to the organizations deserving public support, the Chamber created the committee on benevolent associations. Its duties as outlined were "to protect the giving public against solicitations for unworthy purposes and thus to assist worthy and efficient institutions, whose income had become adversely affected by the existence of much fraudulent solicitation." As a means to this end it was suggested that the Committee investigate carefully all charitable organizations in the city and issue a card of endorsement to such as complied with a certain standard of excellence. As a condition of endorsement the committee has been able to require, in most cases, such reorganization and improvement of methods as has resulted in an adequate meeting of the needs for which the organization was intended, economy of expenditures and intelligent, businesslike operation.

In order to carry out its policy, the committee has stipulated, as far as is practicable, that organizations comply with the following requirements:

1. The organization shall fill a need not already well filled by an existing organization, and not capable of being thus filled.

2. The need shall be relatively great enough to warrant the equipment and support of a separate organization.

3. The organization shall agree to co-operate with other benevolent associations in promoting efficiency, and economy of administration in the charities of the city as a whole, and in preventing duplication of effort.

---

[54] Community pressures led to formation of a fund-raising federation. R101 outlines the proposed plan and the initial response to it.

4. The administrative committee of the organization shall meet at least quarterly.

5. All funds shall be collected according to a method approved by the committee on benevolent associations.

6. The accounts of the organization shall be regularly audited and a copy of its annual report shall be filed with the committee on benevolent associations.

7. The operations of the organization and its accounts shall always be open to the investigation of accredited representatives of the committee on benevolent associations.

Before endorsement was granted the committee usually arranged for a personal investigation . . . and a written statement giving, in detail, the essential facts regarding the organization was required. A card of endorsement was granted to such as complied with the committee's standards. Members of the Chamber and the contributing public in general were requested to contribute only to those bearing the card of endorsement. At first contributors were inclined to rely upon their own judgment, pursuing the policy of previous years, and not realizing that a careful investigation, backed by trained judgment and adequate conceptions, was necessary to determine the need for an organization and its fitness to do charitable work. The committee found it necessary therefore to inaugurate a campaign of education along these lines. When it was found that a contributor had given to an unendorsed institution the contributor was called by telephone, the reason for the committee's refusal to endorse was carefully explained, and an effort was made to impress upon him the justice of this action and the mutual advantage which would obtain through his co-operation with the committee. The Chamber by means of circulars notified its members of hopelessly unworthy institutions which were receiving the support of the public. The newspapers gave their cordial co-operation. Many organizations were prevailed upon, in making their solicitations, to present a card of endorsement, whether the contributor asked it or not, thus bringing to the attention of the public, the existence of the system. After years of education and development the community has come to recognize the value of this committee's work and to rely almost universally on the committee's action. Strong institutions now consider the card of vital importance in collecting funds. Smaller institutions say that the committee's endorsement is essential to their support and that existence would be impossible without it.

As a condition of endorsement of the various organizations each succeeding year, the committee requires evidence that the standard of efficiency is gradually improving. In addition to this, the committee plans to select perhaps half a dozen organizations for special attention. Their methods are carefully studied, conferences are held with boards of management, and, if necessary, fundamental changes are insisted upon to bring about the very highest standard of efficiency.

The committee has endeavored not only to eliminate worthless institutions and prevent the creation of new organizations which do a work similar to one already in existence, but the committee has been directly instrumental in the inauguration of movements to meet needs not already provided for by the development of existing, or the creation of new, organizations.

Twelve years of such intelligent co-operation has resulted in the combination of organizations where duplication of work existed; the reorganization of other institutions or the entire elimination of some whose work was useless, while more economic methods of collecting contributions from the public, by reducing the number of paid solicitors, benefits, fairs, socials and entertainments which are at best very expensive methods of raising funds for charitable support, have been established.

This decade of careful supervision, although producing exceptional benefits to worthy organizations, has not solved certain problems with which the charitable work of the city is confronted. First—some of the most reliable charitable organizations in the city have experienced great difficulty in raising money sufficient to carry on an aggressive and thoroughly efficient work, while other societies doing a less important work have been laying up a surplus of receipts over expenditures from year to year, and some institutions have collected from the public money which has been expended in maintaining an inefficient or needless work. Second—the demands upon a certain class of contributors have continually increased until those known to be charitably inclined have come to be unduly burdened by the present solicitations of the representatives of various charitable organizations. . . .

Desiring to assist the charitable institutions and the contributing public in the solution of these problems, the committee on benevolent associations during the summer of 1907 made a thorough investigation of the budgets of sixty-one charitable institutions. This study covered such particulars as total budgets, the cost of collection, the amount of invested funds, sources of income, and the number of contributors, a list being made of those who contributed in amounts of five dollars or more. . . . It was found that the total income for the work of these organizations was $994,491.00, of which $39,596.00 was given directly by the public in anonymous gifts and in sums of less than five dollars, $442,811.00 by 5,733 people in amounts of five dollars and over, and the remainder or $512,084.00 was derived from endowment, legacies, beneficiaries, etc.

It is to be noted that 2,153 contributors gave only 2.46% of the money, and this in subscriptions of ten dollars or less, while *thirteen people,* or but two-tenths of one per cent of the total number of contributors, gave over *one-third of all money contributed to charity*. Seventy-four people gave more than one-half of the money contributed, and 411 people gave three-fourths of the total.

The results of the canvass of 1907 revealed the fact that the contributing public is not interested in and educated to the broad demands of charity. 72% of the whole number of individuals contributing to charity gave to but one institution. . . . Only twelve contributed to twenty or more, and there was only one who contributed to more than thirty.

The facts in regard to the number of contributors to charity presented in the report were startling, even to those who had made a special study of charitable work in Cleveland. . . . The committee on benevolent associations tentatively suggested the federated plan of collecting and distributing all moneys for charitable purposes as a remedy for this and other conditions which appeared to hinder the largest development of philanthropic work in Cleveland. The printed report covering the results of the first census was mailed to 374 contributors to charity. . . .

136 answers [to questionnaires] were received from these persons.

119 contributors gave unqualified approvals of the plan.

4 contributors gave qualified approvals.

8 contributors gave qualified approvals subject to certain objections.

2 contributors gave qualified approvals subject to further investigation.

3 contributors gave an unqualified disapproval.

Backed by such enthusiastic endorsement the committee was considering a campaign to educate the contributing public to the merits of the federated plan and if it then appeared feasible, to secure its immediate adoption. But before this publicity campaign could be started, the depression of industrial and financial conditions made it seem impracticable to commence the undertaking. . . .

In December of 1909, the matter was again taken under consideration, but two years had lapsed since the first canvass. The increasing demands of charity and the changed conditions among both contributors and institutions made the results of the first canvass of comparatively little value. . . .

The committee determined upon a second canvass.

The letter sent to the various organizations asked for information of a very wide range and very great detail. The co-operation manifested by the organizations in compiling the material desired showed their desire for a change. . . .

In the present census seventy-three institutions were covered. One which was included in the previous canvass was dropped. . . . Three organizations did not report, two organizations had suspended work and did not handle any money during the year of 1909. The Salvation Army was included as three organizations because these branches are separately endorsed by the committee on benevolent associations. The Jewish Federation was counted as one organization although in reality it represented eleven separate institutions. Two of the above institutions had not been endorsed by the Chamber of Commerce.

It was found that the total income for the work of these organizations was $1,893,010.33.

101. *The Federated Plan of Giving*

The Social Year Book: the Human Problems and Resources of Cleveland (Cleveland: the Cleveland Federation for Charity and Philanthropy, 1913), pp. 13–15, 20–21

The Federation is the result of action taken by the Cleveland Chamber of Commerce on January 7th, 1913, adopting the recommendations of its Committee on Benevolent Associations. . . .

The givers-lists of 73 benevolent organizations in 1909 showed only 4,598 different individuals and 788 corporations contributing a total of $5.00 or more. . . .

In order to make certain that such an educational and cooperative effort should bear equally in mind all the interests at stake, the Committee suggested that the Federation be controlled by a board of thirty trustees, one-third to be elected by the participating organizations, one-third by the givers and one-third chosen by the Chamber of Commerce to represent the city at large. On March first the Board as thus created met and organized. Between that time and previous to October 1, it has been forwarding subscriptions as made by 4,118 givers on a subscription blank bearing the explanation of the plan. . . .

I. *Federation subscribers* are not solicited for current expenses by any of the organizations in the Federation.

II. *Current expenses only* are solicited by the Federation; before soliciting funds for other needs, federated organizations are expected to consult with the Federation board. Gifts to such needs are forwarded by the Federation on request.

III. Gifts are forwarded in line with the designation of givers *to any Cleveland organization*, whether listed as a member of the Federation or not. . . .

Seven months . . . of the Federation's first full fiscal year, have shown surprising progress toward the attainment of the organization's four-fold aim: (1) larger gifts to good works; (2) more effective gifts; (3) more givers, and (4) happier givers.

Larger Gifts. A careful comparison of each subscription received by the Federation with the gifts made by the same persons in 1912 shows the use of the federated subscription-blank to cause the following amazing results: [69.1 percent gain in gifts designated to more organizations]. . . .

"The City of Good Will." More gifts and greater efficiency and economy in the use of them, more givers and givers happier in the unselfish use of their means, are important matters and will long be worth all the attention that can possibly be given them. . . .

The Federation for Charity and Philanthropy, thus, is much more than a group of related social organizations working simply for the increase of their own resources or efficiency. The Federation represents the plan of a whole community to pool all its resources of time, energy, intelligence, vision, sentiment and inspiration in the attempt to solve the problem of human welfare as it presents itself in the acute forms so familiar—so unpleasantly familiar—in the modern city. Nothing less than such a combination of the entire resources of the whole community will suffice to meet successfully the challenge of the city of today. Because Cleveland has been the first to recognize this, inquiries come daily from all over the world as to the progress of so daring and timely an enterprise.

102. Conclusions and Recommendations Regarding Federation

Financial Federations, the Report of a Special Committee [55] of the American Association for Organizing Charity, July 31, 1917 (New York: the Association, 1917), pp. 63–67

Our general conclusions are as follows:

1. Measured by total contributions, financial success appears to have been usual in initial federation years except where there has been inadequate preparation and organization. Financial success is much less surely shown when later years are taken into account, and failure is indicated in the one city where there has been a long experience. But the gains achieved have been based almost uniformly upon methods of financial work which in our judgment do not tend to build up as stable a constituency as most organizations in non-federation cities now have. These methods [are] the granting of immunity from solicitation, the use of whirlwind campaigns, and the encouragement of undesignated giving. . . . Moreover, many and wide variations exist in the extent to which the constituent organizations have or have not shared in the total gains, this fact resulting, in some federations, in varying degrees of satisfaction with the situation. Finally, a system of reapportioning the community's gift income among its organizations has been set up, regarding the ultimate benefit of which we have grave doubts. In most federations the cost of collection has probably been reduced below what it might have been under average unfederated conditions, but the gain has not been a marked one.

2. On the educational side there has been an undoubted gain

[55] This committee was charged with the task of evaluating the chest method of financing. Up to this time the American Association for Organizing Charity and the Charity Organization Department of Russell Sage Foundation had been very much opposed to the chests. Members were W. Frank Persons, director of general work, New York COS, chairman (see R82, n. 29); William Baldwin, member of the board of managers, Washington Associated Charities; Fred R. Johnson, secretary, Boston Associated Charities; Eugene T. Lies, general superintendent, Chicago United Charities.

in certain cities, due to their federations' publicity efforts, and some gain in all cities to the extent that joint appealing makes the breadth and variety of social work better realized. But even in the federation cities that have done the best educational work we recognize a tendency, which seems to us inevitable, toward a loss of interest resulting from the lessened contact between givers and the objects of their gifts, and we very much doubt whether this has not more than offset all that has been gained by organized publicity and by the one educational element in joint appealing just referred to. A failure to develop interest makes difficult the development of social intelligence, with unfortunate results on every side. We recognize that in most federation cities there have been increases up to date in the number of people who are interested to the extent that a campaign contribution shows. But because these increases have been gained by whirlwind campaign solicitation we feel it is not yet safe to base any important conclusions upon them.

3. On the social side the gains of the federations that have attempted social work have been considerable, and usually so far they seem not to have been offset by losses, other than . . . the retarding of progress in particular lines which we believe must follow from a federation's approval of budgets. The fact, however, that so many federations have neglected social work indicates a tendency which grows out of the imperative character of the financial problem which it is a federation's first duty to solve.

In weighing the considerable testimony that indicates gains in federation cities along educational and social lines, we have kept in mind the fact that in many of these cities modern unfederated methods of co-operative effort have never been developed. Comparisons of each federation with its own earlier situation are therefore not altogether conclusive.

Alongside of the facts which we record regarding federation cities, we place our conviction that the existing order has not been weighed in the balance and found wanting. In many cities in which no federations exist progress has been steady and important, both in educational lines and in organized co-operative social work—quite as important, even though possibly not as rapid, as that which has taken place in certain of the federation cities.

Throughout our study we have been conscious of the inadequacy of the evidence available, this being chiefly due to the short history that most federations have had. The only federation whose experience has been adequate from this standpoint, the Denver Federation, was unwisely managed until very recently. When federated organizations in that city were asked whether they would recommend the formation of federations elsewhere, the weight of advice received favored delay by other cities. The advice was almost equally balanced from organizations in Cleveland where the Federation, with one exception [Elmira, N.Y.], has had the next longest history. From Baltimore and Cincinnati only six and three organizations respectively replied to the inquiry, and only one from each city advised others to follow their example at once. The four Dayton replies expressed no very clear opinions in one direction or the other. The Federation in South Bend is the only one from whose organizations a clear preponderance of advice was received in favor of the formation of federations elsewhere at once.

We who are in non-federation cities are indebted to those who have been brave enough to be pioneers in this important matter, for it is only through experiments that the plan can be tested. Our recommendation, however, to those for whose sake primarily this study has been made, the social workers and others in cities in which the formation of federations is being considered, is very positively against any adoption of the plan *at present*. Fourteen cities are now experimenting with it under quite varying conditions and with several different types of organization. We feel strongly that this is experimentation enough.

Whether the federation plan in any city means a net social advance or the reverse is yet to be demonstrated. No demonstration, moreover, can be made in the next two or three years. The more far reaching effects can hardly show themselves in that time. It must be recalled also that the forming of a federation means an immense amount of work, which is wasted unless the federation accomplishes more than the constituent associations could do. Unless this result is very probable, federation should not be undertaken.

If those responsible for decision in any city are convinced that federation may safely be tried, a choice must be made among the several quite different plans of organization now in operation.

It is important in this connection to recall that as a result of wide advertising of the Cleveland Federation, and of missionary work on the part of its officials in visiting other cities and presenting the subject, the Cleveland plan of organization was imitated in most of its details in Dayton, South Bend, and Erie, and to a considerable extent also in the reorganization of the Denver Federation, and that now the original Cleveland plan—so far as relates to the Federation's scope and the selection of its governing board—has been discarded by its sponsors, and another substituted regarding which much optimism is felt that it will bring the improvement needed. The fact that after an experience of four years the Cleveland plan needed to be radically and fundamentally changed is as important as any one thing that can be said about it.

We recognize that many of the federation difficulties . . . are due to mistakes of management. The secretary of one of the large federations states that "no important movement has suffered more from hasty organization, inadequate preparation, and amateurish leadership than the federation movement." In reaching our conclusions we have aimed to distinguish between mistakes and essentials. But this distinction is frequently difficult in the early days of a movement. For instance, the secretary just quoted holds that immunity though universal is not essential to the federation plan. . . .

It should be remembered that to a considerable extent when an organization enters a federation it burns its bridges behind it. The secretary of one of the large federations writes: "Obviously, after a few years of giving which is almost altogether undesignated giving it will be very difficult to restore designations or even to restore the old unfederated order." This is of course true only if the federation lasts long enough for what we fear are disintegrating tendencies of the plan upon the organizations' relationship with their constituencies . . . to become effective. It is this that makes an organization hesitate to withdraw from a federation even when convinced that its work is being injured. In the six federations that have been abandoned or suspended there was not time for these forces to operate to any important extent, for the experiments lasted in no city more than a year and a half. In our judgment, this explains the fact that several correspondents from such cities report no difficulty in re-establishing financial relations with their former contributors after the federations were dissolved.

A few months ago Mr. Williams [of Cleveland] stated that "the biggest obstacle to the success of the federation plan is that its logic is too good—it looks too easy." This is very true. It partly explains the great mortality among federations. Five out of twenty have been abandoned and one other has suspended operations. . . . The abolition of competition in the financing of social organizations, for the sake of avoiding its waste, is as attractive a proposition in theory and apparently as logical as the abolition of competition in business, which is championed in part on the same ground. But in the social field, whether we agree or not regarding the economic field, there are spiritual and psychological factors which leave doubts as to the ultimate advantage to be derived from giving up a plan of work which has behind it the experience of more than one generation of social workers, in order to adopt one which, according to many who are in a position to know, is still in its experimental stage.

XXXV
EMERGENCE OF METHOD: RESEARCH

Since the beginnings of the Social Science Association and the National Conference, one of the avowed goals of workers in philanthropy and the public services had been to secure factual information about the extent and causes of need, to determine what kinds of services best met and prevented need, and their cost to the community.

Amos Warner's analysis of statistics on the causes of poverty (R69, 70) had undermined easy moralizing about personal fault on the part of "paupers," and so contributed to growing pressure for social reforms. Studies as to what form changes should take, such as evaluation of different types of model housing, and the results of changes elsewhere (R74, 86), became more frequent.

When Mrs. Russell Sage gave ten million dollars, "the income thereof to be applied to the improvement of social and living conditions in the United States," research and experiments became possible on a new scale. Sufficient funds were now available that well-trained people could give adequate time and achieve a degree of objectivity and nation-wide scope not possible within the confines of single agencies. Statistics became more accurate and sophisticated; data-collection methods were more varied.

The Pittsburgh Survey, started in 1907, probably had the most far-reaching effect, both on research techniques and on organization and methods of services, during the next thirty years. It left no doubt that to get effective results social work must take economic and social factors and the entire service network into account.[56]

[56] A description of the Pittsburgh Survey's over-all method is found in Paul U. Kellogg, "Field Work in the Pittsburgh Survey," in *The Pittsburgh District* (Paul U. Kellogg, ed., *The Pittsburgh Survey*, Vol. V), (New York: RSF, 1914), Appendix E, pp. 492–515. For the extent and types

Amos Warner's pioneering work also contributed to the recognition that more must be learned about the causes of individual behavior. Mary Richmond's six-year study of methodology (R91) was outstanding, but only one of many supported by the Russell Sage Foundation. Later, other foundations also regarded social welfare as a field that deserved financial encouragement. The Commonwealth Fund exerted a great impact in underwriting experimentation with application of psychiatric principles to the treatment of problem children (R93). Most of the schools of social work secured funds for small studies of practice and for experimentation with research methods being developed outside the profession.

This research in techniques was received and accepted at varying rates by practitioners. But it did not help the increasing number of community organizers to answer the questions of skeptical or puzzled local leaders: "What good does such-and-such service do?" or "What do we most need to do with our limited funds?" Many of the answers given had to be as much statements of faith as Mrs. Hale's assertions about the merits of normal family life and pride in appearance (R27). Some approach which would give more directly convincing information seemed essential. The fact-finding procedures of a local survey and financial and service accounting became the research methods of community organization.

The American Association of Community Organization (subsequently, Community Chests and Councils, Inc., and now United Community Funds and Councils of America) assumed leadership in this development, and conducted many surveys. The later ones were more directly concerned with the effectiveness of current techniques and the establishment of standards in the quality of services than the Pittsburgh Survey had been. There were few objective criteria, however, and usually evaluations had to depend on the personal judgments of experienced practitioners. The Hartford Survey is an example of one of the most thorough

---

of surveys, consult Allen Eaton and Shelby M. Harrison, *A Bibliography of Social Surveys* (New York: RSF, 1930).

of these community reviews, and not only illustrates the type of research approach current in the mid-thirties, but also gives a representative picture of the kinds and standards of social work that existed just before the advent of the social security system.

Another tool of research developed with a degree of success during this period was a system of uniform nation-wide service statistics. This was something Warner had longed for but felt was hopeless to achieve. The national Social Statistics Project originated in Cleveland. Its sponsors met with a resistance to following definitions accurately and keeping records consistently that was similar to what the National Conference leaders had experienced in the nineties. Yet such basic information was seen to be essential if the efficacy of methods was to be tested under varying conditions, and if any standards of adequacy in meeting needs were to be developed. In the almost complete absence of governmental data in this field, the Social Statistics Project gave some clues to what was happening in the early days of the depression, and helped to demonstrate the values to be derived from a good governmental system.

The depression of the thirties also stimulated research, evaluating types of solutions, some under Federal and some under private auspices (R105). The Social Security Act itself was in part the product of extended assembly of case information to provide a picture of conditions to be corrected as well as painstaking analysis of systems in the several states and in other countries.

103. Social Welfare Census-taking

Raymond Clapp, *Study of Volume and Cost of Social Work* (New York: American Association of Community Organization and the Welfare Federation of Cleveland, 1926), pp. 1–3; "Service Supplement," p. 2 [57]

Community fund budget committees usually start on their work feeling that their main task is to reduce duplication and promote "business" efficiency in social work. But a very few years brings them to

[57] The author quoted extracts from his article "Seeing Social Work Whole, an Experiment in Devising Community Measuring Sticks," *Survey Midmonthly*, LV (1926), 661–64, which gives more details of the method and findings.

the realization that their great responsibility is to make the best provision possible within the funds available for improved and extended service, the opportunities for which present themselves on every hand.

With this heavy responsibility weighing upon them they begin to look for help. They have surveys and studies and investigations of this agency, of that need, and of the other field of service. Economies are achieved, old institutions change their programs to meet new opportunities, new agencies are established. All these are possible as the community fund is increasing the contribution money available for social work by from 50 per cent to 200 per cent. But sooner or later a saturation point seems to have been reached. There seems to be some limit to the amount the city will contribute. New money comes slowly but new needs continue to be discovered as well as improved methods for accomplishing present tasks.

It is no longer sufficient to know that a project is well thought out and really needed. It must be shown to be of prior urgency.

When we reach the stage of weighing the relative urgency of need for a dispensary, a summer camp, a more nearly adequate fund for the boarding of dependent children and an increased capacity for the aged or incurable, we begin to realize a great lack of standards or methods of comparison between the various fields of service. We see the need for a comprehensive view of the community's welfare facilities as a whole—for development of a community program in which plans for hospital development, health promotion, child care, recreation, etc., will each have its proper place.

Our efforts in the past have been like those of a group of crusading forces, working more or less independently, maintaining themselves by foraging for themselves as they go. The community fund movement is an attempt to organize these foraging groups into an army with a plan of campaign and a central commissary department.

We are now at the point of wanting a census of our army and of our allies, the governmental welfare agencies; and we want to compare this census with similar figures for other cities. If other cities facing similar problems have found need and use for more hospital beds or visiting nurses, or have needed fewer orphanages because they have kept more homes together by adequate relief measures, may not their experience be a guide to us?

Just as the first step in the estimating of an ideal family budget is the study of the actual expenditures of many real families, so the consideration of an ideal community welfare budget needs, as a basis, a tabulation of the actual expenditures of many cities.

It is with these considerations in mind that the American Association for Community Organization, including in its membership 150 councils of social agencies, welfare federations and community funds, is making an experiment in its Study of Volume and Cost of Social Work in which thirty of the larger American cities are cooperating.

The information being secured includes the total expense of services in the fields of family welfare and relief, child care, hospitals and health promotion, recreation and character building, such as are usually financed through community funds and welfare federations. The expense of parallel governmental services financed from tax funds is likewise being included.

This information is being secured in such a way that it is possible to compare not only the total expense of these services for various cities but so that it is possible also to compare the cost of care of children in orphanages and in foster homes; the cost of care of the sick in hospitals, in dispensaries and by bedside nursing; the cost of character building through the settlement, young men's and women's associations, scouting, etc. The services are classified in this way into forty different groups. In addition to the expense, income is classified into contributions, endowment income, earnings from service rendered and tax revenue. This classification of income is secured for each of the above forty groups.

While comparison of financial figures will be of interest, it is of comparatively little value without some indication of the volume and character of service rendered. So the information to be collected includes the simplest possible statistics of service rendered. For the hospitals, for instance, we have the number of beds, the number of patients admitted and the number of patient days care, free, part-pay, and full pay, all classified by character of case where such information is available. We also ask for the number of professional employes, the total paid them in salaries, the total number of other employes and amount paid them and all other current expense.

The questions asked are few and simple because it is an arduous task to collect even the simplest figures for all public and private agencies in a large city and we prefer to get a few basic figures for a considerable number of cities rather than a mass of information from only two or three.

Because of the tremendous amount of work involved, this study could be carried on only as a cooperative enterprise; the council of social agencies or welfare federation or community foundation in each city studied secured the information for that city.

Care has been exercised to get figures which are correct, complete and comparable. Questionnaires were revised and approved at a conference of representatives of twelve cities. Each city is visited by the director of the study, and agency schedules reviewed in detail, then revised and completed before that city's figures are used.

The tabulation presented herewith covers the four main sources of income, and total expense for each of the 40 agency groups, and for 6 main divisions of the study. Figures are given both in dollars total and in dollars per unit of population because comparisons between cities of different size can be made better on the per capita basis.

Tabulations of service and expense detail are in preparation but the service figures which can be secured are much less complete and accurate than the financial figures and there is less uniformity in expense distributions. For these reasons attention was devoted first to the income tabulations. Even with income, it will be appreciated, estimates have been necessary in the case of many agencies. Figures have been included however for every agency known in each of the cities tabulated. It is our belief that the figures given are, as a whole, within ten per cent of the true facts. . . .

No attempt is made to draw conclusions from this material. This study is only a census providing figures which can be made a basis for present study and future comparison.

Chart A shows the grand total income for all cities, classified by source. The large amount of earned income or self support will be noted. The major factors in this item are earnings from hospital patients, Y.M.C.A. and Y.W.C.A. dormitories, class fees, cafeterias, etc.; but almost every type of service has some earnings or refunds from beneficiaries or their families. The varying proportions of self support are shown in succeeding charts and tables.

The fact that public revenue or taxes exceeds in amount the sum of private support from contributions and endowments together, comes as a surprise to many. It shows the great importance of team work between public and private agencies in the administration of present social welfare activities and in the planning of programs for the future. Great differences in practice between cities as well as between services will be noted in the following pages. . . .

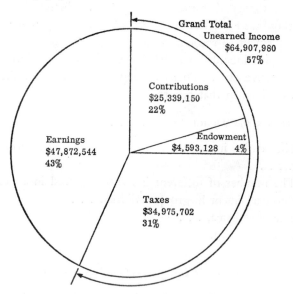

Grand Total
Unearned Income
$64,907,980
57%

Contributions
$25,339,150
22%

Earnings
$47,872,544
43%

Endowment
$4,593,128 4%

Taxes
$34,975,702
31%

Grand Total Income $112,782,073 100%
CHART A

The experimental character of this Study of Volume and Cost of Social Work is best exemplified by the difficulty experienced in getting satisfactory figures on the volume and character of services rendered.

Social agencies and public departments almost universally have become accustomed to recording and reporting dollars received and expended, because of legal regulations, endorsement committee requirements, and contributor demands. The pressure for service reporting has been much less forceful.

Accuracy is much more easily secured in financial than in service accounting because the dollar is the universal unit in the first and the technic of the financial audit is well established and largely applied.

On the other hand there are many units in service accounting and even the simplest of these, such as the day's care, is subject to different interpretations.

On the theory that the best way to get better figures is to study those we have, this tabulation of service figures is presented as a supplement to the report issued May 25, 1926.

The report included a tabulation of income with introduction and illustrative charts. Purpose, scope and method of the Study were explained in that report.

EXPLANATION OF SERVICE FIGURES. . . .

a. The basic information we want is: The normal capacity. . . .

b. The number of different individuals served in a year. . . .

c. The enrollment in group activities. . . .

d. The attendance. . . .

e. The care given.

104. The Hartford Survey

A Study of the Several Services Financed by the Hartford Community Chest, Inc., and Their Relationship to the Social and Health Program of the Community (New York: Community Chests and Councils, Inc., 1934), pp. 1–3, 9–19, 22–26, 30–31, 35–37, 41–44

Recommendation that a "comprehensive survey of all Chest agencies be made" was made originally by the Budget Committee of the Hartford Community Chest. . . .

The findings . . . are based in part on statistical evidence and comparable factual material. . . . The data available in the Council of Social Agencies, the different agencies and various public departments, represent a substantial factual basis for many of the findings.

In part, however, the recommendations are based directly upon the breadth of experience, the professional equipment and objectivity of attitude of the personnel of the technical staff. . . .

The service of the twenty-seven agencies financed by the Community Chest could not be studied in a vacuum. They are part of a total circle of public and private agencies. . . . The general report, therefore, will outline that total program. . . .

Considered as a whole the program . . . is weak in preventive effort. The casework agencies are too largely preoccupied with the treatment of the end results of social troubles; the recreational and group work agencies with the promotion of mass recreation or preconceived activity programs; and the health agencies with the treatment rather than the prevention of disease. . . .

The Community Program and Its Cost

In 1933 the social and health agencies in the Hartford Metropolitan Area consisted of twenty-four public departments, boards or bureaus, and forty-nine agencies under private auspices. Four of the public agencies are state agencies with special programs in Hartford, seven are under the Hartford City Government, and thirteen under the [seven surrounding] Town Governments. . . .

Broadly classified, and with certain agencies falling into more than one field of service, twenty-nine are in the field of family welfare and relief, fourteen in the field of child care, fifteen in the field of recreation and leisure time. There are eight hospitals and clinics, ten agencies in the field of public health nursing, and eight concerned with health education and administration.

The gross expenditures for all social and health service in Hartford in 1933 were $5,828,078. . . .

Of the total expenditures . . . public agencies administered . . . 43.4 percent, and private agencies . . . 56.6 percent. . . .

Thirty-one private agencies are Community Chest members, maintaining, of course, individual autonomy and independence. Four of these do not participate in the Chest annual budget because of adequate endowment income.

The Chest annual budget review over a period of years has done much to bring about a coordinated program within this group of agencies. . . . As a group they occupy the dominating position in privately financed social service, and . . . include important agencies in each field. . . .

Three important factors are significant to the whole problem of community planning.

1. *Metropolitan complications.* Certain complications in organization relationships, program planning, and financing inevitably arise because the smaller governmental divisions cut across the essential unity of the Metropolitan service area. The Chest in its campaign solicits the entire area. Certain of the family service agencies . . . give service in the surrounding towns, but have had to work out relationships with the local public authorities on a quite different basis than in Hartford itself. . . .

2. *Publicly administered services.* . . . The public share in providing service for those who cannot afford to pay the whole cost is clearly the dominating one.

3. *Relative position of the private agencies.* . . . Relatively speaking, the private agencies in Hartford are meeting a larger proportion of the total service than is generally true in other communities. In 1933 for example, the average proportion of total relief expenditures in one hundred twenty cities met from private funds was 6.4 percent. In Hartford it was 31.6 percent.

The relatively small public expenditure for recreation speaks for itself. . . .

During the past four years the character of the social problems confronting American urban communities has been continually changing . . . the traditional programs of both public and private agencies have been in a constant state of flux. That has been true in Hartford, and . . . is in part a reason for this survey.

The Community Chest Unemployment Relief Fund program gave way to the Civil Works Administration. The Farm Camp for homeless men, financed by the Chest in 1933, with city responsibility now being assumed for this problem, has been eliminated from its 1934 budget.

The relief burden has vastly increased, and this has brought changes not only in the division of responsibility between the public and private agencies, in that field, but also has had its influence on the amount of service it has been possible to finance in other fields. . . .

The Hartford Department of Public Welfare has gradually absorbed a larger and larger proportion of the total relief load. . . .

This vastly increased volume . . . had its effect upon internal policies in the different agencies. . . . Administration of relief expenditures has become the dominating concern of the family agencies as compared with service to families whose need is for adjustment of other, and often more fundamentally important, social problems.

Much the same thing has taken place in regard to the care of dependent and neglected children. . . .

The demand for free nursing care and for free hospital care has increased steadily. . . . Preventive service of health supervision has given way steadily to the immediate and emergency demands for care of the sick.

With decreased opportunity for employment, with more adequate relief, and greater consideration for the family unit, mothers are not leaving their children in day nurseries as they did formerly, but are caring for them at home. . . .

The number of homeless and transient persons has markedly increased . . . the Federal Transient Service has now assumed a responsibility which formerly had been entirely local, for the non-resident transient, leaving to each locality responsibility for its resident homeless. . . .

Chest budget policies in regard to the distribution of its funds since 1929 have . . . reflected the changing situation in the community. . . . Appropriations for relief not only absorbed the additional funds which were raised, but . . . accentuated actual curtailment in certain of the other fields, particularly recreation and character building. . . .

[These fundamental changes] demonstrate the necessity for future plans based on a present situation which is very unlike that of 1929. . . .

The Hartford Council of Social Agencies was organized in 1920 and the Community Chest in 1924. The public agencies in Hartford are represented in the Council as are practically all of the private agencies carrying on active programs. Together the Chest and Council represent a central leadership. . . .

Both Chest and Council have shown unusual flexibility and responsiveness to changing needs and conditions. . . . Projects . . . were developed to meet specific community needs of which the Central group became aware, and . . . have in turn been transferred or discontinued as a need for their sponsorship has disappeared. The Emergency Case Conference through which policies of transfer of cases between the Department of Public Welfare and the private agencies have been worked out, is an excellent example of the contributions which the Central body is making to the development of coordinated service between the two groups. . . .

The Chest, very successfully financing a well rounded program, with strategic spearheads in each field of community service, should be able to bring about the simplification and adjustments which will increase the service value of its expenditures. The Council with its broad base of representation and its experience as a directing as well as a planning medium should be able to strengthen further the community services that are most essential and focus them upon the major problems with which Hartford is now confronted. . . .

THE COMMUNITY PROGRAM FOR FAMILY WELFARE AND CHILD CARE. . . .

Generally speaking that part of the Hartford program directed primarily to meeting economic needs . . . compares favorably with other communities. . . .

The case work agencies in Hartford have not been so successful, however, in reaching and dealing with the beginnings of individual and family maladjustment which later come to the surface as acute community problems. . . .

[The Survey] shows clearly certain fundamental weaknesses in the present program which militate against the maximum of constructive achievement.

1. *The agencies think of themselves as fundamentally separate agencies each with its own salvation to be worked out. . . .* Co-operative machinery works largely to smooth out differences when their paths happen to cross rather than to harness them together in a team. . . .

2. *There is no machinery for reaching out into the community to identify developing problems in their early stages and in order to apply the agencies' services to them.* The client's troubles must become a "nuisance" to himself or someone else before he comes into the hands of an agency. . . .

3. *The choice of agency to which the client applies, or is referred, is mainly by chance and is undiscriminating. . . .*

4. *The original diagnosis of a problem is made primarily in terms of thought of the agency receiving the application.* This means that the initial treatment plan is made in terms of the facilities of this agency, not in terms of maximum use of the community resources. . . .

5. *While there is transfer of applications between agencies, this is likely to be made on the apparent facts in the application, rather than on the basis of thorough investigation. . . .*

6. *Lack of continuity in treatment, which adds to the instability of the client. . . .* At present many cases are handled by several agencies in turn, over a long period of time. . . .

7. *Indefinite delay in decisive action where removal of children is indicated.* There is the constant danger that action comes at too late a stage in the development of the problem. The children are too old, habits and tendencies have become too well established and family situations have become acute. . . .

Mental Hygiene a Dynamic Factor . . . Case work service might be arbitrarily described as of two kinds. In the first place, there is the case work administration of relief—the individualized process of providing for the client what he lacks. . . . In the second place there is the much more delicate, complicated process of dealing with the emotional adjustments, personality defects, faulty character development and undesirable behavior patterns which are the outstanding factors in the family and individual "trouble areas." . . . Here the mental hygiene element in the case work . . . is uppermost. The case worker needs to have available in the community a maximum of mental hygiene and psychological clinic facilities and the use of facilities for the treatment of mental disease. She also needs to have learned the principles of modern psychology and psychiatry, to know something of what constitutes the human personality and with this knowledge to have practiced the methods of understanding and of dealing with the reactions which the more or less normal client presents.

No case worker without this equipment is able to cope with the tangled snarl of family relationships. . . . While the treatment of the pathological and the more serious cases lies with the psychiatrist, for the general run of clients whose need is for something more than bread and butter and shelter the case worker must be equipped with the insight and knowledge that the mental hygiene field contributes. . . .

One gets the definite feeling that too many Hartford social workers have a reluctance, a timidity or some emotional bar to yielding themselves whole-heartedly to the values mental hygiene brings to case work. Some few of them using it still insist on terming it "understanding" or "horse sense." Whatever you please to call it, without it case work is mechanics without imagination, manipulation without insight, a lantern without a flame. . . .

THE COMMUNITY PROGRAM FOR RECREATION AND
GROUP ACTIVITY. . . .

Judged by traditional standards the recreation and group-work agencies of Hartford represent an exceptionally high order of service. The money is well administered, the agencies are well staffed, and the programs are good.

Social situations are changing, however. Experimental social science methods involving better techniques are developing. New tests of effectiveness are being applied to this as to the other fields of social work, which means that services and programs must be interpreted by other than traditional standards. . . .

The protective function of social work is a large one, but the enrichment function is also a community social work function and should exist for all classes of people. Some of the educational and recreational agencies have developed historically and have evolved techniques of work as essentially enrichment agencies rather than protective agencies. At any given point it is perhaps unfair to make the sole test of their work in terms of their ability to reduce delinquency, deal with the children of families on relief, or to remedy acute social conditions. If the community chest movement is to represent the enrichment as well as the protective function of social work, recognition needs to be given to the values inherent in this aspect of the agency service. . . .

[The] particular contribution [of group agencies] lies, of course, in the use of group method whereby the interplay of individuals upon each other, the stimulation of interest in hobbies and wholesome activity, the development of habits of co-operation, bring a stimulus to character and personality development. . . .

1. *Technical group work skill.* . . .

[Professional group workers responding to a questionnaire indicated an awareness] that the problems of individual guidance for the boys and girls in their various groups and of leadership supervision of those who are responsible for directing the work of each group were of outstanding importance and needed improving. . . . This is particularly significant in relation to certain lacks in leadership abilities and mental hygiene insights, which other devices used revealed. . . .

2. *Basis of group organization.* . . .

The particular group of children who happen to get together and the method of originally grouping them are much more important than the programs of activities in which they happen to engage. Grouping policies for the neighborhood agencies should be especially important in view of the group life now existent in unsupervised fashion in their communities. Powerful social contacts in small groups where members care about each other should be harnessed to work with the agency, rather than against it.

3. *Mental hygiene insights.* In developing group work in such a way that it will contribute the maximum to the individual members of the group, an understanding of mental hygiene and the use of mental hygiene facilities on the part of both professional and volunteer workers is essential. . . .

Leadership in the Development of Group Work Method. . . .

The program of the [Recreation, Education, and Character-building] Division is weak in the leadership it provides for improving the methods and standards of group work. . . .

Improvement in methods, clarification in objectives and standards, and the development of common kinds of records and terminology are very much needed in the recreational group-work agencies. Group work lags far behind other fields of social work in its techniques and standards.

XXXVI

RESPONSE TO CRISIS

One of the professional responsibilities envisioned by the AASW founders was to point out developing conditions in the community which might harm individuals and lower the happiness and cohesiveness of all society. There is no better example than the foresight of settlement workers preceding the depression, when they collected evidence concerning what was happening to families all over the nation. A professional writer was able to present these facts in a telling description of the impact of unemployment (R105).

Caseworkers, then preoccupied with integrating psychiatric theory into usable method, were not so alert to what was impending, but after it happened they mustered forces to make clear to legislators the imperative need for action. The professional association took initiative in organizing and presenting testimony before Congress.

Ellery Reed and Grace Coyle appraised professional social work activity in the crisis. They not only described professional behavior, but illuminated it with much about the current state of philosophy, method, and professional unity.

Recognition of the expertise of social workers was now a reality influencing legislation, and members of the profession assumed decisive leadership in administration.

105. Some Folks Won't Work

Clinch Calkins,[88] *Some Folks Won't Work* [copyright, 1930, 1958, by Marion Clinch Calkins Merrell] (New York: Harcourt, Brace, 1930), pp. 17, 19-21, 156-58, 160-62

Long before last winter's depression became a matter of public comment settlement workers were aware of a growing increase in the amount of unemployment and a lengthening of the periods during which individual workers were unable to secure jobs. The

[88] Clinch Calkins was a poet and writer of fiction of a social-protest

settlements are in a peculiarly advantageous position to observe. They know their neighbors in good times and in bad, as individuals with tastes, habits, and ambitions. They know that the unskilled and the semi-skilled workers are on the whole an ambitious group, the parents struggling to give their children better opportunities than they themselves had, and the children alert and groping for ways to succeed as success is understood in America. . . .

In June, 1928, the National Federation of Settlements met in conference in Boston. The program committee chosen for that year decided that no one other force at work against the contemporary family compared in magnitude with unemployment. . . . An Unemployment Committee was appointed under the chairmanship of Miss Helen Hall . . . with the task of gathering evidence of the effects of unemployment on the individual and on the family. For although there has been a literature on unemployment, no factual study of its effects upon the family had been made. A machinery was at once put into operation and over three hundred records were brought in from thirty cities in twenty-three States. . . .

There are several widely held ideas about unemployment which this book should dispel. One of them is that unemployment comes only in hard times. . . . A second presumption is that under unemployment only those suffer who have been too thriftless to save. And still a third, the most pervasive of them all, is that if a man really wants to find work, he can find it. . . .

Conclusion

As the reader has seen over and over again, not perseverance, nor skill, education, and health, nor a long and excellent work-record, stand the breadwinner in any certain stead when the bad word is handed down from directors to executive to foreman.

---

nature. This book is a dramatic analysis and presentation of material assembled in Marion Elderton, ed., *Case Studies of Unemployment,* compiled by the Unemployment Committee of the National Federation of Settlements with an introduction by Helen Hall and a foreword by Paul Kellogg (Philadelphia: University of Pennsylvania Press, 1931). Helen Hall is best known for her long service as director of Henry Street Settlement, New York.

To be sure, the best man may be the last to be discharged. But even he has no assurance of security. Laziness, incompetence, and shiftlessness determine the incidence but not the quantity of unemployment.

Nor is a man's need or that of his family an assurance of safety or even of consideration. He may be given a day's notice. He may be given a week or even a month. But whatever the mode of dismissal, the burden falls finally upon the individual who has lost his job and upon the household which hangs upon his earnings. It is up to him and to him alone, or his wife in his stead, and his children to reconnect with the sources of income.

Because labor has been regarded as, if not a commodity, at least the most flexible and easily replaced element in production, the general run of business has long taken an attitude toward its labor supply which it would be too thrifty to take toward raw materials. . . .

The smallest employer and the most modest consumer will have to sense their obligation toward unemployment before the problem can be met. An indifferent producing and consuming public is the first obstacle to overcome. . . .

Within the last quarter of a century we have decreased the number and eased the human cost of industrial accidents in marked degree. When work accidents were first multiplied by congregate production the public invented for that horror, too, a self-absolving cliché. "It's the worker's own fault." The worker and his family were merely out of luck. . . . In twenty years we have closed in upon industrial accidents from two sides. First, safety engineering has cut down the number of accidents. Second, some share of the income loss from those accidents which precaution cannot avoid has, through workmen's compensation laws, become part of the recognized cost of modern production, and is met by the consumer.

Like the work accident, the unemployment hazard is not new. . . .

Production must be regularized insofar as regularization is humanly possible. . . .

Equally clear is the need for some more effective means for

helping the individual in his baffling search for work. At present the jobless man is dependent too often upon inefficient public employment agencies, on newspaper advertising, and upon the doubtful assistance of private employment agencies. After his money is gone, he can depend at last only upon his feet. . . .

But over and beyond the need for industrial regularization, the need for public works and for a Federal employment system, there is the need for some form of protection against what would seem to be unpreventable unemployment. For there are certain situations in which it is hard to fix the blame. The disappearance of the cut-glass trade was probably more mysterious to the factory owners than it was to Zarone [Calkins's fictitious name for an able workman displaced by change in consumer fashion].

Clearly whether unemployment is controllable or uncontrollable its ultimate burden falls upon men least able to bear it and frequently upon those in no way responsible for its incidence. Most of the great modern nations have provided their workers with some form of insurance against such unemployment. We have not. . . .

But whether protection is arranged by individual management, by the trade as a whole, or through public action, as in compensation laws, the burden of unemployment should not be allowed to fall solely on the family of the worker.

106. What Actually Is Happening in Some Families in Philadelphia

Statement of Dorothy Kahn, before the Subcommittee of the Committee on Manufactures, United States Senate, Senator Robert M. La Follette, Jr. (chairman of the subcommittee), December 28, 1931, concerning "A BILL to provide for cooperation by the Federal Government with the several states in relieving the hardship and suffering caused by unemployment," *Unemployment Relief,* 72d Congress, First Sess., S. 174 and S. 262, pp. 73–77

Miss Kahn. Mr. Chairman and gentlemen, I am executive director of the Jewish Welfare Society of Philadelphia, which is a family welfare agency of the Jewish Federation.

The Chairman. Can you tell this committee what happens when these budgets are pared down to spread out the relief?

Miss Kahn. Senator, the things that happen are so legion that it is difficult to be brief on this subject. I think that the best way to approach it, perhaps, is to indicate what actually is happening in some of the families in Philadelphia that are now being cared for under our present funds, the city funds, which will soon be exhausted. . . .

The bureau of unemployment relief, in the creation of which we have all been interested because it was a public agency, for the first time administering direct relief after a lapse of 50 years in our community, has found it necessary, because of the limitations of its fund, to give what it regards as wholly inadequate relief. . . . What impresses me as a family social worker are some of the direct results of our inadequate relief provisions as they come to my attention in a private agency which has attempted to maintain what we call a minimum standard of health and decency in our relief appropriation—and what I say is in no criticism of our bureau; it is operating under an intolerable handicap, caring for 43,000 families, about forty times as many families as have ever received relief at one time in Philadelphia in normal times, and finds itself having to deal with a practical situation. Now, this bureau is providing grocery orders to families in amounts that range from $1.50 for one or two persons to something like $5 or $6 for a family of five persons.

The Chairman. Per week?

Miss Kahn. Per week. It also gives a certain amount of milk for young children in cases of illness. It provides a limited amount of coal, shoes where needed, and clothing on an emergency basis, only secondhand clothing such as is donated to the bureau. It pays no rent, not even in cases of eviction, and that is one of the outstanding problems in this situation, and I think that it illustrates some of the results of inadequate relief.

The Chairman. What happens to these families when they are evicted?

Miss Kahn. The families in Philadelphia are doing a number of things. The dependence of families upon the landlords, who seem to have a remarkable willingness to allow people to live in their quarters, rent free, is something that has not been measured. I think the only indication of it is the mounting list of sheriff's sales where property owners are simply unable to maintain their small pieces of property because rents are not being paid. Probably most of you saw in the newspapers the account of the "organized" representation of the taxpayers recently, where they vigorously and successfully opposed a rise in local taxes, largely because of the fact that they are under a tremendous burden through nonpayment of rents. That, of course, is the least of the difficulties, although I think this is the point at which we ought to stress one of the factors that . . . other speakers have brought out in their testimony, that is the effect on families of the insecurity of living rent free, and in addition to that, the effect on their attitude toward meeting their obligations. Some of us would not be surprised if rent paying became an obsolete custom in our community. There are also, of course, evictions and the evictions in Philadelphia are frequently accompanied not only by the ghastly placing of a family's furniture on the street, but the actual sale of the family's household goods by the constable. These families are, in common Philadelphia parlance, "sold out."

One of the factors that is never counted in all of the estimates of relief in this country is the factor of neighborliness. That factor of neighborliness is a point that I would like to stress here, because it seems to us who are close to this problem that this factor has been stretched not only beyond its capacity but beyond the limits of human endurance. We have no measure in Philadelphia to-day of the overcrowding that is a direct or indirect result of our inability to pay for families. Only the other day a case came to my attention in which a family of 10 had just moved in with a family of 5 in a 3-room apartment. However shocking that may be to the members of this committee, it is almost an every-day occurrence in our midst. Neighbors do take people in. They sleep on chairs, they sleep on the floor.

There are conditions in Philadelphia that beggar description. There is scarcely a day that calls do not come to all of our offices to find somehow a bed or a chair. The demand for boxes on which people can sit or stretch themselves is hardly to be believed. I would not have believed it until I got actual testimony from our workers in the field and workers in this bureau (who have been coming to classes that I have been teaching for these workers), that families were living with the paucity of household goods, to say nothing of the total lack of income, that people in this country, in a civilized community, are having to experience at this time. Of course, that is on the physical side.

I think it is not necessary to go into great detail about the effect of that sort of living conditions on standards of health, personal hygiene, family relationships, and all the rest of it. We are having continued evidence of what we humorously call the "strains on the family tie," that arise out of these overcrowded conditions.

Only the other day a man came to our office, as hundreds do day after day, applying for a job, in order not to have to apply for relief. I think we have already stressed the reluctance of individuals to accept relief, regardless of the source from which it comes. This man said to our worker: "I know you haven't any money to care of [*sic*] the needs of everybody, but I want you to give me a job." Now, we have so many applications of that kind during the day that it has gotten to the point where we can scarcely take their names as they come in, because we have no facilities for giving jobs. In this particular case this individual interested me because when he heard that we had no jobs to give him, he said: "Have you anybody you can send around to my family to tell my wife you have no job to give me? Because she doesn't believe that a man who walks the street from morning till night, day after day, actually can't get a job in this town. She thinks I don't want to work." I think it is not necessary to dramatize the results of a situation like that. And there are thousands of them. It is only one illustration.

Another thing, it seems to me to be important to stress is the effect of this situation on the work habits of the next generation. I think it has not been brought out that in the early period of this so-called "depression" one of the most outstanding features of it was the fact that young people could get jobs even when old people of 40 years and over could not get jobs, and it has become quite customary for families to expect that their young members who are just coming of working age can replace the usual bread-winner, the father of the family. It is easy to forget about these young boys and girls reaching 14, 15, 16, 17, 18 years of age, who have had no work experience, and if we think of work not as merely a means of livelihood but as an aspect of our life and a part of our life, it has a good deal of significance that these young people are having their first work experience, an experience not with employment but with unemployment; that in addition to that they are looked to as potential breadwinners in the family; that they are under the same strain, the same onus that the father of the family is under, suspected of malingering, suspected of not wanting to work—all of these things which the average individual sees not as clearly as we see them in terms of millions of unemployed.

Senator Costigan. Miss Kahn, did you not place the industrial old-age line rather high? Does it not tend to be nearer 35 years than 40?

Miss Kahn. I suppose it does, Senator. We like to be conservative in our testimony. We find that the people who are displaced at 40 are hopelessly old men. That is coming down all the time.

Perhaps in further answer to Senator La Follette's question about standards of relief, it might be interesting to indicate what are, in the opinion of those of us who are working in this relief field, minimum standards of decency. We do talk . . . in such large figures that sometimes we forget what it actually takes for a family to live, and I would like to submit to you a few figures that I submitted to Senator Costigan in a letter, indicating what we regard as a minimum requisite income for a family to maintain what we call a standard of health and decency—and when

I say "health and decency," perhaps these standards would not come up to the standards of most of the working population of our country, because they are considerably below the average normal income of the better group of skilled workers in our midst. But they are figures that we have to use in relief agencies as representing something as close to the actual cost of the number of calories' worth of food that a family requires to maintain health, as we can possibly gauge it. Our organization has a department of home economics which watches carefully changing ideas of what food requirements are for families and prices of this food locally in Philadelphia four times a year, to determine how much money will buy what we require as an absolute minimum. I would like to stress in this connection that when we talk about this "minimum" we overlook the fact that it almost requires a college education to get the maximum value out of our "minimum" because it requires a degree of management that perhaps the average housewife of the working group does not have at her command, in spite of our best efforts. . . .

We would estimate as [the typical] family's needs something just a few cents less than $22 a week. . . .

Senator Costigan. That total is for how many people?

Miss Kahn. Five people. This is about four times as much as our public bureau finds it possible to give at the present time. We consider that an absolute minimum. If we deviate from it we know that we are undermining this family's standard of food, with the resultant threat to health; we know that we are undermining their capacity for maintaining decent family life, not having enough cups and saucers to go around, enough chairs to sit on, and so forth. If we deviate from it on the rent side we know we have the overcrowding evil that I described, and so forth. That, as I see it, is the relief situation for the individual family.

107. Efforts of Social Workers toward Social Reorganization

Ellery F. Reed,[59] *Social Forces*, XIV (1935), 87–93

This paper presents the thesis that social workers are effectively promoting social reorganization. . . .

Only a few aspects of the subject, however, can be here presented. The fields of public health, housing, leisure time, and child welfare will necessarily be neglected and the major attention given to social workers in the family welfare and relief field as these have related themselves to the matter of social reorganization. It will, furthermore, be necessary to omit discussion of some very interesting specialized phases of relief activity recently developed by the Federal Emergency Relief Administration, such as Relief Production Units (Self Help Projects), Civil Works Administration, Rural Rehabilitation, including purchase and withdrawal of marginal lands from agricultural uses and their improvement as public forest and park reserves, relocation of families from "stranded populations," the financing of musicians and artists in production of high class free concerts and art, student aid, etc. Some, if not all, of these appear to bear germs of a new social order and may be highly valuable as experiments in social reorganization, but this paper will deal with the more common and prosaic aspects of direct relief and work relief. . . .

Unfortunately relief is still the principal resource in this country for meeting the needs of the unemployed. Although the majority of social workers are still engaged in such relief work, they recognize it as a symptom of social maladjustment. . . .

Such work when maintained according to good standards by qualified case workers may serve the ends of fundamental social reorganization. . . .

But the relation of social workers to the more far reaching aspects of social development will be the principal object of analysis.

[59] Dr. Reed was director, Research Department, Cincinnati Community Chest.

The depression years have brought radical reorganization of the ways and means of meeting relief needs in this country. For some years social workers, particularly as represented in the Family Welfare Association of America, have advocated that relief of the chronically disabled plus those whose dependency arose out of the maladjustments of society rather than personal deficiencies, should be cared for by public or tax-supported agencies rather than by private agencies. Until recently private agencies in this country were carrying a large share of the general outdoor relief burden.

In 1929, if Detroit is left out of the picture, public outdoor relief departments in 22 large cities contributed only 31 per cent of the outdoor relief while private agencies contributed 35 per cent.[60] Five years later, in August, 1934, these private agencies contributed only 1.9 per cent. Mothers' Aid, Old Age Relief, and allowances for the blind accounted in this recent month for 5.7 per cent, and the remaining 92.4 per cent, including veterans, relief, was from public funds; Federal, State and local. In the second quarter of 1934, 73.9 per cent of the public funds administered by the Federal Emergency Relief Administration were supplied by the Federal Government, 11 per cent by the States, and 15.1 per cent by local governments.[61]

[60] Author's note: "A. R. Griffith, Helen R. Jeter, A. W. McMillen, *Registration of Social Statistics, 1929*. A report submitted to the Joint Committee of the Association of Community Chests and Councils and the Local Community Research Committee of the University of Chicago, Oct. 1, 1930; page 3, Table 1 *a*–29. The remaining 34 per cent of relief in these cities in 1929 was accounted for in Mothers' Aid." (Editors' comment: the Social Statistics Project [R103] was now conducted by the University of Chicago. Private agency groups found it hard to concede that they were not dominant in the administration of relief in 1929. They excluded Detroit, which had no Family Welfare Society, but whose Department of Welfare was a member of the Family Welfare Association of America, from the tabulations. They relegated to a footnote the fact that 34 percent of all relief was in Mothers' Aid.)

[61] The author cites: U. S. Children's Bureau, *Monthly Bulletin of Social Statistics*, II, No. 10 (1934), 8, Table IV; also *Bulletin 3670* (rev.) Federal Emergency Relief Administration, Division of Research and Statistics, Oct. 10, 1934. (Editors' comment: The Social Statistics Project had now been taken over by the U. S. Children's Bureau, while other series of data, especially on public assistance, were being developed nationally. Ulti-

There was thus developed in a very brief period not only an overwhelming proportion of public as contrasted to private relief, but there was also a revolutionary departure from the principle of local responsibility for poor relief embodied in our laws since the colonial period.

In these major aspects of social reorganization in the relief field social workers have played an important part. While federal relief was still in general disfavor and opposed by leading business and capital interests as well as by federal authorities, Mr. William Hodson, then of the New York Welfare Council, on October 13, 1931, addressed an open letter to President Hoover urging consideration of federal relief. The American Association of Social Workers in December, 1931, and January, 1932, took an active part in organizing the notable Senate hearings on unemployment relief needs, and leading social workers there spoke strongly on behalf of carefully administered but outright grants of federal relief. Some social workers, including Mr. C. M. Bookman,[62] although convinced of the need of federal relief grants, counselled the more conservative beginnings represented in the provision of $300,000,000 in the Reconstruction Finance Corporation Act for loans to states and localities for unemployment relief. This act was followed a year later in the spring of 1933 by that establishing the Federal Emergency Relief Administration . . . which represented more nearly the idea of the majority of social workers. Thus social workers, together with a little group of socially minded senators, particularly Senators Costigan, La Follette, Wagner, and Cutting, are to be credited with initiating this revolutionary reorganization of relief in this country. . . .

The American Association of Social Workers and the American Public Welfare Association have both passed public resolutions and are now actively working for a permanent modernized

---

mately, the Social Statistics Project was dropped by the Children's Bureau because, in part, it was dependent upon the voluntary cooperation of nongovernmental agencies in a limited number of cities which were not statistically representative of the nation. The Project has since been continued in a limited form by United Community Funds and Councils.)

[62] Executive of the Cincinnati Community Chest.

system of poor relief, with federal, state, and county participation. . . .

Both Mr. Hopkins, FERA Administrator, and President Roosevelt himself stated quite positively, before the Community Chest Mobilization Conference, September 28, 1934, that the old rule of local responsibility still held and that the Federal Government was still in the relief picture only temporarily. Nevertheless, social workers are striving for and are still hopeful of achieving permanent social reorganization along federal lines for relief and welfare purposes in this country in the near future.

The viewpoint is not uncommon that social workers, in their efforts to present to government officials, Community Chest contributors and others, the extent of need for relief funds are merely playing into the hands of shrewd politicians and capitalists in showing them how far they must yield and what policies they must pursue in order to preserve the political and economic status quo. Community Chests have in fact during the present depression made some use of the argument that beneficiaries of the present social order should regard contributions for social work, particularly for relief, as insurance against riots, crime, and even revolution.

Failure of society to grant relief, when relief is widely needed, tends to produce demonstrations, riots and crime, but not revolution. Vigorous revolutionary movements are not generated or sustained by a starving population. . . .

Periods of revolutionary change have been characterized by a fermentation of ideas—ideas of democracy, of equal rights and worth of all men, of a wider distribution of wealth and opportunity, of the possibility of a higher standard of life for the worker, ideas that the institutions of society can and should be changed. Such ideas grow rank in the mind of the masses when their standard of living and their sense of security is depressed. . . .

Social workers in supplying relief help to avert the disorder and crime born of desperation, and at the same time they supply the physical basis for the more far reaching movements of social reorganization. Well trained social workers particularly are constantly urging adequate relief, not on the grounds of social reorganization it is true, but because they know how important it is for the client himself as well as for society that his physical and mental health and morale be maintained.

Social workers are also promoting social change through the education of clients to a higher standard of life. As pointed out above, one of the elements which stirs people to demand a new social order is the acquirement of a higher standard of living than they are able to maintain and which they feel there is little prospect of achieving under the existing social order. . . . What then may well be their reaction when a regular job is found, the agency withdraws its service, and the client finds that on regular wages he cannot buy some of the things which he and his family enjoyed at the hands of the agency?

A third way in which trained social workers in the relief field are helping fundamentally to bring about a new social order is in the reorientation of clients from the still prevalent viewpoints of "rugged individualism" to the newer social philosophy dictated by the interdependent, complex society of today. It is the common observation of social workers that one of the most general and serious problems which they have to meet is the psychology of defeat and inferiority on the part of their clients, and this is frequently most serious in those clients who have been independent, thrifty, and industrious. The mores of our time and country relative to relief have been the outgrowth of the philosophy of individualism as developed by Adam Smith, Malthus, and other classical economists. The attitude characteristic of America has been that any man who wanted to work could find a job, that dependency was a certain sign of bad management, lack of ambition, resourcefulness and energy. . . .

As a result of such traditional ideology on the part of the unemployed, America has had as a product of the depression a tragic crushing of the spirit of millions of its workers rather than the growth of large and vigorous radical parties. . . .

The untrained worker dealing with the dependent unemployed

client usually evidences one or the other of two extreme attitudes, both of which tend to confirm the client's sense of defeat, discouragement and inferiority. One of these attitudes is that of condescending, patronizing sympathy, characterized by Lady Bountiful, at least until her recipients fail to show proper gratitude, or do something of which she disapproves. The unprofessional person then characteristically swings quickly to the other extreme of hard-boiled intolerance which blames the individual for his unfortunate condition and bids him starve or find work. Unfortunately, from the standpoint of social reorganization as well as that of the individual client, thousands of persons without proper case work training are employed in our relief and work relief programs. Some of the most intolerant individuals in their treatment of clients are observed to be those who have themselves been recruited from the relief rolls.

It is the trained social case worker with a good background of sociology, economics, and psychology, who is laboring tactfully, patiently, and skillfully with the victims of unemployment . . . and calling attention to the fact, that they, along with thousands and millions of others, are the victims of a breakdown of the economic system. Trained workers, although strongly in favor of work for clients when such can be found, at reasonable wages and under proper conditions, avoid using withdrawal of relief as a threat to club clients into accepting jobs which they sometimes resist as representing a further evidence of humiliation and failure. . . . Not only is the client's attention definitely directed toward finding work and toward such limited, temporary and personal adjustments as may be possible, but also the psychology of personal defeat is often changed by a new understanding of the social causes of their unemployment. . . .

There are . . . evidences that the majority of well qualified case workers would be greatly heartened to believe that their efforts were contributing to create a spirited, dynamic working class insistent upon achieving a better social order, rather than developing a cowed, whipped proletariate, capable of indefinite exploitation by a ruling class or a dictator. . . .

Their progressive attitudes toward social change are indicated in many ways. The Recommendations of the Conference on Government Objectives for Social Work held in Washington last February under the auspices of the American Association of Social Workers represented an official expression on the part of qualified members of the profession.

The Conference went on record in its formal recommendations as follows:

We recognize our responsibility as social workers not only to advocate a national program of public welfare, but likewise to point out definite methods by which such objectives can be achieved. We recognize that our social problems arise, not out of inherent limitations in either the wealth or the productive capacity of the nation but rather out of our faulty distribution of wealth.

We urge increases of income taxes, progressive increases in the higher brackets, and increases in the excess profits and inheritance taxes. . . .

Preferment and prestige is freely extended by social workers to members of the profession who by many would be regarded as radical. An illustration of this is seen in the awarding of the two Pugsley prizes at the last National Conference of Social Work to papers,[63] one of which challenged social workers in their professional associations to

define our goals, examine the foundations, and reach our own clear decisions as to whether capitalism, private ownership, and profit making are to be retained, or whether the resources of this country are to be utilized in a socialized, planned economy for the raising of standards of living and the establishment of security of livelihood of the people.

The paper was critical of the New Deal as "designed to sustain property by credits and to encourage restrictions on production in the interest of maintaining profits." . . .

[The] second Pugsley paper stated:

[63] *NCSW*, 1934: Mary van Kleeck, "Our Illusions Regarding Government," pp. 473–85; Eduard C. Lindeman, "Basic Unities in Social Work," pp. 504–16.

Our task is to project a conception of society which is sufficiently revolutionary on the one hand to eliminate accumulated evils and at the same time sufficiently indigenous to our cultural tradition to insure workability. We do not need an either/or symbol for this purpose. But we do need enough clarity of mind and courage to envisage the outlines of a new social order which must include, I believe, (a) a high degree of collectivism in economics, (b) functionalism in governments, (c) integrity in education, and (d) social reality in ethics.

I assume that it might be possible for us to build a new society based upon the following changes:

(a) A redistribution of national wealth achieved through rational taxation and a new index for wages proportionate to production.

(b) Circumscribed control over private property in relation to a national plan.

(c) Nationalization of utilities, currency, credits and marginal lands.

(d) Elevation of a large proportion of housing to the status of public utility.

(e) Socialization of medicine.

(f) Functionalization of government without abandoning entirely the representative system.

(g) Insurance against unemployment, old age, illness, and accident. . . .

It appears that social workers, at least in the case work and relief fields, are making a real contribution to social reorganization. . . .

108. The Limitations of Social Work in Relation to Social Reorganization

Grace L. Coyle,[64] *Social Forces*, XIV (1935), 94-102

The subject of this paper by its terms of definition confines the author to the negative side of the question. . . . She must here confine her efforts to the rather ungracious task of analyzing why [social work] has not done better. . . .

Agencies in their official capacity may endorse legislation and

[64] Grace Coyle was on the faculty of the Western Reserve School of Applied Social Sciences after being executive secretary of the national YWCA.

participate in various movements for social reform. They may adopt policies governing their own activities which have a bearing upon social reorganization, such as a policy for relief for strikers, or the use of their buildings for union or radical meetings, or the inclusion in education programs of discussion or promotion of certain measures for social change. . . .

In addition to such official action many social workers as individuals and through their professional groups may play their part in similar movements. Both types of activity are included in the general compass of social work but in practice the scope and the limitations of each may be quite different. . . .

By social reorganization is meant a fundamental rather than a superficial shift in social relations. At this point, however, one's concept of fundamental is as relative as the terms radical and conservative. To some the shift from private to public support of relief is a fundamental reorganization; to others nothing is fundamental which leaves one stone upon another in our present economic and social system. . . .

Any attempt to bring about social reorganization is likely to express itself most obviously in movements or causes. It may well be claimed that the changes wrought in individual lives through case work techniques are the only sound way to social reorganization. . . . For the purposes of this paper, however, it seems feasible to take as the instruments of social reorganization only those organized efforts which are discernible in the form of movements and to ask what is the relation of social work to these collective efforts.

Dr. Neva Deardorff . . . points out [65] that causes are of two kinds, those relating to the conditions of the poor and to public welfare administration, and more general causes such as good government, economic reform, etc. To the first of these she assumes the social worker may have a special connection because of his knowledge of the problem. With the second type, she

[65] "Next Steps in Job Analysis," *NCSW*, 1933, pp. 619–30. Dr. Deardorff was director of the Research Bureau, Welfare Council, New York City, and had been president of the AASW, 1926–28.

seems to feel the social worker is less immediately involved. . . . It is a distinction often used by social workers themselves in discussing the legitimacy of their participation in movements of various kinds.

With these distinctions in mind, therefore, we can confront the question. Is it in some measure the function of social work (either social agency or social worker) to be related to the movements for social reorganization? If so, is its part limited only to those causes specifically related to its special knowledge of the unfortunate? Or is it related as well to the more remote social forces creating the present type of disorganized society with whose products it deals?

The answers to these questions have been various in the history of social work. Like the smile of the Cheshire Cat, the interest in social reorganization has come and gone and come again. In its early history social work was itself a cause and embraced within itself as well the advocates of many movements. . . . Porter Lee pointed out [66] that social work was outgrowing its cause aspect and becoming instead a function of organized social life, requiring intelligence rather than zeal, administrators rather than prophets. . . . The wide acceptance of this philosophy would limit social work not only in practice but in objectives to a field in which social reorganization would have small part. Any philosopher reconstructing the philosophy of social work would no doubt attach great significance to the fact that this pronouncement was made in the spring of 1929.

Within three years, the climate of opinion had greatly changed. Social workers in their organized capacity through the American Association of Social Workers were playing an active part in advising the government on its relief policies. . . . And further, many of the younger or more radical members of the profession were demanding that social workers assume a more active part in causes of the second type dealing with unemployment insurance, old age pensions, income taxation, and the like. By May 1933, the Committee on Federal Action on Unemployment of the American

[66] "Social Work: Cause and Function," *NCSW*, 1929, pp. 3-20.

Association of Social Workers which was set up to provide a channel for social workers to take up the cause of unemployment relief had proposed a program of National Economic Objectives for Social Work which takes the first steps along the way of fundamental reorganization. . . .

This recrudescence of the interest in social reorganization is, of course, a symptom of the times. But it suggests that . . . the prophetic spirit and the addiction to causes may prove to be not merely a mood of its adolescence but a permanent part of its functional life. . . . Among the social functions of social work is that of playing some part in the process of social reorganization—not only at the point of those services to the poor with which the technical skill of the case worker may deal but also at the point of those social and economic conditions which produce so much of the need for social work.

Those who believe that social work should assume such a responsibility are, of course, all too aware of the limitations which in practice hamper its performance. . . .

One does not have to be an economic determinist to recognize the controlling part played by the source of support of any social activity. As an institution or a collection of services such as social work becomes very large and requires large sums for its maintenance, there are only two sources from which it can draw, the large gifts of the wealthy or the many small contributions of a large group, collected either by taxation or by voluntary methods. . . .

This does not mean that along an extensive front moderate but essential modifications of present social institutions cannot be effected. These include such movements as those which led to the establishment of our juvenile courts, the progress of public health, or shifts in the administration of relief. . . . It is here that the author believes is the most likely field for increasing efforts by social work through the agencies themselves. . . .

The limitations which function here seem to be not so much related to the economic support of the agency as to its conception of its function and to the attitudes of social workers. . . .

Fundamental social reorganization, however, requires a more profound shift in human values and in institutional arrangement than is involved in such changes. There can be little doubt today that any such fundamental change must deal primarily with our economic life. . . . The futility of the case by case method of dealing with the problem is increasingly obvious. The flood must be stopped at its source, not mopped up by the bucket full, however scientifically modelled the bucket. For this reason, many social workers are beginning to look further upstream for the source of the trouble. It is inevitable that where the resulting proposals for reorganization touch the sphere of economic relations social work should feel the limitations arising out of its base of support. . . .

Except in times of revolution, the great majority of the people who have money enough either to give to community funds or to be taxed are not willing to consider proposals for radical reorganization. . . . This is in many ways a necessary and valuable protection from hasty and ill-advised proposals. It means, however, that agencies supported by the large numbers who fall within the contributing class will feel themselves limited as agencies to support of the measures which move only slightly from the existing institutions. . . .

Mr. Bookman of Cincinnati probably voiced the consensus of opinion among community chest executives in his statement . . . that organizations with new or propaganda programs do not belong in the chest. Since few large organizations can survive outside the chest, this policy, reasonable as it is, certainly acts to produce conformity with majority opinion and existing institutions. . . .

Even with public support by taxation, this sensitiveness to economic relations makes itself felt, as for example in the protest last fall on the federal policy of feeding textile strikers. . . .

As the whole of public opinion moves to the left as it has been doing, the support of measures like unemployment insurance, for example, formerly considered radical comes within the purview of social work *because* the proposal has now moved into the range of a slight deviation from the norm of public opinion. . . .

Though the bulk of social work is unlikely to advocate fundamental economic change, certain agencies as agencies are still able to go some distance in this direction. . . . Not all boards of directors are made up of economic men. To the sociologist this inconsistency may be merely the evidence of the tendency to assume varying rôles in different groups. To the psychiatrist, it may represent a dark and illegitimate escape from reality. But to the practical social worker interested in the endorsement of certain measures, the inconsistently liberal position of the economic man (or frequently his wife) on occasion provides a delightful surprise. . . .

Whether the social worker can as an individual or in his professional groups go further than his agency policy is one of those questions to be settled not by deductive reasoning but by observation. Logic would point to the fact that his salary comes from those same funds and that it is upon his actions and opinions that economic pressure is brought to bear. This is often true. Observation, however, shows that the fortunate inconsistency of life frequently allows him a longer tether. He can range, if he wishes, further into the field of those causes related to his specialty or he can even, if he dare, question the foundations of society itself. . . .

Why is it then that more of the forty thousand social workers are not active in the movement for social reorganization? That they are not is a commonly observed fact. As it is stated in the report of the Committee on Federal Action on Unemployment of the American Association of Social Workers,

There has been a tendency on the part of social workers to avoid expression and activity concerning major economic issues. The disadvantage of their attitude inheres in the fact that through a lack of positive expression the social worker thereby aligns himself with reactionary elements and with laissez faire methods of social organization.

Any good Marxian would put such hesitancy down to purely economic motives—rooted in the need for a job and the class alignment of the social worker with the hand that feeds him. While not minimizing the economic motives, even a superficial acquaintance with social workers would make one hesitate to impute to this cause the major part of the lack of active support of the measures for social reorganization.

It is in fact not so much to the vices as to the virtues of the social worker that one must look to discover these causes. The very essence of social work is the concern for the individual and his welfare—the attention to this, individual by individual. While case workers are not all of the social workers, they are the majority and the philosophy and techniques of case work dominate the scene. This very absorption in the problems of the individual turns the mind away from the consideration of social phenomena of a general character. . . . One might think that as case piled upon case, certain similarities would appear and certain generalizations became inevitable—among them generalizations about the coincidence of certain social factors and certain maladjustments. . . . Such a habit of mind would soon reveal significant relations between social and economic factors and the case worker's problems. It is by that road that the promoters of causes went from case work to industrial reform. . . . However, the effect of intensive individuation in treatment has not usually been the development of the habit of generalization, but rather the concentration upon the individual alone. . . .

This tendency to see the individual chiefly and sometimes solely has of course been strengthened by the great contributions of psychiatry within recent years. As case work has "gone psychiatric" it has not only concentrated upon the individual, it has further centered upon his emotional life, giving decreasing attention to environmental factors social and economic. It has even been claimed at times that the ills that beset the unemployed could be met by proper emotional adjustment. A pamphlet on *Morale*, issued by the National Committee for Mental Hygiene in 1933 contains suggestions "for relieving the emotional strains and raising the morale of those who are made insecure." Social workers "leaving to others the task of fundamental reconstruction" are to undertake the job of trying to discover in the morale-stricken unemployed some personal resource that will help them to bear hardship either because it must be borne in order to reach a goal ahead, or because the compensations and emotional outlets of the resource are so satisfying that in them hardship can be partially robbed of its discomfort and made tolerable.

As Harry Lurie has pointed out in a recent article, such an approach to individuals under present conditions not only makes no contribution to the fundamental economic problems of our day, but produces a kind of smoke screen of illusions through which it becomes difficult for social workers to discern the inherently social nature of the problem with which they are confronted. . . .

Psychiatry has further decreased the drive for social reorganization by sometimes adopting the rôle of the passive agent devoid of social aims or norms. While some psychiatrists like Frankwood Williams are recognizing the importance of social reorganization as the way to make individual adjustment possible, one of the influences which has been potent in social work recently has been that which not only made social factors relatively unessential but which made the formulation of social goals a doubtful practice.

Another aspect of the psychiatric approach has had its bearing upon the attitudes of social workers on social reorganization. This is the psychoanalytic emphasis on the early life of the child and on sexual adjustment and a relatively undeveloped interest in adult relations outside the family. In a time when economists and political theorists are emphasizing the growth of the collective spirit, the increasing importance of our complex group life in all phases of experience and the necessity for our understanding how to develop new and adequate collective forms for our economic and political institutions, the rôle of the group in the life of individuals has received relatively little attention from psychiatrists. Certain of them go further and treat group loyalty as an adolescent habit to be superseded normally by the sex relation. Since the interest in social reorganization is not only expressed largely through groups but is concerned necessarily with these new collective forms, this emphasis also serves to divert attention from social action.

While case workers have been drawing the breath of inspiration from psychiatry, many group workers adopted with equal enthusiasm the theories of progressive education. The results in the attitudes here being considered were curiously similar. While case work in some of its aspects was developing the idea of the passive rôle of the worker in relation to his client, the group worker who was nurtured on Dewey and Kilpatrick had become equally passive for fear of dominating his group and so destroying their God-given initiative. As with case work, this position in its extreme form tended to neutralize the worker's social objectives as well and to lead to a disparagement of social conviction and action on social questions. In the case of the group workers affected by this theory, this attitude has recently undergone some change. Not only has all of progressive education tended to react from its extreme position on self-determination but in particular discussion has raged over the problems of social objectives in education. This in turn has tended to restore certain initiative to the group leader and to revive his interest in social reorganization. . . .

[Another deterrent factor] has probably been the contacts which social workers have had with some of the protest groups promoting change. . . . Contacts with the labor movement are likely to be at points which give trouble to the social worker— workers go on strike, and need relief, employment opportunities are only open to union members, men refuse jobs at less than union pay, etc. Otherwise the social worker has as little contact with the unions as any other middle class person. . . .

The recent experience with the organized unemployed undoubtedly tends even more strongly in the same direction. In this case, the agitation is directed against the social workers themselves. They would perhaps be superhuman if they could see these protest movements not as the doings of trouble makers or the evidence of psychological maladjustments but as the healthy and legitimate attempt at social reorganization by a group of those most concerned. Some no doubt do recognize their significance. It is not likely, however, that many social workers have been made more open minded toward either the theories or the methods of such groups by their first hand contact with them. In so far, therefore, as an interest in social reorganization involves an understanding of and perhaps sympathy with the protest movements of our times, the social worker is probably being conditioned by his experience against them.

The discussion of attitudes so far seems to have put much responsibility upon theories of various kinds. It would be entirely unrealistic and certainly indicative of a pre-psychiatric approach to imply that intellectual considerations of any kind played a major part in human behavior. Not theory but the tremendous and overwhelming practice itself limits more than anything else the concern of the social worker. As Dr. Deardorff points out . . . the promotion of causes of any kind does not appear in the job analysis of the social worker. The time and energy required to draw conclusions, to do research, even to belong to organizations promoting social improvement is almost impossible to acquire in the face of the daily demands of the job. . . .

In a day of individualism, it is easy enough to concentrate upon the individual and believe that his social inadequacies are due to his own maladjustment and not to his environment. The typically individualistic bias of all professional workers further strengthens this natural trend so characteristic of middle class America. It is, therefore, not surprising if the social worker in spite of his constant and continuous contact with the results of our social disorganization does not always take hold of his opportunities, draw conclusions in social terms from his personal observation and throw himself into one or another movement for fundamental reorganization.

To admit these limitations is not to succumb to them. Through the bitter lessons of the depression itself, through a broader education providing more acquaintance with sociological concepts; through a research program which will draw the generalizations which the busy social worker cannot make; through contacts with constructive movements, and perhaps through the necessity for collective action on their own behalf, social workers may change their conception of their functions. There is evidence that this is happening to some extent.

XXXVII

SOCIAL SECURITY BECOMES A FACT

Since the days of the Reverend Goodsell (R14) and Benjamin Franklin (R15–17), the health hazards to which people were subject in their quest for economic stability had received the concerned attention of many people. Franklin and Carey (R26) pointed to the precariousness of earnings as a major hindrance to individual financial independence. The younger Griscom (R29) pointed to the disastrous effects of poor housing and sanitation. External economic and neighborhood conditions ranked high on all lists of causes of poverty and "pauperism," justifying special services in substandard areas.

Edward Everett Hale (R67) had enunciated one aspect of the ferment for some form of pensions or insurance which had been widespread since European countries had introduced such measures late in the nineteenth century. The report of the Massachusetts commission in 1910 (R86), pointing out the difficulties of state-by-state action and suggesting that Federal action would be necessary, was realistic in the economic sense, but appeared completely unrealistic from the political standpoint in view of the firm hold of the Pierce doctrine of state responsibility (R38). Such progress as was made in solving these problems in the first three decades of the twentieth century was of a halting nature by states which undertook to set up pension plans for indigent persons with various kinds of handicaps—orphans (R88–90), the blind, the aged.

The depression of the thirties was an economic and social storm of such unprecedented proportions that established patterns had to be reconsidered. The Social Security Act represented an overriding of the Pierce veto after the passage of eighty-one years. It was hailed by its supporters (R110, 111) as a means of

insuring sound democracy (cf. Griscom, R21) and as opening
the door of opportunity for the social work profession to provide
the leadership in a new era of humane, efficient, and constructive
public welfare administration. Whether or not these anticipations
were justified, the issue of the reversal of the Pierce doctrine was
not complete until the supporters of that point of view had had
their day in court. This day was complete on May 24, 1937, when
the Supreme Court handed down decisions in two separate cases,
Steward Machine Company v. *Davis,* and *Helvering* v. *Davis,*
each dealing with a distinct aspect of the constitutional problems
raised in respect to the Act. In both cases the Court held the
provisions of the Act to be constitutional. In the decision here
quoted it is interesting to note the amount of social testimony
which the Court cited in support of its decision. However, from
the constitutional aspect, the significance of this testimony was
that it supported the arguments that (1) the problem being dealt
with was nation-wide and that (2) the benefits provided, though
paid to individuals, were general and not particular.

In this decision, not only was the future course of social welfare
in the United States greatly altered, but one of the basic provisions of the original Elizabethan Poor Law (R4) at long last
fulfilled. Then the burden of excessive need in a single parish was
to be shared first with the hundred and then with the county.
Now, seeing the impossibility of long-range planning for economic need at the local level, the United States as a whole assumed
on a permanent basis a large share of the responsibility for that
planning and provision.

109. The Social Security Act

U.S., *Statutes at Large,* XLIX, Part 1, 620-48 (c. 531,
Aug. 14, 1935)

AN ACT to provide for the general welfare by establishing a
system of Federal old-age benefits, and by enabling the several
States to make more adequate provision for aged persons, blind
persons, dependent and crippled children, maternal and child
welfare, public health, and the administration of their unemploy-

ment compensation laws; to establish a Social Security Board; to raise revenue; and for other purposes.

Be it enacted by the Senate and House of Representatives of the United States of America in Congress assembled,

Title I. Grants to States for Old Age Assistance

APPROPRIATION

Section 1. For the purpose of enabling each State to furnish financial assistance, as far as practicable under the conditions in such State, to aged needy individuals, there is hereby authorized to be appropriated for the fiscal year ending June 30, 1936, the sum of $49,750,000, and there is hereby authorized to be appropriated for each fiscal year thereafter a sum sufficient to carry out the purposes of this title. The sums made available under this section shall be used for making payments to States which have submitted, and had approved by the Social Security Board established by Title VII . . . State plans for old-age assistance.

STATE OLD-AGE ASSISTANCE PLANS

Section 2. (*a*) A State plan for old-age assistance must (1) provide that it shall be in effect in all political subdivisions of the State, and, if administered by them, be mandatory upon them; (2) provide for financial participation by the State; (3) either provide for the establishment or designation of a single State agency to administer the plan, or provide for the establishment or designation of a single State agency to supervise the administration of the plan; (4) provide for granting to any individual, whose claim for old-age assistance is denied, an opportunity for a fair hearing before such State agency. . . .

(*b*) The Board shall approve any plan with fulfills the conditions specified in subsection (*a*), except that it shall not approve any plan which imposes, as a condition of eligibility for old-age assistance under the plan—

(1) An age requirement of more than sixty-five years, except

that the plan may impose, effective until January 1, 1940, an age requirement of as much as seventy years; or

(2) Any residence requirement which excludes any resident of the State who has resided therein five years during the nine years immediately preceding the application for old-age assistance and has resided therein continuously for one year immediately preceding the application; or

(3) Any citizenship requirement which excludes any citizen of the United States. . . .

Title II. Federal Old-Age Benefits

OLD-AGE RESERVE ACCOUNT

Section 201. (*a*) There is hereby created an account in the Treasury of the United States to be known as the "Old-Age Reserve Account." . . .

OLD-AGE BENEFIT PAYMENTS

Section 202. (*a*) Every qualified individual . . . shall be entitled to receive, with respect to the period beginning on the date he attains the age of sixty-five, or on January 1, 1942, whichever is the later, and ending on the date of his death, an old-age benefit (payable as nearly as practicable in equal monthly installments) as follows: . . .

Title III. Grant to States for Unemployment Compensation Administration

APPROPRIATION

Section 301. For the purpose of assisting the States in the administration of their unemployment compensation laws, there is hereby authorized to be appropriated. . . .

Title IV. Grants to States for Aid to Dependent Children

APPROPRIATION

Section 401. For the purpose of enabling each State to furnish financial assistance, as far as practicable under the conditions in such State, to needy dependent children, there is hereby authorized to be appropriated for the fiscal year ending June 30, 1936, the sum of $24,750,000, and there is hereby authorized to be appropriated for each fiscal year thereafter a sum sufficient to carry out the purposes of this title. The sums made available under this section shall be used for making payments to States which have submitted, and had approved by the Board, State plans for aid to dependent children. . . .

DEFINITIONS

Section 406. When used in this title—

(*a*) The term "dependent child" means a child under the age of sixteen who has been deprived of parental support or care by reason of the death, continued absence from the home, or physical or mental incapacity of a parent, and who is living with his father, mother, grandfather, grandmother, brother, sister, stepfather, stepmother, stepbrother, stepsister, uncle, or aunt, in a place of residence maintained by one or more of such relatives as his or their own home. . . .

Title V. Grants to States for Maternal and Child Welfare

PART I. MATERNAL AND CHILD HEALTH SERVICES

APPROPRIATION

Section 501. For the purpose of enabling each State to extend and improve, as far as practicable under the conditions in such State, services for promoting the health of mothers and children, especially in rural areas and in areas suffering from severe economic distress, there is hereby authorized to be appropriated. . . .

APPROVAL OF STATE PLANS

Section 503. (*a*) A State plan for maternal and child-health services must (1) provide for financial participation by the State; (2) provide for the administration of the plan by the State health agency or the supervision of the administration of the plan by the State health agency; (3) provide such methods of administration (other than those relating to selection, tenure of office, and compensation of personnel) as are necessary for the efficient operation of the plan; (4) provide that the State health agency will make such reports, in such form and containing such information, as the Secretary of Labor may from time to time require, and comply with such provisions as he may from time to time find necessary to assure the correctness and verification of such reports; (5) provide for the extension and improvement of local maternal and child-health services administered by local child-health units; (6) provide for cooperation with medical, nursing, and welfare groups and organizations; and (7) provide for the development of demonstration services in needy areas and among groups in special need. . . .

PART 2. SERVICES FOR CRIPPLED CHILDREN

APPROPRIATION

Section 511. For the purpose of enabling each State to extend and improve (especially in rural areas and in areas suffering from severe economic distress), as far as practicable under the conditions in such State, services for locating crippled children, and for providing medical, surgical, corrective, and other services and care, and facilities for diagnosis, hospitalization, and after-care, for children who are crippled or who are suffering from conditions which lead to crippling, there is hereby authorized to be appropriated for each fiscal year. . . .

PART 3. CHILD-WELFARE SERVICES

Section 521. (*a*) For the purpose of enabling the United States, through the Children's Bureau, to cooperate with State public-welfare agencies in establishing, extending and strengthening, especially in predominantly rural areas, public-welfare services (hereinafter in this section referred to as "child-welfare services") for the protection and care of homeless, dependent, and neglected children, and children in danger of becoming delinquent, there is hereby authorized to be appropriated. . . . The amount so allotted shall be expended for payment of part of the cost of district, county or other local child-welfare services in areas predominantly rural, and for developing State services for the encouragement and assistance of adequate methods of community child-welfare organization in areas predominantly rural and other areas of special need. . . .

PART 4. VOCATIONAL REHABILITATION

Section 531. (*a*) In order to enable the United States to cooperate with the States and Hawaii in extending and strengthening their programs of vocational rehabilitation of the physically disabled, and to continue to carry out. . . .

Title VI. Public Health Work

APPROPRIATION

Section 601. For the purpose of assisting States, counties, health districts, and other political subdivisions of the States in establishing and maintaining adequate public-health services, including the training of personnel for State and local health work, there is hereby authorized to be appropriated. . . .

Title VII. Social Security Board

ESTABLISHMENT

Section 701. There is hereby established a Social Security Board. . . .

Title VIII. Taxes with Respect to Employment

INCOME TAX ON EMPLOYEES

Section 801. In addition to other taxes, there shall be levied, collected, and paid upon the income of every individual a tax equal to the following percentages of the wages. . . .

DEDUCTION OF TAX FROM WAGES

Section 802. (*a*) The tax imposed by section 801 shall be collected by the employer of the taxpayer, by deducting the amount of the tax from the wages as and when paid. . . .

EXCISE TAX ON EMPLOYERS

Section 804. In addition to other taxes, every employer shall pay an excise tax, with respect to having individuals in his employ, equal to the following percentages of the wages. . . .

Title IX. Tax on Employers of Eight or More

IMPOSITION OF TAX

Section 901. On and after January 1, 1936, every employer . . . shall pay for each calendar year an excise tax, with respect to having individuals in his employ, equal to the following percentages of the total wages payable by him . . . with respect to employment. . . .

UNEMPLOYMENT TRUST FUND

Section 904. (*a*) There is hereby established in the Treasury of the United States a trust fund to be known as the "Unemployment Trust Fund." . . .

Title X. Grants to States for Aid to the Blind

APPROPRIATION

Section 1001. For the purpose of enabling each State to furnish financial assistance, as far as practicable under the condition in such State to needy individuals who are blind, there is hereby authorized to be appropriated. . . .

110. The Outlook

Harry L. Hopkins,[67] *Spending to Save: the Complete Story of Relief* (New York: Norton, 1936), pp. 179–85

America has spent the last few years in the counting house. . . . From our inventory we have emerged, as a nation, with the conviction that there is no need for any American to be destitute, to

[67] Hopkins was the Federal Emergency Relief Administrator. He had worked at Christadora House, a settlement in New York, and for the New York AICP after college, for the Red Cross during the First World War, and for the New York Tuberculosis Association before the depression. He worked in the first AICP employment bureau set up with special voluntary funds early in the depression, then in New York State emergency programs before joining Franklin D. Roosevelt's staff. Though not pro-

be illiterate, to be reduced by the bondage of these things into either political or economic impotence. . . .

One may believe that the human being should come first, and the serviceability of the economic system in which he functions should be estimated by the number of persons who share in its rewards. There is reason to think that the present system is capable of giving to all its workers those things which are now the expectations of a comparative few: a warm, decent place to live in; a liberal diet; suitable clothes; travel, vacations, automobiles, radios, and college educations for those who want them. Even one who does not pretend to be an expert on the subject can see a few fairly obvious means by which we can approach the problem of redistribution. Wages must be raised and hours lowered. Unfair profits will have to be translated into lower unit price. Some three million persons over sixty years of age should be taken out of the labor market. Most of them are there not because they want to be, but from dire necessity. Compulsory school age, with some exceptions, probably should be raised, and young boys removed from competition with their fathers.

Until the time comes, if it ever does, when industry and business can absorb all able-bodied workers—and that time seems to grow more distant with improvements in management and technology—we shall have with us large numbers of unemployed. Intelligent people have long since left behind them the notion that under fullest recovery, and even with improved purchasing power, the unemployed will disappear as dramatically as they made their appearance after 1929.

Even if they did so disappear, there would still remain with us the people who cannot work, or should not, and who have no one to support them; the too old, the too young, mothers with

---

fessionally trained, Hopkins was so much a part of the social work profession that he was elected president of the AASW, 1923–24. See Robert E. Sherwood, *Roosevelt and Hopkins* (New York: Harper, 1948), esp. Chaps. II and III. Compare Hopkins's position on unemployment with Captain John Smith's (R1), on the inevitability of poverty with Cardinal Gibbons's (R65), on the right of each child to develop to his full potentiality with Sanborn's (R40), and on the possibility of eradicating unemployment with Calkins's (R105).

small children, the sick and crippled. These people cannot be left to fumble their way along alone; to be sent from one vacillating agency to another, given something one month and not the next, with almost nothing in the present and, so far as they know, nothing at all in the future. For them a security program is the only answer. In the past three and a half years more progress has been made in providing security for them than during the whole history of the nation. The Social Security Board has been set up; appropriations have been made, public education has begun, but most important, over one million unemployable persons are already receiving its benefits. We need only to refine, extend and consolidate gains that have been made in order to provide minimum security for all of them.

Many who wanted the continuance of Federal relief by grants in aid to states, contended that if you gave unemployable people back to the care of the states, they would be neglected. In some places, even widely, this has proved to be true. States should never pass them on to the niggardly and degrading practices of county and township poor relief. Federal aid, I believe, should be given through the Social Security Board which, with similar state and local boards, should pass this benefit as a pension without stigma to those who need it. If this is to be done, it is equally clear that the Social Security Board must be given power to regulate standards of administration in states and cities. Too small a benefit will not serve the purpose of a pension. Political control of the manner in which it is administered would destroy it. An adequate civil service made up of permanent employees is absolutely essential to the success of any pension system. . . .

The Social Security Act potentially covers only about half the workers in the nation. One of the first necessities is to see if it cannot be given greater coverage.

To me, the only possible solution for those who cannot be absorbed by long-time or large-scale public works is a work program. I believe we must continue such a program until other forces produce a very substantial increase in the volume of employment. . . .

For all its tremendous natural wealth, the American people are the greatest resource of the country. So far men and women, with few exceptions, have found no substitute for useful work to keep themselves sound of body and mind. In other words, work conserves them as a national asset, and lack of work lets them sink into a national liability. . . .

The unemployed need work, the public needs construction done and services rendered which neither private business nor regular departments of government are in a position to undertake. . . . Communities now find themselves in possession of improvements which even in 1929 they would have thought themselves presumptuous to dream of.

In fact, everywhere there has been an overhauling of the word presumptuous. We are beginning to wonder if it is not presumptuous to take for granted that some people should have much, and some should have nothing; that some people are less important than others and should die earlier; that the children of the comfortable should be taller and fatter, as a matter of right, than the children of the poor.

It finally whittles itself down, I suppose, to a matter of the children, since we ourselves are not likely to see all those ends accomplished toward which we strive. Suppose we place two grown men beside each other. One has been given all the privileges of his time, and has made good use of them; the other has never had a glimpse of privilege. The first is healthy; the second sick from neglect. If we were told that one was going to be abandoned, and the other encouraged to carry on, which one should we choose to keep? In a democracy, no matter how conspicuously we fail to operate upon the principle, we don't admit that one man has more right to live than another. Yet realistically, it would be easy to say which is the more useful member of society.

Put two children in their place. Upon one child privilege has only started to take effect. Neglect of the other has scarcely begun. How shall the choice be made between them, and who will dare to be the chooser?

111. Social Work Aspects of the Social Security Act

Frank J. Bruno,[68] *The Southwestern Social Science Quarterly*, XVII (1936), 262–73

After lagging behind every other modern nation, the United States, for the first time, acknowledges its obligation to equalize some of the sharp differences in economic conditions of its citizens, and this it accomplishes by the two devices in which the other industrial nations have had considerable experience: social insurance and national, public assistance. To social workers it seemed impossible, as short a time ago as ten years, that the federal government could assume any responsibility for social welfare, or attempt to raise the standards of public assistance to a humane plane, or to equalize them through the United States. Nor are social workers entirely free from the fear that the Supreme Court will declare that the whole plan is unconstitutional. Unless, or until, such a catastrophe occurs, the administration of the Act will be a stimulating influence on public welfare services throughout the country to a degree never before reached, and not possible by any other means. Up to the Great Depression, welfare projects outside institutions had been largely left to the initiative and generosity of local units. . . . Consequently, there had been wide variations between communities in the same state, all governed by the same basic law, and between the laws of different states. . . . It was . . . the scandal of the policy of placing not only responsibility but power of initiative in welfare matters with local units that a premium was placed upon niggardliness and barbarous neglect of those whom even the poorer nations of Europe had furnished with some sort of economic defense. The only conceivable method at once to cease penalizing the generous community and at the same time to insure some measure of protection for the economically defenseless is federal participation. . . .

[68] Dr. Bruno was a professor in the Department of Social Work at Washington University. He had been president of the AASW, 1928–30.

On viewing the other side of the ledger, the Act presents some glaring omissions. It has all the appearances of being a compromise: not what the President's Commission on Economic Security believed was necessary, nor what the experience of other nations with social insurance and our own with public assistance have demonstrated as practical, but what could pass the Congress, and —perhaps—run the gauntlet of the Supreme Court. The limiting nature of this compromise is shown in two ways: instead of being a comprehensive law covering the subject matters with which it deals it attacks them piecemeal. Recent legislation has all been in the other direction [in other countries]. . . . Our Act breaks with these precedents; it picks out certain beneficiaries and ignores others in what seems wholly an arbitrary manner, e.g., the crippled child is pointedly indicated for good and potentially adequate care; the child with heart disease, or who is born syphilitic, or who is handicapped by any one of a number of troubles is passed by. The crippled child has been duly publicized, a powerful fraternal order has thrown its weight into the task of caring for him, there is no stigma attached to being crippled, and so on. But social workers are coming to be very critical of any provision for special classes, even though such classes may be determined by medical diagnosis. Contrariwise, social workers feel that the only just method of approaching the problems of dependency is to handle them as dependents, not as special classes, as folks who for some reason cannot support themselves, not because they happen to be widows, or unemployed.

So in the insurance sections of the Act. It singles out two classes for protection: the aged and the unemployed, but it omits any provision for sickness, by far the most needed and most effective form of social insurance anywhere in the world, and it has similarly omitted provisions for invalidity insurance which is almost as widely spread as sickness, and is a provision whereby those who must cease earning before they are eligible for old age assistance may be assured of protection for which they have made some contribution. The two insurance provisions are not going to be spared violent and to some extent justifiable criticism.

That against old age has been aired in the present national election and its precedent oratory. Again, caution to propose only the safest kind of old age insurance has probably led Congress into other evils quite as bad. There is no contribution from the states or the federal government, in order to meet the criticism that it would open public treasuries to increasingly dangerous raids; but it leaves workers who are over forty practically with such little protection that it is all but meaningless to them, and they will have to have their annuities supplemented by the old age pension provision, should they have no other income when they reach sixty-five. And it has made necessary that astronomical reserve fund which has created consternation among the financiers. At least they say it has. Again, it should be pointed out that within the last ten years almost every industrialized nation has passed some old age insurance legislation; each one has faced the same alternative of this mountainous reserve in some far off future, with very slight benefits for the present, or governmental supplementation, and they have all chosen the latter of the two evils. . . .

It is clear that within the framework of the objectionable policy of categorical relief there are some valuable possibilities. Perhaps at the very top a social worker would place the provision for child welfare projects to which the federal government will make grants-in-aid, should the plans of a state meet the approval of the Federal Children's Bureau. This has all the advantage of a general provision for a whole group, leaving the specific application to the initiative of localities and to their peculiar needs. . . .

The policy of the Works Progress Administration and of the Social Security Act in omitting any plan for general public assistance is probably to be understood in the light of the previous experience of two years with the Federal Emergency Relief Administration. During that entire period the central government was waging a losing battle along two fronts. The first was the general conviction of the man in the street that relief for the able bodied was bad and that he should be given work instead.

This criticism is a part of the general stigma under which the whole project of public assistance suffers, which is a long story, and cannot be recited here. It is of no significance that the stigma is unmerited and that public assistance is sometimes the only real way to meet economic defenselessness.[69] The stigma is there; and no one feels it more than the able-bodied. . . .

The most significant effect of the Social Security Act, however, is likely to be less the amount of money the Federal Treasury will grant the states for their social services, but rather the reorganization of the entire state welfare administration and personnel. The amount of money involved is so great and the welfare of so many of the citizens of the state is so intimately tied up with the operation of these provisions that states cannot afford to permit welfare administration to be anything but the most efficient and the most economical attainable. . . . The very continuance of the provisions of the Social Security Act is dependent upon the most efficient administration; and if such an administration is secured, our disgraceful and niggardly treatment of dependents will be a thing of the past.

112. *Social Security Constitutional*

Helvering, et al. v. *Davis*, 301 U.S., 634–46 (U.S. Supreme
Court decision, 1937)

Mr. Justice Cardozo delivered the opinion of the Court.

The Social Security Act . . . is challenged once again. . . . In this case Titles VIII and II are the subject of attack. . . . [Title VIII] lays a special income tax upon employees to be deducted from their wages and paid by the employers. Title II provides for the payment of Old Age Benefits, and supplies the motive and occasion, in the view of the assailants of the statute, for the levy of the taxes imposed by Title VIII. . . .

The scheme of benefits created by the provisions of Title II is not in contravention of the limitations of the Tenth Amendment.

Congress may spend money in aid of the "general welfare."

[69] Cf. Carey, R26; Lowell, R64.

Constitution, Art. I, section 8; *United States* v. *Butler*, 297 U.S.
1, 65; *Steward Machine Co.* v. *Davis, supra.* There have been
great statesmen in our history who have stood for other views.
We will not resurrect the contest. It is now settled by decision.
United States v. *Butler, supra.* The conception of the spending
power advocated by Hamilton and strongly reinforced by Story
has prevailed over that of Madison, which has not been lacking
in adherents. Yet difficulties are left when the power is conceded.
The line must still be drawn between one welfare and another,
between particular and general. Where this shall be placed cannot
be known through a formula in advance of the event. There
is a middle ground or certainly a penumbra in which discretion
is at large. The discretion, however, is not confided to the courts.
The discretion belongs to Congress, unless the choice is clearly
wrong, a display of arbitrary power, not an exercise of judgment.
This is now familiar law. "When such a contention comes here we
naturally require a showing that by no reasonable possibility can
the challenged legislation fall within the wide range of discretion
permitted to the Congress." *United States* v. *Butler, supra*, p.
67. . . . Nor is the concept of the general welfare static. Needs
that were narrow or parochial a century ago may be interwoven
in our day with the well-being of the Nation. What is critical or
urgent changes with the times.

The purge of nation-wide calamity that began in 1929 has
taught us many lessons. Not the least is the solidarity of interests
that may once have seemed to be divided. Unemployment spreads
from State to State, the hinterland now settled that in pioneer
days gave an avenue of escape. . . . Spreading from State to
State, unemployment is an ill not particular but general, which
may be checked, if Congress so determines, by the resources of
the Nation. If this can have been doubtful until now, our ruling
today in the case of the *Steward Machine Co., supra*, has set the
doubt at rest. But the ill is all one, or at least not greatly different,
whether men are thrown out of work because there is no longer
work to do or because the disabilities of age make them incapable
of doing it. Rescue becomes necessary irrespective of the cause.

The hope behind this statute is to save men and women from the rigors of the poor house as well as from the haunting fear that such a lot awaits them when journey's end is near.

Congress did not improvise a judgment when it found that the award of old age benefits would be conducive to the general welfare. The President's Committee on Economic Security made an investigation and report, aided by a research staff of Government officers and employees, and by an Advisory Council and seven other advisory groups. Extensive hearings followed before the House Committee on Ways and Means, and the Senate Committee on Finance. A great mass of evidence was brought together supporting the policy which finds expression in the act. Among the relevant facts are these: The number of persons in the United States 65 years of age or over is increasing proportionately as well as absolutely. What is even more important the number of such persons unable to take care of themselves is growing at a threatening pace. More and more our population is becoming urban and industrial instead of rural and agricultural. The evidence is impressive that among industrial workers the younger men and women are preferred over the older. In times of retrenchment the older are commonly the first to go, and even if retained, their wages are likely to be lowered. The plight of men and women at so low an age as 40 is hard, almost hopeless, when they are driven to seek for reëmployment. Statistics are in the brief. A few illustrations will be chosen from many there collected. In 1930, out of 224 American factories investigated, 71, or almost one third, had fixed maximum hiring age limits; in 4 plants the limit was under 40; in 41 it was under 46. In the other 153 plants there were no fixed limits, but in practice few were hired if they were over 50 years of age. With the loss of savings inevitable in periods of idleness, the fate of workers over 65, when thrown out of work, is little less than desperate. A recent study of the Social Security Board informs us that

one-fifth of the aged in the United States were receiving old-age assistance, emergency relief, institutional care, employment under the works program, or some other form of aid from public or private funds; two-fifths to one-half were dependent on friends and relatives, one-eighth had some income from earnings; and possibly one-sixth had some savings or property. Approximately three out of four persons 65 or over were probably dependent wholly or partially on others for support.

. . . The results of other studies by state and national commissions. . . . point the same way.

The problem is plainly national in area and dimensions. Moreover, laws of the separate states cannot deal with it effectively. Congress, at least, had a basis for that belief. States and local governments are often lacking in the resources that are necessary to finance an adequate program of security for the aged. This is brought out with a wealth of illustration in recent studies of the problem. Apart from the failure of resources, states and local governments are at times reluctant to increase so heavily the burden of taxation to be borne by their residents for fear of placing themselves in a position of economic disadvantage as compared with neighbors or competitors. We have seen this in our study of the problem of unemployment compensation. *Steward Machine Co.* v. *Davis, supra.* A system of old age pensions has special dangers of its own, if put in force in one state and rejected in another. The existence of such a system is a bait to the needy and dependent elsewhere, encouraging them to migrate and seek a haven of repose. Only a power that is national can serve the interests of all.

Whether wisdom or unwisdom resides in the scheme of benefits set forth in Title II, it is not for us to say. The answer to such inquiries must come from Congress, not the courts. Our concern here, as often, is with power, not with wisdom. Counsel for respondent has recalled to us the virtues of self-reliance and frugality. There is a possibility, he says, that aid from a paternal government may sap those sturdy virtues and breed a race of weaklings. If Massachusetts so believes and shapes her laws in that conviction, must her breed of sons be changed, he asks, because some other philosophy of government finds favor in the halls of Congress? But the answer is not doubtful. One might ask with equal reason whether the system of protective tariffs is to be set aside at will in one state or another whenever local policy prefers the rule of *laissez faire*. The issue is a closed one. It was fought out long ago. When money is spent to promote the general welfare, the concept of welfare or the opposite is shaped by Congress, not the states. So the concept be not arbitrary, the locality must yield. Constitution, Art. VI, Par. 2. . . .

The decree of the Court of Appeals should be reversed and that of the District Court affirmed.

Reversed

Mr. Justice McReynolds and Mr. Justice Butler are of opinion that the provisions of the Act here challenged are repugnant to the Tenth Amendment, and that the decree of the Circuit Court of Appeals should be affirmed.

APPENDIX: TOPICAL LISTING

In the text, readings have been grouped according to what seemed to the editors to be their central contribution in the stream of professional development. Many have passages which illustrate other points or subclassifications, not included in major subject divisions, that are useful in considering special methods or settings. In compiling this suggestive list we have included negative as well as positive comments, and examples of missing community resources as well as provision for them. Such references often are useful in stimulating discussion or pointing up the issues in today's systems.

ADMINISTRATION. 4, 13, 15, 19, 21, 22, 30, 32, 40, 46, 51, 78, 89, 90, 111

AGED. 8, 14, 26, 54, 67, 86, 109

ATTITUDES, TOWARD THE NEEDY. 17, 18, 22, 23, 24, 25, 26, 27, 30, 36, 37, 40, 53, 57, 59, 60, 62, 63, 64, 65, 68, 69, 70, 71, 72, 73, 88, 89, 105

ATTITUDES, TOWARD PUBLIC RELIEF. 13, 20, 21, 22, 32, 51, 60, 63, 64, 104

CASEWORK ANTECEDENTS. 25, 27, 30, 32, 36, 44, 45, 51, 53, 54, 56, 60, 72, 78, 79, 85, 88, 91, 92, 93, 94, 95, 104, 106

CAUSATION. 17, 21, 26, 27, 29, 34, 40, 65, 66, 69, 70, 73

CHILDREN. 4, 7, 8, 11, 19, 20, 26, 27, 31, 33, 34, 35, 36, 41, 42, 43, 44, 45, 46, 60, 66, 70, 72, 73, 87, 88, 93, 109

COMMUNITY ORGANIZATION. 15, 17, 21, 22, 25, 26, 36, 37, 46, 51, 52, 55, 57, 58, 61, 62, 71, 74, 78, 87, 90, 94, 96, 99, 100, 101, 102, 103, 104

COMMUNITY RESOURCES, PROVISION AND USE. 21, 25, 26, 27, 28, 30, 34, 35, 37, 51, 53, 99

DELINQUENCY AND CRIMINALITY. 23, 33, 34, 42, 46, 62, 93

ELIGIBILITY FOR SERVICE. 4, 5, 11, 13, 16, 18, 19, IX, 22, 25, 32, 36, 51, 53, 54, 58, 64, 68, 86, 104, 109, 111

EMPLOYMENT AND UNEMPLOYMENT. 4, 21, 25, 26, 27, 53, 62, 68, 70, 72, 73, 74, 86, 104, 105, 106, 107, 108, 109, 110

ENHANCEMENT AND RESTORATION. 16, 17, 25, 27, 28, 40, 41, 53, 58, 59, 66, 69, 71, 72, 97, 110

ENVIRONMENTAL CONDITIONS. 29, 58, 59, 61, XIV, 66, 71, 72, 99

FAMILY LIFE, PRESERVATION OF. 43, 53, 60, 62, 63, 66, 87, 88, 89, 106, 109

FOSTER CARE. 34, 36, 41, 44, 45, 46, 62, 87

GOVERNMENTAL RESPONSIBILITY. 4, 15, 16, 19, 21, 22, 24, 25, 26, 29, 32, 37, 38, 39, 40, 44, 45, 46, 47, 50, 63, 64, 66, 68, 78, 86, 87, 88, 89, 90, 104, 105, 106, 107, 109, 110, 111, 112

SE